The Industrial Revolution in France

1815–1848

BY ARTHUR LOUIS DUNHAM

The Anglo-French Treaty of Commerce of 1860 and the Progress of the Industrial Revolution in France

The Industrial Revolution in France, 1815–1848

The
Industrial Revolution
in France

1815–1848

ARTHUR LOUIS DUNHAM
Professor of History, University of Michigan

EXPOSITION—UNIVERSITY BOOK

EXPOSITION PRESS • NEW YORK

Exposition Press Inc., 386 Fourth Avenue, New York 16, N.Y.

FIRST EDITION

Preface

RESEARCH ON the Industrial Revolution in France is an adventure which brings both the joy of discovery and the knowledge of failure. The literature of French economic history is unsatisfactory. There are great gaps in the evidence that cannot yet be filled; there is widespread ignorance of what does exist, and there are very few statistics that are reliable. Much evidence is also highly prejudiced, or must be used for purposes quite different from those for which it was written. This is particularly true of the tariff, the cause of a series of *enquêtes* and many books and pamphlets in which propaganda is generally given as fact. From such material it is exceedingly difficult to write an account that will be useful, or even interesting, to the economic historian. Also, some of the best evidence is almost buried in sources that would not appear to be concerned with the history of the Industrial Revolution. Thus, the best essay on the general subject is nominally on cotton alone and was published by Professor Laufenburger in the *Revue politique et parlementaire*. A source on the actual condition of the workers in mills that is second in value only to Villermé is the report of Dr. Thouvenin published in the *Journal d'hygiène publique,* where it was promptly forgotten. An investigator in the field of French economic history never knows where he will find evidence, but he does know that in most cases he will find only atoms, which he must fuse together as best he can. He cannot start in the usual way by a careful study of the official archives unless he is assured of years of residence in France. He must go wherever clues may lead him.

Work on this book was begun in 1931, through inspiration from the work of the late Henri Sée, whom I knew personally, and continued until 1948, despite frequent interruptions during the Second World War, which made further visits to France too difficult to attempt and thus made use of the national archives impossible.

For aid in obtaining evidence I am indebted to many persons, besides the officials of the Bibliothèque Nationale, the British Museum, the Library of Congress and the libraries of Harvard University and the University of Michigan. Over a period of several years I obtained books from all parts of the United States through the unfailing courtesy and patience of the Inter-Library Loan Service of the Library of the University of Michigan, directed by Miss Margaret Smith. I received great assistance also from the late Dr. W. W. Bishop, for many years director of the Library of the University of Michigan. At my request he bought the fifteen volumes of the report of the French commission on the Exposition of 1851 and asked the director of the Bibliothèque Nationale to send to Michigan on loan the file of the rare *Journal de l'industriel et du capitaliste* (1836–40). Dr. Bishop also bought the Guizot Collection, which contains several valuable pamphlets on the economic history of France. Another valuable collection is that presented by Mr. Kress to the School of Business Administration of Harvard University, which I was able to use through the courtesy of its librarian, Professor Arthur H. Cole. At the Widener Library much help in the preparation of this book was received from the late Walter Briggs of the Circulation Department and his successor Mr. Haynes. I am indebted also to Professor John Worley, for many years director of the valuable Transportation Library of the University of Michigan, and to his successor, the late Professor Roger Morrison, who also kindly read my chapter on roads. The chapter on capital has been strengthened greatly and clarified by the keen interest of Dr. Fritz Redlich in European banking in the early nineteenth century, and by his remarkable ability to find facts and appreciate their importance.

Some of the early chapters of this book were read critically by my teacher, the late Professor Edwin F. Gay, by Professor John U. Nef, of the University of Chicago, and by Professor Herbert Heaton, of the University of Minnesota. More chapters were read and criticized most patiently by my colleague Professor A. E. R. Boak. The chapters on machinery were read by Professor Usher and the whole second half of the book by Professor Arthur H. Cole, both of Harvard University, and the entire book by Colton Storm, long the assistant director of the William L. Clements Library, who, like Professor Cole, made numerous and helpful suggestions. To all these kindly critics I extend my hearty thanks, and my regrets for errors and omissions. In the preparation of the bibliography and the footnotes I have received skilled and kindly advice from Mrs. Patricia Irwin.

Other forms of valuable assistance I wish to acknowledge here. For the academic year 1933–34 I was granted by the regents of the University of Michigan a sabbatical leave, which I spent chiefly in Paris and London. I returned there in the summer of 1935 with my wife through a grant in aid from the Social Science Research Council. Thereafter, for two years, I received a grant from the Faculty Research Fund of the Rackham School of Graduate Studies at the University of Michigan. This enabled me to obtain the services of Dr. Robert Sethian, now in the Department of Commerce at Washington, in cross-indexing several thousand pages of notes. His knowledge of French and economics and his enthusiasm and loyalty were invaluable in the preparation of the manuscript.

Parts of several chapters of this book have been published in periodicals. For permission to reprint these I am indebted to the editors of the *Journal of Economic and Business History,* the *Journal of Economic History,* the Michigan Academy of Science, Literature, and the Arts, the *Journal of Modern History,* and the *Michigan Alumnus Quarterly Review.*

I wish to acknowledge gratefully the courtesy, encouragement and skill of my publisher, the Exposition Press, in particular its president, Mr. Edward Uhlan. Publication at this time has been made possible by the generous assistance of the dean and the Executive Committee of the Horace H. Rackham School of Graduate Studies of the University of Michigan.

This book is dedicated with respect and affection to Charles Schmidt, inspector emeritus of the Archives and Libraries of France, who has put his great knowledge at my disposal since I first began working in French economic history thirty-five years ago and who has always been a loyal and devoted friend.

ARTHUR L. DUNHAM

Ann Arbor, June 5, 1955

Contents

The Industrial Revolution in France

1815–1848

CHAPTER ONE

France in 1815

FRENCH HISTORY EMPHASIZES so strongly the creation of a great national state by its kings and their centralization of its administration that it is difficult to think of the country in any other terms. The Revolution, after numerous mistakes, increased this centralization, and Napoleon, heir both of the Bourbons and of the Revolution, strengthened and perfected the system so well that it has endured greater tests than any even he could have dreamed of. The economic historian must return to nature and study the geology and geography of the country. The picture thus obtained is very different from that painted by the political or legal historian. Though geography shows the possibility of unity and clearly points to Paris as the geographical capital, it shows even more strongly a most amazing diversity among the many districts, or *pays*. This diversity is apparent enough to be striking to any observant traveler, but it also extends deep into the soil. The charm of the constantly changing scene really portrays both a remarkable variety of natural resources and the distribution of those resources. The economic historian, then, while impressed by the unity of France, must always bear in mind the diversity. If one has been made out of many, there remain many in one.

Local differences in France are many because the country is large, and the two facts of diversity and size have created a transportation problem of great complexity. Until the middle of the nineteenth century there was little industrial concentration, and the scattered natural resources and such obstacles as frequent changes of elevation and numerous streams, some of which are swift, have made it difficult to connect local markets with each other and with Paris. This was a problem in an age of highways and waterways, even if less serious than it became with the advent of the railroad. In addition, so many parts of France are fertile that the country is still almost half agricultural, and in the earlier nineteenth century it was overwhelmingly so. Although the industrial tradition in France is ancient as well as honorable, it was followed by only a minority of the population until after the Revolution of 1848.

France has a long coast line, and so is maritime as well as continental; but that coast line is, on the whole, too straight. Harbors are numerous but are almost always small, so that the country has few natural ports able to hold large ships or to handle any great volume of trade. There was also another difficulty of equal importance. None of the important natural ports is in, or really close to, an important industrial region. This was not nearly so serious in 1815 as it is now; but if the size of ships, the volume of trade, and the concentration of industry were all far less then than they are now, so were the means of coping with them. The industrial resources of France, like the agricultural, were mainly in the north, while the best port, Marseilles, was in the south and served the Mediterranean. For expansion France needed rather ports on the Atlantic. She had Bordeaux, but that was some distance up the Garonne, and on the wrong side of the river. Le Havre was still small and somewhat difficult of access from the interior, while the greatness of Rouen, now the most-useful and best-equipped port in France, was undreamed of in 1815, because no one had yet conceived of the possibility of digging great basins out of the plain on the opposite side of the Seine, nor had the means of safely navigating the lower river yet been devised.

The fertility of much of the soil, the varied beauty of the countryside, and the comparative mildness of the climate have combined to produce in the French people a passionate devotion to the land and a burning desire in each to possess a bit of it, no matter how small. This has been strengthened by the fact that throughout her history France has had to fight off invaders. She has nearly always displayed extraordinary tenacity in doing this, and when she has been forced to submit, she has generally absorbed the invader. After each invasion she has resumed her usual agricultural productivity as if nothing had happened. This occurred after 1870, after the First World War, and seems to be occurring again at the present. The influence of this devotion to the land on the economic development of France has been great. Ownership of land has not been a mere matter of social prestige but a passion in nearly all classes of the population. Those with money nearly always invested it in land, either through direct purchase or through mortgages. In comparison, an industrial enterprise was apt to seem both unsafe and unattractive. The industrial worker was even more devoted to the land than his employer, because he helped bring forth its fruits with his own hands. In most cases he remained a peasant and returned to his farm for the summer and often for week ends as well. Thus the French manufacturer of the early nineteenth century found labor abundant, cheap, and intelligent; but he found it also obstinate, difficult to keep and to train, and still more difficult to get into mills. Like the peasants from whom he had generally sprung and whom he employed, the manufacturer used and abused the domestic system, partly because it seemed the most profitable, but more because his laborers would accept no other willingly. The employer himself often had the temperament of the peasant. He was interested in thrift as well as in profits, but not in expansion as a means of decreasing costs nor in improvement of methods. In most cases he knew little about science, economics, or planning. Like his workmen, he followed tradition. Since the French were singularly intelligent, however, then as now, and produced able scientists, engineers, and economists, they did learn new and better methods, but they learned slowly and reluctantly; and in 1815 they had scarcely begun to learn. This is perhaps the strongest reason why in France the Industrial Revolution developed slowly.

If her long coast line on two oceans made France maritime, her long land frontier made her continental. The Alps, the Pyrenees, and the Vosges may have served frequently as barriers to invasion, but there are passes through or around them. To the north there was no barrier between France and the Netherlands, but a plain that was an invitation both to invasion of France and to expansion by France to the north. And the valleys of the Rhône and Saône and the low hills of Champagne made contacts between southern France, Italy, and the Netherlands easy and frequent, just as the Trou de Belfort facilitated both trade and invasion from and to southern Germany and Switzerland. The effort to make the Rhine the frontier of France has been quite as persistent as the contrary effort to make it wholly a German river.

Geography, then, gave France ready access to the rest of the continent, and while it facilitated invasion and expansion even more than defense, it also facilitated trade. On the whole, the continental influences upon France were stronger than the maritime. Contact with the Netherlands was easier by land than by sea. While the Mediterranean coast and the port of Marseilles would appear to make easy contacts by sea between France and Italy, in actual fact contacts by land proved more important, even during the centuries before the advent of the railroad. The choice of Louis XIV to dominate the continent of Europe rather than to strengthen his colonial empire was not really deliberate any more than the support of his people in this policy was due to the king's personal magnetism. Similarly, Napoleon, in fulfilling the French Revolution, gloriously conquered the continent eastward to Russia, but failed completely on the sea.

Yet, if the continental influence on France was stronger than the maritime, it never won a complete victory. If France lost many colonies under Louis XV, and more still during the Revolution, she created a new colonial empire in the nineteenth century; if her navy and merchant marine were decimated more than once in her history, they were always rebuilt. The significance of 1815 in French history is that it marks the shattering of the most glorious era of continental expansion that France had ever known, and also demonstrates with unusual clarity the loss of many of her colonies and the destruction of much of her shipping. That year marks the beginning of a new era of reconstruction which France had to undergo at the very moment that she was called upon to face the rising tide of the Industrial Revolution.

The position of France is shown more clearly if we contrast it with that of England. The British lived near the Continent, but on an island that, despite its great size, is a true island and gave them remarkable security from invasion up to the twentieth century. This island had a markedly indented coast line which supplied many good natural harbors and frequently made communication by sea between different parts of the kingdom easier than communication by land. England had to expand by sea if she was to grow at all, while the foreign influences that stimulated her, as they did France, could come only over the ocean. Although England's industrial and agricultural growth are now regarded as having been gradual, and while her commercial expansion was also probably evolutionary rather than revolutionary, they all depended, from the beginning, upon her relations with countries overseas. The Industrial Revolution did not come until England had expanded commercially and accumulated through foreign trade the capital with which to develop her iron industry, her coal-mining, her cotton industry, and her system of inland transportation. Even coastal shipping, for obvious geographical reasons, played a greater part in British economic development than in French. England was fortunate also in her natural resources of iron and coal, which were both near each other and near the sea. While her iron was often less rich than the French, she could get the best ore from Sweden far more cheaply than France could transport ore within her own territory by land. The English, as a truly maritime people, were ready not only to explore and trade, but to emigrate, as the French never have been. Their navy became important in the seventeenth century, and supreme from the eighteenth to the twentieth, and was supported by an expanding merchant marine. In the same way English traders became bankers in order to finance their enterprises overseas, whether those markets were colonial or belonged to foreign states. This essentially maritime position of England proved in the twentieth century a cause of dire peril, but in 1815 England was riding on the crest of the wave commercially, financially, and industrially. This was the empire that continental France faced as Napoleon was carried off by the British to exile on St. Helena.

France never felt as keen an interest in her colonies as did England, because her attention was focused more on the Continent. For the same reason, her explorers, while able and courageous, were few, as were the settlers who followed them. France had many well-informed and able merchants, and the economic historian must always be heavily indebted to them for the evidence they have supplied regarding the industrial growth of their country and for the breadth of their views and the soundness of their judgment. But they were not eager to extend credit in foreign markets and colonies, because they were not supported by the manufacturers whose goods they were asked to sell, nor were they supported by public opinion or the government. Their position in 1815 was peculiarly difficult. Not only was the spirit of their countrymen no more maritime than before, but in almost every market overseas they found the British entrenched and well armed with cheap goods and credit. At the moment when French continental expansion had been checked so grievously and the country might have turned for relief to maritime expansion, it seemed as if every desirable market was held in political, financial, or commercial domination by Great Britain. The French also had no banking system that would make the development of foreign trade on a large scale possible. Banks were few and still inspired fear rather than confidence, even in the government. This point of view was soon to change, but the change had scarcely begun in 1815.

We have seen that the industrial workers in France were still peasants early in the nineteenth century and that the great majority of the manufacturers were moved chiefly by thrift and tradition. This meant that industrial expansion would be slow, certainly at the start. The development of natural resources of France also made slow growth inevitable. Potential water power was abundant in France but was little used because much manufacturing was still done in homes and the few mills that existed were small. In the early nineteenth century there was scarcely any production on a large scale and labor was cheap. Therefore there was no need for speed. Canal barges were frequently towed by men, and such machines as existed were usually wooden and run by hand or winches moved by horses or oxen. Only in Alsace was there any important use of water power, although in Normandy the change had also begun. Similarly, the power of steam, while known in France, was the possession of scientists rather than manufacturers. There was little need for such power, in the first place, while the coal necessary to produce it was too expensive to make its use profitable in a very small mill.

The greatest single reason for the great expense of coal was the general absence of adequate and economical means of transportation. Another reason was that coal was not mined on a large scale in 1815. We should remember that England did not begin to mine coal on a large scale until she had suffered for some time from a serious shortage of wood, despite the fact that her coal mines were seldom far from the sea and sometimes extended under it. In France there was no general shortage of wood until metallurgy began to develop rapidly about 1825.

The cost to France of the long period of civil and foreign war had been great, although some of it had already been paid through bankruptcy during the Revolution. Many roads and bridges had been damaged by the enemy or through neglect. For more than twenty years the greater part of the country's energy had gone into reform, revolution, or conquest, rather than into industry. As has been mentioned, a great part of the French merchant marine had been captured or destroyed, and for several years after 1815 France was occupied by foreign garrisons, while money had to be found not only to run the government and maintain order, but also to pay claims and indemnities due both to citizens and to foreigners.

But great as these difficulties were, it would appear to the economic historian that the greatest obstacle France had to overcome was the effect of her isolation from England for a quarter of a century. During that period France had made little economic progress, for existing methods had sufficed to wage war on the Continent. In the meantime, however, England had forged ahead, waging war less with her own armies than with her navy, her merchant marine, and her money. The nation of "contemptible shopkeepers" was far stronger financially, commercially, and industrially in 1815 than she had been in 1793, and infinitely stronger than France. England had in those years acquired many new colonies and other markets overseas, had dug many canals and begun the improvement of her roads, while she had developed on a large scale the power of steam and was applying it vigorously to industry and was beginning to apply it to transportation. France knew little about these improvements across the Channel. Her people were weary, humiliated, and uncertain of the future. Their restored monarch was old and unpopular and seemed likely at any time to be forced off the throne again by another revolution.

France, in overthrowing the Old Regime, had destroyed much that was bad and some that was good. The *corvée* had been greatly abused, but it had supplied labor with which to build and maintain roads. The *gabelle,* or salt tax, had led to even greater abuses, but it had been a valuable source of revenue. How were the roads and waterways, which were needed more than ever in 1815, to be paid for? The forests had suffered from neglect and from excessive cutting during the long period of disorder and warfare. These were some of the economic problems that faced the Bourbons on their return. Another problem arose from the loss of the French conquests under Napoleon. France now found herself separated from Piedmont, Lombardy, Rhenish Prussia, and Belgium, who were now competing against her as foreign states in the production and manufacture of silk, wool, flax, and iron. The competition of England seemed bad enough, but England was the hereditary foe. France's new competitors were her immediate neighbors on the Continent and had been a part of her empire during the period of her greatest power and glory. France had forgotten what competition in trade is like, and now it arose to threaten her on every side.

France had not, however, suffered serious destruction, whether in life or property, nor had the conditions of peace been harsh enough to leave her permanently weakened. Her great Revolution and the rule of Napoleon had purged her, and while they had inflicted some injury, they had also removed many impurities that would have impeded her economic progress. Her administration and her laws had been modernized and improved by the Convention

and by Napoleon. It is easy to forget the importance of these reforms because we associate the Convention with the Jacobin Club
and the Reign of Terror, and we think of Napoleon as a military
genius. The Convention, however, contained a considerable number
of men of great intellectual distinction, and it laid the foundations
for an excellent system of schools and for the development of the
universities. Among reforms of economic importance, it produced
the metric system, so useful now that it is difficult to understand
why it was not generally applied in French industry and trade for
forty years. Napoleon's codes put an end to interminable conflicts
among local laws and customs that had helped to paralyze the
administration of justice under the Old Regime and had greatly
hampered the progress of industry and trade. They combined the
principles of Roman Law with others derived from Canon Law and
the feudal customs of the Middle Ages, the decisions of the royal
courts, and the edicts of the Crown, while they added interpretations and amendments that made them practicable at the beginning
of the nineteenth century. The work was done by a group of jurists
of great distinction who completed it because they were urged on
by their emperor. In this same revolutionary period France built up
a chemical industry that proved of incalculable value to her in
metallurgy, engineering, printing, and dyeing.

The loss of Belgium, Piedmont, Lombardy, and Rhenish Prussia
has been mentioned as a calamity and as confronting France in
1815 with new and serious competition. But there is another side
to the picture. The incorporation of these states and provinces into
France had greatly benefited the French textile industries and
metallurgy, and the great French Empire of Napoleon had been a
powerful stimulant to French trade by making the whole of continental Europe up to the frontier of Russia, and even beyond it,
for a brief period, one great market for French goods. If humiliation and frustration were keenly felt in France on the downfall of
Napoleon, the glory and power of his empire were vividly remembered, as they are to this day. France had also made progress in
industry even during the Revolution. The mechanization of the
preparation and spinning of cotton had begun in the last years of

the Old Regime, and this continued. The best machines from England were introduced, at least until 1793, and spread thereafter, and mills were built. It is true that progress was very slow and the mills exceedingly small, while the cotton yarn they produced was coarse and poorly spun. The long period of civil and foreign war, one aspect of which was an economic struggle between France and England, made good American cotton very difficult to obtain. Even poorer cotton from the Levant was scarce, while prices were high and speculative. Under Louis XVI, merino sheep had been introduced from Spain. This was continued and, through interbreeding, a very considerable supply of fine wool was created within France itself, while during the first years of Napoleon's government were invented the merino cloths that proved so important to French industry and trade in the period 1815 to 1848.

Other gains in the period before 1815 were the creation of the Bank of France and the perpetuation and modernization of the medieval *commenda*. It is true that in 1815 the Bank of France was still young and was more useful to the government than to industry; but it gave a unity and strength to the financial system of France that were badly needed, and it began the slow process of teaching the French people to use banks and sound paper, whether as currency or as commercial notes. The *commenda,* generally known in the nineteenth century as the *société en commandite,* had evolved slowly in the Mediterranean world during the Middle Ages. It was modified in practice during the Revolution and formally in the Napoleonic Code of Commerce, so that it could be used to facilitate the transition from small partnerships with unlimited liability and nontransferable shares to the modern corporation. It is interesting to note that France, with her small, individualistic manufacturers and her fear of large companies was the first of the great countries of modern Europe to use extensively this valuable legal institution that was more useful and flexible than any possessed at that time by the powerful British Empire.

By 1815 France had suffered much, but her injuries were not permanent, and in many ways she was stronger than she had been before. Her territory was not devastated, her loss of life had not

been crushing, and her humiliation had not been too great for her
to bear. Her industries had not been destroyed; they had merely
suffered from speculative crises caused chiefly by internal disorder
and foreign war. Her financial structure, as we have seen, was far
better than any she had known. If her iron and cotton industries
looked fearfully across the Channel, there was no important evidence of fear in the other textile industries of wool, linen, and silk.
She had some very able manufacturers capable of adjusting themselves to the problems of mechanization and industrial expansion.
She had a considerable number of scientists and engineers, some of
whom were among the best in Europe, and she had excellent institutions for training them and organizations through which they
could work, such as the Corps des Ponts et Chaussées and the
Service des Mines. Her greatest material handicaps were probably
her small merchant marine and her inadequate system of inland
transportation, which had not been really modernized effectively,
was based as yet upon no national plan for expansion, and was
quite incapable of meeting unusual strains from large-scale mining
or manufacturing.

Psychologically, France suffered in 1815 from a fear of England's economic power, which had resulted partly from her defeat
by her ancient rival, partly from the reality of England's economic
strength, and partly from France's long isolation from industrial
and commercial contacts with her. Because of this, France was not
fully conscious of her own economic strength. She did not realize
that she must go through the Industrial Revolution almost from
the beginning, at the same time making the difficult readjustment
from war to peace which England also had to make. France clung
to the old domestic system and to small-scale manufacturing because
they seemed to meet her needs and were well suited to her actual
resources. To face the great changes ahead, she had courage, ingenuity, and many assets which needed only to be mobilized.

CHAPTER TWO

Roads

THE ADVENTURES OF MR. PICKWICK and the scientific and administrative skill of McAdam and Telford have made the nineteenth century familiar as a period when travel by stagecoach was quick and delightful in England. When we think of France after the overthrow of Napoleon we are apt to recall the enthusiastic descriptions of the royal roads which Arthur Young gave before the outbreak of the Revolution. It is an unpleasant surprise to find that most contemporary and many modern writers were loud in their complaints of the bad condition of French roads—that they were badly built, or badly maintained, that there were extensive gaps where they were almost impassable, and that the cost of traveling on them was high. They felt, in short, that the roads were a grave hindrance to the industrial and agricultural development of France in the early nineteenth century.

While the building of roads on a considerable scale had begun in France about the middle of the eighteenth century, the monarchy was most interested in straight and wide roads that should radiate from Paris or Versailles and meet the needs of the government or court. It was advised by the corps of engineers gradually brought together by Trudaine between 1743 and 1769 and called the Corps des Ponts et Chaussées. The school of this corps was producing regularly a small number of thoroughly competent highway engineers long before the outbreak of the Revolution, and its council planned and administered their work. Numerous great roads that impressed both French and foreign travelers were probably the best highways of the time in Europe; yet they were built primarily for administrative purposes, as had been the roads of Rome, upon which they were modeled. A solid foundation of large stones was considered necessary and the surface was usually paved. Since this made roads very expensive, only a few great highways between important cities, and usually near Paris, were built. But the government of France, like that of Rome, had the great resource of the *corvée,* by which poorer peasants could be required regularly to build or repair roads for brief periods each year without pay or, if the local authorities were unusually arbitrary, for periods as long as thirty, or even fifty, days. This meant that the funds assigned by the Treasury could be devoted chiefly to the erection of bridges or the salaries of engineers, but it meant also that the work was often done hastily and carelessly, since most of the labor was ignorant, unskilled, and reluctant. Many of the roads thus built aroused admiration when new, but deteriorated with considerable rapidity because of either faulty construction or inadequate maintenance. The royal government, furthermore, did not have more than partial control over the work in those provinces, such as Languedoc and Brittany, with Estates which voted the necessary funds. Other defects in the roads built in the eighteenth century, which were not apparent at the time, were very wide, soft shoulders, wide and deep ditches, and steep grades necessitated occasionally by the insistence upon straightness. These were not recognized as defects, because the volume of traffic was light and vehicles were seldom heavily loaded.

In some parts of France in the eighteenth century really excellent roads were built. The most notable example is the Generality of Limoges, where the great Turgot was *intendant* for many years before his brief tenure of office as minister at Versailles. He employed an unusually able highway engineer, Trésaguet; he abolished the *corvée* and paid his laborers; and he was fortunate in finding for his roads an unusually good quality of hard stone. Trésaguet developed a system of building roads that was very successful in the Limousin. He made a foundation of large stones carefully fitted together, and added a layer of smaller stones carefully broken; a surface of small stones was then spread carefully with shovels.

Trésaguet's method was adopted also by the province of Languedoc in the eighteenth century, but it did not prove as successful there, probably because the labor was neither as skilled nor as well paid and because the supervision was less thorough. These defects were shown by the necessity of rebuilding about half of the roads of Languedoc under the July Monarchy. This probably explains also why the method of Trésaguet, while it did spread widely through France under the Restoration, did so very slowly and was not preferred by most of the highway engineers to the method of McAdam, which was simpler. But Trésaguet made another contribution of greater importance through his insistence on constant inspection of roads after their construction, and immediate repair as soon as deterioration had been noted. In the periods of the Restoration and the July Monarchy this method was insisted upon by the best highway engineers and was gradually adopted by the government.[1]

During the Revolution the roads of France deteriorated rapidly, chiefly because of administrative and financial anarchy, supplemented by an increase of traffic that was probably considerable as warfare became more serious within the expanding frontiers of the republic. The whole responsibility for highways was transferred by the national government to the newly created *départements*. This was a serious mistake, because it meant a change from partly unified control to complete decentralization and to administration by incompetent, young, and wholly inexperienced authorities. The Revolution also abolished the *corvée* because of its abuse by arbitrary officials. Yet the loss of the *corvée* was serious, because it had been the chief source of labor for both construction and maintenance of roads, and it had provided this labor at a cost that appears to have been very low indeed.

In 1797 the republic found the condition of the roads deplorable. Assuming that this was because little or no money had been spent upon them since the abolition of the *corvée*, the Directory ordered tolls levied on vehicles using the main roads—a measure that

---

[1] Alphonse F. M. Léon, "Considérations sur les différents modes de construction et d'entretien des routes," *Annales des ponts et chaussées*, Série 1, v. 11 (1836), 139–43.

was resented widely because the government took no pains to improve the condition of the roads upon which the tolls were levied. With the advent of Napoleon came important reforms. The Law of 28 Pluviôse, Year VIII, gave municipal councils the power to use volunteer labor on the roads, and the Decree of 4 Thermidor, Year X, transferred this power to the executive officials of the local governments. As a result, some work was done on the local roads; but as the local officials had no power to compel labor and as the laws laid down no uniform rules for their own enforcement, little was accomplished beyond the statement of the idea that some substitute for the hated *corvée* must be found. In 1806 Napoleon imposed a new tax on salt, the proceeds of which were to be used for building or repairing roads, and he took administration of the more important roads away from the departments and restored it to the national government in 1811. He accomplished little by these changes, however, because gradually most of the proceeds from the new tax were spent either on roads outside the permanent frontiers of France or for the increasing needs of war; the change in administrative control became finally of little importance, because the Empire was absorbed first in the attempted conquest of Russia and then in the defense of France itself.

During the Restoration the condition of most French roads was unsatisfactory, and in many districts it was deplorable and grew worse, at least until 1824. In that year much information regarding the main roads was published in the report to the king by Becquey, director general of the Ponts et Chaussées.[2] In those districts where the traffic was unusually heavy, conditions were worst, as in the region around Saint-Etienne and Lyons, the main road down the valley of the Rhône, the district around Marseilles, and the low-lying districts in the Department of Nord. In the region around Saint-Etienne and Lyons, much of the trouble was due to the rapid development of coal-mining and metallurgy and to a lesser extent

---

[2] France, Ministère des Travaux Publics, *Les Travaux publics de France*, par Félix Lucas *et al.*, v. 1 (Paris, 1883), 56. France, Ministère de Travaux Publics, Administration Générale des Ponts et Chaussées, *Statistique des routes royales* [par Becquey] (Paris, 1824).

that of other industries, such as silk. Elsewhere we find the worst roads in rural districts, such as the plateau of Morvan and the Department of Nièvre, through which should have run the most direct main route between Paris and Lyons, and such as several districts in southern Normandy and Brittany and, in the former province of Languedoc, the Department of Gard. Many more districts probably could be added to this list if there were more local histories dealing with roads, or if the government had published more information regarding the less-important roads, which were not described adequately until the highway census of 1837.

One of the most distinguished of French economic historians, the late Henri Sée,[3] and a leading authority on finance, Clamageran,[4] have both stated, on the basis of the information available to them, that the government of the Restoration was indifferent to the condition of the roads. Other writers show that the government spent far too little on both construction and maintenance, that it made few major repairs, that, although it sent several of its best engineers to England to study the system of McAdam and received admirable reports from them, it neither adopted that system generally in France nor substituted for it a better system, and that it did not devise a system of general labor on the roads that could take the place of the *corvée*. Finally, the Restoration has been compared very unfavorably in its policy regarding highways to the monarchy of Louis Philippe. These accusations are important and are based upon a considerable body of evidence, but they are unjust.

The government of Louis XVIII confronted very serious problems in 1815. It was weak and unpopular. It had to pay the war indemnities exacted by the allies in order to free the country from foreign occupation. It had to pay, or fund, the debts incurred during more than twenty years of war, and it needed to repair the damage done to the roads and bridges of France by two allied invasions. In addition, it had to cope with the strain of a very consider-

---

[3] Henri Sée, *La Vie économique de la France sous la monarchie censitaire (1815–1848)* (Paris: Alcan, 1927), 141.

[4] Jean Jules Clamageran, *Etudes politiques, économiques et financières* (Paris: Alcan, 1904).

able increase in traffic, much of it very heavy traffic, which had begun during the Revolution, continued under the Empire, and continued with ever greater intensity after the restoration of peace. Not only, then, did the highway system of France need to be repaired, but it had to be prepared to withstand strains far greater than those for which it had been constructed. While in some respects the situation in France was less acute than in England, because industry and trade had developed much more slowly and with far less concentration in certain areas, in other respects the problems were greater because the country was much larger and more mountainous in many districts. Also, it was a part of the Continent, so that most of the industrial centers were not close to the sea. France could not, therefore, send any appreciable amount of her goods by water unless a great and expensive system of artificial waterways was constructed and the existing rivers were greatly improved. Even if all that were fully realized, France could not hope to send nearly as large a proportion of her goods by water as England did, and could never, therefore, protect her roads from undue strain as fully as her insular neighbor. The fact, also, that French industrial centers were numerous, small, and scattered meant that a great network of local roads had to be constructed, or repaired, in order to keep pace even wtih the slow development of French industries.

The government of the Restoration solved its principal financial problems well. It paid off the indemnity even more rapidly than the allies had expected and it funded the floating debt. By meeting its obligations honestly it established public credit, an essential foundation for the future development of business. With regard to transportation, the government undoubtedly was more interested in the development of waterways than of roads, as its critics have said, but it did not neglect the roads. The annual government grants for highways were increased from 14,000,000 francs at the beginning of the Restoration to 20,000,000 francs.[5] While this was scarcely

[5] Gustave F. Margueron, *Le Droit routier: Etude complète, historique, administrative et juridique du régime de circulation sur les routes françaises* (Paris: Dunod, 1930), 102.

half of what should have been spent, it may easily have been as much as the government could afford, for there had not been time to recover from the strain of prolonged war and the people were not accustomed to the flotation of large government loans for public works. Another serious handicap was the political dependence of the monarchy upon the landowning class, which was expressed in the restricted suffrage and in greater solicitude for agriculture than for industry. While the influence of the larger landowners on national legislation is well known, their influence upon local legislation has been overlooked; yet it affected seriously the development of highways.

The Restoration was slow in judging the merits of the system developed in Great Britain by McAdam. By 1820 the French government was well informed of the improvement of English roads. Engineers such as Cordier, Polonceau, and Baron Charles Dupin studied the highways across the Channel and recommended macadamization in France; but Becquey, as the official responsible for authorizing the change, hesitated. He reported in 1824 that tests of macadamized roads in France were being made, but were not yet conclusive.[6] He said that he doubted the wisdom of building roads without a foundation of large stones, and he evidently retained that conviction, for no action towards general macadamization was taken before he had been replaced by Legrand after the Revolution of 1830. It seems probable, however, that fewer paved roads were built than before and that most of the new roads were surfaced with small stones or gravel.

Maintenance of roads was inadequate during the period of the Restoration and the condition of many roads deteriorated, but one important improvement was made about 1816 with the establishment of road patrolmen to repair the roads regularly, instead of once or twice a year.[7] This was evidently done on a small scale because of lack of funds, and was increased slowly, so that the fact

---

[6] France . . . *Statistique des routes royales*, p. xxx.
[7] Pierre Dominique Bazaine, "Considérations générales sur les routes," *Bulletin de la société industrielle de Mulhouse*, v. 7 (1834), 321.

that the new system of maintenance had been adopted escaped the attention of most observers.

Some of the evils from which the highways of France suffered under the Restoration were due to the extreme centralization of the government and to the control of the bureaucratic Corps des Ponts et Chaussées. While this system of administration ensured better planning of the highway system as a whole, it meant also frequent interference with local authorities, frequent shifting of able engineers from districts where they were doing good work before it had been completed, and denial of many opportunities to use their initiative in local highway problems. On the other hand, evidence indicates that the number of departmental and communal officials was so great that no one, whether in Paris or in the district concerned, could take the initiative or be held fully responsible. These bureaucratic problems undoubtedly affected somewhat the improvement of departmental roads, and even more that of local roads. If funds were scarce, or other difficulties proved great, responsibility might be shifted from national to departmental or local officials by changing the classification of a road. We know that this was done frequently with unfortunate results. Some of the worst cases of it, in the Department of Bouches du Rhône, were recorded by one of the ablest prefects of the Restoration, Villeneuve-Bargemont.

The problem of creating an adequate system of local roads, which was vital to the development of both industry and agriculture in France, was not solved during the Restoration, because of the shortage of funds and the influence of the larger landowners in local as well as national legislation. The public was also not sufficiently aware of the problem to bring pressure to bear in time. We have seen that under the Consulate local officials had been authorized to employ labor for the construction or maintenance of their roads and that, in principle, local landowners could be taxed in money or labor for this purpose. But the larger taxpayers and the municipal officials who made such decisions were frequently also the larger landowners and were most reluctant to tax themselves for the benefit of the community. In fact, they often not only opposed the widening of local roads but actually encroached upon them in order to increase their landholdings. The Act of 1824 changed from ownership of land to citizenship the basis of liability for taxation in money, labor, or materials for the improvement or maintenance of local roads. Every able-bodied male resident of a commune who was a taxpayer was declared liable to two days' labor on the roads and, if head of a household, owed the same amount for every means of transportation in his possession. This was an improvement in principle, but not in practice, for the new law did not compel villages to collect taxes for roads in money or labor, and few did so, because of the opposition of the local landowners.[8]

After the Revolution of 1830 the government was in a better position to improve the roads. The floating debt had largely been funded, the government's credit had been firmly established, and suffrage had been widened, so that the landowners were no longer dominant. Furthermore, industry and trade had increased to a point where the demand for better means of transportation had become irresistible. Accordingly, in the new reign the government spent more than twice as much on roads as before, partly by increasing the usual annual appropriation from about 20,000,000 francs to about 30,000,000 francs[9] and partly by several special grants, such as that of 84,000,000 francs in 1837.[10] The policy of trying to limit the weight of loads in vehicles was no more successful than before, because there were not enough weigh bridges; and the policy of insisting on wheels with wide rims, which had been borrowed from England, where it had proved a failure, was dropped because it could not be enforced in the face of almost unanimous popular opposition. While far too little was said about the maintenance of roads, it is clear that it was improving steadily, that repairs were being made more frequently and promptly, and that their supervision was more thorough. The government was learning that mate-

---

[8] Antoine Ségalat, *L'Impôt de prestations: Son origine, sa législation, sa réforme* (Toulouse: Imprimerie Coopérative Toulousaine, 1906), 101–3.

[9] Margueron, *op. cit.*, 104.

[10] Michel Chevalier, *Cours d'économie politique fait au Collège de France,* 1st ed., v. 1 (Paris, 1842), 291.

rials spread thickly on roads not only helped little but were often harmful. It was getting far more complete and reliable information regarding the condition of roads, whether they were main roads or local ones; and it is estimated that, through knowledge of better methods of construction and better use of materials, the government reduced the amount spent on new main roads from 80,000 francs per *lieue* of four kilometres to 52,000 francs.[11]

The most important event in the history of French highways in the reign of Louis Philippe was the enactment of the Law of May 21, 1836, making compulsory the maintenance of local roads by local authorities and the collection of the tax called *prestation en nature*—that is, payment in money or labor by every able-bodied male taxpayer. If such a taxpayer did not choose within a specified number of days whether he would pay in money or give three days' labor each year, he could be compelled to pay in money; and if the local authorities did not vote the necessary sums from their funds, or enforce the law compelling labor, compulsion could be exercised by the prefect.[12] The need for this law was shown by the fact that, despite repeated orders, only thirteen departments had completed the classification of their local roads in 1836. This work was now done rapidly and thoroughly. Preference was given to the more important local roads, called "vicinal," because their mileage was less than a tenth that of the smaller local roads, called "communal"; but the latter were not neglected, for approximately half the funds raised were spent on them. Government officials helped the villages to do the work on their roads properly and to spend their funds wisely, and they brought pressure to bear when needed.

The report of M. Duchâtel, Minister of the Interior, to the king in 1843 shows that the Law of 1836 was enforced efficiently. Of 37,000 towns affected, only 7,000 had to be forced by the prefect to supply adequate funds.[13] The tax of *prestation* supplied a little

---

[11] Jules Burat, "Etat actuel de la question du roulage," *Journal de l'industriel et du capitaliste,* v. 1 (1836), 203.

[12] Ségalat, *op. cit.,* pp. 111–12.

[13] France, Ministère de l'Intérieure, *Rapport au roi sur l'exécution pendant l'année 1841 de la loi du 21 mai 1836 relative aux chemins vicinaux* (Paris, 1843), 12.

more than half of the funds needed for the local roads, the balance coming chiefly from other local taxes, or from funds belonging to the department concerned. The government of the July Monarchy, like that of the Restoration, refused firmly to renew the unpopular expedient of tolls on the roads, which had been tried by the Directory and given up within a few years. In this it acted against the advice of some of its ablest engineers, such as Cordier, Polonceau, and Michel Chevalier. It did concede construction of longer and more difficult bridges, as had the government of the Restoration, to private companies who were authorized to levy tolls. These toll bridges were frequently of the suspension type and made of iron.

There is little information available regarding traffic conditions on the highways of France between 1815 and 1848, beyond frequent complaints of the high cost of cartage, often accompanied by a request for a railroad or a waterway. There were frequent complaints, also, regarding the slowness of transportation; but indications are that conditions were probably better in France with regard both to speed and to cost than in other continental countries, except Belgium, and that in England, although the speed of vehicles on the roads was probably double that attained in France, the cost was very much greater. It is clear, also, that conditions in France improved steadily between 1815 and 1848, although we must not give all the credit to better roads, because there was also distinct improvement in the construction of public vehicles, and probably some in carts. Ordinary cartage was usually handled by peasants in two-wheeled carts supplied only when they could be spared from the farms, so that charges were lower in winter, when the roads were bad, than in summer, when they were good. About 1840, the usual charge appears to have been about 80 centimes per ton per *lieue*, compared to 2.25 francs in England and 1.80 francs in Germany and Italy, but these carts usually traveled only eighteen to twenty-five miles a day.[14] The chief improvement seems to have come through the development of fast cartage by using relays of horses.

---

[14] Emile Levasseur, *Histoire du commerce de la France depuis 1789,* v. 1 (Paris: Rousseau, 1911), 56.

This service was common, apparently, by 1832 and improved steadily because of better roads and increasing competition. Through a well-organized service of correspondents, shipments could be made to most parts of France and even abroad. The cost was approximately double that of slow or ordinary cartage. For very long trips, four-wheeled carts were used which were sometimes drawn by as many as eight horses and did great damage to some of the main roads, such as those between Paris and Havre, and Lyons and Marseilles. Many manufacturers must have been dependent upon such cartage.[15] We know the cotton manufacturers of Mulhouse had a regular cartage service between their city and Havre that took six days under the best conditions and a month under the worst, and it seems probable that there was a similar service between Mulhouse and Marseilles. The fast-cartage business was so important that between 1825 and 1850 it supported a large population of workers, manufacturers, and merchants, many of whom were organized in companies.[16] On several occasions they instituted boycotts and lawsuits in an effort to check some of the early railroads, and, in one or two cases, they tried to organize companies to build or control the railroads.

Travel by stagecoach developed extensively in France under the Restoration, and its growth continued until the latter part of the reign of Louis Philippe, when, we know, it was greatly affected by the opening of the railroad between Paris and Orléans and somewhat by that between Paris and Rouen. But coaching was not as successful as in England, because it was never as fast or as comfortable for the passengers. Turgot had found many private companies running stages under royal concessions, but because they did not satisfy the needs of the public or the government, he canceled the concessions and organized the Messageries Royales, which ran until

---

[15] Jean Baptiste Schwilgué, "Mémoire sur les routes et sur le roulage," *Annales des ponts et chaussées*, Série 1, v. 4 (Paris, 1832), 222–24.

[16] Philippe Barrey, *Le Havre maritime: La Batellerie et les transports par terre du XVIᵉ au XIXᵉ siècle,* in Hayem (ed.), *Mémoires et documents,* v. 6 (Paris: Hachette, 1921), 67–126.

the Year VI of the republic.[17] In 1805 it was reorganized and controlled most of the roads to Paris even after the government permitted the resumption of competition in 1817. It was a useful organization, for it gave the quick and regular service that the government wanted and it put an end to the anomalous situation Turgot had found of postmasters with horses but no carriages, and of stage companies with carriages but no horses.[18] All went well until 1827, when rival interests headed by the banker Laffitte organized the Messageries Générales, which proved a serious competitor, but this threat was met by an agreement of the two organizations to divide the main routes and charge the same rates.[19] Despite their power and the capital behind them, however, these two big companies do not appear to have controlled more than a third of the coaches of France,[20] but they were strong enough to prevent the organization of other companies of equal power and to survive several prosecutions for monopoly, one of which, in 1841, has supplied us with valuable information. They were not able to earn profits and pay large taxes to the government[21] by carrying passengers alone, although the number they carried daily increased

---

[17] Georges, vicomte d'Avenel, *L'Evolution des moyens de transport* (Paris: Flammarion, 1919), 96. Compagnie des Messageries Royales, *Observations de l'administration des Messageries royales sur le discours prononcé le 5 janvier 1841, à la tribune de la Chambre des Pairs, par M. le baron Charles Dupin, à l'occasion de deux pétitions d'entrepreneurs de messagerie* (Paris, 1841); in Guizot Collection of Pamphlets, v. 66, no. 5, p. 6, University of Michigan.

[18] Compagnie des Messageries, *op. cit.,* 7–8.

[19] Henri d'Alméras, *Au bon vieux temps des diligences* (Paris: Michel, 1931), 117–19.

[20] Jules Burat, "Des voitures publics," *Journal de l'industriel et du capitaliste,* v. 6 (May, 1839), 262.

[21] Pierre Edmond Teisserenc de Bort, *Les Travaux publics en Belgique et les chemins de fer en France* (Paris, 1839), 182. The postal service founded by Louis XI had been a government monopoly, as was the Administration of the Messageries established by Turgot. The Revolution had abolished the monopoly of the postmasters and thus deprived them of most of their income. In compensation the Law of 15 Ventôse, Year XIII, required that every entrepreneur of public vehicles pay 0.25 francs per horse to the postmaster whose relay he would otherwise have used. The revenue derived by the government was reported in 1831 as 5,600,000 francs from this indemnity and 10,300,000 francs from the rental of horses.

between 1810 and 1839 from 220 to 900.[22] They therefore carried
parcels at four times the cost of ordinary cartage, but a little more
rapidly than fast, or express, cartage. In this also they seem to have
been successful, for the volume of merchandise carried doubled in
the same period. While these two big companies checked the growth
of powerful competition, and thus undoubtedly prevented many
improvements, they did build better and lighter coaches and increased their speed considerably, cutting in half the time required
to reach some of the principal provincial cities, such as Bordeaux
and Brest. This was done through improvement of the coaches,
through improvement of roads, and, under Louis Philippe, through
increasing the number of horses pulling each coach and by continuing the journey during the night.

---

[22] Jules Burat, "Des voitures publics," 264.

CHAPTER THREE

Waterways

FRANCE IS A COUNTRY rich in rivers; it is not surprising that they were freely used by the Gauls as the main routes of communication. But many of the rivers proved ill suited to the needs of modern transportation. The problem of connecting them, so clear to the logical French mind because some of them, such as the Loire and the Seine, are close together, was actually difficult to solve, and in several cases the solution did not seem likely to give valuable results. Most French rivers, especially the Loire and Garonne, are irregular in flow; others, like the Rhône, are torrential; and many are shallow. Before the Revolution, because they seemed adequate for existing traffic, the Old Regime tried merely to connect them by canals. It was not realized that increase of trade would soon constitute a formidable problem that would be intensified by the decreasing flow of water caused by deforestation.

The most successful canal planned and completed before the Revolution was the Midi, or Canal des Deux Mers, connecting the city of Toulouse, at the head of river navigation on the Garonne, with the port of Cette (now Sète) on the Mediterranean. It was dug jointly by the national government and the Estates of Languedoc and, when largely completed, was sold at auction for 400,000 francs to Riquet, in 1669,[1] because it was believed that it could not be operated at a profit. It was wide and well built, and under private management it became extremely productive.

It is true that before embarking on this great and expensive undertaking, the monarchy had dug a short and narrow canal from

---

[1] *Journal de l'industriel et du capitaliste,* v. 4 (Paris, 1838), 236.

Briare on the Loire to Montargis on the Loing, a small tributary of the Seine. Completed in 1642,[2] it was thus actually the first canal in France, but it was not really useful until it had been supplemented by the Loing canal begun in 1719 and completed in 1724,[3] which gave the necessary connection with the Seine itself and, through the Seine, with Paris. An alternative route to the Briare, the Canal d'Orléans, running from the city of Orléans on the Loire to Montargis, had been begun in 1679 and was completed in 1692. These canals were much less successful than the Midi. They were narrow and shallow, and were small, although their strategic importance was far greater than that of the Midi, for they formed a vital connection between the greatest river of central France and the chief artery of the north.

It is interesting to note the precedent set when both the Orléans and the Loing canals were conceded to the duke of Orléans. Although they both reverted to the state during the Revolution,[4] they were sold by Napoleon in 1808 and were soon again in the hands of the Orléans family, which thus found itself in possession of the most decisive link in the system of French waterways in 1830, when it unexpectedly acquired the throne as well. This singular opportunity for personal profit by the sovereign at the expense of the nation was utilized fully.

The old monarchy can be condemned justly for its indifference to the waterways of France, despite its important contribution in the Midi canal. It not only neglected the rivers but allowed private landowners to make navigation on them difficult and dangerous through the operation of mills and fishing weirs. It did not regard

---

[2] *Ibid.*, v. 9 (Dec., 1840), 299. The Midi canal was opened to navigation in 1684.

[3] Alphonse C. Courtois, "Notices historiques et statistiques sur les canaux entrepris en vertu des lois de 1821 et 1822," *Journal des économistes,* v. 29 (July, 1851), 213. Dupérier gives the date of 1792 and Courtois 1692 for the completion of the Orléans canal, and 1793 for that of the Loing. Antoine Louis Ravinet, *Dictionnaire hydrographique de la France,* v. 1 (Paris, 1824), 87 and 107, agrees with Courtois.

[4] Richard von Kaufmann, *La Politique française en matière de chemins de fer* (Paris: Librairie Polytechnique, 1900), 804 (Decree 15 January, 1790). Napoleon ordered the sale of these canals in Decree 8 March, 1808.

the waterways as a public service, did not make provision for them in its budgets, and did not put them under the control of the Corps des Ponts et Chaussées until late in the eighteenth century. But it planned other canals of real importance—that from the Rhône to the Rhine; that of Nivernais, from the Loire at Decize, near Nevers, to the Yonne at Auxerre; the canal of Burgundy from the Saône to the Yonne; the Centre, connecting the Saône with the Loire; the Cher, or Berry, connecting the upper with the lower Loire and opening up a district containing excellent iron ore and abundant supplies of both wood and coal; and finally, a canal connecting the Somme with the Oise in the north. The Old Regime, however, did not complete any of these, and in most cases, it did not even begin construction. The only one of them which the old monarchy nearly completed was the Centre, but it was so narrow and shallow and had been dug so badly that it was of little use and had to be almost entirely rebuilt.[5]

The periods of the French Revolution and the Empire were not important in the development of French waterways. A few canals were opened during the early years of the Revolution, such as the Centre in 1793. Napoleon had great plans, such as that of building a canal connecting Dijon with Paris—although this had been planned previously by the Bourbons—and that of connecting the Rhine with both the Saône and the Scheldt. He is generally credited with having added 205 kilometres of canals to the 1,067 already open, whereas his Bourbon successors built 930 kilometres under the Restoration and 1,442 under the Orléans monarchy.[6] Napoleon was going to raise considerable sums to finance his program of waterways by selling canals owned by the state and by levying on boats using both canals and rivers navigation dues based upon the cost of the improvements required on each waterway. But, as happened so frequently under the Empire, most of the funds so raised were diverted to other purposes, and the navigation dues, which

---

[5] Dupérier, "De la navigation intérieure," *Journal des économistes,* v. 7 (June, 1844), 250.

[6] Paul Boiteau, *Fortune publique et finances de la France,* v. 1 (Paris, 1866), 90, 101.

seemed logical from the financial point of view, proved subsequently to be highly detrimental to the increase of traffic. The emperor did force the digging of the Ourcq Canal and the basin of La Villette, although they were not opened to navigation until after his death; and he issued a useful decree in the Year XI dividing France into basins, and each basin into districts, with a resident engineer appointed for each.[7]

The most important single step in the development of French waterways between 1815 and 1848 was the comprehensive scheme prepared by Becquey, director general of the Ponts et Chaussées, on the orders of a majority of the Cabinet and presented to the king on August 16, 1820, by Comte Siméon, the Minister of the Interior.[8] This first general plan of a system of inland waterways in France utilized the work of the predecessors of Louis XVIII and the rivers provided by nature, and it called attention to the fact that canals to be dug or completed could not be fully utilized until the rivers which they would connect had been put in good condition. It distinguished between the main waterways of capital importance to the kingdom and a great number of small ones rightly classified as of minor importance. An excellent map showing all the different types of waterways was attached to the report.

From the points of view of geography and cartography, the plan was admirable. It is only when we consider other aspects of France that the defects of the plan appear. It contains no thorough discussion of the cost of construction or operation of either existing or future waterways. It scarcely mentions the important problems of construction, except in a few matters of detail, nor does it make any recommendations for the improvement of those rivers it declares need improvement. It says that the need for the canals was so great that any method of securing the funds for their construction or completion should be approved if it would give quick results. The

<hr>

[7] François Maury, *Le Port de Paris hier et demain* (Paris: Guillaumin, 1904), 23–24.

[8] François Louis Becquey, "Rapport au roi sur la navigation intérieure de la France," *Annales de l'industrie nationale*, Série 2, v. 1 (1820), 138–52, 193–209.

choice between government or private construction and control, the length of leases, and the control of rates are all treated as questions of minor importance. Still more serious is the lack of any attempt to estimate the future growth of traffic, or to ensure a wide and deep canal connecting the Loire with the Seine. This was the key to the whole system of waterways at that time, when the region watered by the Loire and its tributaries provided a very large part of the grain, wine, iron, and coal used by Paris and other important centers.

In 1821 and 1822 the French government made practical arrangements to dig many of the waterways recommended by Becquey. The financing of the work, which was criticized afterwards more than any other feature, was sound and reasonable. The government had no sources of income which could be applied exclusively to the construction of canals; in fact, it had hardly enough cash for its immediate needs. It had recently floated loans at home and abroad for the payment of indemnities to the victorious allies and had thereby freed France from occupation by foreign armies, and it had laid a sound foundation for public credit. It had also guided the country through the crisis caused by the crop failures of 1817 and the ensuing financial depression. The government, realizing that it must borrow in order to dig the desired canals and that its credit was not yet very good, signed an agreement with the promoter Urbain Sartoris, who was supported by the Parisian banker Greffulhes, for a loan of approximately 18,000,000 francs at 6 per cent for the completion of the canals of the Somme, Manicamp, and the Ardennes, and the improvement of the Aisne and Oise rivers.[9]

In the next year the government borrowed about 98,000,000 francs in a series of loans bearing an average rate of interest of 5½ per cent for the construction or completion of the canals of Brittany, the Loire, Berry, and Nivernais, which were soon merged in an

---

[9] Dupérier, *op. cit.*, 245. Jacques Bresson, *Histoire financière de la France,* 1st ed., v. 2 (Paris, 1829), 349. Alexandre Léon Joseph, comte de Laborde, *De l'esprit d'association dans tous les intérêts de la communauté,* 2d ed., v. 2 (Paris, 1821), 244.

organization known as the Company of the Four Canals; for the completion of the canal from the Rhône to the Rhine, known as the Canal de Monsieur, by a group composed chiefly of Alsatians and led by Humann, the future Minister of Finance and partner of the Duc Decazes in the great metallurgical establishment of Decazeville; and for the completion of the canal of Burgundy.[10]

Little information is available regarding the bankers and other financiers involved in these transactions, but it seems probable that the interests afterwards merged in the Company of the Four Canals, and probably some others, such as the canal of Burgundy, were represented by Parisian bankers such as Jacques Laffitte, Bartholony, Pillet-Will, Mallet Frères, Lapanouze, André Cottier, Ardoin, Hagermann, and, probably, the Rothschilds themselves.[11] Some of these bankers, such as Bartholony and Pillet-Will, had close connections with the financial center of Geneva; others were connected with the Bank of France, and Hagermann, who supplied funds chiefly for the canal of Burgundy, was probably an Alsatian. These facts and inferences indicate that the government found its credit growing stronger and that it was able in 1822 to secure the financial support of some of the principal bankers of Paris, Alsace, and Geneva for its comprehensive plan for the construction of canals.

In justice to the critics of these agreements, it should be noted that, although the government secured its funds at rates of interest that cannot fairly be called unreasonable, since the 5-per-cent *rentes* were then well below par, it had also to pay between 1 and 2 per cent for amortization and was forced to agree in most cases that, after the loans had been paid off, the lending companies should

---

[10] Dupérier, *loc. cit.*

[11] Laborde, *op. cit.,* v. 2, 243. Jacques Bresson, *loc. cit.* Henri Melchior de Lagréné, "Statistique de la navigation intérieure," in France, Ministère des Travaux Publics, *Les Travaux publics de la France,* v. 3 (Paris, 1883), 7. Jean Baptiste Capefigue, *Histoire des grandes opérations financières,* v. 2 (Paris, 1856), 104. Gonsalve, baron de Nervo, *Etudes historiques: Les Finances françaises sous la Restauration,* v. 2 (Paris, 1866), 104. Pierre de Joinville, *Le Réveil économique de Bordeaux sous la Restauration: L'Armateur Balguerie-Stuttenberg et son œuvre* (Paris: Champion, 1914), 130.

enjoy half the net income from the canals for periods running from forty to ninety-nine years. The loans had to be paid off within a given term of years, and if the canals were not completed within the time set by the government—and none of them were—the companies should receive indemnities in compensation. Finally, the companies should have the right to inspect the government's financial and administrative records concerning the canals and must give their consent to any change in the freight rates charged on the canals covered by the agreements of 1821 and 1822. The companies immediately issued shares of stock, called *actions de jouissance,* approximately equal in number to the ordinary shares, giving the holder a claim to the future earned income of the canals. These were dealt in on the Bourse, as were the other shares, and were frequently raised in value by speculation.

The questions raised by these *actions de jouissance* seemed of slight importance when the agreements were signed under the Restoration. They became highly significant under the July Monarchy when widespread complaints against the high rates charged on the canals and against the profits made by the companies (or what the public believed were made) forced the government to seek the consent of the companies to a general reduction of rates. Despite the threat to exercise its right under the constitution to take over the canals after indemnifying the companies, the government accepted the refusal to consent to reduction of rates by the companies of the Loing and Orléans canals, the majority of whose stock was owned by the royal family. The rights of the two companies rested upon perpetual concessions, but even more important was the strategic situation of the canals in connecting the Loire with the Seine, forcing their use regardless of the rates charged. Finally, the Cabinet hesitated to defy the king by taking over his canals. The high rates continued, as the public believed, to paralyze traffic on the waterways of France until the strong government of the Second Empire bought the canals after Louis Philippe had died in exile.[12]

---

[12] Ernest Grangez, "Des droits de navigation intérieure sur les rivières et canaux," *Journal de l'industriel et du capitaliste,* v. 9 (Oct., 1840), 210. Dupérier, *op. cit.,* 250.

The plan presented by Becquey to the king in 1820 emphasized speed as the most important consideration; but it was executed slowly, for many reasons. No thorough study of the engineering problems involved in the construction of the canals had yet been made, although the plan had been asked for in 1818. Critics friendly to Becquey and the Corps des Ponts et Chaussées, among whom one of the most important in this case was the reforming highway engineer Berthault-Ducreux, insist that many of the difficulties of construction could not have been foreseen. We know only that much time and money were consumed in these studies of engineering problems after Becquey's plan had been presented. Another important cause of delay was the inadequacy of the funds supplied. The sums raised through the loans could not have sufficed even if they had been used quickly and efficiently. The cost of building and completing the canals authorized by the Laws of 1821 and 1822 actually was nearly three times what had been estimated. The government was criticized severely for the inadequacy of its estimates, but we find that similar and sometimes greater errors were made in estimating the cost of construction of canals in England. It is not just, therefore, to support the criticisms of the government of the Restoration, nor can we blame it for not supplementing the inadequate loans by grants from the budget.

Further investigation shows also that the government, in digging the canals, encountered much opposition from the landowners affected, who insisted upon fantastic indemnities for the loss of the land actually taken for the canal and the depreciation of the remainder. In far too many cases the government had to institute condemnation proceedings in the courts, which greatly delayed the progress of the work. Similar difficulties were encountered in the building of many of the roads, and we find records of them in England also. The delays in executing the plan of 1820 were, therefore, largely inevitable, although not wholly so. The government was partly responsible for digging most of the important canals itself through the Corps des Ponts et Chaussées. Sartoris objected that greater speed and efficiency could have been secured if the same engineers had worked under the control of private companies who could have selected them for their competence alone and could have controlled also their contractors and workmen.[13] This mistake by the government was due partly to the pride of the Corps des Ponts et Chaussées, and partly to the fact that the government had always distrusted private initiative in public works.

The new monarchy following the Revolution of 1830 continued the program of the old and by the year 1843 completed practically all the canals it had found unfinished. These amounted to approximately 2,700 kilometres; an exact figure is difficult to give because authorities differ as to the dates when certain canals were finished. Some canals are known to have been officially opened before they were really finished; and Eugène Flachat, one of the ablest engineers and soundest writers on the subject, goes so far as to say that most of the canals were never entirely finished.[14] The canals officially completed included in central France that of Nivernais, finished after a delay of fifty-eight years, the Berry (or Cher), the lateral canal of the Loire, and the canals of Burgundy and of the Rhône to the Rhine.[15] The canals of Brittany were dug primarily for military reasons and were never expected to be profitable. In the north the canals completed were the Ardennes, the Somme, the lateral canals of the Aisne and Oise, and the canalized section of the Oise River. To this list we should add the canal from Roanne to Digoin, conceded under the Restoration but opened only in 1838. The delay was due to the fact that the company had been financed largely from Geneva and was therefore not fully organized until 1831. Then it had soon to be reorganized because of need for more capital. This canal should really be considered a part of the lateral canal of the Loire, because it follows the course of that river closely, but it has not generally been so classified.

---

[13] [Urbain Sartoris] *Note sur les canaux adjugés en 1822* (Paris, 1822), 6, 21.

[14] Louis Joseph Gras, *Le Forez et le Jarez navigables: Historique de la navigation de la Loire et sur le canal de Givors et des projets de canal de la Loire au Rhône* (Saint-Etienne: Théolier, 1930), 103. He quotes an address by Eugène Flachat, 1872.

[15] Léon Faucher, "Des projets de loi sur les chemins de fer," *Revue des deux mondes,* Nouvelle série, v. 13 (1 May, 1843), 360. He lists the following delays: canal Rhône–Rhine, 35 years; canals Brittany 34, Nivernais 58, Burgundy 61, Somme 65, canalization Ill and Tarn rivers 74.

The July Monarchy, in its turn, planned several new canals which it was unable to finish. Among the most important were those of the Marne to the Rhine, from the Marne to the Aisne, and the lateral canal of the Garonne. Much of this work was possible because the revenue of the kingdom had increased greatly and because the credit of the government had grown stronger. Thus, where the Restoration had been able to spend only 142,591,000 francs on the canals, the government of Louis Philippe spent 248,499,852.[16]

While we have been considering at length the development of canals we have scarcely mentioned navigation on any river except the Oise. The rivers were neglected by the government and for some time also by public opinion; but, under the July Monarchy, demands for the improvement of the rivers increased until they compelled official attention. Michel Chevalier, an engineer by training and an economist by choice, wrote a few years after the accession of Louis Philippe that the canals of France did not tap the great mineral wealth of the country and did not connect well the towns on their banks, and that they should be regarded only as a tribute to the skill of French engineers and the resources of France. The canals were useless, he said, because the rivers they connected had not been improved; and most of them had become more dangerous to navigation than they had been in the days of the Gauls. He described nearly all of them as irregular in flow, or even torrential, or else full of shoals or rocks. Finally, he said, the engineers were not sure what was the best method of improving the beds of rivers.[17]

While Chevalier went too far in condemning the canals as useless, he was quite correct in his description of the difficulties of river navigation and of the unfortunate effect of these upon the canals. Goods could be sent down the Loire above Roanne, where

---

[16] Félix B. Lucas, *Etude historique et statistique sur les voies de communication de la France* (Paris, 1873), 102.

[17] Michel Chevalier, "Navigation du territoire," *Journal de l'industriel et du capitaliste,* v. 3 (Jan., 1837), 45; *Des intérêts matériels en France,* 4th ed. (Paris, 1838), 68–70.

the traffic in coal from the mines of Saint-Etienne was of great importance, only during flood. Almost all parts of that great river, until tidal navigation became possible, were full of sand bars, and the river was also wide enough and the country flat enough to make wind a real difficulty. On the Yonne River below Auxerre, which was the outlet for the Nivernais and Burgundy canals, there were sixty-nine shoals in a distance of 120 kilometres. Boats could be sent down only by shooting a sudden flood of water out of the Nivernais canal. We hear also of great difficulties encountered on the Saône, which had to be used for some distance by boats wishing to enter the canals from the Rhône to the Rhine, Burgundy, and the Centre, connecting the Saône with the Loire. The Oise, through which all traffic from the north had to pass to reach Paris, was full of obstructions; the Seine, perhaps the best of all French rivers for commercial purposes, contained shoals, rapids, fishing weirs, islands, and dangerous sand bars. The difficulties of navigation on the Rhône and Garonne are too well known to need description.

A remedy for many of these difficulties was found at almost the exact moment when complaints were compelling action by the government. In 1834, Poirée, the chief engineer of the canal of Nivernais, invented a movable dam which could be installed at a moderate cost in the bed of the river, to be raised when water was low and lowered when it became too high. This invention, which had been made at Clamecy on the Yonne, was improved at Decizes, on the Loire, in 1836, and still further at Bezons on the Seine. There it solved successfully the problem of getting boats through the rapids of La Morue, which had formerly required at least thirty horses for each well-loaded barge. Poirée's invention, while little used abroad, was well adapted to the small rivers of France, where the fall of water is small and the banks high. It became a favorite method of French engineers and enabled them eventually to canalize the Seine successfully and secure a uniform depth of 3 metres of water from the mouth of the Aube to Saint-Aubin near Elbeuf. Their aim was not achieved completely until 1888, however, because of excessive caution on the part of the government, first concerning the merits of the movable dam, and then over the expense of installing an adequate number of dams.[18]

Despite these great delays, much was done for the improvement of French rivers under the July Monarchy. The great route from the north was fully opened at last in fulfillment of the plan of the Restoration by the completion of the canal of Saint-Quentin after its concession to M. Honorez in 1827. He had stopped the seepage of water through its sandy soil by opening the lateral canal of the Oise in 1831 and that of the canalized Oise in 1836. The results of these improvements were prompt and striking.

The government was less successful in its handling of the problem of the Seine, but it was not inactive. The upper Seine was canalized for 44 kilometres from Troyes to Marcilly between 1840 and 1846. The passage through Paris, where the river falls more rapidly and where the traffic was dense, was finally made safe and easy by enclosing the river between stone quais, beginning in 1845, and by towing boats by a sunken chain instead of by horses on towpaths. On the lower Seine the government, on the advice of its engineers, proposed in 1833 a series of permanent dams in the bed of the river with locks which would cost 20,000,000 francs and would ensure a uniform depth of water of between 1.8 and 2 metres. This was opposed by the Chambers of Commerce of Paris, Rouen, and Le Havre and by the navigation companies, which asked the government simply to widen the arches of the bridges, improve the towpaths, and regulate the channel so that horses would not have to cross the river so often. The government, unable to decide between the merits of these contradictory plans, did nothing.[19] A few weeks later, however, a final and completely successful test of Poirée's movable dam was completed at the rapids of La Morue at Marly, tested from 1838 to 1840. Poirée advised the construction

---

[18] René Musset, "La Canalisation des rivières en France," *Annales de géographie*, v. 47 (15 September, 1938), 502–4.

[19] "De l'amélioration des rivières en France," *Journal de l'industriel et du capitaliste*, v. 3 (Oct., 1837), 653–67. Taken from reports of Marquis de Dalmatie and Comte Daru to the Chambers of Peers and of Deputies.

of thirteen dams between Paris and Rouen to give a depth of 2 metres, and the government secured passage of the Law of May 31, 1846, authorizing the construction of six dams to give a uniform depth of 1.6 metres.[20]

More general measures for the improvement of the rivers had been taken earlier in the reign of Louis Philippe. The first response to the growing number of complaints came in the year following Poirée's invention in the form of the Law of 1835 creating a permanent fund of 6,000,000 francs for the maintenance and improvement of the rivers Scheldt, Moselle, Ill, Baïse, and Adour, together with an annual appropriation of 3,750,000 francs for the improvement of certain other rivers.[21] In 1837 the government was given 60,990,000 francs to divide between the Aa, Meuse, Marne, Yonne, Seine, Vilaine, Charente, Dordogne, Tarn, Lot, Saône, and Aisne.[22] Other measures were taken later, but many of them were justly criticized on the ground that the government should not have insisted on simultaneous improvement of the bed of a river and construction of a lateral canal. This error was committed in the cases of both the Loire and the Garonne, and a greater error was added when the government continued all these waterways after asking the building of parallel railroads. Teisserenc, in making this criticism, said that he could not state the causes of so faulty a policy, but hinted at envy, the pressure of local interests, and rivalry between the government's engineers and private interests.[23]

Before any important improvements had been made on the rivers of France, steamboats had been introduced. The first one, mentioned in 1814, was an English steamer running to the French port of Le Havre. We hear of a service, in 1822, of fast freight on the Saône, and by 1826 there were twenty-four steamers on the

---

[20] "Application du barrage mobile de M. Poirée à la navigation de la Seine," *Journal de l'industriel et du capitaliste*, v. 9 (July, 1840), 24. Maury, *op. cit.*, p. 133.

[21] "De l'amélioration des rivières," 627.

[22] *Ibid.*, 696.

[23] Pierre Teisserenc de Bort, "La Crise des chemins de fer," *Journal des économistes*, v. 28 (March, 1851), 230–35.

lower Seine (below Paris) and three on the upper, six on the Saône, seven on the Loire, and, shortly afterwards, ten on the Garonne, or a total of approximately fifty. This number increased slowly but steadily until 1837, when there were 124, after which there was a more rapid increase to 227 in 1841 and 242 in 1843, according to the figures given. These last figures, although from good sources, seem exaggerated. They are probably to be explained by the sudden addition of new classes or types of steamboats not listed before, such as packets built by the government for use in the Mediterranean or in Senegal, or by errors in official computations, which were not infrequent.[24]

The first steamers were probably imported from England, and later the engines were probably imported but the boats built in France. The early dependence upon England caused certain difficulties and delayed the general adoption of steamers in France. The tariff duties on ships and iron were very high, and those on machinery far from low, while coal as fuel was expensive in France. The French needed time to learn how to make the engines themselves, and at first they were afraid of possible explosions. It was discovered gradually, however, that the English steamers and engines, designed primarily for coastal navigation, or for use on tidal rivers, were too big and heavy for any French rivers except the maritime part of the Seine; and if the engines were put into light and shallow French boats the vibration was terrible. The French, therefore, began to manufacture their own steamers, and by 1834 we find Manby and Wilson of Charenton, Hallette of Arras, and Cavé of Paris listed as manufacturers of engines, most of which were of Watt's low-pressure type, although about one third were the high-pressure type of Evans. Later we find engines made for steamers on the Saône and Rhône by the Creusot iron works and by the establishment of the navy at Indret.

---

[24] Most of the statistics are from a series of short articles in the *Journal de l'industriel,* 1836–40, many of them by Amédée Burat, an eminent geologist and secretary of the Comité des Houillères. In most cases figures are based on the annual or biennial reports of the Ingénieurs des Mines.

Competition between different steamboat companies and between steamers and stagecoaches brought considerable improvement in steamers on the Saône. The small, wide, and slow boats of 1826 were narrowed and lengthened to increase their speed and, by 1840, were made with hulls of iron, while a few years later propellers began to replace paddle wheels.[25] Steamers for both passengers and freight soon became popular on the chief French rivers, but they were seldom profitable. Most of the companies were organized by relatively obscure men with inadequate financial support. Tugs were very useful on the Seine, where, below Rouen at least, the water was deep but curves and sand bars made sailing difficult, though the volume of freight was great. They were used on other rivers also, but probably to a lesser extent, except on the Rhône. There the swift current and frequent floods made towing barges impracticable, although steamers with more powerful engines were able to go upstream and the time from Arles to Lyons was reduced from eighty-eight hours in 1829 to thirty-four hours in 1844.

Any attempt to judge the utility of the French waterways in carrying traffic is rendered difficult by the almost universal complaints against excessive dues, though it is quite clear that other considerations must have played a greater part. It is almost impossible to determine the exact rates charged, because few writers use the same measurements of volume or distance and few distinguish between navigation dues and the actual cost of hauling the boat. Other writers critical of the French government speak with enthusiasm of the great earnings of the English canals, the enormous volume of traffic they carried, the speed of their service, and their ability to use large barges of uniform size for through shipments. It is known, however, that many English canals were not prosperous, that more than half were of small sections, and that many were shallower than most French canals and had smaller locks. While a few English canals gave excellent service and used big barges, many others did not and could not have done so because of

<hr>

[25] W. Manès, "Notice sur la navigation à la vapeur de la Saône et du Rhône," *Annales des ponts et chaussées,* Série 2, v. 5 (1843), 10–46.

their smaller dimensions. The good service and big barges in England were largely in the hands of private firms, such as the Wedgwoods, or in the hands of shipping companies, of which there were far too few in France.

The fundamental error made in such comparisons lay in the fact that England built her canals to care for existing and dense traffic in a few districts. Most voyages on British waterways were short, and inland transportation was aided powerfully by excellent ports and coastal shipping. In France, on the other hand, serious traffic problems existed in few districts when the waterways were planned; distances were much greater; well-equipped ports scarcely existed; and coastal shipping was small in volume. The inland waterways of France, therefore, had a much greater burden to bear, although there was compensation in the fact that the volume of traffic was seldom heavy and that it grew rather slowly. The industrial growth of France was not rapid like that of England. In the period which we are considering, 1815–48, France was still overwhelmingly agricultural.

Most of the canals of France were well planned by competent engineers and were wide with sloping sides, but the actual digging and grading were sometimes badly done. The government's engineers had either labor of poor quality or contractors whom they could not control fully because of lack of adequate authority or because of delays through official formalities. Many canals suffered from excessive seepage or from lack of water because of insufficient reservoirs. Thus both the Briare Canal, built in the early seventeenth century, and the canal of Givors, built in the late eighteenth century, had to build extra reservoirs about the middle of the nineteenth century. Others that could not, or would not, such as the Burgundy and the canal from the Rhône to the Rhine, had to close for long periods annually or limit the draft of barges. In the case of the Centre Canal, connecting the Saône with the Loire, the shortage of water made it almost useless when first opened, but after 1822 additional reservoirs were provided and the principal watershed was lowered. In such cases it would be easy for a critic to complain of unreasonable rates when actually the cost of transportation to the shipper was high because he had to send his goods in a small barge only partly loaded.

Many of the problems of French inland navigation are clarified if we consider first comments by two able French writers, Charles Comte, the son-in-law of Jean Baptiste Say,[26] and Baron Jean Jacques Baude,[27] one of the principal owners of coal mines in the district of Saint-Etienne. We may then compare the history and efficiency of the two greatest highways of inland navigation, the Loire and the canals connecting it with the Seine, and the Oise and its connections with the north and Belgium. Comte said in 1826 that the network of canals authorized by the Laws of 1821 and 1822 was based upon the memoirs of Dutens on the public works of England, published in 1819, and on similar sources. These sources showed neither the cost of transportation before the canals had been opened nor the economies effected by them; nor did they show the influence of the canals upon English agriculture, industry, and trade. Consequently, said Comte, France had no sound basis for judging whether canals were good or bad. Although Becquey does not give any of his sources of information in his plan of 1820, we do know that Dutens had been sent to England by the French government; and Becquey's neglect of commercial and industrial matters in his plan has been emphasized here.

Baude had complained a year earlier that the French government did not consult representatives of business before digging new canals, as England did through Parliamentary hearings, and that the French canals, when opened, were run by men who were not interested in business or in the products to be transported. That is why, he said, the French canals, although built better than the Eng-

---

[26] Charles Comte, *Des garanties offertes aux capitaux et aux autres genres de propriétés, par les procédés des chambres législatives, dans les entreprises industrielles et particulièrement dans la formation des canaux* (Paris, 1826), 85.

[27] Jean Jacques, baron Baude, "Sur les canaux de la Loire, du Nivernais et du Duc de Berry, concédés à la Compagnie financière des Quatres Canaux," *Bulletin de la société industrielle de Saint-Etienne,* v. 3 (1825), 58–59.

lish, were less useful and earned less. It could be argued, of course, that the Laws of 1821 and 1822 authorizing the construction of many canals were voted by both chambers of the national legislature after public debates and discussions in committee. At that time, however, most of the deputies and peers were landowners with little knowledge of business, and there is no evidence that businessmen outside the legislature were consulted or invited to appear before committees of either chamber. In any event, these comments of Comte and Baude are important, for both men were well informed and both point out that business interests were neglected by the government in planning the waterways, while Baude, who was vitally interested in transportation, shows that they were neglected also in the operation of the canals.

If we now consider the great waterway of the Loire and its connections with the Seine, we shall see more clearly how the rivers and canals of central France met the needs of that region and of Paris. This was the great route by which the coal from the mines of Saint-Etienne, which were among the most productive in France early in the nineteenth century, was shipped nearly 600 kilometres to Paris. The coal was carted a few miles to the Loire (until the opening of the railroad from Saint-Etienne to Andrézieux in 1826) and then sent down the river in boats made from pines grown on the near-by mountains. The river there was so shallow and swift, and so full of dangerous rocks, that the boats had to be small and loaded to only one third of their capacity, and they could go down only when the water was high, during less than a third of the year. Below Roanne conditions were better and it was possible to build a canal to Diguin in 1838; but even there the boats could be loaded to only two thirds of their capacity. When they reached the canal of Briare, after a long voyage on the shallow and windy river, the coal had to be reloaded again so that the boats should have only one third of their capacity, or between 35 and 50 tons, because of the shallowness and narrowness of the canals of Briare and Loing and the narrowness of their locks. Compliance was enforced by heavy surtaxes on all boats that had a draught of more than 24 inches. The Briare Canal did increase the depth of its water and widen its locks about 1840, but this was useless because the Loing canal, through which all traffic from the Briare to the Seine must pass, made no improvements at all. It refused also to lower its rates, to which the Briare company had consented. When the boats reached Paris, they were broken up and sold for a small part of their value. It would have been impossible to send them back up the Loire, and even if the return trip had been possible, there would not have been sufficient cargoes to make it profitable. We know also that the shipment of grain and wine through the canals of Briare and Loing was considered expensive and was avoided when possible. There is little mention of the shipment of ore, and the metallurgical establishments of the Nièvre and near-by departments sent most of their goods by road rather than use the Loire River, or the canals of the Centre, Briare, and Loing. That is interesting, because that region was then probably the most important in the iron industry of France.

The history of the northern waterways is different and shows what might have been done, partially at least, in central France if the canals of the Centre, Briare, and Loing had been widened and deepened, provided with good towpaths, and the barges hauled by horses instead of men. The strategic waterways from the north to Paris, the canal of Saint-Quentin, the lateral canal of the Oise, and the canalized Oise, were so greatly improved between 1825 and 1836 that traffic more than doubled. Time for passage was greatly reduced, and the congestion in Paris became so great that drastic improvements in its port were forced in 1845. Another important result was a marked decrease in the price of coal, a great and steady increase in its supply, and the stimulation of the mines of the north, which were soon able to drive out the coal of Saint-Etienne from the market of Paris. It is true that the distance from most of the mines of the north to Paris is much less than from Saint-Etienne, and that the Oise was an easier river to regulate than the Loire; but the fact remains that the great artery of central France was not made available to traffic as it might have been, and the development of French industry was delayed.

Had the government felt strong enough to defy the king and compel the consent of the Loing canal company to widen locks and lower navigation dues, it might have succeeded in establishing uniform rates on the waterways of France. With the exception of the Loing canal and that of Givors, which charged rates so ruinous that it hastened the construction of the railroad from Saint-Etienne to Lyons and its own death by absorption, the rates charged do not appear to have been unreasonable. But the variations in rates did constitute a serious obstacle to the growth of traffic, and they were based upon the needs and costs of each waterway, not upon those of the nation. French business needed rates that were less than reasonable, because distances were great. It needed also quick and regular service by night as well as by day. The service had to be improved. The closings of the canals had to be shortened and arranged so that they were not simultaneous in most parts of the country. The towpaths had to be paved or given a hard surface, and some canals needed to be deepened, widened, and straightened so that trains of big barges instead of single barges of very moderate size could be used. The lowering of navigation dues would have helped little without these essential improvements, because the cost of navigation would have remained high.

In conclusion, it can be said that the system of internal waterways in France under the Restoration and the July Monarchy did not meet the needs of the country adequately. It probably delayed its economic development somewhat, as did the dearth of good roads; but the responsibility cannot be placed upon the government alone. It is true that the government neglected the rivers for many years. It also showed much ignorance of economic questions and greatly distrusted private initiative in public works. Furthermore, it sought to build canals or improve rivers where the resources of the country would never have justified the expense, as in parts of central and southwestern France; and it tried to build economically a great many canals when it should have tried to build a few that were vitally needed, without regard to the expense.

The government could have replied that it was only slightly responsible for the difficulties of navigation on the rivers of France. Public opinion also was ignorant of economic questions and showed too little interest in them. Private initiative seldom came to the assistance of the government and, when it did, seemed interested more in profits than in serving the nation. Finally, it was public opinion that insisted upon a great network of waterways and upon such economically foolish projects as the connection of the Loire with the Garonne. The chief error of the French government with regard to the waterways was that, for the most part, it followed and did not lead public opinion, and in that it resembled most other governments. The distances were so great, however, the watersheds so high and numerous, and the volume of traffic was so slight and grew so slowly that even the wisdom of Solomon could not have provided France with an adequate system of waterways before the advent of the railroads. The French people, despite their impatience, felt this instinctively; to the love of speed and progress of the Anglo-Saxon mind they opposed the love of leisure and the wisdom of *la juste mesure.*

CHAPTER FOUR

Railroads

THE PERIOD 1815–1833

NOT LONG AFTER the Peace of Vienna the transportation problem
in France became acute in the mountain region between the Loire
and the Rhône, where it was becoming increasingly difficult to
bring together the rapidly increasing quantities of iron ore and coal
and to market the coal dug in the basin of Saint-Etienne. Local
opinion realized that the roads were quite inadequate and favored
an extension of the Givors Canal over the steep watershed between
the Rhône and the Loire, which there were only a few miles apart.
Yet it was understood that the cost of such a waterway might be
prohibitive and the problems of construction almost insuperable.
While the discussion was at its height, in 1817, one of the government's mining engineers at Saint-Etienne, de Gallois, published a
pamphlet[1] describing the English tramroads, particularly in the
region of Newcastle. These had been cheap to build, had connected
highways and waterways, and were quite feasible in mountainous
districts where canals might be impractical.

On May 15, 1821, a colleague, Louis Beaunier, supported by
Claude Hochet, secretary general of the Council of State, applied
for permission to build such a tramroad with cast-iron rails. It was
to connect the Rhône with the Loire and run through the town of
Saint-Etienne. He asked also the right to condemn land under the
Law of 1807. Two other applications were made in that same year,

---

[1] L. de Gallois, "Des chemins de fer en Angleterre, notamment à Newcastle dans le Northumberland," *Annales des mines,* [Série 1] v. 3 (1818),
129–44.

the first in the name of the Compagnie des Mines de la Loire, and the second by the Compagnie des Fonderies et Forges Frèrejean.[2] Opposition to these applications was expressed formally by the carters of the district of Saint-Etienne, and the opposition of many landowners was a matter of public knowledge. The government, on the advice of Becquey, director general of the Corps des Ponts et Chaussées, ignored the opposition and told the promoters to restrict their tramroad to the short route between Saint-Etienne and the Loire. It ordered the three groups of applicants to amalgamate, put them under the strict supervision of the Corps des Ponts at Chaussées,[3] and on February 26, 1823, granted them a perpetual concession for the line from Saint-Etienne to Andrézieux, a small port on the upper Loire River.[4]

This little line, usually called the first railroad in France, was about eighteen kilometres long, followed the undulations of the ground like a road, and had a single track of parallel cast-iron rails. It was too short and too light to bring about any revolution in local transportation, or to make the fortune of its promoters; but it deserves study as a precedent and because we possess unusually full evidence concerning the interests of its promoters. In this case the government granted a perpetual concession, as had been done with the older canals, and it ordered the combination of the different applicants instead of accepting, or even requiring, competitive bids, as it did subsequently in most cases.

The first railroad in France was promoted chiefly by a group of metallurgists with important interests in both local coal and iron mines and in metallurgical establishments outside the region of Saint-Etienne. Many of them were personal friends or relatives. They included the Boignes brothers of Imphy and Fourchambault, Frèrejean of Terrenoire and La Voulte, and the engineer Beaunier, who with Milleret owned the local mill of La Bérardière. There

---

[2] Georges Lefranc, "The French Railroads, 1823–1842," *Journal of Economic and Business History*, v. 2, no. 2 (Feb., 1930), 303.

[3] *Ibid.*

[4] Armand Audiganne, *Les Chemins de fer chez tous les peuples aujourd-hui et dans cent ans*, v. 1 (Paris, 1858), 120.

were no bankers or Parisian capitalists in the group, but Bricogne, as a Receiver-General of Taxes, should be regarded primarily as a capitalist, and later railroad companies nearly always had among their organizers at least one Receiver-General. When the Andrézieux company had been incorporated, however, we find among the directors the Minister of the Navy, a member of the Court des Comptes, and a former Director-General of the Domain, indicating a desire for stronger political and financial support, although on a very small scale.[5]

The second railroad in France, authorized in the spring of 1826 and finished in 1832, nearly five years after the completion of the short line to Andrézieux, was that from Saint-Etienne to Lyons, a distance of fifty-eight kilometres. This was a true railroad from the beginning and connected an important manufacturing and mining town with one of the chief centers of commerce in France. It was promoted and built by a group of engineers. The Séguin brothers were Jews from Annonay—a family of recognized ability and probable wealth. The eldest, Marc, was a well-known scientist, a member of the Academy of Sciences, and inventor in 1828 of the tubular boiler used by Stephenson shortly afterwards in his famous locomotive. They had organized a company in 1825 for towing barges by steam on the Rhône, in which they had been joined by Edouard Biot, the engineer, son of a colleague of Marc Séguin in the Academy of Sciences, and son-in-law of Becquey, director general of the Ponts et Chaussées. The five Séguins and the younger Biot were the winners of the concession and the actual builders of the railroad from Saint-Etienne to Lyons. One of them, probably Marc Séguin, had been to England, where he had studied the Stockton-Darlington railway, and he was keenly interested in the development of the locomotive.

As a result, the railroad from Saint-Etienne to Lyons was built with wide curves, with embankments, with two sets of tracks and, despite the strong disapproval of the Ponts et Chaussées, with one

---

[5] Louis Joseph Gras, *Histoire des premiers chemins de fer français* (Saint-Etienne: Théolier, 1924), 17–20, 67, 107. Audiganne, *op. cit.*, v. 1, 122–23.

long tunnel under the watershed between the Loire and the Rhône. The grades from Saint-Etienne down to the Rhône at Givors were so steep that the cars could descend by gravity, but the economy from this was more than offset by the cost of hauling the empty cars up again. The line was not built originally to carry passengers, and only single tracks were laid through the tunnels, which proved inconvenient when passenger traffic did develop. The change was necessary because of the lack of sufficient cargoes from Lyons to Saint-Etienne and because, in order to win the concession, the promoters had offered so low a rate for the transportation of coal from the basins of Saint-Etienne and Rive de Giers that they found themselves losing money. They also introduced locomotives, the first in France, on the more level part of the line between Lyons and Givors. Later, after the locomotive had been improved by Stephenson in England, and by others in France, it was used on the steep grades up to Saint-Etienne, where it cut the cost of traction by two thirds but forced the replacement of the light rails by heavy ones and the rebuilding of much of the masonry supporting the embankments.

From the financial point of view, the railroad company founded by the Séguins and Biot in 1826 and incorporated in 1827 differed as greatly from the little Andrézieux line as it did in its economic importance and in the interest of the problems of its construction. While the founders, with the help of Edouard Biot's father, subscribed for a quarter of the original shares, they were more interested in engineering and invention than in making money, and soon lost full control of the business affairs of the company, although at least one Séguin remained on the board of directors. The two largest original shareholders were Henri Boulard, a deputy and retired notary who owned 500 shares (as many as all the Séguins combined) and Laurent Garcias of Paris, who also owned 500, but of whose occupation we know nothing. There is no record of any well-known metallurgist or owner of coal mines among the early stockholders of the Lyons–Saint-Etienne railroad, or of any well-known Parisian banker—only of the Bodin brothers, who were bankers at Lyons but owned only 50 shares. There was no other shareholder from Lyons and none from Saint-Etienne, nor was there any connected with the railroad from Saint-Etienne to Andrézieux. We can surmise only that the necessity of fighting the rich and monopolistic company of the canal of Givors, together with almost unlimited opportunities for profit from close relations with the more important coal-mining companies in the basins of Saint-Etienne and Rive de Giers, were the decisive factors in the gradual change of financial control. It is not surprising to find that within ten years the railroad company had won control of the Givors Canal and that in 1845 it was practically identical with the great coal trust of the Saint-Etienne region.

The third railroad built in France was also in the Loire region. It connected the line from Saint-Etienne to the port of Andrézieux with the town of Roanne much further down the Loire, and it cut in half the distance coal had to travel down the river between the two ports. It also provided a certain means of transportation at all seasons. It was thus much more important than the little line from Saint-Etienne to Andrézieux, and it had a length of sixty-eight kilometres; but Roanne was a small town instead of a great city like Lyons. The new railroad also tapped only the coal basin of Saint-Etienne, while the line to Lyons served the basins of both Saint-Etienne and Rive de Giers. As the traffic on the Roanne line was expected to be light, construction was light, and although the line was graded for double tracks, only a single track was laid and the line followed the undulations of the ground as had that from Saint-Etienne to Andrézieux. When it reached the steep range of hills barring access to Roanne, a series of inclined planes was built and the cars were pulled over by two stationary engines. This was the best method of traction according to the prevalent opinion when the concession was granted to Mellet and Henry in 1828.[6] The only notable improvement over the line from Saint-Etienne to Andrézieux was that the rails were of forged instead of cast iron, but they were still too light for heavy traffic, weighing about a third

[6] Gras, *op. cit.*, 133.

as much as the rails on the main lines built under the Second Empire.

François Noël Mellet and Charles Joseph Henry were much criticized for lack of judgment and business ability, because the line from Andrézieux to Roanne was not a financial success, as were the other railroads of the Loire. Yet the real causes of failure were beyond their control. Their railroad could hardly have been a success unless it had been part of a line running to Paris and bringing coal from one of the most important basins of France to the greatest market in the country. Unfortunately, no one under the Restoration, except a few idealistic followers of Saint-Simon, of whom Mellet was probably one, thought of railroads in national terms. The proposed railroad from Roanne to Digoin would have helped the Andrézieux line a little, but it was rejected by the government in 1829, probably because plans for the canal between those points had already been completed. The railroad from Andrézieux to Roanne was regarded as a feeder for this canal, and its financial support came in considerable part from men interested in the waterways, not from metallurgists or engineers. While the largest stockholder, Jobal de Pagny, was active in raising money among his friends in the nobility, the second largest stockholder, Eugène Mévil,[7] held the concession for the canal of the duc de Bordeaux, and the company's Parisian banker, Ardoin, was a member of the consortium that had formed the Company of the Four Canals. The railroad to Roanne was partly sacrificed to the canal interests and did not fight them as did the line from Saint-Etienne to Lyons. It was thus the victim of the long delay in the construction of the canal from Roanne to Digoin, which instead of being opened in 1830 was not finished until 1839, while the railroad was opened in February, 1834.[8] Other errors were committed, it is true, which could have been avoided, such as issuing too little stock when the railroad company was organized, because the cost of construction

---

[7] *Ibid.*, 284.

[8] Napoléon Chaix, *Annuaire officiel des chemins de fer* (Paris, 1847–48), 18.

was greatly underestimated; but that error was committed by every railroad company in France, and by most in other countries. Another mistake was the failure to build a bridge over the Loire at Roanne so that the terminus of the railroad should be on the same side of the river as that of the canal to Digoin.[9]

Most writers have attributed the bankruptcy of the Andrézieux–Roanne railroad company in 1836, and the end of its liquidation only in 1841 after the grant of a loan of 4,000,000 francs from the government, to the Revolution of 1830 and the following business depression, which continued at least into the year 1832. This view can hardly be sustained, for the depression had begun in 1827 and the revolution had merely prevented continuance of the recovery that was just beginning. Furthermore, there is no evidence that either the little line from Saint-Etienne to Andrézieux or the very important line from Saint-Etienne to Lyons suffered severely from the long business depression between 1827 and 1832. It seems probable, therefore, that the depression was only a contributory cause of the bankruptcy of the railroad from Roanne to Andrézieux and that the most important cause was the delay in the completion of the canal to Digoin.

The three railroads of the Loire have been discussed in detail because they were the first railroads in France. We have an unusual amount of information regarding both their construction and their financing, chiefly because of the researches of Louis Joseph Gras of Saint-Etienne. Furthermore, they illustrate in simple form certain problems of economics and governmental policy which became more complex later when railroads became numerous and the sums of money required very large. They also fall chiefly within the first period of railroad construction in France, from 1823 to 1833, as defined by Audiganne, the best of the more thorough historians of French railroads and a witness of what he describes. These lines were mainly of local interest, although they were only partly financed locally. Two of them were regarded primarily as feeders to waterways, and all were intended in the eyes of their promoters

---

[9] Gras, *op. cit.*, 321.

to carry coal, as did the Stockton-Darlington railway in England. Like it, they soon began to carry passengers as well. The policy of the government towards them shows that while each had to be authorized by a royal ordinance, there was no discussion regarding them in the Chambers, and no general law was considered necessary, because there appeared to be no question of national policy involved. The many formalities that were required were dealt with by the Corps des Ponts et Chaussées. The concessions granted were perpetual because those of the older canals had been and no one thought, under the Restoration, that a railroad would ever be a matter of vital concern to the nation in both peace and war.

The attitude of the Corps des Ponts et Chaussées toward these early railroads was natural and intelligent, but bureaucratic. As a body of highly trained engineers clothed with authority by the government, the corps advised the government regarding all applications for concessions for railroads, and on its recommendation all but four were rejected. It thought that no railroad should compete with an existing or even with a proposed highway or canal. It insisted upon a plan for the line being filed with the application for a concession, after which, following much deliberation, it declared the enterprise a public utility. Then there followed local hearings, usually conducted by the prefect of the department or departments through which the proposed railroad would run, while legal problems were considered by the Council of State, and engineering problems were studied by the corps itself.[10]

In most cases formalities and studies took at least two years. In addition, the Corps des Ponts et Chaussées laid down regulations regarding grades, the radius of curves, and other matters within its competence so severe that many applicants gave up their schemes at once, and the expense of building a railroad was greatly increased. Yet, although the severity of these requirements is stressed by several writers, we know that some of them were not strictly enforced, as in the case of the railroad from Saint-Etienne to Lyons, the construction of which was carefully supervised by Brisson, one

---

[10] Lefranc, *op. cit.*, 311–14.

of the highest engineers of the corps under Becquey, and by the elder Biot, member of the Academy of Sciences. The strict policy of the government, in most cases framed largely by the Corps des Ponts et Chaussées, is supported by most French writers on the ground that it saved France from many useless railroads and from many failures that would have discouraged promoters and ensured public hostility to railroads. This may be questioned. It would seem as if milder regulations combined with a little financial assistance during construction would have protected adequately the interests of the public and also have promoted more rapid progress.

THE PERIOD 1833–1842

The second period of French railroad construction, as defined by Audiganne, began in 1833 with a law appropriating funds for planning a network of railroads. It ended at the beginning of 1842 with the introduction of the bill that became the first general law authorizing such a network of railroads in France, and laying down rules for its construction, financing, concessions, and supervision by the government. It has been described frequently as a period of study and comparative inaction, yet it saw the completion of two or three railroads of considerable importance and the beginning of two others of great significance. Writers have dwelt upon the eloquent speeches in the Chambers on the policy that should govern the construction of the French railroad system and on the methods for securing funds. They have emphasized perhaps even more the legislative squabbles on these subjects that prevented useful action for several years.[11] They should have given more attention to the serious business depression beginning in 1837 and to the numerous writings of engineers and promoters that did much to arouse public interest in railroads. If we consider first how the French public

---

[11] The most important of these writers are Audiganne, in his book of 1858, and Richard von Kaufmann, *La Politique française en matière des chemins de fer* (Paris: Librairie Polytechnique, 1900).

became interested in railroads as essential to the development of the country, it will be easier to understand the delays in construction and the variations in governmental policy.

The influential advocates of railroads in France during the decade following the Revolution were nearly all followers of the idealist Saint-Simon, who died in 1825 but whose sect, under the leadership of Enfantin, remained a closely knit body until 1832. Among the most important writers in this group were Michel Chevalier, Emile Péreire, Lamé, Clapeyron, and Stéphane Mony and his half-brother, Eugène Flachat. Chevalier was the editor of the Saint-Simonian newspaper, the *Globe*, and published in it in the spring of 1832 a series of letters in which he urged the creation of the Système de la Méditerranée through the construction of railroads, canals, and steamers and the improvement of rivers. He thought of great arteries of travel along which both men and goods could be carried rapidly and efficiently whether by water or by land. After the failure of the *Globe* and the breaking up of the Saint-Simonian Church, Chevalier was active as a writer on the staff of the *Journal des débats* and the *Revue des deux mondes,* and as a teacher on the faculty of the Collège de France. His most significant writings in arousing interest in railroads were his *Lettres sur l'Amérique du Nord,* published serially by the *Journal des débats* in 1834 and 1835 and as a book in 1836, his technical book on the railroads of North America, his *Intérêts matériels* of 1838 and his *Cours d'économie politique* of 1842–43. He had influence because of the charm of his style, the clarity of his exposition, and the soundness of his training at the Ecole Polytechnique. He was also an economist of real ability and wrote more about matters of general interest than about technical problems.

Other important advocates of railroads, while they were also followers of Saint-Simon, were not merely writers and teachers, like Chevalier, but remained professional engineers, and as such helped actually to build the railroads about which they wrote. In 1832, the year that saw the publication of the Système de la Méditerranée, two mining engineers, Lamé and Clapeyron, co-operated with two civil engineers, Stéphane Mony and Eugène Flachat, in publishing a book entitled *Vues politiques et pratiques sur les travaux publics en France*. They urged the construction of main lines of communication with wide canals and railroads using locomotives, and minor lines with narrow canals and railroads using horses.[12] They advised also that the government guarantee a minimum rate of interest to the companies building and operating such waterways or railroads, an idea which, as we shall see, aroused heated controversies, but ultimately proved of great practical value. Most of these men were not teachers, but were active as journalists[13] and as actual builders of railroads.

A third type of railroad promoter, still a follower of Saint-Simon, is found in Emile Péreire, aided by his brother Isaac. He was an exceedingly adroit journalist, writing articles on finance and railroads for *Le National* of such ability that they not only aroused the interest of the public but also won the practical support of bankers such as James Rothschild, Thurneyssen, and the d'Eichthals. He had also a genius for organization, and boundless enthusiasm. It was he who supplied the stimulus for the building of the railroad from Paris to Saint-Germain and obtained for the enterprise the capital, which he did not possess, and the technical skill in construction in the persons of Stéphane Mony and his brother Flachat. He was active also in organizing the company that built the railroad from Paris to Versailles by the right bank of the Seine, for which he won almost identical financial and technical support. He was possibly the first to make practical plans for the construction of a railroad from Paris to Belgium and the English Channel.

Péreire seems to have understood better than most of his contemporaries that most capitalists were quite ignorant of industry and its needs, while the public was fond of gambling and preferred dazzling to sound enterprises. He understood also the powerful in-

---

[12] Arthur Louis Dunham, *The Anglo-French Treaty of Commerce of 1860 and the Progress of the Industrial Revolution in France* (Ann Arbor, Mich.: University of Michigan Press, 1930), 30–33. Audiganne, *op. cit.*, 333, 336. Maurice Wallon, *Les Saint-Simoniens et les chemins de fer* (Paris: A. Pedone, 1908), 45.

[13] Mony was on the staff of *Le Constitutionel* and Flachat on that of the *Journal du commerce.*

fluence exercised by the Corps des Ponts et Chaussées, which both judged the merits of enterprises such as railroads and competed as entrepreneur with capitalists for their actual construction. Emile Péreire is reputed to have been the man who did most to arouse the interest of Legrand, director of the Ponts et Chaussées since the Revolution of 1830, in the building of railroads as a national problem of urgent importance.[14]

The first important railroad built in this second period of construction was the short line from Paris to Le Pecq, authorized by the Law of July 9, 1835, and opened on August 24, 1837, and generally called the railroad from Paris to Saint-Germain. Because it required crossing the Seine and the hill upon which Saint-Germain stands is steep, it was actually completed only in the spring of 1847, through the invention of the atmospheric engine by Eugène Flachat and its construction by that excellent builder of locomotives and other machines, Hallette of Arras. This railroad, although short, was of great importance, because, as the first line starting from Paris, it attracted the attention of the entire country. It was also the first railroad built originally to carry passengers, the first line to be an unqualified financial success from the beginning, and the first to win the support of the future railroad czar, Baron James de Rothschild. As we have seen, it was planned in detail by the engineers Lamé, Clapeyron, Mony, and Flachat in their book of 1832, and promoted skillfully by Emile Péreire, who organized the actual railroad company and remained its manager with the help of his son Jacques. The line to Le Pecq was built by Mony and Clapeyron, and the last section to Saint-Germain, as has been mentioned, was added by Mony's half-brother Flachat.[15] The capital, originally 6,000,000 francs, but soon increased to 9,000,000 francs in stock, was subscribed almost entirely by Rothschild, Thurneyssen, Davillier and the d'Eichthals, and remained in their hands and those of Emile Péreire, who received 2,000 shares as founder and manager. There were also at least two bond issues floated for a total of 10,000,000 francs, making a total capital investment of approxi-

[14] Wallon, *op. cit.*, 62, 73–75.
[15] Audiganne, *op. cit.*, 365–72.

mately 16,000,000 francs, on which between 1837 and 1845 the average net income was 6.7 per cent.[16]

The brilliant success of the railroad from Paris to Saint-Germain should have been a great stimulus to the building of railroads in France and should have led rapidly to the planning and construction of a national network. Yet almost immediately afterwards there were built the two railroads from Paris to Versailles, which were not successful financially. Their early failure not only frightened promoters and investors, but brought to light one of the most serious problems to plague the government in its efforts to create a national network of railroads—the rivalry of local interests, whether provincial, municipal, or commercial. Many historians have claimed that one railroad between Paris and Versailles would have been sufficient, which is quite correct, but they explain the construction of two by the rivalry of the Rothschilds, who supported the line on the right bank of the Seine, and the Foulds, who were interested in the shorter line on the left bank. It might also be claimed that the serious depression beginning in 1837 and lasting until about 1843, which was a general one affecting many industries, was a factor in the failure of these Versailles lines. Yet it seems clear that the true reason for the failure was simply the building of two lines where only one was needed, and that this was due chiefly to the rivalry of the two quarters of Paris from which they started and of the two quarters of Versailles in which they ended and which treated each other like independent municipalities.[17]

The government had planned only one line, but the second was added by the commission in the Chamber of Deputies and the law was enacted as amended. Almost immediately the line by the left bank of the Seine fell into disfavor. It had able engineers in Bergeron and Perdonnet, but the company had great difficulty in raising capital and in collecting payments after subscriptions had been

---

[16] *Journal des économistes*, v. 16 (March, 1847), 381. Chaix, *op. cit.*, 82–85. Alfred Legoyt, *Le Livre des chemins de fer, construits, en construction et projetés; ou, Statistiques générales de ces voies de communication en France et à l'étranger* (Paris, 1845), 145–47.

[17] Chaix, *op. cit.*, 99–100. Audiganne, *op. cit.*, 375–76.

pledged. It could not get the support of many important capitalists, and its directors were men who inspired little confidence in the public. Despite loans floated commercially and a loan of 5,000,000 francs from the government, the line by the left bank was unable to earn as much as 2 per cent on its capital.[18] Yet the line on the right bank, promoted by the Rothschilds and the Péreires and supported by most of their banking friends who had invested in the railroad to Saint-Germain, with the important addition of the Mallet brothers, who were close to the Bank of France, did not earn more than 3 per cent and was, consequently, operated at a loss. This unfortunate situation was an important factor in delaying the construction of a national network of railroads and was remedied only in the period beginning in 1846 by the merger of the two railroad companies under pressure from the government.[19]

In the meantime, railroads had been begun to connect Paris with two important provincial centers at a moderate distance, Rouen and Orléans. A line to Rouen had been proposed as early as 1825, and other proposals for lines to Rouen or Havre were made in 1830 and 1832, but all were rejected by the Corps des Ponts et Chaussées.[20] There were probably defects in those early plans and there was probably also inadequate financial support. Another serious difficulty was that the government found it difficult to decide the route of the line. A line by the plateaux via Pontoise and Gisors would be shorter and cheaper and would give better connections with the port of Dieppe and the cities in northern France, while the line following the valley of the Seine would pass through more important towns and would help the textile centers of Elbeuf and Louviers.

In 1838 a concession for a railroad from Paris to Le Havre by the plateaux was granted to Lehobe, Chouquet and Company, but the next year the company surrendered the concession.[21] They had

---

[18] Legoyt, *op. cit.*, 154.

[19] *Ibid.*, 148.

[20] Lefranc, *op. cit.*, 311.

[21] Marcel Marion, *Histoire financière de la France depuis 1715*, v. 5 (Paris: Rousseau, 1914–31), 198.

been unable to collect the subscribed capital, because of the panic on the Bourse and because they failed to secure modification of the severe regulations for construction imposed by the government, owing to the opposition of the Chambers. These regulations imposed expensive grades and curves, provided for a short concession with cancellation by the government on brief notice, fixed rates that were far too low, and limited profits to 10 per cent. Government engineers had estimated the cost of building the line to Le Havre at slightly more than 80,000,000 francs, and the company had, therefore, limited its capital to 90,000,000 francs; but when its own engineers surveyed the line they estimated the cost of construction at 157,846,691 francs. The Lehobe Company felt that this enormous deficit, together with the difficulty of collecting funds and the refusal of English interests to give their support, made the continuance of the concession under its original conditions impossible.[22] Furthermore, they were offered no financial assistance by the government, although at almost the same time the government helped the company holding the concession for the railroad from Paris to Orléans, and also that from Paris to Versailles by the left bank of the Seine. Public opinion was very timid regarding railroads in 1839, partly because of the difficulties encountered by the railroads to Versailles, but chiefly because of the business depression and the squabbles of the legislature over government policy towards the railroads. It is interesting also to note the opinion of one of the Séguin brothers, who had built the railroad from Saint-Etienne to Lyons, expressed in 1838 that the government had been foolish to grant the concession for the line from Paris to Havre hastily without waiting for a stronger company, because the organizers of this one lacked the technical knowledge necessary for construction of a railroad and would supply credit rather than cash.[23]

In 1839 preparations for the organization of a company to build the line from Paris to Rouen were begun by the banker Charles

---

[22] "Etat de la question des chemins de fer," *Journal de l'industriel et du capitaliste,* v. 7 (Aug., 1839), 28–30.

[23] Jules Séguin, *Chemins de fer: De leur exécution par l'industrie particulière* (Lyon, 1838), 1–3.

Laffitte and the directors of the London and Southwestern Railway. This group engaged the able English engineer Locke, and the well-known Mackenzie and Brassey as contractors, and insisted upon the route down the valley of the Seine. They were able to raise enough capital, and in the spring of 1840 obtained the desired concession from the French government together with a loan of 14,000,000 francs, which represented about a third of the original capital. This is the first case recorded of a French railroad whose capital was obtained partly from England and which was built chiefly by English engineers and contractors. It was a precedent that was followed in extending the Norman line to Le Havre and also in connecting Paris with the narrows of the English Channel and with Bordeaux. All of these were clearly of benefit to British business, and also in the cases of railroads from Paris to Lyons and from Paris to Strasbourg, where the benefits to the British partners were much less obvious except from the point of view of investment or speculation.[24]

A railroad from Paris to Orléans entered into the plans of the government at an early date, but here also engineers differed as to the routing, finding it difficult to choose between the most direct route and the longer route by way of Versailles, which would probably have brought more traffic. Extensions of this line were also discussed very early, and both the government and the promoters found it difficult to decide between alternative routes beyond Orléans. Each route developed its partisans, raised its subscriptions, and mobilized the members of the Chambers, the prefects, and the mayors of the districts and towns concerned. In the face of this political pressure the government compromised or, rather, postponed some of the difficulties. It conceded only the direct line from Paris to Orléans to a company headed by Casimir Leconte, former manager of the most important company of stagecoaches, the Messageries Royales, in August, 1838. He had collected some 30,000,000 francs in subscriptions from the cities of Orléans and Etampes, but he soon

---

[24] Joseph Devey, *Life of Joseph Locke, Civil Engineer* (London, 1862), 156–58. "Des lois sur les chemins de fer votées pendant la dernière session," *Journal de l'industriel et du capitaliste,* v. 8 (June, 1840), 345, 349.

proved more interested in obtaining further financial support from local centers and in running the affairs of the company himself than in co-operating with his fellow directors. Unfortunately for Leconte, and fortunately for the railroad, the Rothschilds had promised a credit of 2,000,000 francs and the bankers Pillot-Will, Odier, and Bartholony brothers had pledged 21,000,000 francs.[25]

François Bartholony had been a highly successful banker and had also been interested in railroads for some time. He was an intimate friend of Beaunier, who built the railroad from Saint-Etienne to Andrézieux; he had made plans with the Mallet brothers for a line from Paris to Le Havre in 1825, and had been an unsuccessful bidder for the railroad from Saint-Etienne to Lyons in 1826. He proved to be a sound financier, not a speculator. He soon replaced Leconte as head of the company and guided the Orléans railroad through the brief period of governmental harshness until the severe conditions which had discouraged the first Rouen company had been modified and the government had guaranteed payment of interest at 4 per cent on the company's capital. He remained the real head of the company throughout the long depression and was dominant at least until the Revolution of 1848. The company had erred in issuing its stock above par, for that discouraged many sound investors; but the guarantee of interest on its capital by the government was won by Bartholony against the strong opposition of Legrand, director general of the Ponts et Chaussées, and Bartholony also wisely insisted on paying his shareholders 4 per cent during the building of the railroad, which lasted five years.[26]

Before considering the developments of the government's railroad policy in the period from the Law of 1833, providing for the planning of a network of railroads, to the Law of 1842, which made provision for its construction, we must describe briefly a provincial line that was built and opened to traffic during this period. This was the railroad from Strasbourg to Bâle with its branch from

---

[25] Audiganne, op. cit., 385–87. René Crozet, "Contribution à l'histoire de la voie ferrée de Paris à Toulouse, et du réseau ferré entre Loire moyenne et Cher," Revue d'histoire moderne, v. 11 (June, 1939), 241–60.

[26] Ibid.

Mulhouse to Thann. The Alsatian line was built rapidly, chiefly with capital from Mulhouse, and under the leadership of one of that city's great captains of industry, Nicholas Koechlin. Capital was undoubtedly obtained also from Bâle and Strasbourg, both of which were important financial centers, and probably from some of the many small industrial centers of the rural districts of Alsace. Yet the 29,000,000 francs raised proved insufficient when more than half of the railroad had been built, probably because of underestimating the cost of construction; an appeal for help was sent to the French government, which granted a loan of 12,600,000 francs in 1840.[27] In 1841 the line was opened with single track except for the entrance into Strasbourg, which was difficult, and that into Bâle, which required international negotiations. The final steps were taken in 1844, and in the meantime the whole line had been double-tracked.

Having described the construction of the more important railroads completed or begun during the period when the government was trying to plan and commence a national network, we should pause to survey the evolution of governmental policy and inquire why it was so remarkably slow. The opening of the Liverpool and Manchester railroad in 1830, followed by the opening of the line from Saint-Etienne to Lyons and the use of locomotives upon it in 1832, made the French government realize that railroads might become a national question of great importance. Their significance was understood more quickly than it had been by the British government. No continental state could treat the railroads as individual commercial enterprises for two reasons. The problem of defending the country against invasion by land was always present, and the power of the governmental bureaucracy, partly because of the need of defense, was a tradition. The fact that many leaders in the French government saw quickly that a national policy must be formed does not prove that such a policy was formed quickly. It is true that in 1833 some action was taken. The Corps des Ponts et

[27] Henry Ferrette, *Etude historique sur l'intervention financière de l'état dans l'établissement des lignes de chemins de fer* (Paris, 1896), 21-22. Chaix, *op. cit.*, 107.

Chaussées had rejected an application for the building of a tramway on the road between Montrond and Montbrison in central France. This constituted not only competition with an existing means of transportation, but also expropriation of the public domain. The promoters appealed the case to Parliament, and the Chambers passed a law granting the concession and stating that every future concession must be authorized by an individual law. Then, in the same year of 1833, Thiers, who had previously scoffed at railroads, asked, in his capacity of Minister of Public Works, for a grant of funds with which to plan a railroad from Paris to Le Havre. The Chambers, torn by local and sectional rivalries, voted instead the sum of 500,000 francs for the planning of railroads in general.[28]

The planning of railroads was, as we have seen, in the hands of the Corps des Ponts et Chaussées, an organization of highly trained engineers, some of whom displayed outstanding ability. Yet this body was part of the official bureaucracy and generally used its power despotically and with outspoken distrust of individual initiative. It was interested not in trade or industry, nor in the problems of economics, but in engineering, and it had no body of sound statistics which might have helped it broaden its point of view, because the government itself did not have really good statistics under the July Monarchy. The corps promptly put its engineers to work, and at the end of the next year it had in its possession plans for railroads from Paris to Orléans, both by the direct route through Etampes and by the longer route through Versailles, from Paris to Lyons and Marseilles, and from Paris to Belgium. In the course of time further grants were made and more lines studied by the engineers of the corps. Their quick and excellent work was done so quietly that many people in France were unaware of its thoroughness and significance.

Yet, accurate as the surveys of these engineers undoubtedly were, we have seen that they underestimated the cost of building a railroad from Paris to Le Havre by the plateaux by approximately 50 per cent, and there is reason to believe they made other similar

[28] Paul Boiteau, *Fortune publique et finances de la France*, v. 1 (Paris, 1866), 183.

errors. Their natural tendency was to consider only sound construction and to ignore the cost. Their standards of construction remained high, and the great rigidity of their application was not relaxed as rapidly as the improvement of the locomotive would have permitted. They believed also in making railroads as straight as possible, no matter what important centers of trade or industry they might miss on the way. They felt not only that they were able to plan railroads better than anyone else, which was probably true, but also that they should build and operate them, and their director, Legrand, supported the policy of government construction and ownership firmly, despite criticisms in the Chambers, falling ministries, and shifting public opinion. Unfortunately, French experience with highways and waterways had shown that government construction was usually slow and costly, and government operation more adapted to the collection of dues than to speed and efficiency of service. France needed railroads badly, and she ought to have them well built; but the increases in her traffic and population were slow, her distances considerable, and her financial resources difficult to mobilize. This made it vitally important to build her railroads at moderate cost.

The problem of financing the construction of a network of railroads in France was exceedingly complex, for it involved both psychological and material factors that were only partly understood. The great majority of French people were still peasants and inclined either to hoard their savings or to invest them in land. The middle class were more inclined to invest than to hoard, but usually selected real estate or government securities. There were few banks in the country, and in the smaller towns and rural districts usury was still common. It was difficult to form even a vague idea of the volume of private capital that could be drawn upon for building railroads, and it was also difficult to make what did exist available because of the scarcity of banks. Nearly every French writer on economic subjects under the July Monarchy complained of the scarcity of capital and of the high rates of interest. We may have legitimate doubts as to the scarcity of the capital, but there can be no doubt of the cost and difficulty of obtaining it. Too many people had read of the disastrous experiment of John Law in the early eighteenth century and distrusted banks because of it; but they did not realize how grievous had been the dishonesty of the government in helping to bring about that swindle.

Funds sufficient to finance the construction of important railroads could be obtained only by the co-operation of the government, as the only organization having the confidence of any great body of investors, and that of the great bankers of Paris and a few other centers, such as Lyons and Rouen. Help from other towns could be expected only if the railroads actually passed through them. Few French centers were willing to contribute to the construction of railroads that would benefit them only indirectly through the enrichment of the country as a whole. It was futile, then, to complain of the evils of the organization of railroad companies by Parisian bankers, because their leadership was essential; yet they could not have supplied enough capital, nor could they have inspired enough confidence in the public without the active support of the government. A further element that must be considered was the tradition that the initiative in public works should come from the government and that, to protect the public interest, governmental regulation and supervision were essential. This tradition was strengthened by the needs of possible defense of the country in time of war, for which the government alone could provide.

Many historians have felt that France was fortunate in having a bureaucratic government that planned its railroads and created a unified system while in England railroads were being built as individual enterprises without any plan or guidance, so that there was much useless or purely competitive construction. Yet in France there were years of delay and friction in carrying out that plan which hindered the development of trade and industry and greatly increased the cost of the railroad system to the nation. These delays were due less to the failure of men to realize the need of co-operation between the government and the Parisian bankers than to the mutual distrust of the two groups that were forced to co-operate. The government felt that it alone could protect national interests and ensure sound construction and honest financing. It realized that it could not obtain all the funds needed through taxation, but it wanted bankers simply to provide money and share in the risks without sharing in control. The bankers felt that if they provided a large part of the money and shared in the risks they had a right to share in control; that they could build railroads more cheaply and more quickly than the government, provided they were allowed to do it in their own way. They wanted the government to give them substantial assistance through guaranteed interest on their investments in railroads or through loans, or subsidies, and also by paying for much of the land.

The period from 1835 to 1842, when attempts were made to organize the first really important railroad companies, was the period during which the government was displaying resentment against the profits made by some of the canal companies and was trying to buy back the shares that might enable them to make greater profits in the future. Some of those companies had brought together considerable sums of capital, as had a few of the more important insurance companies, but on the whole the railroad companies needed much larger amounts of capital than any of their predecessors. The government showed little understanding of the problems confronting these companies. In most cases it sought to drive as hard a bargain as possible. It not only granted concessions for a brief term of years and under stern and costly regulations, but enforced taxes of great variety and weight and threatened fines or confiscation if there were not compliance with all the conditions imposed. The government sought in these measures not only to protect the public interest, as was its duty, but to do so in a dictatorial spirit as if all the companies were composed of speculators and profiteers, or would be if not frightened into wisdom and honesty. The result was to keep many able financiers and sound investors out of the field of railroad construction, or to make them feel that their only chance of profit lay in the very speculation the government wished to prevent.

The difficulty of overcoming the mutual distrust of the government and the bankers was increased by the whims of the legislature and public opinion and by the uncertainties of business. The deputies, and to some extent the peers, were engaged in the exciting game of politics. They might themselves be able engineers or bankers; they might also be gifted writers or speakers; they might even be economists able to understand the railroad problem from the point of view of the welfare of the nation; yet they could rarely resist the opportunity of using railroad legislation to favor their local constituents and to weaken or overthrow political opponents. Great harm was done in this way to the railroad cause, particularly between 1837 and 1840, when political rivalries were keen because of the struggle for power between Thiers and Guizot, combined with the attempt of Louis Philippe to rule by using weaker and more compliant ministers.

It seems futile to discuss whether the government had a continuous railroad policy and public opinion alone was changeable, as Kaufmann has contended in opposition to Audiganne. No government in those years held office long enough to do more than appoint a commission to study the railroad question and to introduce one bill, while the Chambers reflected public opinion with enough accuracy to make a distinction between them and the government difficult. Thus in 1837 the government introduced a bill for building six important railroads, chiefly by companies, and in 1838 another government introduced another bill, framed largely by Legrand, favoring construction by the government itself. Both bills were defeated through a combination of legislative maneuvers and changes in public opinion. It has been a mistake to try to isolate as a constant one of the three forces acting on this problem—the government, the legislature, the public opinion—for all were variable.

Finally, in completing our explanation of the delays in planning and building the French railroads we must consider developments in business. The period from 1833 to 1837 was one of rising prosperity and industrial development. Many more companies were formed and there was a great increase in the securities listed on the Bourse. Towards the end of this period there was a boom in France, as in the United States and England, followed by a serious business crisis from which France was not exempt, as has generally been supposed, on the ground that her industrialization was slight. Far too many companies had been launched in France, especially those with partnerships of limited liability called *commandite par actions,* in which the majority of the partners who had simply bought stock were in the event of failure not liable for more than the amount of their subscriptions, but in which they had no control of the management of the company. Just when a reaction against this overdevelopment of companies had begun, in 1837, came the introduction of railroad securities on the Bourse followed by the difficulties of the railroad being built from Paris to Versailles by the left bank of the Seine. In 1838 there was a lull in these developments, but in 1839 there was a severe business depression and a sharp drop in the values of railroad securities on the Bourse. At the same time the diplomatic situation, which had been growing worse for several years, became suddenly tense, and the country was seriously alarmed in 1839 and 1840 over the danger of war over the eastern question.

The delay in planning and building a network of railroads in France was due to no single factor, but to a balancing of forces that were in conflict when they should have been co-operating. Thus, the ability and intelligence of the government's engineers were balanced by the bureaucratic methods and intolerance of the Corps des Ponts et Chaussées; the advantage of a centralized government in planning a uniform network, by political strife and undue distrust of individual initiative; and the great resources of the country, by the difficulty of mobilizing them effectively because of both governmental and popular distrust of financial leaders. Finally, the whole railroad question became acute when the country was alarmed by the danger of war and was sinking into a serious business depression.

Yet, even during the worst period of the depression, progress in planning and building railroads did not cease. As we have seen, the government revised the harsh conditions of the concession to the Orléans railroad company in 1839 and guaranteed it 4 per cent interest on its investment in 1840. In that same year, when the crisis over the eastern question was at its height, the government conceded the line from Paris to Rouen on terms that were acceptable to English capitalists. Similarly, the government went on planning a network of railroads, and commissions of the legislature and experts continued to consider it, so that the introduction in February, 1842, of the bill that became the Law of June 11 was neither sudden nor unexpected. Another defeat was averted because the government had an able Minister of Public Works in Teste, who had replaced the rather weak Martin du Nord, because public opinion was more anxious to have railroads and the legislature was therefore less obstructive, and because recovery from the depression had begun and capital was again seeking investment.

The Act of June 11, 1842, was no more surprising in its terms than in its successful enactment, nor was it remarkably wise. It should be regarded as the inevitable compromise between divergent points of view and hostile interests that had been unwilling to co-operate before, but it cannot be said to have provided a permanent solution of the railroad problem. The Act did provide for several main lines with a mileage of approximately 3,600 kilometres, but the details of the routing were left to be settled by future laws. It stated also that the railroads built would be the property of the government, but might be leased to companies provided each lease was sanctioned by a separate law. The Act of 1842 stated that the land would be supplied or bought by the national government, but that the departments and communes through which each line passed would pay two thirds of the cost. The government was to prepare the roadbed and build structures, while the lessee company would supply all equipment and maintain the railroad in good condition. The length of the lease, the regulations governing operation, and the rates to be charged were to be decided separately for each lease, approved by the Minister of Public Works, and ratified by law.

The Law of 1842 authorized construction of a line from Paris to Belgium by way of Amiens and Lille with a branch to some port on the English Channel, which would almost certainly be either Calais or Boulogne; a second line to Germany by way of Nancy and Strasbourg; a third to the Mediterranean via Lyons; a fourth to the Spanish frontier by way of Tours, Poitiers, Angoulême, Bordeaux, and Bayonne; a fifth from Tours to Nantes; a sixth from Orléans into central France via Bourges; a seventh connecting Lyons and Dijon with Mulhouse; and an eighth connecting Bordeaux with Toulouse and Marseilles. This was the most valuable and permanent part of the statute, for it decided the general routing of the main lines, even if it stipulated routes that were quite obvious. It seemed to contemporaries to end decisively a period of futile discussion with little accomplishment, although to the historian it seems indecisive.

The Act of 1842 was unfortunate also in providing for building railroads by the government, with operation by lessee companies. This was a useful compromise between advocates of government construction and operation and proponents of railroads built and managed by private companies. In principle also the government retained title to the railroad, but, although the Law of 1842 made no stipulation regarding the length of leases, and although many leases granted subsequently were very short, in practice the railroad belonged to the operating company in time of peace, and in actual fact many railroads were also built by private companies. The Law of 1842 was an ordinary statute and could easily be modified by later laws, so that it should not be regarded as a sort of "railroad constitution." Some of the provisions, such as the payment for two thirds of the land by the departments and communes affected, proved impossible to enforce and were soon repealed. Others, like that providing for the building of railroads by the government, were maintained in principle and violated frequently in practice. The Law of June 11, 1842, was, therefore, a useful compromise that provided a convenient basis for the construction of the national network of railroads which nearly everyone desired; but, like the constitution of the Third Republic, it satisfied no one and was vague enough to leave everyone with the hope that his view would finally prevail. To the legally-minded writers of continental Europe, this statute has appeared to be of decisive importance, but to the economic historian it served only to facilitate activities that would have occurred in any event because of the revival of business and because the time for a compromise settlement had come.[29]

THE PERIOD 1842–1848

The period between the enactment of the Law of June 11, 1842, and the revolution which broke out in February, 1848, was characterized by indecision, contradictions, and compromises in the policy of the government which reflected fairly accurately the opinions of the legislature and the public. The strongest tendency was probably that favoring construction by the government and operation by companies through leases of approximately forty years. Actually, most of the railroads were both built and operated by private companies under the supervision of the government and, in many cases, with financial assistance in the form of loans or subsidies, and sometimes gifts or loans of land or structures. Some laws were enacted, as in 1845, which indicated the desire of the government to lay down a general policy regarding concessions, but no such general policy was ever adhered to consistently. The government remained suspicious of companies able or rich enough to build an important railroad quickly. It ensured sound construction and tried to prevent large profits by companies and to control speculation. Those were worthy objectives, but exceedingly difficult to attain, as was being shown by experience in contemporary England. The French government made vigorous efforts but failed as completely as did the government of its neighbor, which scarcely even tried to control individual initiative.

While it seems certain to us now that the French government

[29] Audiganne, *op. cit.*, 252–329. Kaufmann, *La Politique française,* 19–24. Napoléon, comte Daru, *Des chemins de fer et de l'application de la loi du 11 juin 1842* (Paris, 1843), 4–7. Ferrette, *op. cit.*, 23–26. Marion, *op. cit.*, v. 5, 203–6. Adolphe Blaise, "Etat de la question des chemins de fer: Exécution de la loi du 11 juin 1842," *Journal des économistes,* v. 5 (July, 1843), 401–13, esp. 403; "Les Chemins de fer et le crédit," *Journal des économistes,* v. 18 (Aug., 1847), 44–53, esp. 46.

could not possibly have succeeded in controlling either profits or speculation in the earlier nineteenth century, it did not seem certain then. The error lay not in making the effort but in lack of understanding of the needs of private companies, which then required a consistent policy on the part of the government and concessions granted on principles drawn up in advance and applied to all concessionaires alike. The concessions also had to be long enough that the company could regard the railroad as a long-term investment and not as a potential source of immediate profit. Finally, we should consider the country, which needed railroads built quickly and at moderate cost. It would have gained most from a small number of lines completed rapidly, but received instead many lines, most of which were not completed because all had been begun simultaneously. The country, therefore, had derived no immediate economic benefit from them when the economic crisis began in 1846 and reached its disastrous climax in the Revolution of 1848.

The unfortunate effects of the combination of governmental inconsistency and severity were shown in the cases of most of the important railroads built or begun in the period between 1842 and 1848. Let us consider first the Nord, whose main line was to run from Paris to Belgium through Amiens and Lille, with one or two branches to ports on the English Channel. The importance of trade between France and England, the Netherlands, and northern Germany made large profits from such a railroad probable, while its location made strategic considerations very important. For these reasons the government desired either to build and operate the Nord railroad itself or to control both construction and operation with unusual rigidity. It was urged by the Corps des Ponts et Chaussées both to build and to operate the line, which the corps had surveyed with its usual thoroughness.

On the other hand, the Rothschilds were keenly aware of the probable profits and were anxious by 1843 to acquire control of the Nord and complete its construction. James de Rothschild had ample financial resources to perform such a task rapidly, with the help of other French bankers. He could also prevent undue influence by English financial and metallurgical interests eager to acquire control of this valuable and strategic route, to the probable detriment of French financiers and ironmasters. Rothschild was the most powerful French financier and had the closest connections with the government. Through his English relatives and associates he was in a position to get the necessary capital from England while preventing English interests from acquiring control of the railroad. It is certain that Rothschild wanted to acquire the Nord in 1843 and that the government was tempted by his offer, but it did not yield because the Chamber of Deputies wanted the government to control the railroad until an offer was received that would be highly profitable financially to the government. The result was the imposition of severe conditions by the government and the withdrawal of Rothschild's offer. Finally, in 1845, when the railroad boom was at its height, the Nord railroad was conceded to a great merger headed by Rothschild and other members of the *haute-banque,* such as Laffitte and Blount, and Hottinguer.[30] It is doubtful that the terms of the concession for forty-one years were much more favorable to the government than could have been obtained in 1843, and any such gains were neutralized by the fact that two years had been wasted.

Other aspects of the railroad problem are seen in the building of the great line from Paris to Lyons and Marseilles, whose economic importance to the country could not be exaggerated. Its profits, however, appeared less certain than in the case of the Nord line, if we consider the southern route as a whole. Strategic considerations in the south were less important under the July Monarchy. This line had been one of the first discussed by the Saint-Simonians and was one of the main arteries named in the Act of 1842. When the problem of actual construction was faced, the route was immediately divided into three sections, with the dividing points at Lyons and Avignon. Thus we find the centralized and bureaucratic government of France committing the same error as the individualistic English, whose early railroad lines were all local, with the result that many of them proved weak and unprofitable. The same results followed in France. The section from Avignon to Marseilles nar-

---

[30] Boiteau, *op. cit.,* 189. Kaufmann, *op. cit.,* 37. See also Appendix B.

rowly avoided bankruptcy in the crisis beginning in 1846. It probably owed some of its relative strength to the fact that its concession was direct, made promptly in 1843, and supported by a government loan of considerable size. The company was directed ably by Paulin Talabot and his associates, most of whom had had excellent experience in building and operating the railroad from Alais to Beaucaire.

The companies building the other sections both went bankrupt, that of Lyons to Avignon in 1847, and that of Paris to Lyons in 1848. It is true that these two sections meeting at Lyons were both longer than that from Avignon to Marseilles and had more difficult problems of construction to solve. On the other hand, they had both adequate capital and able management. The guiding spirit in the Lyons-Avignon company was Paulin Talabot himself, while the company of the Paris–Lyons railroad had several very able directors, such as Arlès-Dufour and Enfantin, and placed at the head of its engineers Adolphe Jullien, who had built the railroad from Paris to Orléans with consummate ability. The difficulties of those companies arose rather from the delays and confusion of their organization. They were not conceded directly, but by the usual system of public bids. As a result, in each case many companies were formed and after much wrangling were compelled by circumstances to merge; and the concession was not granted in the case of the Paris-Lyons company until the end of 1845, and in that of the Lyons-Avignon line until June, 1846. It is notable also that neither of these two northern sections received any loan from the government, or assistance in any other form, with the exception of the construction of the section from Dijon to Châlons by the engineers of the Corps des Ponts et Chaussées. It is true also that the troubles of the Paris-Lyons and Lyons-Avignon companies were not due wholly to the manner or slowness of their concessions but even more to the crisis beginning in 1846, for which the government can hardly be held responsible. It remains a fact, however, that, as in the case of the Nord, much time and energy were wasted without any benefits to compensate for the delay.

Another interesting case is provided by the great route from Paris to Bordeaux and its logical continuation through Toulouse to

Cette on the Mediterranean. The first section to Orléans had been conceded in 1838, and the line had been opened in 1843, as we have seen. The Orléans company had strong financial support and remarkably able direction, yet it was unable to extend its control over the rest of the route, even as far as Bordeaux, although it did dominate the new company building the line south from Orléans to Vierzon, Bourges, and Châteauroux, a route generally called the Centre Railroad and intended ultimately to extend directly south to Toulouse. This may have been due to governmental policy or to the general belief that the line from Orléans to Bordeaux would not be very profitable, with the exception of the section between Orléans and Tours. We do know that the government insisted on conceding the entire line from Orléans to Bordeaux as a unit, on the ground that it might be very difficult to find a concessionaire if the section to Tours were separated from the rest of the line running through Poitiers and Angoulême to Bordeaux. The government wished to grant a concession for forty-seven years, a longer period than that of any other main line authorized between 1842 and 1848, but the Chamber of Deputies reduced the duration to twenty-eight years— the shortest of any. On this revised basis it was granted, after very little competition, to a company organized by Laurent, Luzarches (a retired ironmaster of central France), and Mackenzie, the well-known English contractor. This company had been able to defeat one organized by the Rothschilds, although after the lease of October, 1844, the successful company named the Rothschilds as its bankers.

It is curious that the railroad from Bordeaux to Cette was considered much more desirable than that from Orléans to Bordeaux and that the competition for it was so keen that a merger had to be formed. This required too much valuable time, and the company received the concession in 1846, only to go bankrupt from the effects of the crisis in 1847. It seems probable that so little money had been paid in on the shares of the Bordeaux-Cette company that there was no serious possibility of averting reorganization, so that the French government should not be blamed for not trying to save the original company. The Orléans-Bordeaux company was two years older and presumably had a considerable part of its capital paid in before the crisis became acute. This explains its survival despite a concession less than half as long as that of the Bordeaux-Cette company.[31]

The indecisive and often contradictory policy of the government towards the railroads, with its taxes, threats, and concessions of short duration, was an important factor in the development of transportation in France, and it reflected fairly accurately the attitude of the legislature and public opinion. But there were other factors of importance, such as the period of business prosperity ending in the crisis of 1846–47. Business had begun to recover from the depression of 1837–39 in 1841 and was exceedingly prosperous from 1842 until 1846. This produced a great increase in the demand for railroads and in the supply of capital which came not only from France but also from England, which was enjoying a similar period of prosperity. Thus the railroad Law of June 11, 1842, which had been planned in a period when recovery had only begun, bore fruit in a time of rapid business expansion. A further stimulus came in the spring of 1843 with the opening of the railroads from Paris to Rouen and Orléans, both of which were successful and highly profitable from the beginning of their operations.

Many investors in France had doubted that their railroads would ever be really profitable, and they now went to the other extreme and assumed that all railroads would yield large dividends. In England, in 1843, began the period known as "the railroad mania" which had great influence on France, partly because of England's predominance in trade and many forms of industry, and partly because approximately half of the capital invested in French railroads between 1840 and 1848 crossed the Channel. This does not mean that France indulged in a mania of railroad construction, as did England, or that she planned to build many lines that could not be justified on economic grounds. It cannot be said that France was reckless in these matters, but only that, after being much too reluctant to build railroads at all, she suddenly began to build simul-

---

[31] The details of these concessions are given in the *Journal des chemins de fer.*

taneously many lines that had long been badly needed. This sound construction reached its height in the critical year 1846. This was unfortunate, but not in itself enough to cause a crisis. Much more serious was the rapid increase of speculation on the Bourse and still more, perhaps, on the Curb in Paris. The French people had found a new and fruitful field for their love of gambling, and it was all the more tempting because it had the appearance of sound investment.[32]

The government tried in vain to check the growth of speculation in railroad securities. After the merger of most of the different companies that had planned to bid for the concession of the Nord railroad, it passed a law that all who had subscribed for shares must be given the exact number of shares for which they had subscribed regardless of the terms of any merger. This did no good, because the companies concerned in the Paris-Lyons and Paris-Strasbourg mergers simply postponed action until the last moment, so that speculation was increased rather than diminished. Another law forbade trading in promissory shares—that is, in certificates for shares that were to be issued when a railroad company had been legally organized. Since such organization had been delayed until the last possible moment, the trade in such promissory shares had become important. By this second law the government drove such trading from the Bourse to the Curb and made it impossible to list the securities concerned. This tended at first to make the speculation worse because of increased uncertainty and irresponsibility, but in 1846 there appears to have been a considerable decrease in this type of trading, possibly because of prosecutions of curb brokers.

In the meantime the inevitable crisis was approaching. The first warning came from England in 1845, when the railroad boom in France was reaching its height. During that year 118 railroads calling for an investment of £60,484,000 had been authorized in England and bills for more than 500 additional lines with an investment of £304,000,000 had been introduced. The panic came at the end of October in England, after which the worst enterprises disap-

[32] Adolphe Blaise, "Les Chemins de fer en 1845," *Annuaire de l'économie politique,* v. 3 (1846), 271.

peared, so that by the summer of 1846 the mania was considered over.[33] The effect was seen in France in a sharp decline in railroad securities on the Bourse in November, 1845, but there was not a serious amount of liquidation, nor do many securities of French railroads, whether belonging to French or English owners, appear to have been sold. The warning seems to have been ignored in France, and after a brief interval the movement of speculation was resumed. But securities did not rise as high again; there was a slight feeling of general uneasiness, and thoughtful observers began to warn the public that too many railroads were being built and too many securities being issued simultaneously in the face of rapidly rising prices and wages.

In the summer of 1846 the wheat crop failed in most of western Europe, but especially in England and France, and the potato disease caused acute distress in Ireland, and in France deprived swine of their chief source of food. In England signs of pressure on the money market appeared in March, 1847, and much gold had to be sent to the United States to buy grain and cotton. Then in the summer of 1847 the price of wheat fell sharply and unexpectedly in England because of the prospect of a good crop, and many speculators in grain were ruined. Their failures began in August and were followed by those of general merchants in September and of provincial banks in October. The result was a severe panic, the raising of the discount rate of the Bank of England to 8 per cent, and the suspension of the Bank Charter Act of 1844 limiting the amount of notes that could be issued. Before the end of 1847 securities in general were rising again and confidence was returning slowly, but railroad securities remained weak and stationary.[34]

We have far less information regarding the crisis in France, and only recently has one of the most eminent of French economic historians said without qualification that this crisis was one of the most important causes of the Revolution of 1848. The failure of the wheat crop meant in France, as in England, the purchase of

---

[33] David Morier Evans, *The Commercial Crisis, 1847–1848* (London, 1848), 18, 37–38.

[34] *Ibid.*, 86.

grain abroad, which cost the government 125,000,000 francs in 1846 and 231,000,000 francs in 1847.[35] This resulted, as in England, in a serious loss of specie, but in France this seems to have affected business rather more because of the less extensive use of credit. The large purchase of French *rentes* by the czar was a real help to the government and the Bank of France, but not to business in general, unless temporarily. Although we do not yet know the details, it is clear that the agricultural crisis in France in 1847 was acute and the business crisis severe. It is clear also that financial stringency continued and that unemployment was rising to serious heights, with an alarming increase in begging and disorders in several districts, such as the Department of Nord, Normandy, and Alsace, the very regions where mechanized industry was then developing most rapidly. There was also increasing hostility to the government of Louis Philippe and a growing feeling that political as well as financial liquidation was imminent. It is interesting to find the *Journal des chemins de fer* saying on December 4, 1847, that the *rentes* were as depressed as if the government were going to fall.

The effect of the crisis of 1847 on French railroads was serious, as was inevitable, in view of the considerable amount of speculation in which the public had indulged. The companies began to have serious difficulties collecting payments on subscriptions to stock, although refusals to pay or sale of partly paid-up shares appears to have been more general among their British shareholders, because of the greater severity of the panic across the Channel and because many English investors had regarded French railroads chiefly as a source of speculative profit. Whatever the reasons, it is clear that the withdrawal of English capital was quite substantial before the Revolution of 1848 and much more serious after its outbreak. The French railroads had other weaknesses, however, than their great dependence upon English capital. Many of them were still under construction when the crisis came, had no earning capacity, and had had the usual misfortune of greatly underestimating their expenses. They also suffered from concessions of short duration and

[35] Henri Sée, *Französische Wirtschaftsgeschichte*, v. 2 (Jena: Brodnitz, 1936).

the fact that many of their companies were mergers of temporary groups organized for speculation or financial competition. Many of their shareholders had subscribed far beyond their means during the years of apparently permanent prosperity, and some of their bankers and brokers had pyramided loans. Apparently, also, most of the funds used for investment in the railroads in France had come from circulating capital to the injury of other forms of business. Finally, it is quite clear that the burden of financing railroads and most other public works was borne almost wholly by the money market of Paris, so that the strain was much greater than if it had been spread over the country as a whole.

It is a pity that we have so little information regarding the businessmen who must have invested in the French railroads. There is much work to be done in this field of French economic history, and there is only one really good French monograph, the monumental and admirable doctoral thesis of Jouffroy[36] on the Est railroad, which the writer of this book has used freely and gratefully, as he has the excellent book of Professor Jenks.[37]

---

[36] Louis Maurice Jouffroy, *Une étape de la construction des grandes lignes de chemin de fer en France: La Ligne de Paris à la frontière d'Allemagne (1825–1852)* (Paris: Dorbon-Aîné, 1932).

[37] Leland Hamilton Jenks, *The Migration of British Capital to 1875*, 2d ed. (New York: Knopf, 1938), 377.

CHAPTER FIVE

Fuel and Power

THE USE OF COAL AND WOOD

NEXT TO transportation, there are probably no questions more fundamental to the development of the Industrial Revolution in France than those of fuel and power. That Revolution developed rapidly in England because the shortage of wood that had held back the growth of the iron industry had been overcome by the discovery that coal could replace wood as fuel, and the further discovery that it gave far more heat in proportion to its bulk than wood had done. England was fortunate also in having coal in abundance and unusually accessible. The use of coal in England, which began from a necessity, thus soon became a great means of further progress. Furthermore, it served as the basis for the development of steam instead of water as a source of power. This revolutionized many forms of manufacturing and transportation and promoted greatly the integration of industry. In France, on the other hand, while there was a shortage of wood before the period of the Restoration, it was not even then a serious factor. There was also a much greater supply of water power than in England. Finally, France had not developed her coal mines sufficiently and she had such inadequate means of transportation that in 1815 coal was available at a reasonable cost and in adequate quantity in only a few parts of the country, whether as fuel for smelting or refining iron or as a source for steam power. France, therefore, neither needed nor found it possible to effect rapid development of the Industrial Revolution in either fuel or power.

It is difficult to estimate the production of wood in France between 1815 and 1848, for the best writers rarely go further than to say that wood was scarce or abundant in a given year and then dismiss the subject by adding that its price was high. Certain inferences seem justified, however, even if they cannot be supported by statistics. The supply of wood in France appears to have been ample for the needs of the country until the iron industry began to grow rapidly in the period following the crisis of 1817–18 and culminating in the boom of 1825–26. It is probable that during the Revolution and First Empire much timber was destroyed and the forests neglected. With the Restoration this was stopped; government forests were given care, and many of those that had belonged to private individuals, chiefly members of the nobility, were restored to them. But even under Louis Philippe it seems probable that the forests did not produce as much as they should have, whether those owned by the national government, those owned by local governments, or those in the hands of individuals. It would appear that the shortage of wood was not serious at any time during the period from 1815 to 1848. The supply neither increased nor decreased appreciably, and complaints of scarcity were due to purely local conditions in each case, of which the most common was the lack of adequate means of transportation at moderate cost or at reasonable speed or convenience.

The price of wood was necessarily quite as important as the supply. The few figures available indicate quite clearly a considerable rise in the price during or shortly after the period of the Revolution and First Empire. Between 1821 and 1826 there was another increase in the price of wood which varied from a 25 per cent rise to double or even triple, according to local conditions. There are indications that this increase was greatest in the year 1826 and that it was largely permanent, but not wholly so. After 1828 we have no figures for the price of wood that seem reliable.

The increase in the price of wood between 1821 and 1826, or, as seems more probable, between 1819 and 1826, was due to several factors, some of which can be determined clearly. This was a period of increasing prosperity which followed many years of war and the crisis of 1817–18, reaching the proportions of a boom in 1825–26.

It was accompanied by speculation in building and real estate in Paris, and probably in other large cities as well. The dates of 1821 and 1828, commonly given in most sources, are actually misleading, because they emphasize unduly the importance of the tariff of 1822 and the *enquête* of 1829, which aroused the fear that the tariff might shortly be lowered. It is important to realize that witnesses at the *enquête* naturally wished to give the impression that their prosperity had been due primarily to the tariff of 1822 and would end promptly if that tariff were revised downward. It is interesting to note that the price of the wooded hectare sold by the government (the right to cut timber in the governmental forests) rose from 641 francs in 1816 to an average of 1188 francs for the period 1821 to 1826. We have no figures for the next few years, which were a period of depression, but in 1831 and 1832, which were the last years of that period, the prices were 919 and 828 francs, while the average for the following three years, 1833–35, which were prosperous, was 1,153 francs, or almost exactly the same as the average for the years 1821–26.[1]

There were other factors which determined the increase in the price of wood between 1821 and 1826 and the general continuance of that increase until 1848, except during years of marked industrial or commercial depression. These were, first, the influence of the landowners, the ironmasters and the government, which was exerted in both the economic and political fields; second, the tariff, which was both economic and political; and third, such purely economic factors as the inadequacy of the means of transportation and the proximity of iron ore in most districts to the forests rather than to the coal mines. It is difficult to separate these factors, however, because they frequently acted together and often were identical. The landowners who controlled the forests usually belonged to one of three groups: the nobles who had recovered their estates during the Empire or the Restoration; the national or local governments or, in a few cases, the Crown; and those ironmasters who were rich enough to invest in a permanent supply of fuel which seemed likely

---

[1] "Chronique," *Journal de l'industriel et du capitaliste,* v. 1 (March, 1836), 203–4.

to ensure high profits indefinitely. The nobles and the governments and those ironmasters who owned forests wished the price of wood to be high. The ironmasters who did not own forests were usually helpless, because inadequate means of transportation made it impossible for them to obtain fuel from any other source. They were kept alive and able to fight each other by the tariff of 1822, directed primarily against iron smelted or refined with coal. This came generally from England and was usually treated by the British processes of puddling and rolling, against which nearly all the French ironmasters desired protection. This tariff had been obtained through the co-operation of the government, the landowners, who were either government officials or the most influential voters under the system of restricted suffrage or both, the ironmasters, and other manufacturers. It gave the iron industry of France so much more protection than it needed that its healthy growth was retarded greatly.

The influences that raised and kept up the price of wood are illustrated very well in the Department of Haute-Marne, probably the most important part of the old province of Champagne from the point of view of metallurgy. The iron industry there cannot be called progressive. At first sight this seems surprising, because the supply of wood was abundant, even if slightly below the needs of the ironmasters, there was a large supply of ore, usually excellent in quality, there were many streams available for washing the ore and supplying power to the mills, and, finally, the great market of Paris was not far away and that of Lyons was accessible. Yet we find the iron industry there towards the end of the period 1815–48 burdened by a price of charcoal that was probably the highest in France and apparently unable to adapt itself to the use of coal except in forging. One reason for this situation has been stated. The high tariff, by protecting French manufactures from foreign competition, enabled them to produce inefficiently and at high cost by the good old methods to which they were accustomed, because they could still sell their iron in the French market at a high price.

Perhaps the greatest single difficulty in the Haute-Marne, however, was the large number of small foundries and forges. There is no evidence here of the fairly steady progress of integration in industry which appeared in the Nivernais in central France. There we find great establishments, such as Fourchambault and Imphy, using many of the best English methods and tools and slowly driving out the small mills. This did not happen in the Haute-Marne. That district was rather isolated in the mountains, and the ore, although excellent in quality, was usually scattered in small pockets. Even the numerous streams rarely supplied enough water power for really large mills. Under these conditions most metallurgical establishments remained small, and being far too numerous they bid against each other for the supply of wood and kept the price as high as the greediest landowner could have desired. It would have been difficult for them to improve their methods because they lacked the capital. Many improvements would not have paid for themselves unless operations could be upon a large scale. They did adopt coal in their forges, but reluctantly, because it had to be brought great distances and was little cheaper than charcoal.

The government was fully informed regarding the imperfections of the iron industry in France and regarding the high price of wood by its exceedingly competent Corps of Mining Inspectors, whose reports form one of the historian's most valuable sources of evidence. Many of these engineers went to England, Scotland, and Wales to study metallurgical methods and then tried to apply the improvements at home. But they encountered serious obstacles. While the national government of France urged the increasing use of coal as fuel and worked hard to improve the means of transportation, it was itself interested, as were the local governments, in the use of wood as a much-needed source of revenue.

Another serious obstacle encountered by the mining inspectors was the continued enforcement through bureaucratic methods of the very rigid regulations governing the use of mines and streams and the installation and operation of metallurgical establishments. These rules hindered greatly the development of water power and made improvements in mills difficult. Every change had to be authorized officially by the government after thorough investigation; that meant months or even years of delay, unless the mining inspector concerned was willing to take the risk of authorizing the improvement himself before it had been approved by higher officials. These rules, although clearly burdensome, were not revised until 1866.[2]

Many ironmasters, either forced to continue the use of wood as fuel or believing that it really was the best, tried because of the high prices to use as little of it as possible. Experiments were made with both green and scorched wood as substitutes for charcoal, particularly during the depression that began in 1837, but they provided no permanent relief and were gradually abandoned. It was found that they slowed down the smelting by chilling the furnace, or that they altered the quality of the cast iron. It was not practicable to use them without constant supervision, because of the prevalence of unskilled labor. Unfortunately the ironmasters who suffered most from the high cost of charcoal were the very ones least able to supply adequate supervision.

Yet despite the failure of these improvements and all the other difficulties encountered, such as rigid rules, scarcity of available capital, and small-scale operations, the French iron industry made considerable progress in its use of fuel in the period from 1815 to 1848. The high tariff and the influence of the landowners and governments as owners of forests delayed but could not prevent the adoption of coal as the principal fuel in both smelting and refining. By 1838 as much iron was refined with coal or coke as with charcoal, and by 1848 the proportion had increased from 50 per cent to 70 per cent.[3] Progress in smelting was much slower. The first blast furnace to use coke was Le Creusot in 1782; in 1819 only one other had adopted it, and in 1840 only 41 out of 462 blast furnaces used coke. Yet the mills that did smelt with coke were the largest and best in France and their production of cast iron increased from 2 per cent of the total in 1819 to 46 per cent in 1846,[4] while in that same period the total production increased fivefold.

[2] Georges Hottenger, *L'Ancienne industrie du fer en Lorraine* (Nancy: Société Industrielle de l'Est, 1927), 120.

[3] Paris, *Exposition nationale de produits de l'industrie, agricole et manufacturière de 1849: Rapport du jury central*, v. 2 (Paris, 1850), 297.

[4] Achille de Colmont, *Histoire des expositions des produits de l'industrie française* (Paris, 1855), 405.

The continued use in France of wood as fuel in manufacturing iron was not, then, a wise economy justified by an abundant supply, any more than the decrease in its use was due to scarcity. The problem was not one of supply but of price. As has been shown, the high price was due to many factors of importance, such as the ownership of forests, the influence of the government, the tariff, the prevalence of small-scale industry, and the lack of adequate means of transportation. At first, the use of wood was a necessity because the supply of coal at a reasonable cost was grossly inadequate. Soon, however, we find its use advocated to justify prejudice, routine, and opposition to industrial progress by vested interests or merely by the ignorant. The prices of wood and charcoal did not increase seriously after 1826, in most cases, yet they appeared to: the price of iron continued to fall, so that a constant expense for charcoal formed an increasingly large percentage of the cost of manufacturing. Also, coal, chiefly through improvement in the means of transportation, increased steadily in abundance and cheapness, both absolutely and relative to charcoal. The high prices of wood and charcoal were actually a blessing in disguise, for they were not nearly as serious a problem as most writers have stated, but they were serious enough to force improvements in metallurgical methods that might otherwise have been delayed for many years.

COAL-MINING

The development of coal-mining in France was negligible before 1815, partly because the necessary means of transportation were not available and partly because there was little demand for it from either industrial or domestic consumers. We have seen that the use of coal in smelting and refining iron had not begun and that the country had been able to obtain a fairly adequate supply of iron goods through importation and still more through manufacture with wood, which was available in reasonably sufficient quantity. But another explanation of fundamental importance for the neglect of coal is the location of the deposits within the boundaries of France. French writers usually speak of many coal basins and list between thirteen and fifty-eight. Further study eliminates nearly all of them as too small or too inaccessible to be important. Most of these deposits are on or near the borders of the great plateau known as the Massif Central. The basin of Saône et Loire lies a little to the northeast. The great basin of the Loire is further south on either side of the watershed between the Loire and the Rhône. Finally, the small but rich basins of Alais and Aubin are on the southeast and southwest borders. Other basins on the north border, as on the plateau itself, were both too small and too difficult of access to be of economic importance. In other parts of France we find some deposits of anthracite in southern Normandy, which in the earlier nineteenth century were used chiefly for slaking lime, and in the small basin of Ronchamps in the Vosges.

The great basin of coal in the Department of Nord, a continuation of the deposits of the Ruhr and of Belgium, is the only important one not in central or southern France. In production it ranked next to the basin of the Loire, yet it was difficult to mine because the coal was generally far below the surface. What is now the richest part of this coal field, the basin of Pas de Calais, was discovered only at the end of the period 1815–48, because as they continued westward the veins of coal sank ever deeper and then suddenly turned sharply northward towards the English Channel. The part of this great northern coal field which was mined effectively in the earlier nineteenth century was the northernmost portion in the Department of Nord, known as the basin of Valenciennes.

Much of the coal available in France between 1815 and 1848 was thus in hilly or mountainous districts in the central part of the country, or in the south. In most cases it was far from any useful deposits of iron or, if not far away in actual distance, was so in effect because of the lack of cheap means of transportation. None of the French coal mines was near a really good seaport and few were near the sea. The most productive basin of this period, the Loire, was between two of the greatest French rivers, but as we have seen, they were difficult and costly to use. The Loire was full of rocks in its upper reaches and of sand bars in its middle course, and the flow of water was irregular, while the Rhône had an unusually strong current and flowed to the south away from the most important markets. Artificial waterways were much used in France and, as we have seen, were greatly developed under the Restoration and the July Monarchy. But only in the north were they united with the rivers into a system of waterways that could carry great quantities of coal economically. This system served the coal basin of Valenciennes only. In central France the canals were too narrow and shallow, and in the south they scarcely existed.

Deposits of coal in France were thus so placed that they did not make easy or economical the use of coal in manufacturing. Alsace, which had so brilliant an industrial development in the period 1815 to 1848, was really dependent for coal upon the German basin of the Saar until the opening of the canal from the Rhône to the Rhine made available the coal of central France, but even then the price was very high. Normandy, whose industrial development was important in our period, had no adequate supply of coal of its own and depended in practice chiefly upon importations from England by sea and from Belgium by inland waterways. Northern France alone had its own supply, yet too frequently that was expensive because waterways could not reach all the many industrial centers and carting was almost prohibitive in cost.

It is not surprising to find that in 1815 the production of coal in France was only 882,000 tons, importations 249,000 tons, and consumption 1,112,000 tons, while in 1847 the consumption had increased to 7,000,000 tons and production to 5,000,000, with importations of 2,000,000 tons.[5] In general, increase in the use of coal corresponded to the industrial development of France, especially to that of the iron industry, and was promoted also by the improvement of transportation and the marked decrease in the duties on importations of coal in 1836. Because of all these factors the demand for coal became great under the July Monarchy. In consequence there were no serious complaints against the increasing use of foreign coal, whose rate of increase was considerably greater than that of domestic production. Also, the consumption of coal did not

[5] François Simiand, "Essai sur le prix de charbon au XIXe siècle," *Année sociologique,* v. 5 (1900–1901), 17, 25.

decrease appreciably during industrial depressions, as did that of most other commodities, except during the economic crisis that accompanied the Revolution of 1848.

France produced numerous varieties of coal in the period from 1815 to 1848; this fact has been emphasized by many French writers, but in practice it was not of great importance, because the only basins that were able to ship great distances were those of the Loire, Saône et Loire, and Valenciennes. Inadequate means of transportation and high prices to the consumer were decisive factors in most cases. Most mines were compelled to sell to local markets exclusively, and the concentration of industry on a large scale would have been therefore prevented, had the tendency to it existed to any marked degree.

Complaints of the poor quality of coal shipped by some basins to industrial consumers were often justified, but sometimes for reasons different from those given. When it was said that the coal of Anzin was inferior for both forging and coking, we must agree, but add that the best concession for those types of coal, that of Denain, was not developed effectively by the Anzin company until about 1839. Also, much of the coal shipped out from Anzin was poorly sorted, sometimes mixed with coal dust, and always sold at a high price. Similar explanations can be given for the inferiority of the coal of Blanzy for forging and coking, although in that case more emphasis should be placed on quality and less on price. The coal from Epinac was very clearly of inferior quality and was full of pyrites; but here, as at Blanzy and Denain, better veins were discovered later. Much French coal seems also to have been poorly cut and to have crumbled too much when shipped considerable distances. Many of these defects were probably characteristic of the coal from the basin of the Loire, but on the whole it was the best in France for forging and was quite satisfactory for coking, so that it was in great demand and would have been used in most parts of the country, had cheap transportation been available.

It is difficult to compare prices of coal for different regions of France and for different years within the period 1815–48 for various reasons. The quality of coal is rarely named when the price is given, and in most cases the price is based upon the average of several different qualities with no information as to how the average was obtained. There is also much careless use of the available figures. But the greatest difficulty is one that harasses nearly all investigators of French economic history before the later nineteenth century, the lack of any general unit of measurement until approximately 1840. Coal before that date might be measured in any one of three units: the hectolitre *comble* of 120 litres, the hectolitre *ras* of 105, or the metric quintal, whose theoretical content was 100 litres. Not until towards the end of our period did the ton come into general use.

It seems clear that until 1833 the coal of Saint-Etienne was very cheap, probably less than half the average price at the mine given by Simiand in his table of 1900. This was due to extensive strip mining in that basin with cutthroat competition between mines, numerous sales at or below the cost of production, and few markets accessible because of inadequate means of transportation. It seems probable also that much of the coal mined was of poor quality and badly sorted. The price of coal in the basin of Rive de Gier throughout the period 1815 to 1848 was much higher, but there the mines were deeper and, until the opening of the railroad from Saint-Etienne to Lyons, much more accessible. Competition between them also was less severe. After the number of mining companies in the basin of Saint-Etienne had decreased in the late 1830's, prices seem to have risen a little. It is difficult, however, to use price figures for distant markets, such as Paris, because they do not usually distinguish between the two parts of the basin of the Loire, and because the cost of transportation to Paris was so high that the selling price there was frequently ten times the price at the mine.

The cost of mining in the really important French basins averaged considerably higher than in England, and was about the same as in Belgium, for although costs in the basin of Saint-Etienne in the Loire and Blanzy in the Saône et Loire were about the same as in the basin of Newcastle, and less than in Lancashire, in the basin of Valenciennes they were considerably higher than in the more expensive of the two great basins of England. Costs in France were raised by the irregularity of veins in nearly all mines, by great masses of subterranean water in the basin of Valenciennes, and by the small scale of operations of all French companies except Anzin until 1835 or even 1840.

There were great difficulties to overcome in most of the French mines, even if they did not all appear at the start because the demand for coal grew slowly and many mines were able to continue strip mining through part or even the whole of the period from 1815 to 1848. Examples of strip mining are to be found at Le Creusot, in some of the mines in the basin of Saint-Etienne, at Commentry in the Department of Allier, and in the rich basins of the south—Alais in the Gard and Aubin in the Aveyron, of which the latter was better known through the great metallurgical establishment of Decazeville founded in 1826. In other cases mining was difficult almost from the beginning, as in the whole of the basin of Valenciennes in the Department of Nord, where the land was soft, with great subterranean bodies of water, and the coal was far below the surface. In addition to these difficulties the veins were often thin and were irregular in both slope and direction. Frequently sharp breaks were encountered, and towards the west of the basin of Valenciennes the veins grew deeper until they finally seemed to disappear.

The problem of water was not as serious in most French basins as in that of Valenciennes, nor was the coal usually as far below the surface; but in most of them the veins were thin and very irregular in their course with frequent breaks. Mining was thus difficult from the start or as soon as the veins near the surface had become exhausted. It was fortunate that the French had excellent schools which trained their mining engineers well. In the basin of the Loire all these problems were present. The oldest mines were those of Rive de Gier not far above the Rhône where, by 1815, many of the shafts were deep and pumping had become vitally important and the cost of extraction rose. The next mines to be developed were those of Saint-Etienne high up in the mountains and on the western side of the watershed dividing the Rhône from the Loire. Here strip mining was common in 1815 and shafts were sunk only gradually, although many of them were deep before 1848.

In both of these parts of the Loire basin the veins were irregular and frequently broken.

Another characteristic of much of the coal in France which presented a serious problem to the industry was the ease with which it was broken up or pulverized. It has been estimated that 75 per cent of English coal was mined in large pieces and only 45 per cent of French coal.[6] This meant that French coal was more difficult to sell and was much more difficult to ship for long distances without considerable loss. It helps explain also the frequent complaints of bad sorting of coal which were made even against the great company of Anzin.

The slow growth in the demand for coal, combined with the difficulties of mining offered by the thin and irregular veins, helps to explain also the great delays in the full exploration of the basins. Where strip mining was possible no exploration seemed necessary and equipment could be simple. In the basin of Valenciennes, however, good equipment was necessary from a very early date. It is natural to find that the great company of Anzin, which is said to have mined a quarter of all the coal produced in France in the period from 1815 to 1848, and which certainly was the most important mining company, was the leader in improving pumps and extracting machines. The mines of central or southern France were usually far behind, sometimes because the equipment really was not needed, and sometimes because there were too many small companies, each with inadequate resources and all eager to compete rather than to co-operate. Towards the end of our period many of the local differences in equipment were removed and many of the mines of the center and south were as well equipped as those of the north, but in the Loire basin at least, this did not happen until most of the small companies had been removed.

In nearly every basin in France exploration was pushed very slowly indeed, because the demand for coal increased slowly until after the depression of 1827, which ended in 1832. Only after 1832, therefore, was much progress made in organizing large mining com-

[6] Amédée Burat, *Le Matériel des houillères en France et en Belgique*, v. 1 (Paris, 1860), 7.

panies with adequate resources to produce really good equipment and to think beyond immediate profits to greater riches obtainable by scientific study of the full extent and resources of each basin. The rate of progress of coal-mining in France was thus closely connected with the rate of growth of business and industry in general and with that of the Industrial Revolution.

A closer study of the cost of carrying coal shows that transportation was the most serious problem of all and served more than any other factor to keep up the price and restrict the consumption. At the beginning of the period from 1815 to 1848, most coal was consumed locally, and manufacturing centers or large cities not near coal mines used it very little. From the point of view of the coal merchant, France was divided into noncompeting regions by the expense and slowness of transportation. The fact that there were notable exceptions to this should not blind us to the fact that it was true in general. No coal basin could then play a part on the national stage unless it was virtually on the banks of a waterway or connected with one by a railroad. We must, therefore, admit the fact that, although French writers describe a great many coal basins in France, only about three played a part of any importance in the industrial development of the country between 1815 and 1848.

The three basins that played a really important part in the industrial development of France as a whole were the Loire, Valenciennes or the Nord, and Blanzy, or the basin of Saône et Loire, which includes Le Creusot. The Loire was the most productive throughout this period, and as we have seen, much of its coal was good for smelting and forging—it was the most important basin qualitatively as well as quantitatively. Yet its situation raised difficult problems in an age of waterways. The Loire, which was not far from Saint-Etienne, was rocky in its upper reaches and the flow of the water was very irregular. During the period a railroad was built beyond the worst rapids to Roanne and a canal eased the passage from there to Digoin in 1839. Finally, other canals connected the Loire with the Seine, yet the route to Paris and northern France remained long, slow, and expensive. None of the improvements were decisive.

On the other side of the Loire basin, Rive de Gier was not far from the Rhône and was connected with it in the eighteenth century by a canal and, after 1832, by the railroad to Lyons, which started at Saint-Etienne. It was feasible, then, to send the coal of the Loire basin through the Rhône valley; but in the Saône valley above, there was competition from the basins of Blanzy and Epinac, and the canals leading to Paris from Burgundy had many locks and were shallow, so that the route was more expensive than that by the Loire, and it was also longer. The average price of coal of the Loire basin was 6.80 francs per ton at the mine and 19.40 francs, on the average, at the place of consumption,[7] so that two thirds of the amount paid by the consumer was for transportation. Even so, the coal was in such demand that it traveled further than that of any other basin in France.

The basin of Blanzy was much less productive than that of the Loire, and the quality of most of its grades of coal seems to have been somewhat inferior; so, although it traveled an average of 126 kilometres to the place of consumption as compared to 166 kilometres for the coal of the Loire,[8] and although the cost of transportation was only 47 per cent of the price to the consumer instead of 65 per cent,[9] it played a much less important part in the development of the country than did that of the Loire. The system of waterways by which the coal reached centers such as Paris was unsatisfactory. Almost the whole of the production of the northern part of the basin, where Le Creusot was situated, was used locally. Finally, the resources of the basin were neither fully exploited nor adequately utilized as early as those of the Loire.

The basin of Valenciennes had deep shafts and subterranean lakes that made the extraction of coal expensive; but it was well placed in northern France, where industry was developed far more

---

[7] "Du mouvement commercial des combustibles minéraux en France pendant l'année 1838," *Journal de l'industriel et du capitaliste,* v. 9 (Aug., 1840); based on *Compte rendu des ingénieurs des mines pour l'année 1839.*

[8] Eugène Flachat and Alexis Barrault, *Traité de la fabrication du fer et de la fonte envisagée sous les rapports chimique, mécanique et commercial* (Paris, 1842), 1063.

[9] "Du mouvement commercial des combustibles," *loc. cit.*

than in central or southern France and where there were more important cities. It was within reach of Normandy and Picardy, both of which had many important textile centers, as had the departments of Nord and Pas de Calais, and was little more than half as far from Paris as was the basin of the Loire. The rivers and canals of northern France were better and had fewer locks than those of central France, and more was done to improve them between 1815 and 1847. The improvement of the canal of Saint-Quentin in 1828 and the canalization of the lower Oise in 1835 were of decisive importance. Such improvements in transportation were almost wholly responsible for the decrease in the price of coal at Paris between 1835 and 1851 from 37 francs per ton to 25 francs.[10]

It is interesting also to recall that the average barge of northern France or Belgium carried twice as much as the barge of central France because the waterways were deeper and wider. The part of the price paid by the consumer of the coal of the basin of Valenciennes for transportation was only 34 per cent,[11] the lowest of any French basin that shipped coal to distant centers. This was only half the relative cost of transportation of coal from the Loire basin. The advantage of the basin of Valenciennes in facilities of transportation and in favorable location with regard to important markets resulted in a steady increase of its sales in Paris after 1830, where those of coal from the Loire remained stationary; in fact, its chief rival in the French capital came to be Mons rather than Saint-Etienne.

The cost of transportation, as has been said, was the most important factor in determining the price of coal to the consumer. In many cases under the Restoration it increased the price of coal to eight or ten times the price at the mine, and in many others it prevented the use of coal altogether. The cost of transportation decreased markedly under the July Monarchy, chiefly through the improvement of waterways, but somewhat also through the improve-

---

[10] Amédée Burat, *Le Commerce des houilles en France* (Paris, 1852), 28.
[11] "Du mouvement commercial des combustibles," *loc. cit.*

ment of highways and the construction of local railroads, such as those serving the mines of the Loire and Epinac. The Nord was the only main line completed before 1848 that could have had any appreciable effect on the coal industry. The conclusion seems justified that in many cases the price at the place of consumption decreased from eight or ten times to double the price at the mine and that relatively few towns in France in 1848 were unable to obtain coal at all.

The tariff did not have an important influence on the price of coal, if we consider France as a whole. The only powerful coal-mining company capable of exerting great political influence was Anzin, and it received ample protection under the Act of 1816, which imposed a duty of 10–11.50 francs per ton, depending on the nationality of the transporting vessel, on coal imported by sea, and duties of 6 francs on coal imported from Belgium, 1.50 francs on coal from Rhenish Prussia, and 3 francs from other countries by land.[12] The mining companies of the Loire basin wanted even more protection than this, as did Anzin, but they were not united and were not really threatened by coal from abroad. Their real enemy was the high cost of transportation on French waterways. They could not compete with English coal under any but a prohibitive tariff in the ports along the Atlantic coast or the Mediterranean. Their most desirable markets were Paris and other industrial and commercial centers, where they met coal from other French basins, or from Mons, which did not come in quantities large enough or at prices low enough to restrict the production of the basin of Valenciennes. These facts were brought out at the *enquête* of 1832, called by the government in reply to repeated demands from northern manufacturers. While the witnesses for the Anzin company were able to show that the tariff was partly responsible for the very high prices they paid for pumps and other mining equipment, they were unable to prove that the prosperity of their mines was ever endangered by foreign competition, whether Belgian or English, and their

---

[12] Léon Amé, *Etude économique sur les tarifs des douanes,* 2d ed. (Paris, 1860), 181–82.

opponents were able to show that the prices and profits of Anzin were high.

The Act of 1836 retained the zones through each of which coal was imported under a specified duty, and the proportions of the rates remained the same, but all were cut practically in half. The only other change of importance was permission to import coal free of duty for steam navigation. The chief result of these modifications in 1836 was a large and continued increase of importations from Great Britain and a further increase of importations from Belgium. There is no evidence that these increased importations injured any important French mining company; in fact, it can be shown that in the period between 1836 and 1848 production of French coal increased greatly and ever more rapidly.

It was inevitable that disputes should arise regarding the conflicting rights of owners of the soil and exploiters of the mineral wealth which was usually some distance below the surface. Further disputes arose when concessions were granted, since these had to be authorized by the government or its local representative, had to specify the rental to be paid to the owner of the soil if he were not also the exploiter of the mine, and had to fix the boundaries of each concession.

The legal aspects of coal-mining raised serious questions in the basin of Saint-Etienne and, to a lesser extent, in that of Rive de Gier under the First Empire. But, as we have seen, the economic aspects were also difficult and confusing. In the district of Saint-Etienne, where there was at first much strip mining at very low cost, there were many small veins reaching the surface. The problem of the rights of landowners was, therefore, serious. There appear to have been many landowners involved and also many exploiters, some of whom evidently had begun operations without the consent of those who owned the soil. Under the Restoration the government gave full ownership of mines to the larger landowners, but dispossessed small ones after compensation and turned their mines over to the exploiters. The Law of 1810 limited the size of mining concessions. It forced the separation of those of Blanzy and Le Creusot in the basin of Saône et Loire and probably also clipped the wings

of the Anzin company for many years. Yet the decisive factor, in
the basin of Saint-Etienne, at least, appears to have been not the
statute cited but the great number of small veins at the surface and
the ease with which they could be exploited. Evidently the competition for them was keen, as was the struggle between the many
small ironmasters in the Haute-Marne. This explains the excessively
high rentals paid the landowners by exploiters at Saint-Etienne. It
explains also the policy of the government in buying off as many
landowners as it could and then in granting a great number of
small concessions and subsequently allowing their subdivision until,
instead of the 56 listed, there were actually 105 competing mines.
This was clearly a violation, or a series of violations, of Article 7 of
the Law of April 21, 1810.[13]

The important factors in the situation at Saint-Etienne were
thus the character of the coal deposits and the administrative practices of the government officials involved, rather than the Law of
1810. The law was interpreted, as the government desired, to sustain
the big landowners, but the practice of coal-mining was not changed
under the Restoration except through the beneficent influence of
the Ecole des Mines at Saint-Etienne, which helped the coal industry
more than all the codes of Napoleon.

With the advent of the July Monarchy in 1830 and the end of
the depression of 1827 in 1832, the development of coal-mining in
France became much more rapid. Other causes, not always mentioned, were probably of even greater importance. The ever-increasing expansion of the iron industry now created a demand for coal
so great that, as we shall see, the better coal-mining companies went
on growing throughout the next depression, from 1837 to 1842.
Secondly, strip mining virtually ended with the exhaustion of the

---

[13] Amédée Burat, *De la houille: Traité théorique et pratique des combustibles minéraux* (Paris, 1851), 414. "Notice sur les mines de houille de
l'arrondissement de Saint-Etienne," *Journal de l'industriel et du capitaliste,*
v. 4 (1838), 184. Ambroise Clément, "De la concentration des entreprises
industrielles et spécialement de la réunion des concessions houillères du
bassin de la Loire," *Journal des économistes,* v. 16 (March, 1846), 337–55,
esp. 344. Louis Joseph Gras, *Histoire économique générale des mines de la
Loire,* v. 1 (Saint-Etienne: Théolier, 1922), 254.

veins on the surface, so that shafts had to be sunk in almost all mines, better equipment supplied, and capital found to make possible exploitation on a more costly but permanent basis.

Under the new circumstances it was obviously necessary to end the situation in the Loire basin, where a great number of small exploiters were fighting each other in both the markets and the courts. At Rive de Gier, where there were relatively few concessions, because the shafts were already deep, the hatred between the companies was so great that they would not co-operate to fight floods, so that the government was obliged to intervene to save the mines. We have, therefore, a change in governmental policy, reflected to some extent in legislation, as in the Acts of 1837 and 1838,[14] but still more, undoubtedly, in the administrative actions of local officials. Simultaneously came a marked change in the attitude of the financiers and the public towards investment in coal mines.

The government had been studying carefully the situation at Rive de Gier since 1833, so that its intervention, through the Law of 1838, had been planned for some time and was effective.[15] The pressure brought to bear sufficed to force co-operation of the companies and the installation of a great pump run by steam, which stopped the floods. We know also that through the Law of 1838 the government allowed the absorption of several concessions in the basin of Valenciennes by the Anzin company, of twelve in the basin of Alais by another company, and of five in the basin of Blanzy, which covered an area larger than the entire basin of the Loire. The Blanzy company was also exempted from meeting the statutory requirement of operating all its concessions simultaneously, and it seems safe to assume that the more influential Anzin company received the same privilege.

As we have seen, there were economic forces of considerable strength working towards integration in coal-mining in France. In the Loire basin a veritable trust was organized through a series of purchases and combinations that extended from 1837 to 1845, when

---

[14] *Journal des chemins de fer* (Aug. 21, 1847), 655, and (Aug. 28, 1847), 669. Gras, *op. cit.*, 269–73.

[15] *Journal des chemins de fer*, Aug. 21 and 28, 1847.

there emerged the powerful Compagnie des Mines de la Loire, which controlled a majority of the mines in the entire basin, including all the best shafts, and at least two thirds of the production of coal. It also acquired control of the canal of Givors and of the railroad from Saint-Etienne to Lyons. There is reason to believe that the government approved the formation of this trust, and actually may have encouraged it, although it did not give it legal authorization as a joint-stock company with limited liability.

The Compagnie Générale des Mines de la Loire was organized with a capital of 64,000,000 francs in shares of 1,000 francs each. This capital was expected soon to be increased to 100,000,000 francs.[16] While there were protests against it made to the government by the cities of Lyons and Saint-Etienne and by many interests which felt aggrieved, possibly because they had not been taken into the trust, there is every reason to believe that much more important interests supported the combination. We know that during the formation of the trust from 1837 through 1845 capitalists at Lyons were working for it in the basin of Rive de Gier, while others, chiefly from Paris, were organizing or buying up the many small concessions in the basin of Saint-Etienne. This division of financiers was natural, for the lower part of the Loire basin, being near the Rhone, supplied Lyons, while the upper part, being nearer the Loire, could more readily send its coal downstream in the direction of the capital.

It is interesting to observe that among the directors of the trust about whom information is available, we find not only organizers of the railroad from Saint-Etienne to Lyons, such as one of the Séguin brothers, or of the short line from Saint-Etienne to the Loire, represented by the ironmaster Hochet, but also four men closely concerned with the management of the railroad from Paris to Orléans, opened in 1843, and with its extension southward through the company of the Centre, whose line was then being built and would eventually bring the coal of Saint-Etienne to Paris by

---

[16] Ambroise Clément, "Nouvelles observations sur le monopole des houilles de la Loire," *Journal des économistes*, v. 16 (December, 1846), 21–22. Gras, *op. cit.*, 296–98, 303.

rail. One of the directors was no less a person than the retired banker François Bartholony, who was president of the Paris-Orléans railroad and one of the ablest business executives of the time.[17]

In the north of France we have another example of integration in coal-mining in the Anzin company. This was organized first between 1717 and 1720, but failed. Then it passed into other hands, and through a series of lawsuits in the course of which two of the great landowners involved, the Prince de Croy and the Marquis de Cernay, were sustained by the courts. In 1757 was drawn up the partnership agreement that continued to govern the company for many years. Its most notable feature was the council of six regents which held all the power, was not obliged to call meetings of the shareholders, and was self-perpetuating. About the beginning of the nineteenth century the Anzin company came under the control of the Périer family, including Scipio, the banker, who died in 1821, and his brother Casimir, who died in 1832 when president of the company and prime minister of France.[18] He was succeeded by Adolphe Thiers, who is much better known as a minister of Louis Philippe and as first head of the Third Republic.

No organization in France seems to have been so successful as Anzin in keeping its archives inviolate and its business affairs from the knowledge of the public, but few have been directed throughout their history with more ability or more continued success. From the beginning of the nineteenth century, if not earlier, land was bought for possible mining in the future and funds were set aside as a financial reserve that enabled the Anzin firm to emerge from each depression unscathed.

The Anzin company was a leader in developing the use of steam for running both pumps and extracting machines and set a valuable example in promoting better methods of exploitation. It seems also to have been a leader in keeping wages down and prices up and was evidently strong enough to follow its own policy unham-

---

[17] Gras, op. cit., 307.

[18] Bulletin de la société d'encouragement pour l'industrie nationale, v. 20 (1821), 118. Julien François Turgan, Les Grandes usines, v. 15 (Paris, 1884), 3.

pered, for it has been described several times as quite indifferent to the needs or wishes of consumers. In the period after 1832, when the development of coal-mining increased very rapidly, the Anzin company was one of the most active in underselling and buying up weaker competitors. But it was also a leader in the search for new and richer veins of coal, by means of which it began in 1832 the development of what proved to be the most valuable of all its concessions, that of Denain, which, towards 1848, was becoming also a metallurgical center of great importance. The growth of the Anzin company is reflected in the value of its shares. Under the Restoration each share increased in value from 22,000 to 90,000 francs; in 1836 the share was worth 160,000 francs and in 1843 200,000.[19]

The power and success of the Anzin company are enhanced by comparison with the company of Aniche, whose mines were adjoining. Aniche was organized in 1773 and reorganized in 1786, 1837, and 1839. It refused an offer of purchase from its powerful neighbor in 1777, but in 1828 begged Anzin in vain to take it over on any terms short of almost unconditional surrender. During most of the period from 1815 to 1848, it suffered from bad management and inadequate capital. Attempts to find new and better veins of coal rarely succeeded, and the company was run almost continuously at a loss until 1839. Then a group of capitalists from Cambrai finally defeated a rival group from Valenciennes, after a struggle of more than three years, and promptly doubled the capital invested in two years, adding a third more in 1844. New and richer veins of coal were found and operated successfully from the commercial as well as the engineering point of view. All losses were paid off, and the value of a share of the Aniche company increased from 1,500 francs in 1830 to 16,000 in 1847.[20]

We have little information of interest concerning other coal-mining companies in France in the period 1815 to 1848. Most French writers on the subject have been more interested in the

---

[19] Léon Cahen, "L'Enrichissement de la France sous la Restauration," *Revue d'histoire moderne,* Nouvelle série, v. 5 (1930), 185.

[20] Henri Tribout, *Un grand savant, le général Jean-Victor Poncelet, 1788–1867* (Paris: Saffroy, 1936), 283.

eighteenth century, or in the period after 1847, when the development of the basin of Pas de Calais began. But we should mention the coal mines in the neighborhood of Boulogne, which had been prosperous in the eighteenth century, but which were noted in the earlier nineteenth for their amazingly high prices and costs of operation and for their almost negligible development. These were the mines of Hardinghen, Fiennes, and Ferques. The explanation of their troubles is simple, but rarely mentioned. They were nearly ruined by reckless and excessive exploitation during the Revolution of 1789, and reconstruction was so costly that it had not been completed in 1827. But in 1837 the tide seems to have turned when capitalists from Paris and England bought the mines, apparently combined them into a single enterprise by 1840, and probably also used them to supply the iron mills of Marquise, which we know passed into English hands at about that period.

Another company which deserves mention is that of Blanzy, which seems to have developed on a small scale and in complete obscurity in the basin of Saône et Loire until 1834, when reorganization with new capital, followed by another reorganization in 1838, set it firmly on the road to prosperity. We have seen also that under the Law of 1838 the Blanzy company was able to combine five different concessions and that the government exempted it from the statutory requirement of operating them all simultaneously. In spite of these improvements, the Blanzy company remained puny by comparison with the great companies of Anzin and the Loire, but it seems to have had in its management men interested in developing the selling of coal on sound commercial principles, and it may have been unique among the smaller companies in selling its coal not at the nearest river port but through agencies at Chalon on the Saône, with warehouses at Lyons and Mulhouse and, shortly after 1848, with another agency at Paris. Professor Amédée Burat, the eminent geologist of the middle of the nineteenth century, tells us also that the Blanzy company was able to double its circulating capital, presumably through the reorganizations of 1834 and 1838, and that it was the only coal-mining company besides Anzin that met all its financial obligations in the revolutionary year of 1848.

During the period from 1815 to 1848 the coal-mining industry of France passed through the pioneer stage. At the beginning the greatest basin of all, the Pas de Calais, had not been discovered, and almost none of the other basins had been fully explored. Strip mining was prevalent, but coal was sorted carelessly and frequently crumbled so much that it depreciated in value. Anzin was almost the only company strongly organized with an adequate supply of capital and reasonably good equipment. Transportation was so inadequate that most mines were wholly dependent on local markets and many industrial and commercial centers were unable to obtain coal at all. Most of the mines were occupied with cutthroat competition and lawsuits, and the demand for coal was so small that even the government seems hardly to have realized the importance of the industry.

In 1848 the exploration of the basin of Pas de Calais was beginning, and the full resources of most other basins were known. Nearly all mines had shafts and adequate equipment, and cutthroat competition had been ended because of governmental pressure and financial reorganization with considerable supplies of capital. The more-important mines had been connected with waterways by short railroads, and the waterways and even the highways had been improved until nearly all important centers were able to obtain coal at reasonable cost. Finally, the immense growth of the iron industry had created an almost indefinite demand for coal, and the beginning of the construction of a network of main railroad lines was providing the basis for unlimited expansion of coal-mining in the future.

STEAM AND WATER POWER

The development of the use of power to run machinery in France in the period from 1815 to 1848 was closely connected with the nature and amount of the machines utilized, with the progress of coal-mining, and with the construction of motors, wheels, or winches to transmit the power to the machines. It was conditioned also by the number and equipment of machine shops which made both the machines and the motors or wheels to run them. Finally, it was affected by the very slow decline in France of the domestic or putting-out system and by the existence of a very large number of streams able to supply hydraulic power, but usually only in quantities sufficient for small mills.

The location of cotton mills in Normandy north of the Seine illustrates some of the problems involved. At first most cotton was spun and woven in the homes of the peasants on the plateaux; that meant that the work was done by hand without the use of artificial power. Then, about 1815, spinning began to move into mills in the narrow but deep valleys cut through the plateaux by swift streams which supplied a considerable amount of hydraulic power; but weaving was still done chiefly by hand on the plateaux. Later, after 1837, power came very gradually to be applied to weaving; spinning moved from mills in the valleys into mills in the larger towns, and the power used was generally steam because the streams were usually too small to supply enough power for both spinning and weaving.

In Alsace, on the other hand, numerous and very swift streams, and a long tradition of successful commerce and manufacturing characteristic of a frontier people, caused a rapid transition to the use of both hydraulic and steam power. The skill of the Alsatians in manufacturing textiles and in construction of machines and the motors to run them enabled them to keep pace with the rapid and extensive progress of England, as scarcely any other part of France was able to do, and to specialize to a considerable extent in the production of both fine yarn and fine cloth. This required a use of power so extensive and an increase in its utilization so rapid that many mills were rebuilt two or three times from 1815 to 1848. Fine spinning and weaving meant that spindles and looms had to move much more rapidly than was necessary in manufacturing coarser materials; that explains why the need for power was great and why it increased rapidly. Yet the courage and ability of the Alsatians met the test and were not daunted by the relative scarcity of coal and its very great cost.

In the Nord conditions resembled neither northern Normandy nor Alsace. There were many streams, but there was little hydraulic power, because the country was flat. Coal was abundant, yet not very cheap—in the earlier part of our period, at least. There was, as in Alsace, an ancient tradition of trade and manufacturing, for the Nord comprises part of Flanders and adjoins the rest of that ancient and productive region. Yet mechanized industry did not, on the whole, develop as rapidly as in Alsace, possibly because of the extent and importance of intensive agriculture, and possibly also because of strong conservatism on the part of the people and the marked strength of the domestic system. There were some notable exceptions, such as Roubaix, which, finding itself unable to develop steam power as it wished, dug a canal and thus brought both the coal to heat the engines and the water to cool them. In general, however, the Nord developed steam, if more rapidly than Normandy, because of the inadequacy of hydraulic power, yet more slowly than Alsace, and this despite the relative abundance of coal.

Other parts of France developed the use of power much more slowly. Two examples will suffice as illustrations. In Calvados, south of the estuary of the Seine, progress was far slower than in northern Normandy; mills remained small and the use of hand or horse power persisted. The best mills adopted hydraulic power, but there was scarcely any use of steam. In the Somme there were larger mills and more important towns, with active trade with the more progressive region of the Nord on one side and with northern Normandy on the other. Yet progress was slow. The domestic system was unusually tenacious, and while the mills grew in number and size they adopted hydraulic power slowly and steam very slowly indeed. Even in the great city of Amiens we find conservatism and provincialism so strongly entrenched that merchants and manufacturers did not wish to exhibit at the national expositions in Paris. They resented the holding of those important and valuable meetings, and almost the existence of Paris itself. The examples of rural Calvados and semi-urban Picardy are important to bear in mind, for they are typical of many parts of France in the period of 1815 to 1848. It is easy for the economic historian to fix his attention on Alsace and Normandy, from both of which information is relatively abundant, and on the Nord, also because of its obvious importance, although there is much less information available about it, and to overlook the rest of the country with its numerous small industrial districts but its deep-rooted provincial conservatism. At the beginning of the Restoration, most industrial establishments were small and neither used nor needed much power. In the more progressive districts cotton was being spun in mills, but only the best ones used water power. Steam had been introduced into mills in both Alsace and Normandy, and within a year or two made its appearance in the Nord, but it was everywhere the exception and was often simply a curiosity in places where even the use of water wheels was relatively uncommon. Probably the majority of such mills as existed had machines operated by hand, if for spinning, and, if for preparatory processes such as carding or roving, by horses pulling winches.

During the Restoration there were several important inventions that could be used to increase greatly the utilization of potential water power, which in many cases was only 15 to 20 per cent. The first was a water wheel devised by the British engineer Fairbairn, which was in use on the continent as early as 1825 and was described as excellent and powerful. It was adopted by the leading textile mills and machine shops of Alsace, which had close relations with the mills of Manchester and its outstanding producer of machines and motors, the firm of Sharp and Roberts. In 1825, Poncelet[21] in France won the Montyon Prize awarded by the Academy of Sciences for the invention of a water wheel with curved blades that increased very greatly the amount of power obtainable from flowing water. In the previous year the mining engineer Burdin[22] had invented his first turbine, although it appears to have been both improved and promoted by Benoît Fourneyron,[23] whose name is the one most commonly mentioned in connection with it. In short, the inventive achievements in the period of the Restoration in the hydraulic field

[21] *Ibid.*, 208.

[22] Michel Chevalier, *Lettres sur l'exposition de 1851* (Paris, 1851), 583.

[23] Emile Eude, *Histoire documentaire de la mécanique française: [Fragments] d'après le musée central de la mécanique à l'exposition universelle de 1900* (Paris: Dunod, 1902), 31, 35.

were highly creditable, but, unfortunately, we know little regarding their application. We have no information regarding the relative merits of the water wheels of Fairbairn and Poncelet and of the competition between them in France. We can say only that neither they nor the turbine were used extensively in France as a whole under the Restoration, but that they were so used when industry recovered from the depression of 1827 in 1832.

It is difficult to say when the first steam engine was used in France as a source of power for running machinery. It is known that one was brought from England for use in pumping late in the eighteenth century, and another was set up near Saint-Quentin in 1803, although we do not know for what it was used. A third was set up near Mulhouse in Alsace by Dollfus-Mieg in 1812 and was used to run a cotton-spinning mill. We have reports of at least one steam engine in use in a cotton mill at Lille in 1817, of another in a woolen mill at Louviers in the same year, and of two in woolen mills at Elbeuf in either 1819 or 1821. We are told that steam was introduced into the cotton-spinning mills of Rouen between 1817 and 1820, and into a mill making silk braid at Saint-Chamond, in the Department of Loire, in 1816. Other cases could undoubtedly be found, and Jules Burat, in his excellent book on the Exposition of 1844, says that in 1818 France had between 150 and 200 steam engines, of which only 50 had been made in the country.[24] In that year a duty of 30 per cent[25] was imposed upon their importation; that probably means that at that time the legislators first distinguished between steam engines and machines in general, which paid 15 per cent. Thereafter France made most of her own steam engines and imported from England only a few that were unusually powerful.

The engines used in France in the first years of the Restoration

[24] Paris, *L'Exposition des produits de l'industrie française de 1844,* rédigé par Jules Burat, v. 1 (Paris, 1845), 23. William Otto Henderson, *Britain and Industrial Europe, 1750–1870: Studies in British Influence on the Industrial Revolution in Western Europe* (Liverpool: University Press, 1954), 58.
[25] "Du mouvement commercial des combustibles," *loc. cit.,* 180.

were chiefly English and of the type manufactured by Boulton and Watt, that is, low-pressure. We are told that the one set up by Dollfus-Mieg in Alsace in 1812 produced only ten horsepower, was made chiefly of wood, and stopped running frequently. It seems probable that many others were as unsatisfactory, for Dollfus-Mieg was one of the best textile firms in France. Doubling the duty on these engines in 1818 appears to have started the manufacture of steam engines in France on a considerable scale, for in that year we hear of the founding of the machine shops of Risler brothers and Dixon at Cernay, in Alsace, which made them and water wheels until it was ruined in the depression beginning in 1827. It was succeeded by one of the greatest of all machine makers in France, André Koechlin of Mulhouse. In 1818 also, Cazalis and Cordier, who had been trained at the Ecole des Arts et Métiers at Châlon-sur-Marne, set up a machine shop at Saint-Quentin with capital supplied by the Duc de La Rochefoucauld-Liancourt.[26] Other shops were those of Manby and Wilson at Charenton on the Seine, of Cavé, Périer, Calla, Edwards, and Decoster at Paris, and of Hallette at Arras. All seem to have been small, with simple equipment, few machine tools, and a volume of business too slight to permit them to specialize in the manufacture of a single type of machinery.

Early steam engines in France consumed an enormous amount of fuel, and most of them were evidently small and weak, with an average of not more than ten horsepower. Since the high price of coal was the chief obstacle to the development of steam engines, the low-pressure engine of Watt was soon dropped by French machine shops. By 1820, they made almost exclusively Woolf engines of medium pressure which had two cylinders and a pressure of approximately three atmospheres each, used about half as much coal as the Watt engine in theory, and were just as safe to operate but required more supervision and cost more to repair. A few engines of high pressure without condensation were used where water was difficult to obtain for condensing, but they used too much fuel and required too much supervision to be adopted by most

---

[26] *Bulletin de la société d'encouragement pour l'industrie nationale,* v. 21 (July, 1821), 202.

manufacturers. It seems doubtful, however, if in practice the French saved as much fuel as they had hoped by adopting almost exclusively the Woolf engine. With the high price of iron, and the small number of machine shops, the engines were so expensive that manufacturers were nearly always required to run far more machines than were economical; and the situation tended to grow worse with the passage of time, for as machines for spinning cotton were improved their speed increased and more power was needed to run them. This must have been a serious problem in Alsace, where, as we have seen, many cotton-spinning mills were rebuilt three times between 1815 and 1848. In coal-mining also there was a steady increase in the power of the steam engines for running both pumps and extracting machines as the shafts grew deeper, and in many foundries and forges also the demand for power increased very greatly.

The rather fragmentary statistics published by the Administration des Mines with comments from a few other sources indicate that there was little real growth in the number of steam engines in France before 1820. The growth was slow but steady from 1820 to 1827, slackened during the ensuing depression and increased with great rapidity again during the period of prosperity between 1832 and 1837. It increased more slowly during the next depression, and then with greater speed than ever during the boom that ended in 1847. These figures agree fairly well with the estimate of Jules Burat that the number of steam engines in France was between 150 and 200 in 1818, approximately 572 in 1830, and 2,807 in 1841.[27] Yet in the Census of 1847 the figure given is 2,494, which Henri Sée says should really be 5,000, with a total horsepower of 60,000.[28] In view of these discrepancies, we cannot state the actual number of steam engines with confidence, but, knowing the inaccuracy of most official statistics in France during the first half of the nineteenth century, the safest guide would appear to be the estimate of the late Professor Sée. The discrepancies do not, however, invalidate

---

[27] Henri Sée, *La Vie économique de la France sous la monarchie censitaire (1815–1848)* (Paris: Alcan, 1927), 74.

[28] *Ibid.*

our very rough estimate of the growth in the use of steam engines between 1815 and 1848.

The *Journal de l'industriel*, published between 1836 and 1840 and edited chiefly by Jules Burat and Professor Amédée Burat, throws a little more light on the use of steam engines in France. It appears there that between 1834 and 1838[29] the number of engines in the five departments that used them most increased as follows: in the Nord, from 200 to 422; in the Seine, from 173 to 300; in the Seine Inférieure, from 108 to 221; and in the Haut-Rhin, from 48 to 80. The Seine includes the city of Paris with some of its nearest suburbs; the Loire includes Saint-Etienne, with its coal mines, metallurgical establishments, and ribbon industry, together with the small cotton-manufacturing center of Roanne but not the coal basin of Rive de Gier, with its industrial establishments; the Seine Inférieure corresponds fairly closely to northern Normandy; and the Haut-Rhin includes the greater part of the industrial region of Alsace.

The same source gives us the number of steam engines for approximately the same period distributed according to industries. Those using the most were the spinning mills, which had 319 in 1834 and 575 in 1838;[30] the mines increased from 246 to 360; the foundries, forges, and rolling mills increased from 67 to 132; the machine shops used 31 in 1834 and 105 in 1838; and the sugar mills and refineries increased from 33 to 210. The mines produced chiefly coal, but some iron ore, although most of the iron was obtained by strip mining and would not have required the use of much power. In this period nearly all cotton was spun mechanically in mills, as was a great part of the carded wool and some of the combed, while the mechanical spinning of flax was just beginning and some power was used in the spinning of silk. We have good reason to believe that the spinning mills increased their use of steam engines very

---

[29] Jules Burat, "Des machines à vapeur en France," *Journal de l'industriel et du capitaliste,* v. 1 (June, 1836), 341. "Statistique des machines à vapeur en France," *Journal de l'industriel,* v. 4 (June, 1838), 359; v. 6 (June, 1839), 388–89; v. 8 (June, 1840), 377; based on *Compte rendu des ingénieurs des mines* for 1836, 1837, 1838, and 1839.

[30] "Du mouvement commercial des combustibles," *loc. cit.*

greatly indeed between 1838 and 1848, largely because of a rapid increase of mechanization in the spinning of carded wool and flax and a considerable increase in the mechanical weaving of cotton; so did the machine shops for the same reasons, but probably not the foundries, forges, and rolling mills.

It is interesting to observe that probably half the steam engines in France were in the five departments of Nord, Seine, Loire, Seine Inférieure, and Haut-Rhin, with the Nord having far more than any other. This is easily explained by the unusual variety of industries in the Nord, which included cotton, wool, and linen among the textiles, very important coal mines, the beginning of metallurgical development that was to be very important later, and a considerable part of the beet-sugar industry. We have seen also that the supply of water power was rather less satisfactory in the Nord than in the other important industrial regions of France.

In conclusion, it seems possible to estimate briefly and very approximately the different sources of power used in 1848. There can be no question that hand spinning had declined greatly since 1815 and had almost disappeared in the cotton industry; and at the end of our period there is scarcely any mention of the use of winches pulled by horses or oxen, which were quite common in 1815. Nearly all mills, unless so small as to be almost insignificant, used either hydraulic or steam power in 1848. Moreau de Jonnès says that in 1856, only eight years later, of 734 cotton-spinning mills in France, 478 used water power and 244[31] steam, to which we can add that some of them used both. While few other industries had gone so far, there can be no doubt that they had progressed considerably in developing the use of power by which machinery could be driven at a reasonably effective speed. The book of that very able engineer Eugène Flachat shows us that in 1845 most blast furnaces and forges were run by water power, supplemented in many cases, and supplanted in a few, where coal was readily available, by steam power. It is clear, however, that in the few really large metallurgical establishments the use of steam was of great importance and that it was

---

[31] Alexandre Moreau de Jonnès, *Statistique de l'industrie en France* (Paris, 1856), 88.

sure to spread widely as integration increased. It had already ceased to be necessary to place forges or blast furnaces on streams. This meant that they were often far from the ore, because water power had ceased to be the primary consideration. In most industries, however, and in most places using power to run machinery, water power was used rather than steam, except in the Nord. This contrasts sharply with contemporary England, where the use of steam was general. It is explained by the high cost of coal available to most French industrial establishments as compared to its low cost and greater abundance in Great Britain, and by the very slight progress towards integration of French industry as compared to very considerable progress across the Channel. But the prevalence of water power in France was not detrimental to industrial progress provided the supply of water was adequate and the wheel or turbine used was efficient. We know that utilization of hydraulic power had increased very greatly through mechanical inventions and improvements during the period of prosperity between 1832 and 1837. It seems safe to assume that really good hydraulic equipment was used much more widely during the next industrial boom, between 1842 and 1847.

CHAPTER SIX

The Iron Industry

THE SITUATION IN 1815

THE FRENCH iron industry in 1815 had met the needs of the French army during twenty years of war, but had learned little regarding metallurgy and nothing regarding steam or coal, because it had been cut off completely from England. Iron was produced in small establishments of ten workers or less, for the most part, by a proprietor who was primarily a landowner, frequently financially interested in a forest, and in most cases a good merchant on a very small scale. Such a typical ironmaster knew little or nothing about science and relied chiefly on the practical experience of one or two skilled forgers or founders. He was as ignorant of planning, routing, and economics as of metallurgy and carried on his business in the manner of his fathers, with little knowledge of what went on outside his own district. Even there, he was an individualist, proud of anything that distinguished his methods, or rather those of his founder or forger, from the methods of his neighbors. His mill usually was old, badly planned, and ill adapted to possible improvements and expansion. Most of his workers were unskilled, obstinate in nature, and lacking in education. He did not need steam because his small stream supplied what little power he required and the surrounding forest provided fuel. Such a man and such a mill, multiplied by thousands, produced a very large part of the iron used in France.

The ironmaster's ignorance, provincialism, love of routine, and individualism are characteristic of the industry in France in 1815 and are of vital importance to our understanding of its condition and lack of progress. To describe inadequate means of transportation, remoteness of coal, and scarcity of capital is not an adequate explanation of the prevalent backwardness. Small-scale production in France was not due simply to those important economic, geographical, and geological factors; it was due also to profound love of individualism combined with devotion to thrift and to tradition, and it has remained typical of French industry and agriculture right down into our age of mass production at ever increasing speed.

Because of her isolation during the Revolution and the Empire, France had learned little of the two great inventions that had revolutionized the iron industry in England: the steam engine invented by Watt in 1769, but not produced on a large scale until about 1800, and the puddling process devised by Cort in 1784 and soon to be greatly improved by Rogers in 1818. If confronted with a steam engine, the French manufacturer rejected it because he had enough water power for his existing needs, or because he felt the necessary coal would be too expensive. If told about the puddling process, the ironmaster would reply, first, that he could not get the coal needed, and then that he was proud of the quality rather than the quantity of his iron and that puddling as known in 1815 often produced defective wrought iron. But behind this obstructive attitude would always be his love of his own little business and a realization that those inventions would not be profitable unless used in production on a very considerable scale. There was much good sense in the French ironmaster's point of view, in his respect for good quality, in his love of tradition, and in his appreciation of the value of leisure. His error, too, was one with which we can all sympathize in the present age. He believed that through his adherence to these standards and with the help of a prohibitive tariff he could continue his business unchanged. In short, he really thought that he and his country could and should maintain their isolation.

MINING

France was fortunate in having an abundant supply of ore of rather good quality lying near the surface. It was usually cheap and easy to mine, but it was generally found in many small and scattered deposits in wooded and mountainous districts. This wealth of an essential raw material was, therefore, far less helpful to industrial progress than would seem probable. We hear of scarcely any very large deposits of ore in the period 1815 to 1848, and of virtually no well-organized mining companies of considerable size. The average yield of French ore was approximately 35 per cent, with some unusually good deposits giving 50 or even 55 per cent. The great and rich bed of the Ardèche, close to the Rhône, was a striking and almost singular exception. Either the other deposits frequently described as rich proved not to be so or their richness was greatly exaggerated, or else they were almost inaccessible to anything but railroads, which were not generally useful in France before the period of the Second Empire. Great hopes were built upon the deposits of carbonated ore discovered in the coal field of Saint-Etienne by de Gallois and others soon after 1815, but further exploration showed that the deposits were actually scanty and not unusually rich. In the basins of Aubin and Aveyron on the southern edge of the Massif Central, supplies of carbonated ore were good, but far from any important industrial centers. The richest deposits of ore were in the Haute-Marne and the Pyrenees, and were thus expensive to ship to markets, while in almost every case the individual deposit was small. This fact proved more important than the rich quality of the ore and, by encouraging the prevalent tendency to operation on a small scale, checked industrial progress.

Another very serious difficulty that hindered greatly the efficient use of the abundant supplies of rather good ore in France was the existence of a considerable percentage of phosphorus, making virtually useless for wrought iron or steel the abundant supplies of minette ore in Lorraine. Most of the ore of the many small basins of southern Normandy and of northern and western Brittany were also either rendered useless for the same reason or had to be mixed with considerable quantities of ore brought from northern Spain by sea. On the other hand, steel was not widely used in the period 1815 to 1848, even in England, and cast iron which could be made from moderately phosphoric ore was relatively far more important then than at later periods. But this was most unfortunate, since, like the smallness of the ore deposits, it tended to discourage improvement in French metallurgy. When we realize in addition that much French coal contained sulphur, which many ironmasters did not then know how to remove, the added difficulty of excessive phosphorus in much of the iron ore makes us wonder that the puddling process developed at all in the period before 1848. It did grow, however, first in districts where ore free from phosphorus could be obtained, such as the districts of Berry and Nivernais in central France, and next in districts where coal could be obtained at reasonable cost, such as Saint-Etienne and the Nord.

Most ore in France in the period 1815 to 1848 was strip-mined in shallow pits or trenches, for which little equipment and capital were required. In nearly every case the mining enterprise seems to have been either an individual, a family concern, or a very small company. Most of the workers, like the majority of men in the foundries and forges, were peasants who spent much of their time in the fields. When they had dug the ore, if their time was not required for tillage, they hauled it in carts over crude roads or tracks to the nearest stream, where it was washed, again with the simplest equipment and by cheap and routine methods.

Several French writers have emphasized the legal difficulties connected with transporting and washing ore. They tell us that it was so difficult to obtain authorization to buy land for a light railway that mine-owners were obliged to use horses and carts whenever the farmers could spare them. When they did get the ore to the streams they had to await periods when there was a considerable flow of water. But if, in such a period, a flood occurred and ore or slag were washed onto farming land on either bank, they were liable for full damage to all the farmers injured. These complaints were undoubtedly justified. There was much red tape to be cut and the legal codes involved were too rigid, but economic factors were even more important. The small size and slight capitalization of most mining enterprises in the iron industry made it neither possible nor necessary to build railroads or buy considerable areas along the banks of streams. The result was that, whereas iron ore at the mine cost between one third and one half the average price in England, by the time it reached the French foundry it cost as much or more.

Hence, nearly all the advantages of greater abundance and cheaper extraction were lost. There seems reason also to believe that there was little improvement in methods of mining or washing in France before 1848. Ore was sufficiently common and cheap to make economy unnecessary, and there was no serious pressure from competition, whether regional or international.

Smelting and Casting

The smelting of the ore improved but slowly in the period from 1815 to 1848. In consequence, the development of the iron industry, and through it of the whole Industrial Revolution, was retarded. The problem of fuel is the one most frequently emphasized in explaining the slow improvement of smelting. After that, liberal French writers, and most foreigners, mention the prohibitive tariff and the scarcity of capital. In addition, we have seen that small-scale production appealed strongly to the French people, with their tenacious devotion to the family in business as well as social life. All these problems, therefore, affected the development of smelting and many of them are bound together almost inextricably. Thus, the problem of fuel involved the increasingly inadequate supply of wood and its rising price, the relative inaccessibility of most coal, and also the change from one form of fuel to the other. The adoption of coal in smelting forced a great increase in the height of the furnace and the power of the blast, and to be economical, the whole plant had to be operated on a much larger scale. In many cases it must have been impossible in France before the Second Empire to accumulate enough ore, coal, *castine* (flux), capital, and labor to promote such an undertaking. It would have been difficult to solve simply the problem of transportation, both of the raw materials involved and of the marketing of the pig or cast iron. We know that it would also have been exceedingly difficult to accumulate sufficient capital.

We find that after the crisis of 1818 to 1819, when the puddling process was being introduced in France, the height of the blast furnace was increasing very slowly. In 1820 the average height was probably less than twenty feet, while in 1848 it was at least thirty feet, with numerous furnaces forty-five or even sixty feet high.[1] At the same time the shape of the furnace was being changed slowly from square, hexagonal, or octagonal to round so that the heat would strike the whole of the interior equally. There were also important changes in the blast and the method of its production, but these, like alterations in height and shape, were gradual.

The hot blast, which had been applied successfully in Scotland before the great French Revolution, appears to have been introduced into France at about the same time at various places about 1830. We hear of it first at La Voulte in the Ardèche. Almost simultaneously it appeared in the region of Saint-Etienne and also in that of the Gard and, shortly afterwards, in the Department of Nièvre, which contained the important and wealthy establishments of Fourchambault and Imphy. We are told that in each district it was introduced by a different person. In the Isère it was ascribed to Gueymard, one of the ablest of the government's mining inspectors; in the Nivernais, to Boignes, a member of the distinguished family of ironmasters which owned Fourchambault and had played so prominent a part in building the first railroad in France. With its partners it had introduced the puddling system. Other writers insist that the hot blast was introduced simultaneously into several parts of France by Charles Taylor of Beaugrenelle, a suburb of Paris, in or about 1834.[2]

We can explain these rather confusing and conflicting accounts. Even in 1848 the hot blast was not regarded as an unqualified success. It was not accepted by French metallurgists as a great in-

---

[1] Jean Antoine, comte Chaptal, *De l'industrie française,* v. 1 (Paris, 1819), 84. Muel Doublat, "De la fabrication de la fonte en Champagne," *Journal de l'industriel et du capitaliste,* v. 2 (July, 1836), 33. Gaultier de Claubry, "Rapport sur les établissemen[t]s de la Compagnie des fonderies et forges de la Loire et de l'Isère," *Bulletin de la société d'encouragement pour l'industrie nationale,* v. 26 (May, 1827), 30.

[2] "Etat actuel de l'industrie du fer en France," *Journal de l'industriel et du capitaliste,* v. 3 (August, 1937), 472–75. "Industrie du fer: Des progrès réalisés dans les usines à fer pendant les dernières années," *Journal de l'industriel et du capitaliste,* v. 5 (August, 1838), 122–24. Paris, *Exposition des produits de l'industrie française de 1844: Rapport du jury central,* rédigé par Jules Burat, v. 1 (Paris, 1845), 37. Achille de Colmont, *Histoire*

vention, and its origin was foreign. It appears to have been tried successfully first in the Isère, but with anthracite as fuel. After some delay, the hot blast was used with soft coal and then with wood, but seldom with charcoal. Even in 1848 it was used in less than a quarter of the blast furnaces of France. It was felt that it made pig iron too soft and that it was really beneficial only when the ultimate produce was to be cast iron. It was admitted that it helped cause much more complete fusion of the ore, more regular operation of the furnace, and great economy in fuel. But these benefits, although great, were not considered to outweigh the alleged injury to the tenacity of the pigs. The historian cannot escape the suspicion that the use of the hot blast did not become popular under the July Monarchy because its greatest benefits came only through the use of coke in smelting on a very considerable scale. For this neither the coal nor the capital was yet available in sufficient quantity.

The means of producing the blast in French furnaces were certainly improved greatly during the earlier nineteenth century. We have little information about them, probably because they were made so slowly that they did not attract the attention of contemporaries. It is clear, however, that wooden pistons had begun to replace leather bellows under the First Empire. They came probably from Germany, either directly into Champagne and Burgundy, or indirectly through Luxemburg into Périgord in the southwest. A considerable immigration of forgers into Périgord occurred early in the French Revolution, and the descendants of these immigrants remained leaders in the iron industry of their new home for several generations at least.[3] It can be said also that the increasing use and improvement of water wheels and of steam helped greatly to produce a stronger blast in most French furnaces.

Smelters using charcoal learned to economize their fuel greatly,

---

des expositions des produits de l'industrie française (Paris, 1855), 235. Emile Gueymard, "Rapport à M. le directeur général des ponts et chaussées et des mines, sur la conduite des fourneaux à l'air chaud," *Bulletin de la société d'encouragement pour l'industrie nationale,* v. 32 (November, 1833), 386–92. William Otto Henderson, *Britain and Industrial Europe, 1750– 1870: Studies in British Influence on the Industrial Revolution in Western Europe* (Liverpool: University Press, 1954), 62.

[3] "Etat actuel de l'industrie du fer en France," *loc. cit.,* 468.

reducing by half or even three quarters the amount of charcoal needed per ton of ore, but since the quantity of iron smelted increased, the cost of the fuel used remained about the same to the manufacturers. The quality of pig iron produced, however, did not improve much. We find that the best machine makers of Paris and Alsace and the leading founders of Normandy had a poor opinion of the pigs sent them for casting from various parts of France. They complained that, while they were often soft enough, they lacked tenacity. Also, they varied so in quality that founders were often afraid to use them. The explanation seems to be that irregular operation of many blast furnaces caused unpredictable variations in the degree of fusion of the ore. There also appears to have been carelessness in sorting the pigs before shipping them to market. At first, pig iron smelted with coal could hardly be sold in France at all. It was said to be too soft and too full of sulphur, probably because of poor methods of making coke, but the situation improved in time.

Methods of casting in France seem also to have been unsatisfactory, chiefly from lack of adequately trained workmen and partly also from frequent loss or destruction of forms, because workers did not like to use the same form twice. English founders had to show foundries using coal how to run in Normandy, and probably in Alsace and other districts as well. We know also that a considerable number of English workmen were used by many leading French ironmasters for a number of years. Eventually French founders learned to cast well and economically. At the Exposition of 1844 it was shown that they could make accurately the largest cylinders for rolling iron, most of the machines needed for preparing and spinning textiles, and steam engines. There can be little doubt that improvement in the art of founding in France was delayed greatly by the prohibitive tariff, but we must always remember other difficulties. Most owners of capital were reluctant to invest in industrial enterprises, and transportation developed slowly. Much of the rapid growth of the French iron industry after 1840 was due to the construction of railroads, and there was no serious reduction of the tariff on iron until 1860.

PUDDLING, "THE ENGLISH METHOD"

Progress in refining iron in France, like that in smelting and casting, depended to a considerable degree on the change from wood or charcoal to coal as fuel and also upon the development of an adequate supply of power. The English method, by which was meant the puddling process invented by Cort in 1784, involved both stirring, or puddling, the molten iron and rolling rather than hammering it to remove defects and secure the shape desired. It must have been known to French scientists and government officials within a few years, but little was done about it, probably because the nation was absorbed in the great Revolution and because the methods then generally used in France produced enough refined iron to meet the needs of both industry and the army.

It is possible that puddling was practiced at Le Creusot before the end of the eighteenth century.[4] If that did happen the experiment was not a success, for refining iron at that great establishment was described as unsatisfactory as late as 1827. It is inconceivable that the Creusot company, if it had really established the new method, would have remained in a state of practical bankruptcy for approximately twenty years before the formal declaration of failure in 1833. If we assume that the attempt really was made, failure was probably due to the impossibility of getting enough English workmen during the war and to the further impossibility of persuading French manufacturers to buy iron refined by the English method.

We may never know when the puddling process was first successfully introduced into France. The first case for which there is indisputable evidence is the attempt made by Dufaud in 1817 at Grossouvre in the province of Berry, which was famous for its good ore.[5] This plant which was moved shortly afterwards across the

---

[4] Louis Joseph Gras, *Histoire économique de la métallurgie de la Loire* (Saint-Etienne: Thomas, 1908), p. xxvii.

[5] *Bulletin de la société d'encouragement pour l'industrie nationale,* v. 18 (Feb., 1819), 5. Paris, *Exposition des produits de l'industrie française de 1819: Rapport du jury central,* rédigé par Louis, baron Costaz (Paris, 1819), 156. Henderson, *op. cit.,* 52–57.

Loire to Fourchambault in the Nivernais, was financed and directed by the Boignes brothers and their partners, who owned both Grossouvre and Fourchambault and shared in the control of the great establishment of Imphy in the same part of France. They appear to have had an ample supply of capital and to have been among the ablest metallurgists in France. Shortly afterwards we find the English method adopted by other leading metallurgists in France, such as the de Wendels in Lorraine in 1819, by de Gallois and Joseph Bessy in the district of Saint-Etienne in 1819 or 1820, and by Manby and Wilson, who owned great establishments at both Charenton and Le Creusot. Blumenstein and Frèrejean introduced it at Vienne. They were closely connected with the development of both the iron industry and the early railroads in the districts of Saint-Etienne and Rive de Gier, as well as with the great iron mine and smelting plant at La Voulte in the Ardèche. Finally, Renault introduced the English method at Raismes near the great coal mines of Anzin in the Department of Nord.[6]

It is clear, then, that the puddling process was brought successfully from England to France and introduced almost simultaneously at several widely separated establishments run by metallurgists of outstanding ability and possessed of substantial resources. We are given few details even by contemporary observers, but we can say with substantial accuracy that several of these pioneers went to England and studied the puddling process there before starting it in France. We know that this was done by Dufaud of Grossouvre, by de Gallois, and by Joseph Bessy, while Manby and Wilson were themselves English. The de Wendels copied the work of Dufaud,

---

[6] *Bulletin de la société d'encouragement pour l'industrie nationale,* v. 18 (Feb., 1819), 51. Gras, *op. cit.,* 402–3. Philippe Hedde, *Indicateur du commerce, des arts et des manufactures de Saint-Etienne,* v. 1 (Saint-Etienne, 1831), 40. François Emmanuel Molard, Jr., "Rapport sur les fonderies et établissemen[t]s de l'industrie de MM. Manby et Wilson à Charenton," *Bulletin de la société d'encouragement pour l'industrie nationale,* v. 24 (April, 1825), 124–26. Paris, *Exposition universelle de 1851 à Londres,* travaux de la Commission Française sur l'Industrie des Nations, v. 3: *Les Machines et outils spécialement employés à la fabrication des matières textiles,* par général Jean-Victor Poncelet, Partie 1, Section 2 (Paris, 1855), 22. Henderson, *op. cit.,* 59.

and we know that Blumenstein and Frèrejean had close connections with de Gallois and may have had also with Bessy. It is interesting to observe further that the introduction of the English method in France came almost immediately after the restoration of peace in 1815. It was closely connected also with the improvement of the process by Rogers in 1818, and with the ability of skilled English workmen to emigrate on a considerable scale. We are told that Joseph Bessy brought no less than forty-two English families to the district of Saint-Etienne,[7] and it is known that English foremen and many English workmen were used for many years by all the leading forgers of France. Hundreds of these families must, therefore, have been brought across the Channel in a few years, for the English method had been adopted by twenty French iron mills as early as 1823 and by forty in 1827, when the great speculative boom ended in both England and France.

Rapid progress in the adoption of puddling and rolling in France did not continue unchecked, however. While the radical change in the mechanical equipment of mills which the new method required began in 1825[8] and spread widely through the efforts of English ironmasters, engineers, or constructors, the cost was great. One French authority estimated that in 1827, when a severe depression was underway, the cost of building a reverbatory furnace in France large enough to use the pig iron of three typical blast furnaces was 502,000 francs—120,000 francs for the rolling mill, 100,000 for the steam engine, 72,000 for the eighteen reverbatory ovens, and 60,000 for the preparation of the ground.[9] This was a large sum of money for that period and would have been difficult to raise for all but the more important ironmasters. Other difficulties were the inadequacy of the supplies of coal until after 1835, the prevalence of water power, with its inefficiency and variability as then used in France, and, finally, the prohibitive tariff, which made easy the widespread use of routine and operations on a small scale. It is not surprising

---

[7] Gras, *op. cit.*, 49.

[8] Paris, *Exposition . . . de 1851* (Poncelet), 23.

[9] Pierre Dufrénoy and Elie de Beaumont, *Voyage métallurgique en Angleterre,* v. 1 (Paris, 1827), 533.

to learn, in view of these obstacles to progress, that in 1848 probably not more than a quarter of the French forges were both puddling and rolling.

Opposition to the English method in France took various forms. One was the widespread belief that puddling and rolling produced iron that was too soft and of very uncertain quality. This was considered to be due partly to the use of coal—which in France frequently contained sulphur, although it was quite possible to refine iron without having it touch the coal at all—and also due to rolling, which was felt to be less effective than hammering in removing defects. Here again was great inaccuracy; the hammering, done very slowly by hand, can have no effect in hardening the iron, any more than rolling can. Furthermore, it is obvious that by rolling the iron can be shaped much more effectively and at about one third the cost in labor. This was a very serious factor in France, despite low wages and long hours, because of the prevalent lack of skill. This sort of wishful thinking, therefore, was common in small mills and isolated districts, such as the part of Picardy known as Vimeu, where thousands of locks were made by individual workmen, and in the villages of the Ardennes, where nails were produced in great quantities and without adequate supervision.

More serious opposition was encountered in the Champagne method, widely used until after 1835, and in the Catalan forges of the Pyrenees and similar establishments in Corsica, which were still of great importance in 1848. The Champagne method was a compromise which allowed puddling in small ovens, but shaped the iron through hammering by hand. It was successful for a long time because it relieved the ironmaster of some of the rising cost of wood, or charcoal, and because it enabled him to continue to operate a small establishment on a small stream. He thus avoided the expense of a large steam engine or a great reverberatory furnace. But the Champagne method was abandoned between 1835 and 1848 because of the economy of labor in the English method, the rapidly increasing supply of coal, and increasing competition from powerful mills in many different parts of France which were near coal fields.

The Catalan forge was a much more effective form of opposition to the introduction of the English method. It is true that its importance depended upon some of the negative factors upon which the strength of the Champagne method rested, such as inadequate supplies of coal, water power, capital, and means of transportation. But it was exceedingly cheap because of the mountain forests and unusually fine ore which frequently yielded 55 per cent and was the best in France for both wrought iron and steel. The Catalan forge had, further, economies resulting from the direct method that had been prevalent in Europe for centuries. The typical forge required the services of only seven men, who were paid very low wages, and it could be closed temporarily with little loss in the summer when the supply of water was low. But the difficulties of the Catalan forgers increased with the passage of time. The forests could not supply enough charcoal even for them, so that they had to cut wood further and further up the slopes of the steep mountains and bring it down on the backs of mules at ever greater cost from ever-mounting distances. Then the workers, who were isolated and ignorant, were more devoted to routine than in almost any other part of France and the markets for the iron were few and inaccessible, except by carting over roads of indifferent quality. Yet, despite these difficulties, some improvements in methods of production and marketing were made, and although the Catalan forges were unable to lower their prices much or to increase their production appreciably, they were able to maintain themselves without any absolute decline.

STEEL

The manufacture of steel appears to have been almost in its infancy in France when the Peace of Vienna was signed in 1815. France could, of course, make natural steel in her Catalan forges, and she had good ore for this in the Pyrenees and in the foothills of the Alps in Dauphiné. Additional amounts of suitable ore, or pig iron, could be obtained from the Rhine Valley or Savoy. This natural steel, made partly by the old direct method and partly by rather crude applications of the indirect, was evidently good enough in quality for most of the agricultural tools used in the eighteenth century and even for carriage springs. The difficulty was that its quantity could not be increased much when the demand came in the nineteenth century, because the use of charcoal as fuel was considered essential and the supply of wood in the lower Alps and Pyrenees was limited. Hence, a fairly good supply of ore in those districts did not lead to the creation of an important industry. The cementing of steel, which had long been known in the German states, was not used in France before the Restoration, and crucible steel, invented by Huntsman in England in 1750, seems scarcely to have been heard of across the Channel. All truly refined or tempered steel was, therefore, imported—in the case of agricultural tools, usually from Austria or Prussia; in the case of crucible steel for the finest cutlery, such as surgical instruments, from England.

Progress in France came with the advent of peace. In 1814 the German Jagerschmidt[10] came to Toulouse and, forming a partnership with Garrigou and Massenet, developed the German method of cementation on a considerable scale. He used chiefly the very good ore of the Pyrenees, with the addition of a little from Sweden or Russia imported through Bordeaux. The partners chose an excellent site for their principal mill, at the falls of the Tarn, near the ancient town of Albi and the coal basin of Carmaux.[11] In a few years scythes and sickles were made of cemented steel; imports from Styria of such agricultural tools declined, and the forges of the Pyrenees ceased to sell an appreciable quantity of natural steel.

A few years later, and evidently quite independently, the manufacture of cemented steel was introduced into the Department of Loire with its coal basins of Saint-Etienne and Rive de Gier by two men. Milleret, a capitalist, had been Receiver-General of Taxes in the Department of Moselle under the Empire, and Beaunier was a

---

[10] Jules François, *Recherches sur le gisement et le traitement direct des minerais de fer dans les Pyrénées*, v. 1 (Paris, 1843), 328.

[11] Jules François, *Extrait d'un rapport à M. le ministre de l'agriculture et du commerce sur la question de l'importation des fers au bois du nord de l'Europe* (Moulins, 1845), 5.

former mining inspector in the Saar and Ruhr. Both were thoroughly familiar with the best German methods. They seem to have done well at their mill of La Bérardière,[12] which is always spoken of with respect, although production seems never to have been very large. The German method was also brought to the district of Saint-Etienne by the Holtzer family, who likewise were successful and respected.[13]

The greatest progress in manufacturing steel in France did not come, however, from developing cementation according to the German method, but rather from the English use of both cemented and crucible steel. Little has been written about the introduction of the English methods into France. Huntsman's invention must have been known to French metallurgists, including the excellent Corps of Mining Inspectors, even if knowledge of it failed to become public. We hear much of the manufacturing of files at Amboise by Saint-Bris as early as 1785,[14] which resulted in a large and flourishing establishment in the earlier nineteenth century. One French authority tells us that a Frenchman named Sauche produced at Amboise in 1782 excellent crucible steel from Swedish iron.[15] But there seems to have been no further discussion of crucible steel. The explanation of this silence seems to be that no development of this early success resulted, because of the insistence upon formal trials by the government and the hostility of public opinion. Sauche and his works were forgotten, like those of the Marquis de Jouffroy and Philippe de Girard.

In 1814 occurred the second and successful introduction of the English method of making crucible steel by William Jackson, who came to the district of Saint-Etienne with his family with the en-

[12] Maxime Perrin, *Saint-Etienne et sa région économique* (Tours: Arnaud, 1937), 221.
[13] Germain Martin, *Histoire économique et financière de la France,* in v. 10 of Gabriel Hanotaux (ed.), *Histoire de la nation française* (Paris: Plon, 1927), 332.
[14] Paris, *Exposition . . . de 1819* (Costaz), 181.
[15] Pierre Guillaume Frédéric Le Play, "Mémoire sur la fabrication et le commerce des fers à acier dans le nord de l'Europe," *Annales des mines,* Série 4, v. 9 (1846), 140.

couragement and partly at the expense of the French government. It is interesting to note that this is the same year in which Jager-schmidt came to Toulouse. Jackson was a typical English entrepreneur, having been a former manufacturer of iron, speculator in land, and cotton spinner in his native Lancashire for some thirty years. De Gallois tells us that Jackson came to France because steel mills had become too numerous in England. He also came, however, under the personal protection of Chaptal, the distinguished chemical manufacturer and former Minister of Commerce, who recommended him strongly to the emperor and promised him financial support and a house. Proof of some governmental patronage is supplied by the actual payment of a subsidy in 1822 after seven years of almost complete neglect which had nearly resulted in his going to Prussia. During that period he lived on loans and a small allowance from France made necessary by the confiscation of his property in England. He encountered also the treachery of a French partner, Robin, who learned his method and then established a rival firm with one of the leading businessmen of Saint-Etienne, J. B. Peyret. Jackson brought over his sons and at one time had as many as sixty-five English workmen.

Personal jealousy and scanty financial resources help to explain the slow progress of the Jackson firm, which was still small when its founder died in 1829. There is evidence also that the task of training French laborers was difficult, for we hear of English workmen employed under long contracts and at high wages as late as 1832, when William Jackson's sons acquired a new mill at Assailly and were steadily enlarging the business. But success did come, for a company with adequate financial resources was organized in 1839 and the quality of the steel was assured by importation of Swedish iron at great expense.[16]

The development of steel manufacturing in France in the period of 1815 to 1848 was amazingly slow, even when we remember that the Industrial Revolution itself moved at a very leisurely pace. There is evidence of the presence of all the usual difficulties—small-

---

[16] *Bulletin de la société d'encouragement pour l'industrie nationale,* v. 23 (Nov., 1824), 328.

scale operations, scarcity of capital, unskilled labor, and the spirit of routine—but it is clear also that the tariff and the nature of French iron ore played decisive parts.

The influence of the tariff and the types of ore found in France are emphasized by a controversy between the mining engineer Le Play, father of the famous sociologist, and François,[17] another mining engineer who spent years in the department of Ariège trying to persuade the ironmasters owning the Catalan forges to adopt progressive methods. François, who was well informed and able, nevertheless was really engaged in propaganda for the government, and his objects were to justify the prohibitive tariff and emphasize the excellence and variety of the mineral resources of France. He contended that most of the ore in France could not make good steel, either because of phosphorus or because of lack of sufficient manganese. But he insisted the ore of Dauphiné and that of the Pyrenees were quite suitable and that a real steel industry could be based on them if manufacturers and laborers were trained to use more progressive methods in making cemented and crucible steel. Le Play pointed out in opposition that the steel manufacturers of Sheffield were unable to use English ore, yet never bought any ore from the Pyrenees, although they imported ore regularly from Sweden and Russia at considerable expense. Since the French were able to import Swedish and Russian ore through Bordeaux and Marseilles for the steel center of the falls of the Tarn and in the Department of Loire, it is obvious that the English, with far better shipping facilities, could have come to the Pyrenees for ore, had they felt it desirable.

Le Play contended that no one in France at that time could produce more than mediocre steel and that the finest qualities could be made only from the iron of certain mines in Sweden or Russia.

---

[17] Paris, *Exposition nationale de produits de l'industrie agricole et manufacturière de 1849: Rapport du jury central*, v. 2, Quatrième Commission, Sect. 3: *Aciers*, par Pierre Guillaume Frédéric Le Play (Paris, 1850), 346. Joseph Duplessy, *Essai statistique sur le Département de la Loire* (Montbrison, 1818), 342. Gras, *op. cit.*, 27, 30; the best source on Jackson. See also Le Play, "Mémoire sur la fabrication," *loc. cit.*, and François, *Extrait . . . de l'importation.*

He was supported in this view by such sound authorities as Perdonnet, the distinguished railroad engineer, Jules Burat, one of the ablest writers of the period on French industry and brother of the well known geologist Amédée Burat, and Dufrénoy, another very able writer on industrial subjects. Le Play showed that France had increased her production of steel but had never succeeded in improving the quality without the introduction of Swedish or Russian iron, and that the improvement was in direct proportion to the amount of iron imported from northern Europe.

The steel industry of France was growing, it is true, and seemed to be increasingly prosperous; but its strength rested entirely upon the prohibitive tariff which forced French consumers to accept mediocre steel made from French iron at a high price, because duties raised the cost of Swedish or Russian iron to approximately three times its price in England. The French steel industry seemed doomed to permanent inferiority, and the consumer compelled to import really fine steel from England, as long as the prohibitive duties were retained. Both the government and public opinion in France supported François in this controversy, and the tariff on iron remained almost prohibitive until 1860.

Cost and Production of Iron and Steel

It is difficult to give adequate figures covering the growth of production of iron in France in the period 1815 to 1848, because most French writers give very few and they are frequently indifferent to accuracy. They consider that statistics interfere with the flow of narrative and elegance of style and often apologize to the reader for giving any figures at all. It is also clear that the writers of the earlier nineteenth century are not greatly interested in the accuracy of figures, whether in their own writings or in those of others. Thus we find that most of the few figures given for the production of pig iron cannot be used. Costaz, a member of the governmental bureaucracy in Paris, who wrote a small volume of official reports on the Exposition of 1819, says that in that year France produced 14,500

tons of pig iron and 64,000 tons of wrought iron.[18] The figure for
pig iron is obviously incorrect, since it took from 1.3 to 1.45 tons of
pigs to make one ton of wrought iron. Eugène Flachat, one of the
few writers whose figures are generally accurate, gives the production of pigs for 1819 as 112,500 tons and that of wrought iron as
74,200.[19]

The error of Costaz is important, because his figures were copied
by Héron de Villefosse in 1828,[20] although he was a distinguished
metallurgist, one of the best-informed men in France on the progress
of the iron industry, and occupied an official position that made a
widespread acceptance of his figures inevitable. Even as late as 1844
we find the incorrect figures of Costaz repeated by Blaise in his
excellent book on the French exposition of that year,[21] although he
had been quite accurate in writing about the Exposition of 1839.

Fortunately for the economic historian of France, Eugène Flachat, a distinguished engineer and builder of railroads, has given
a table of figures covering the production of pig and wrought iron
from 1819 through 1843 and for cemented and forged or cast steel
from 1831 through 1843 without a single important error.[22] This
makes it possible to state with some confidence that the production
of pig iron in France increased from 112,500 tons in 1819 to 442,622
tons in 1843, while another reliable estimate gives us the figure of
522,385 tons for 1847—representing a nearly fivefold increase in the
production of pig iron in France from 1815 to 1848. In this same
period the production of wrought iron increased in the same proportion from 74,200 tons to 376,000.[23] In the case of steel, the
figures given by Flachat show an increase in the production of
forged or crucible steel from 2,967 tons to 3,527, and of cemented

[18] Paris, *Exposition . . . de 1819,* 157.

[19] Eugène Flachat and Alexis Barrault, *Traité de la fabrication du fer
et de la fonte envisagés sous les rapports chimique, mécanique et commercial* (Paris, 1842, 1846), 1250–51.

[20] Antoine Marie Héron de Villefosse, *Recherches statistiques sur l'état
actuel des usines à fer de la France en l'année 1825* (Paris, 1828), 37.

[21] Adolphe Blaise, *Exposition des produits de l'industrie nationale en
1844* (Paris, 1844), 23.

[22] Flachat and Barrault, *loc. cit.*

[23] *Ibid.*

from 2,412 tons to 5,812[24] between the years 1831 and 1843. After that we have no figures that seem reliable or that indicate clearly the kind of steel produced. Even the figures of Flachat himself do not inspire the same confidence as those he gives for iron, partly because we cannot be sure even of the quality of the steel referred to, and partly because his figures are not as clearly confirmed by others as are the figures he gives for the production of iron.

The price of iron in France also is not easy to determine, although there are more figures given and more opportunities, therefore, to determine the accuracy of any one source. The chief uncertainties regarding figures for prices are the quality of iron referred to and whether the cost of transportation from the place of production to the place of sale or of final preparation is or is not included. In general it can be said that the price of iron fell considerably from 1815 to 1848; it would seem almost justifiable to say that it was cut in half. But if the general trend was downward, it was not uniform during the whole of the period, for there were some important forces at work that tended to raise prices, or to prevent their decline.

We know that the cost of production of both pig and wrought iron decreased through better methods, improvement in equipment, better transportation, and cheaper coal. Cheaper labor was obtained by the elimination of great numbers of highly paid English foremen and other workmen who had trained their French pupils. On the other hand, we know also that many French mills remained so small that they could not reduce their costs of production substantially. It was those small establishments that usually persisted in the use of charcoal, the price of which continued to rise as the demand increased, because the supply could not increase. It is clear that competition increased greatly within France because of better transportation and a growing use of coal. Competition from abroad could not increase effectively because the tariff, which was high in 1815, was made prohibitive in 1822, and remained so until after 1848.

It is interesting, however, to observe the smaller cycles of price changes in French iron within the general decline. In 1823, follow-

24 *Ibid.*

ing the imposition of prohibitive duties on the importation of pig and wrought iron, French prices rose somewhat. They rose even more in the next two years, and then fell sharply, because from 1823 to 1826 there was a period both of rapid industrial expansion and of speculation, which was followed by a financial crisis and a period of deflation prolonged by the Revolution of 1830. Thus in the Department of Loire, pig iron rose from 190 francs in 1823 to 250 in 1826 and then fell slowly to 135 francs in 1831.[25] These prices are those of mills using coal that were so ably managed that they had learned to eliminate most of their expensive English workmen. They are, therefore, unusually low, but the changes in them are probably typical of those of France as a whole.

We lack sufficient figures to say in detail what happened to the prices of iron in France during the crisis of 1837 and the ensuing depression. We can say only that prices rose considerably between 1843 and 1846 because of railroad-building and a renewed period of industrial expansion and speculation like that of 1824 and 1826. In the later period of the 40's, however, prices of iron did not rise as much as they had twenty years earlier, because costs of production were lower and competition within the country far more intense. There can be little question that if subsequent research makes further figures available, the prices of French iron will be found to have been influenced by much the same factors of industrial expansion and construction that affected the iron industry of England, except that the first great period of railroad construction across the channel from 1830 to 1836 has no parallel in France.

THE FINANCING OF IRON MILLS

The financing of the French iron industry, like that of most French industries in the earlier nineteenth century, has received scarcely any attention from historians, yet a little information is available and more could undoubtedly be found. Unfortunately,

---

[25] Alphonse Peyret, *Statistique industrielle du Département de la Loire* (Saint-Etienne, 1835), 108.

what little evidence we have deals chiefly with those mills using coal in whole or in part, which could be said to dominate the iron industry in 1848 but nearly all of which did not exist in 1815. The government paid little attention to them at first, and Baron Pasquier, in summarizing the *enquête* of 1828 into the iron industry, said that the forty English forges—meaning iron mills using coal or coke and possibly making some use of puddling—were capitalized for 4,000,000 francs.[26]

Baude, a wealthy owner of coal mines in the district of Saint-Etienne and one of the most reliable writers on the French iron industry, gave a list of the French establishments using coal, with the capitalization of each in 1829, and the total figure obtained from his calculations is 45,700,000 francs.[27] There is no means for knowing the accuracy of Baude's figures, and he probably included several mills that used coal only in part; but it is certain that he was well informed and was a shrewd and careful observer, whereas Pasquier had only official sources of information and was a Parisian bureaucrat interested chiefly in the law.

Interesting conclusions can be drawn from the figures of capitalization presented by Baude in 1829. If the principal establishments are grouped by regions, we get for the Department of Loire a capitalization of 10,200,000 francs, for those of the Centre 15,500,000, for the east 8,400,000, and for the northeast 6,200,000 francs. The Nord is represented by two establishments capitalized for 1,600,000 francs, the west by one in Brittany worth 1,000,000 francs, and the south by the great establishment of the Duc Decazes, capitalized then for 1,800,000 francs.[28] This regional capitalization corresponds closely with the known relative importance of the regions in the development of the French iron industry in the period from 1815 to 1848. It shows also how each region was dominated by a small number of financial groups or individual financiers.

---

[26] France, *Enquête sur les fers de 1828,* faite par une commission formée avec l'approbation du roi sous la présidence du ministre du commerce et des manufactures (Paris, 1829), 287.

[27] Jean Jacques, baron Baude, *De l'enquête sur les fers* (Paris, 1829), 89.
[28] *Ibid.*

In the Loire the Compagnie de l'Isère et de la Loire was capitalized for 5,000,000 francs in 1829[29] and for much more later. Through some of its partners it controlled the establishment of Lorette, worth 1,200,000 francs, and it also had an important voice in the establishment of Janon, run by the Compagnie des Mines de Fer and capitalized for 2,000,000[30] francs, which it succeeded in absorbing in 1840. This joint-stock company thus virtually controlled 80 per cent of the capital invested in the iron industry of the Loire (if we accept completely the figures of Baude), the iron mines of Ardèche, among the richest in France, and the great foundries of La Voulte and Vienne further south. Of the men in this great company, or trust, the most important were undoubtedly Frèrejean, a wealthy manufacturer of Lyons, Blumenstein, a well-known and wealthy promoter, and the Neyrand brothers. The only important firm in the Loire whose connection with the Frèrejean company is not shown is the forge of Saint-Julien, worth 2,000,000 francs and owned almost entirely by Ardaillon, a silk-ribbon merchant of Saint-Etienne who appears to have bought out the heirs of his partner, the ironmaster Joseph Bessy, after his death in 1825.[31]

In the Centre, financial power among the great iron mills was divided between the Boignes family of Fourchambault and their allies, who included the powerful de Wendels of Lorraine, the Guérins of Imphy, closely connected with the French government through their work for the navy, and the interests behind the great establishment of Le Creusot. This was run in 1829 by a joint-stock company in which the chief investors were Manby and Wilson, who must have brought capital from England, by the Chagot family, who owned the near-by coal mines of Blanzy, and by Napoleon's great minister Chaptal, with his son. Of these three groups Le Creusot was by far the most powerful, with a capitalization of 10,000,000 francs, but we know that in actual fact the company was bankrupt in 1829 and probably had been in poor financial condition since the later years of the Empire. There were financial connections

---

[29] *Ibid.*
[30] *Ibid.*
[31] Gras, *op. cit.*, 50.

between Fourchambault and Imphy, but it appears certain that in the Centre there was no effective concentration of financial power such as we saw in the Loire.

Of the other parts of France little can be said about financing. The power of the de Wendels in Lorraine is well known and was well earned. Further south in eastern France the most important mills were Audincourt, in the old province of Franche-Comté, which was owned almost entirely by Georges Humann, an Alsatian promoter long since residing in Paris and well connected both financially and politically, who became Minister of Finance under Louis Philippe. The other great coal-using establishment of the east, Châtillon-sur-Seine, was owned by the duke of Ragusa, a former marshal of Napoleon.

In the south the only important establishment in 1829, other than the foundries of the Frèrejean company in the Ardèche and Isère departments, which have been discussed in connection with the Loire, was Decazeville on the south western edge of the Massif Central. It was financed chiefly by the well-known politician of the Restoration, the Duc Decazes, who had served as ambassador to Great Britain and Prime Minister under Louis XVIII, and by Georges Humann. The investment in Decazeville, where there were rich deposits of both coal and iron, was only 1,800,000 francs at first, but by 1845 the enterprise had absorbed no less than 14,000,000 francs,[32] partly through the investment of new capital, and partly by paying no dividends for fifteen years and reinvesting all savings in the establishment. In short, Decazeville seems to have been largely the toy of a small group of wealthy men, and it never became a great financial success.

Le Creusot, which we have mentioned in discussing the most important metallurgical region of France in the period, the Centre, was probably the greatest establishment in the French iron industry in 1815. Yet it was not a financial success, even under its English owners Manby and Wilson, who did so much to train Frenchmen in the English methods of manufacture. It was bought by the

---

[32] *Journal des chemins de fer* (Paris, May 23, 1846).

Chagot family, who owned the coal mines of Blanzy, about the beginning of the Restoration, for less than 1,000,000 francs; and by Manby and Wilson in 1826 for approximately 2,000,000. The reasons for the failure of this great organization are various. Manby and Wilson tried to run both the works at Le Creusot and those at Charenton, nearer Paris; finding this too difficult, largely because of the high cost of transportation, they closed Charenton. Further difficulties were caused by the widespread reluctance of French consumers to use iron smelted with coal and by the expense of maintaining a large force of English workmen.

It is probable also that the English owners were too much interested in improving methods and not enough in producing at low cost and selling at a profit, and it is possible that the joint-stock company they had formed was not well administered. Such companies were few under the Restoration and were regarded with suspicion, both by a watchful government and by the majority of much smaller firms that were partnerships. Many of the directors of such companies were usually Parisian bankers, or others with little knowledge of metallurgy, and they met in the capital far from the establishments they were trying to administer. But the chief reason for the failure of Le Creusot was that Manby and Wilson acquired control at a moment that was singularly unfortunate. The speculative boom that had begun in both England and France was drawing to a close, and it is clear not only that the crisis and the period of deflation that followed shortly helped to ruin some of the chief stockholders of Le Creusot, such as Chaptal and his son, but that the whole enterprise was unable to weather the storm.

In 1836, after the formal bankruptcy with a loss of approximately 11,000,000 francs, Le Creusot was brought by the Schneider brothers, whose descendants still were among its controlling directors at the outbreak of World War II a century later. They were fortunate in obtaining the greatest metallurgical establishment in France after a thorough liquidation, and also after English methods had been learned well. They owed much to the ability and idealism of Manby and Wilson. They were fortunate also in that the crisis that began in 1837 did not affect seriously either the coal or the iron industry as the crisis of 1826–27 had. But they also showed good judgment in reorganizing Le Creusot as a partnership with limited liability rather than as a joint-stock company. Furthermore, they secured the financial support of François Seillère, one of the ablest and soundest bankers of Paris, who had made a fortune as an army contractor under Napoleon and who had very valuable business connections in the great mercantile and financial center of Lyons, which was not far from Le Creusot. The Schneiders were thus able to obtain almost continued credit in the city that was their nearest money market, and it is not surprising that their capitalization was increased rapidly from 4,000,000 francs to 14,000,000.[33]

GOVERNMENT POLICY TOWARD THE INDUSTRY

Finally, we must consider the attitude of the government towards the iron industry in the period 1815 to 1848. This policy was not simply paternal and protective, as has often been supposed, for the attitude and actions of the government affected the iron industry in many different ways. The easiest form of governmental influence to understand is the tariff, because that tariff remained high throughout the period considered in this book and most of the time was prohibitive. The government on the whole would have liked a lower tariff, but through the restricted suffrage under the Restoration the Chambers were dominated by the large landowners of the country, among whom were many important ironmasters and other private owners of forests. Under Louis Philippe, when the

[33] Adolphe Blaise, *Exposition des produits de l'industrie nationale en 1839* (Paris, 1839), 84. Henri Chazelle, *Le Creusot* (Dôle: Imprimerie Presse Jurassienne, 1936), 83–86; he shows that Le Creusot was left practically bankrupt at the conclusion of the Napoleonic wars in 1814. Louis Reybaud, "Rapport sur la condition morale, intellectuelle et matérielle des ouvriers qui vivent de l'industrie du fer," *Mémoires de l'académie des sciences morales et politiques*, v. 13 (Paris, 1872), 543. Napoléon Vadot, *Le Creusot* (Le Creusot, 1875), 320.

suffrage was widened, the ironmasters simply combined with other manufacturers for a pact of mutual assistance.

A few years after the return of peace in 1815, it became clear that English pig iron smelted with coal was entering France in considerable quantities, and there was anxiety felt also concerning the importation of wrought iron that had been puddled and rolled. The result was the passage of the Law of 1822 raising the duty on pig iron to 90 francs per ton, if imported by sea, and 60 if imported by land, and the duty on wrought iron was increased from 150 francs to 250 per ton.[34] As a result of this tariff, pigs were imported only for casting and for wrought iron used mainly for making steel or for other purposes for which unusual homogeneity or special qualities were needed. It can be said that on the whole the French iron industry was completely protected from foreign competition and was affected only by internal competition, which was negligible in 1815 but was extremely important long before 1848. The government was more liberal than the Chambers regarding the tariff and sought to lower the duties on iron after the *enquête* of 1820 had shown that this could be done without serious injury to the French industry. But the government was neither strong nor brave and succeeded only in reducing by 25 per cent the duty on wrought iron refined with coal in the Act of 1836.[35]

The tariff policy of the government was thus pleasing to the ironmasters on the whole. But the laws and regulations regarding mines, forests, and streams were frequently irritating, or even harmful. The Law of 1810, which has been considered in the previous chapter on coal, required a formal concession from the government for every mine; that meant delay and expense for the ironmaster seeking the concession, but almost complete security once the concession had been obtained. We should not consider this law too important, however, for we have noted that most iron ore in France in the period of iron, 1815 to 1848, was dug from the surface in

[34] Baude, *op. cit.*, 66. France, *Enquête sur les fers*, 5–9.
[35] Léon Amé, *Etude économique sur les tarifs de douanes*, 2d ed. (Paris, 1860), 184.

shallow ditches, which were legally called *minières* to distinguish them from true mines. The operators were usually organized in small and temporary mining companies that required no concession but simply a declaration to the local authorities.

The use of forests and streams by the iron industry created problems of greater complexity. As we have seen, most French forests were owned by the national or local governments, which were anxious both to conserve them and also to obtain from them the largest possible income. The policy of the government was thus contradictory, the Treasury rather favoring the growth of the iron industry and the Forestry Service tending to oppose it. It is probable that, on the whole, governmental control of forests served to check the progress of the iron industry in the earlier part of the period from 1815 to 1848, and served to hasten that progress in the later part of the period by increasing the advantage of using coal. Probably the influence of the government made it more difficult for ironmasters to build light railways through the forests from mines to streams, and it may have increased the difficulty of establishing new foundries and forges in many wooded districts.

Even greater difficulties were encountered, however, in the use of streams, because the needs of the ironmasters for water to wash ore and supply power were opposed to the interests of the farmers, who wanted to irrigate their fields but not to flood them. They were opposed also to the interests of the nation, which needed a greatly developed system of waterways, including both canals and canalized rivers. The government under both the Restoration and the July Monarchy was keenly interested in both the prosperity of agriculture and the development of waterways and was supported strongly by public opinion. The farmer could legally take as much water as he desired for his fields from the smaller streams and the government as much as it needed for navigation from the larger. The result was that ironmasters rarely established foundries or forges on large streams, even if they possessed sufficient capital to develop the equipment for using a considerable quantity of water power, while on small streams they often found their mills idle from lack of water. If the aggrieved ironmaster sued the farmer, or if the farmer sued the ironmaster, whether for lack of water or for flooding the fields with both water and impurities injurious to crops, the decisions of the courts were uncertain. In important cases that were appealed the decision was likely to be affected by the ancient feud between the Council of State and the Corps des Ponts et Chaussées, with the odds in favor of the landowner, backed by the Council of State, which was the supreme court in administrative cases. In consequence, the ironmaster could not be sure of using any small stream undisturbed except by the vagaries of nature. Besides, even the erection of a water wheel required, under a strict interpretation of the law, a royal ordinance, which was likely to be issued only after a long delay. In most cases, therefore, the ironmaster sought and obtained the consent of the prefect of the department for the erection of his wheel, but here again he could not be sure that the prefect's permit would be recognized by a court of law.

Finally we should consider the influence of the mining inspectors on the development of the iron industry in France. These men were organized in an efficient corps by the regulations of Napoleon, and during the whole of the period from 1815 to 1848 they exercised great influence over the ironmasters, who did not develop the powerful Comité des Forges to govern their industry until the time of the Second Empire. The activities of these officials were often galling, because they inspected all mills and were required to approve all changes in them. They also decided the amount of the taxes to be assessed upon them. The ironmasters, therefore, frequently regarded them simply as tax collectors. The information the owners supplied regarding production and earnings was usually calculated to deceive rather than to enlighten the government, and was certain to emphasize losses and difficulties and to minimize profits. Yet these mining inspectors were highly trained engineers and in most cases both enlightened and tolerant. There can be no question that on the whole they guided the ironmasters wisely and taught them to use both better equipment and improved methods. Through them the government counteracted much of the harm done by the tariff and by the rigidity of laws and regulations, and promoted much of the very considerable progress made by the iron industry of France from 1815 to 1848.

SUMMARY

In conclusion we must recognize the fact that nearly all decisive improvements in metallurgy realized in France between 1815 and 1848 were made by establishments using coal and often by only a small number of them. The mills using wood remained, for the most part, small and somewhat isolated, and where they were able to hold their own it was frequently through the adoption of coal for part of their production. Most of these mills did raise the height of their furnaces, improve their blasts, and learn to use gas for reheating, but they did these things primarily to economize fuel.

The mills using coal were increasing in number and even more in efficiency. Before 1848 their relative importance had risen and they were coming rapidly to dominate the industry as a whole. Improvements made by mills using coal thus served not merely to economize fuel but directly to increase production. It was due chiefly to them that the iron industry, which had suffered considerably from the depression of 1826 to 1832, scarcely felt the depression of 1837 to 1842. The industry was thus fully prepared for the boom that came with the building of the great network of railroads. It was the mills using coal that trained a large body of skilled French workmen through highly paid workers brought from England. They attracted the largest investments of capital and did the most to increase the size and efficiency of individual establishments. It was these mills, therefore, that brought down the cost of production and cut in half the price of iron.

An observer at the end of the July Monarchy could still have found many Catalan forges using the direct method and many other small mills using wood in whole or in part that were run by the owner as a family business, with high costs and the tendency to routine that frequently characterize operation on a small scale.

These backward establishments were not doomed as yet, but they were to be found increasingly on the sidelines as progress swept on. Superficially the picture of the iron industry in France in 1848 bore many resemblances to that of 1815, but the spirit of life was passing from the wooded landscape of Champagne or the Pyrenees to the sooty forges of the Loire, the Nivernais, and the Nord.

CHAPTER SEVEN

Textile Raw Materials

IN THE DEVELOPMENT of the Industrial Revolution in France in the earlier nineteenth century, the supply of raw materials was as essential as the development of transportation, fuel and power. The most important of all raw materials, iron, has been considered first because it was used in nearly all machines in transportation and the production of power as well as in manufacturing. Next to iron the most important raw materials were those used by the great textile industries, in which many of the great mechanical developments occurred, partly because their fibers were unusually well suited to manipulation by machinery, and partly because of the need of clothing by all classes of the population. Three of these raw materials, wool, flax, and silk, were produced in France and were closely connected with the development of French agriculture. They were also imported in considerable quantities, however, so that foreign competition was often a serious factor. The fourth, cotton, was produced wholly outside France, yet it had a depressing influence upon the raising of sheep and the growing of flax, because the ease with which its fibers could be manipulated mechanically and its low price resulted in its manufacture on so great a scale that its cloths competed extensively with woolens and very seriously indeed with linens. The four principal raw materials must, however, be studied separately, because the problems involved in increasing or maintaining the supply of each are peculiar and affect the development of the manufacturing industry concerned just as they are themselves influenced by it.

Wool

It is surprising to find that France, which in Colbert's day had become famous for fine woolens, and which throughout her history had raised large numbers of sheep in proportion to her population, was not wholly successful in producing the wool needed by her deservedly famous woolen and worsted industries. In the eighteenth century, as in the seventeenth, France regularly imported from Spain, England, or Germany, the wool needed for finer cloths. Shortly before the Revolution she began to raise merino sheep and under the Restoration was able to produce wool finer than any in Spain and almost equal to that of Electoral Saxony. Under the Restoration she started importing from England sheep with the long and shiny wool needed for the rapidly growing worsted industry and raised her tariff high enough to make the importation of wool very expensive. Yet under both the Restoration and the July Monarchy complaints never ceased regarding the abundance, quality, and price of French wool. These complaints were varied and contradictory and were usually related to the complainer's opinion of the tariff. It is difficult to estimate their value, but it is clear that they seldom dealt with the fundamental problem of securing a suitable supply of native wool for French manufacturers. This could be done only by fitting the raising of pure or well bred sheep with fairly fine fleeces into the existing framework of French agriculture with its increasing number of small farms owned by peasants with little capital.

France probably had about thirty million sheep in 1815 and forty million in 1848. Our period, then, was one in which the raising of sheep increased; but it did not increase enough to meet the needs of expanding industry or the danger of competition from the superfine wool of Saxony, the long wool of England, and the amazingly cheap wool which began to come in ever-increasing quantities from Australia. It was clearly a period in which the quality as well as the quantity of the wool produced was greatly improved, yet here again the progress made was not great enough to enable France to meet her industrial needs.

France had several breeds of native sheep before the Revolution. On the low plains of the Camargue between the Rhône and the Mediterranean grazed great flocks which required no shelter in winter and which could spend the summer in the cool and juicy pastures of the Alps. Further north we find frequent mention of breeds or types of sheep in the provinces of Berry, Normandy, Picardy, Champagne, and Flanders and in the regions of Beauce and Brie not far from Paris. Most of these sheep, however, produced wool that was short, coarse, and curly. At its best, this wool was good enough for carded cloths of medium quality, although most of it was woven into coarse cloths for the working classes. Only the fleeces of the sheep in French Flanders appear to have been long and straight enough to be combed easily. It was necessary, therefore, in the period from 1815 to 1848, either to import for making worsted long wool that was not curly, or to use some of the shorter and curlier French wool with excessive waste of the valuable material in combing and spinning.

The first significant importation of foreign sheep to supply better wool for French manufacturers and, ultimately, to improve the native breeds occurred in the last years before the Revolution. In 1784, a certain Delporte brought in a flock of sheep with long wool of a breed described as "Romney Marsh" to his farm near Boulogne.[1] This did not, unfortunately, lead to an important increase in France of sheep whose wool could be used for combing, because the flock was not kept pure but was crossed with merinos whose characteristics eventually became dominant. In 1785 and 1786, Louis XVI imported about six hundred Spanish merino sheep[2] and

---

[1] Sir John Harold Clapham, *The Economic Development of France and Germany, 1815–1914* (Cambridge, Eng.: University Press, 1921), 176. Professor Clapham says: "Continental cultivators have never succeeded in fitting sheep into the system of mixed arable farming as practised in England. The reasons are many . . . chief among them are the smallness of the holdings, their dispersion, and the lack of enclosures."

[2] Julien François Turgan, *Les Grandes usines*, v. 8 (Paris, 1868), 51. *Bulletin de la société d'amélioration des laines,* v. 2 (Paris, 1826), 14.

began the famous flock at Rambouillet which influenced the breeding of sheep in France for many years. A much larger importation was made under the Consulate through the Treaty of Bâle in 1799 of approximately five thousand of these valuable sheep.[3] Under the Empire the breeding of merinos in France made great progress, and at its close the wool of these sheep in France was finer than that of those in Spain, although in fairness it would probably have to be admitted that this result was due to Spanish neglect as well as to French skill.

At the accession of Charles X, the Prince de Polignac had increased his flock of merinos in southern Normandy from seven thousand to eleven thousand,[4] but we are told that he was obliged to board them out with other landowners at great expense. This must also have made it difficult to control their diet and breeding sufficiently to insure continued production of the finest wool. A smaller flock of approximately eighteen hundred merinos was kept by Perrault de Jotemps and Girod de l'Ain,[5] heads of a sheep-breeding organization known as Naz. It was handled with much greater care and not only produced for many years the finest merino wool in France and the only fleeces comparable in quality to those of Electoral Saxony, but also through judicious sales and propaganda influenced profoundly the improvement in the quality of wool in many parts of France.

There can be little doubt that in the last years of the Restoration landowners and textile manufacturers of France were merino-minded. Some writers rejoiced over the prevailing fashion, while others said that it had become almost a mania and had resulted both in an excessive production of merino wool and in the neglect of other kinds of wool, particularly that needed for combing. We can say only that, relying upon the figures published by Baron Charles Dupin in 1827, the production of merino wool in the whole of France was only 766,310 kilograms compared to a production by

---

[3] *Ibid.*

[4] Turgan, *op. cit.,* 51–52.

[5] Achille de Colmont, *Histoire des expositions des produits de l'industrie française* (Paris, 1855), 175.

mixed breeds, known as *métis,* of 4,578,748 kilograms and of native or unimproved wool of 30,852 kilograms.[6] Even if great allowances are made for possible errors in these figures, it is clear that fine merino wool, when interest in its production was greatest, was only a small proportion of the total amount of wool grown in France. Even if we included all the wool of mixed breeds, although they cannot all have had in them merino blood, we should still have a total of only one sixth, approximately, of the annual clip of France. It does not seem possible, therefore, either that the production of common wool was ever seriously neglected between 1815 and 1848.

France, through her increasing flocks of merinos, was coming to have an excellent supply of wool for carding in the last years of the Restoration, but her supply of wool for combing remained seriously deficient. Yet interesting attempts were made to solve the problem. As early as 1817 importations of English sheep with long, silky wool began, chiefly those of the New Leicester or Dishley breed, whose wool was both long and fine. Three men appear to have been engaged during most of the Restoration in fairly systematic importations: Wollaston at Rouen, Colvert at Dieppe, and the younger Hennepin at Villepreux, a village in the Brie district not very far from Versailles. They seem to have acted occasionally as agents for the king or the French government, and frequently for wealthy landowners. Among these were the Prince de Polignac, Baron de Mortemart-Bosse, Camille Beauvais, the retired manufacturer of Lyons who made valuable experiments in the culture of silkworms, and F. A. Seillère, the Parisian banker who had powerful financial connections with Lyons and was later to be the principal supporter of the Schneiders at Le Creusot.[7]

A society was formed for the improvement of wool in 1825 by a group of great landowners, many of whom were members of the nobility, and a few manufacturers of woolens or worsteds. In their

---

[6] *Ibid.,* 173.

[7] To this list of importers of English sheep should be added the name of Baron Ternaux, the great woolen manufacturer, who brought English sheep in, imported the famous Kirghiz goats, which produced Cashmir wool, and bred them in France, and began the construction of proper establishments for washing wool.

Bulletin[8] they described various breeds of sheep and how to improve or maintain them in France, but they were interested primarily in importing English sheep with wool suitable for combing and in seeing that after arrival they became acclimated and crossed with suitable breeds of native French sheep. We do not know precisely how long this society continued to exist and to spread its propaganda, although there is reason to believe that it did not survive the Revolution of 1830 and was probably rendered almost powerless by the depression that began in 1827. It succeeded in importing many English sheep, however, and in establishing permanently in France a considerable proportion of them. Nevertheless, it is doubtful if the number of English sheep acclimated in France during the Restoration was sufficient to affect appreciably the quality of any considerable proportion of the annual clip. It seems probable also that these importations of English sheep did not continue on any large scale during the July Monarchy. On the other hand there can be little doubt that the quality of French wool improved steadily throughout the period from 1815 to 1848, even if, as seems certain, most French wool remained short and curly.

Information regarding the price of wool is confusing and contradictory and seriously inadequate. Yet certain conclusions can be drawn. It is clear that the price of wool, like that of iron, was greatly affected by the business cycles in France,[9] such as the speculative boom that culminated in 1825, the long depression from 1827 to 1832, and the ensuing period of rising prices. We can be sure also that prices fluctuated greatly during each year. There was no national market for wool in France, but rather a small number of important regional markets and a great many local ones. The inadequate development of transportation must also have helped to increase regional and local price differences. In short, the uncertainty of the price of wool made the growing of sheep speculative for most landowners and, therefore, undesirable for the small farmer without capital.

The tariff had an influence on both the production and the

[8] Clapham, *loc. cit.*
[9] *Ibid.*

price of wool in France, but less than many contemporary French writers claimed. In 1815 foreign wool was admitted free, and a duty was imposed upon the exportation of fine wool, while exporting coarse wool was forbidden. Shortly afterwards, duties were levied upon the importation not only of wool, but even of sheep and lambs, and these were increased rapidly. In 1822 the duty upon imported wool reached 30 per cent, although the classification of wools was so complicated that the rate actually levied varied considerably.[10] These duties were clearly imposed in the interests of the larger landowners, who had the franchise and were the principal supporters of the restored monarchy. This was made doubly clear in 1826, when all duties upon the exportation of merino sheep were repealed and also the prohibition against exporting common wool.

The tariff was clearly injurious to manufacturers of woolens and worsteds, partly because it increased the cost of their raw material and partly because it resulted in reprisals by other countries which restricted appreciably the sale of French cloth abroad. It is doubtful that the average French farmer raising sheep was directly affected extensively by these duties, or that importation of wool before the voting of high duties was large enough to injure most French raisers of sheep. While there is reason to believe that imports of fine wool increased greatly after 1834, it is not clear that the increase was due to the reduction of the duty to 20 per cent in 1836,[11] or that it injured French agriculture seriously. The expansion of the woolen and worsted industries was then so rapid that they could easily absorb a great increase in importations, whether resulting from legal operations or smuggling, and also use whatever fine wool could be produced in their own country. The chief effects of the tariff on wool were probably to increase the price of woolens

---

[10] Charles, baron Dupin, *Forces productives et commerciales de la France,* v. 2 (Paris, 1827), 368. Dupin gives the production of wool of each department of northern France separately in chapters scattered through the whole of his two volumes, and the totals for northern and southern France.

[11] Léon Amé, *Etude économique sur le tarif des douanes,* 2d ed. (Paris, 1860), 109–46.

and worsteds in France, to restrict and retard their development by limiting their sale abroad, and to put large and unearned profits into the pockets of a considerable number of large landowners, most of whom were already prosperous.

To inquiries as to why the production of fine wool in France did not increase more, the historian can answer that the reasons were economic. There is evidence that merino sheep adapted themselves admirably to the French climate and pasturage, and it seems safe to assume that English sheep with long wool could have become acclimated and increased considerably. But our limited knowledge of French prices and agricultural conditions indicates that it is among them that we shall find the true reasons why merinos never made up more than a small percentage of the millions of sheep in France and why English sheep never became numerous. Although merinos are small sheep and are not very good eating, every French town levied in the *octroi* a fixed tax per head regardless of weight. English sheep, especially those of the Dishley breed, are large and excellent to eat but they are hearty eaters themselves, and also require greater care and regulation of diet than most French farmers could give. We know also that both their fleeces and their flesh begin to lose their excellence after the age of two years. In short, it is clear that these sheep with long wool were too expensive to raise and that their introduction into France was the work of a small number of large and wealthy landowners with a little help from the government. Under the conditions then prevalent in France they could not be fitted into the system of agriculture.[12]

Even merinos required fairly skillful care and it is interesting to observe that the figures of Dupin,[13] published in 1827, show that nearly two thirds of all the pure merinos in France were in the provinces close to Paris, including the regions known as Beauce and Brie, where large estates were numerous, and also considerable supplies of capital and large and accessible markets. It is in these same provinces, for the most part, with the addition of Normandy and

---

[12] See Note 7.
[13] Dupin, *op. cit.*

possibly parts of Picardy, because of favorable climate and pasturage, that we find most of English sheep with long wool. Even the *métis*, or mixed breeds, most of whom had merino blood, were found in great numbers only in these same provinces and districts.

Finally, it might be asked how the growth of the worsted industry of France, which is known to have been great, could have occurred in the face of the failure of French landowners to breed sheep with long wool in great numbers and in the face of the high tariff. The answer seems to be that the high tariff did not stop importations of English wool, particularly after the reduction of the duty to 20 per cent. It seems probable also that there was some increase in the supply of long wool produced in France. Finally, there were technical improvements, such as better sorting and washing of wool and improvements in both combing and spinning, that made it possible to use relatively short wool with much less waste. In the end, of course, the problem of the worsted industry, like that of the woolen, was solved by importing wool from Australia on a large scale, and also by the invention of the mechanical comber by Josué Heilmann of Alsace, which became effective about 1850.

LINEN

Wool was produced in France, as we have seen, as the raw material for an industry that was conspicuously strong and healthy and expanding rapidly. It conformed to the pattern of a textile industry that we should call normal for the earlier nineteenth century. It is well to turn, therefore, to an industry that was strong but not healthy and not expanding at all. Linen was suffering from the overwhelmingly great and rapid growth of the cotton industry, resulting largely from the ease with which its fibers could be manipulated by machinery, but also from the fact that the cotton itself could be grown cheaply and in great quantities. Since cotton cloth is light and cool, and since it could already be manufactured at very low cost, it competed directly with all but the finest linens. The darkening shadow of the great cotton industry was felt, therefore, by every manufacturer and merchant of linens and should have been felt by every farmer who grew flax.

The linen industry was so ancient and spread so widely throughout France that it was really indigenous. All districts within reach of the damp winds from the Atlantic had a climate very favorable to the growth of flax, while many parts of those districts had soil that was eminently suitable. France had always produced considerable quantities of flax of good quality, for the most part, and some of it excellent. Nature had been bountiful. She had required only that flax should not be grown on the same soil for more than seven years and that, for the best results, the soil be light. Flax was, however, easily injured by bad weather at certain stages of its growth, so that the yield varied greatly from year to year. These facts were well known to the farmers, who still continued to take the risks involved for the sake of the profits, which were frequently great. It is probable that the yearly crop would have been larger if the peasants had cultivated flax only when they had capital sufficient to carry them over bad seasons and labor sufficiently skilled to ensure the thorough weeding that the young flax plants need for their best growth. They should also have had a knowledge of the composition of the soil that would have made them realize that lightness or sandiness is more desirable than great quantities of manure. In general, however, the quality of French flax when harvested was good and the quantity was apparently sufficient in most years until the advent of mechanical spinning about 1837.

It is difficult to estimate the acreage sown to flax in France in the earlier nineteenth century, partly because the figures are few and partly because the best authorities differ sharply. Chaptal said that in 1017 flax was grown on 40,000 hectares,[14] but it seems probable that he considered only cultivation on a large scale, whereas thousands of peasants in many districts grew it in small quantities

---

[14] Jean Antoine, comte Chaptal, *De l'industrie française,* v. 1 (Paris, 1819), 185. France, *Enquête sur les fils et tissus de lin et de chanvre,* par le Conseil Supérieur du Commerce, novembre 1838 (Paris, 1838), 94; testimony of Comte Defitte, member of the Conseil Supérieur at the session of June 9, 1838.

so that the aggregate of small-scale production must have been considerable. In the *enquête* of 1838 we are told that the average was 55,000[15] hectares, and this figure was accepted by Charles Coquelin in 1839 in the first of his two admirable writings on the linen industry.[16] But we are told also that Brittany alone in 1838 had an average of 20,400 hectares,[17] and it is well known that the cultivation of flax in that province was extensive, while Renouard tells us that about 1840 the acreage in the Department of Nord had increased to 15,000 hectares.[18] If these two important districts alone had an acreage of 35,000, it seems improbable that the rest of France had only 20,000. Other estimates which seem more likely to be accurate are that of Moreau de Jonnès, the statistician, who gives 98,242 hectares as the acreage of flax in 1840,[19] and the agricultural census published by the government in 1842 which gives the acreage for 1838 as 97,672.[20] In conformity with these larger estimates we have that of Legentil, one of the ablest of French writers and investigators, who tells us that the acreage in 1836 was 97,000.[21]

It is even more difficult to determine whether the acreage sown to flax increased or decreased during the period from 1815 to 1848.

---

[15] France, *Enquête sur les fils,* 226; testimony of M. Moret, justice of the peace and spinner of Moy, near Saint-Quentin, Aisne, at the session of July 3, 1838.

[16] Charles Coquelin, "De l'industrie linière en France et en Angleterre," *Revue des deux mondes,* Série 4, v. 19 (July 15, 1839), 194.

[17] Louis François Benoiston de Châteauneuf and Louis René Villermé, "Rapport d'un voyage fait dans les cinq départements de la Bretagne, pendant les années 1840 et 1841," *Mémoires de l'académie des sciences morales et politiques,* v. 4 (1844), 770.

[18] Alfred J. Renouard, *Etudes sur le travail des lins,* 4th ed., v. 1 (Lille, 1879), 45.

[19] Alexandre Moreau de Jonnès, *Statistique de l'industrie de la France* (Paris, 1856), 175. He states on pp. 168–69 that Chaptal had access to the manuscript documents from which the Exposé de l'Empire was prepared, but did not use them, and that for the late eighteenth century he used without analysis the figures supplied by Tolosan, which had been computed inaccurately.

[20] Louis Estancelin, *De l'importation en France des fils et tissus de lin et de chanvre d'Angleterre* (Paris, 1842), 26.

[21] Paris, *Exposition universelle de 1851 à Londres,* travaux de la Commission Française, sous la présidence du Baron Charles Dupin, v. 4 (Paris, 1854), 32.

Here again there are differences of opinion. The greatest cause of confusion as to the actual acreage and changes in it is probably the necessity of allowing land on which flax was grown to be fallow at least every seventh year. This caused many farmers to alternate flax with other crops, so that the determination of the actual acreage of flax in a given year was rendered difficult for the authorities. It is impossible then to give figures proving that the cultivation of flax increased or decreased between the Peace of Vienna and the Revolution of 1848, but careful scrutiny of the evidence available and the opinions of competent writers indicate that the acreage increased until about 1840. This date corresponds fairly closely to the revolution in the spinning of flax and a sudden increase of flax from Russia. After 1840 the acreage would appear to have declined slowly. The supply of flax grown in France seems to have been adequate and of reasonably good quality up to the introduction of mechanical spinning on a large scale about 1837 and importation of Russian flax in considerable quantities. Yet the exports of flax decreased alarmingly, and the farmers of France would undoubtedly have cut their acreage sharply and have suffered severe losses if greater activity in the manufacturing of linen had not increased the domestic demand for flax.

Able critics have agreed that most of the flax grown in France was of far better quality than that grown in the Baltic provinces of Russia, but distinctly inferior to much of the flax of Belgium and Holland. Why was it not better? There is reason to believe that most of it could have been and that some of it was, for some flax grown in France near the Belgian frontier is described as so good that it was never put on the market and the price received by the farmers who grew it was never made public. The whole of this limited supply of superfine French flax was reserved for the manufacturers of batistes and other very fine linens in which France still excelled, although the demand for them had declined greatly owing to the sale of fine cottons at much lower prices. If, then, the finest flax could be grown in France, why was there so little of it?

The quality of French flax when harvested seems to have been very good indeed, but preparation for manufacturing appears to have been careless and even slovenly in so many districts that we are justified in saying that faulty preparation is the explanation of the inferiority of French flax as compared to Belgian and Dutch. A small quantity of French flax was evidently prepared with great care for the manufacturers of batistes, but most flax was not retted and scutched as well in France as in the Netherlands. It seems probable that the farmers of Belgium and Holland were more skilled in retting and scutching than those of France, and that they were more interested in doing their unpleasant and tedious work as well as possible. There is no evidence that they knew of methods unknown to the French, and it is quite clear that in retting, at least, there was no important improvement during the period from 1815 to 1848. Scutching mills did come into use in England in districts where great quantities of unscutched flax were available, but the work done by them does not appear to have been good enough to make their use profitable unless labor was very expensive. We are forced to the conclusion, then, that the better preparation of flax in Belgium and Holland was due chiefly to more careful supervision by merchants and manufacturers of linens. The same skill could have been attained in many parts of France, but was not, except along the Belgian frontier and probably, to a lesser extent, in the district of Moy near Saint-Quentin and in the district of Berney in southern Normandy.

The importation of flax was unimportant for many years. The duty of 0.20 francs per kilogram[22] was not significant in checking imports. Belgian flax was needed for certain qualities of French linens and was imported over the duty, but not in amounts sufficient to influence flax-growing in France significantly. Imports from Russia were not serious in the earlier part of the period from 1815 to 1848, partly because the shipping facilities to France were not as good as those to England, but chiefly because Russian flax was coarse, so that it was not as well suited for hand spinning as was the flax of France. But in 1836, although duties on iron and coal in the French tariff were lowered, the duty on green flax was increased

---

[22] Alphonse Arnauné, *Le Commerce extérieur et les tarifs de douane* (Paris: Alcan, 1911), 163.

to 0.50 francs, that on dried flax to 0.60 francs, and that on retted flax to 0.75 francs.[23] The reason for this change was a great increase in importations of Russian flax[24] because of mechanical spinning then being adopted on a considerable scale in France as a result first of the introduction of English machinery and later of the construction and improvement of similar machinery in France. The coarser flax of the Baltic was well adapted to the rougher treatment it received by machinery, so that the softer French flax, which had been suited to spinning by hand, no longer had an advantage. In addition, Russian flax was cheaper, even after paying the cost of transportation and the duty. It cost about half as much to grow flax in Russia as in France because the value of land was less and taxes and wages were lower, and it could be grown on a larger scale than was possible on most French farms. These advantages were probably increased by the development of mechanical hackling at about the same time as the introduction of mechanical spinning on a large scale in France.

In conclusion, it can be said that while there was progress in France between 1815 and 1848 in the spinning of flax and some also in hackling, there was no progress in retting or scutching, and the inadequacy with which they were frequently done was probably the chief cause of the inferiority of French flax to Belgian and Dutch. Most French flax remained, therefore, as inferior to the Flemish as before, and after the advent of mechanical spinning, accompanied by increasing imports from Russia, its production in France appears to have diminished somewhat and to have been inadequate for the needs of the domestic market. There is no evidence of any serious decline of the linen industry of France at that time, because any deficiency in the supply of French flax was made up by imports from Russia and Belgium; nor have we any reason to believe that the decrease in production was serious. Yet it could be said that the linen industry in France, and with it the raising of

---

[23] *Ibid.*, 168.

[24] Charles Coquelin, *Nouveau traité complet de la filature mécanique du lin et du chanvre* (Paris, 1846), 154. This book was begun in 1840, completed soon afterwards, and then rewritten.

flax, was always on the verge of a crisis because of the continued expansion of the cotton industry, with whose products it was necessarily in direct competition.

COTTON

The cotton industry differed from the other textile industries in that its raw material was produced entirely outside of France. It had numerous advantages over the others in the early nineteenth century. It obtained its cotton far more cheaply than the other textile industries could get wool, flax, or silk, despite the fact that the material had to come from America, Egypt, or even India. Even more important was the fact that cotton fibers are the most easily manipulated by machinery of all natural textiles, and a series of inventions which began in the middle of the eighteenth century revolutionized nearly every stage of the preparation and manufacturing of cotton from picking to finishing of the cloth. One of these, the invention of the cotton gin by Eli Whitney in 1793, made possible the immense development of cotton growing and picking in the United States at an amazingly low cost. The growth of this industry in most parts of France was relatively slow, however, because both tradition and fear of England's commercial and industrial power dictated a rigid tariff policy which made importations expensive; this policy was rendered even more restrictive by the regulation and protection of shipping.

The most reliable statistics available indicate that French importations of cotton between 1816 and 1848 increased from 12,000,000 kilograms to approximately 65,000,000.[25] This fivefold increase is impressive, although despite this expansion the cotton industry of France remained about one quarter the size of its gigantic rival across the Channel. Even more interesting, however, is the decrease in the price of cotton. A report from Mulhouse, which probably refers to either long-staple cotton of Georgia or Jumel cotton of Egypt, since Alsace specialized from necessity in the manu-

---

[25] Moreau de Jonnès, *op. cit.*, 84.

facture of fine yarn and cloth, tells us that the price fell from 6.38 francs per kilogram in 1815 to 1.43 francs in 1848.[26] This indicates remarkable improvement in both the production and the transportation of cotton which cannot have been simply the result of the great increase already noted in the quantity imported.

The decrease in the price of cotton was a great achievement, because the difficulties overcome were very notable. The tariff which had been imposed in 1816, against the better judgment of the government, was rigid. The duty was 15–30 centimes per kilogram for cotton of short staple and 30–50 centimes for cotton of long staple.[27] This was a reasonable rate in 1816, as it could then have been hardly more than 10 per cent of the value. But the rate was specific and remained the same, while by 1848 the price of cotton in France had fallen to approximately one fifth the figure of 1816, so that in effect the duty was increased from approximately 10 to at least 25 per cent of the value. Even this was not the whole story, for the French shipping regulations imposed a tax of 8–10 per cent on cotton imported in ships that did not come directly from the country where the cotton was grown.[28] This meant, in most cases, that the French manufacturer tried to import cotton directly from the United States, because the more favorable rates frequently obtainable in the great market of Liverpool would be more than overcome by the French shipping tax.

The manufacturer of Alsace, which produced about one sixth of all the cotton cloth made in France and a much larger proportion of the finest cloth, was at a serious disadvantage. Economy would have caused him to bring cotton up the Rhine, but the French government forced him to bring it across the whole of northern France from Le Havre by canal boat and cart, or from Marseilles up the valley of the Rhône and over the mountains, since by its

---

[26] Emile Dollfus, "Notes pour servir à l'histoire de l'industrie cotonnière dans les départements de l'est," *Bulletin de la société industrielle de Mulhouse*, v. 27 (1856), 460.

[27] Arnauné, *op. cit.*, 156.

[28] Jean Dollfus, "De l'industrie cotonnière," *Journal des débats* (July 24, 1855), 20. Adolphe Blaise, *Exposition des produits de l'industrie nationale de 1844* (Paris, 1844), 179.

regulations he must import the cotton directly through a French port. This meant not only great expense for transportation itself, but great delay. It might take several weeks for the cotton to reach Mulhouse, for the Seine was full of treacherous shoals and rapids and did not then have the present excellent service of skilled pilots or the dikes in its lower reaches, while the current of the Rhône was so swift that in most cases carting was preferred. The delay was serious, because fluctuations in the price of cotton were frequent, so that the Alsatian manufacturer planning his purchase could never calculate exactly the cost of his raw material. He could not avoid possible difficulties by buying great quantities of cotton in advance, for he seldom had great storage space himself and governmental regulations, until 1834, at least, permitted public warehouses for storage only in the seaports, where the facilities were few.

The British blockade had made importation of cotton from the United States very difficult, and Napoleon had found it impossible to grow cotton at all in France or in sufficient quantities in Spain or Italy. It was necessary, therefore, to rely on the inferior types of cotton grown in India or the Levant, although importing even from them was difficult. After the return of peace in 1815, however, France imported chiefly American cotton. For coarse or medium cloths Louisiana ordinary could be obtained in sufficient quantities, but for fine cloths, for which cotton of long staple was desired, there was difficulty. The best supplies of Georgia long-staple cotton were usually taken by the English, partly because they sent agents to Georgia itself and partly because they bought in much larger quantities. An alternative source was Egypt, where about 1820 a Frenchman named Jumel had begun to grow cotton from seeds from Pernambuco in Brazil.[29] The result was a new type of cotton with longer staple and great fineness and softness which became very popular in Alsace, although it was expensive because it was usually very dirty and difficult to card. Mulhouse appears to have bought considerable quantities of Jumel cotton, although her mainstay remained the cotton of Georgia. Tarare, famous for its fine muslins,

---

[29] Jean Baptiste Brayer de Beauregard, *Statistique de l'Aisne,* v. 1 (Saint-Quentin, 1826), 392.

seems to have followed the same policy as Mulhouse; but the centers in Normandy and the Nord used American cotton exclusively because their location made shipments from the Levant more expensive.

Finally, the purchase of cotton was highly speculative, not only during the Napoleonic period but also during the years of peaceful development that followed. The few statistics that seem trustworthy show that the price of cotton varied greatly, and that it did not simply follow the cycles of business that helped to cause them. France felt the same influences as England in these fluctuations, and, although the cotton industry was on a much smaller scale, she suffered almost as much as her neighbor, because her supply of cotton was less adequate and more uncertain, because it was more expensive, and because it reached her manufacturers more slowly.

The cotton industry of France was, then, more speculative than either the woolen or the linen industry—partly because of the immensely greater power of the competing industry in England, and even more because the price of the raw material was higher because of purchases abroad on a smaller scale than those made by England, inadequate means of transportation, and rigid tariff and shipping dues. In the case of the cotton industry of France we can say more clearly than in any other that the commercial policy of the Restoration and the July Monarchy was definitely harmful.

SILK

The production of silk in France in the period from 1815 to 1848 presents problems that differ strikingly from those of other textile raw materials, because of the delicacy and short life of the silkworm and because of the unusual strength, fineness, and value of the fiber it spins. The period is marked by great and rapid expansion in the growing of worms and the mulberries upon whose leaves they feed. There was notable progress in scientific research into the health and productivity of the silkworm and the mulberry and a remarkably efficient and sustained effort by leading manufacturers and the government to apply the results of that research. Finally, there was great improvement in reeling and pulling, considerable progress in weaving, milling, and dying, and a really revolutionary expansion in manufacturing from waste silk. Yet it is clear, a century afterwards, that this golden age of the silk industry was unsound in many important respects and contained the seeds of the overwhelming catastrophe that came under the Second Empire.

The silkworm cannot endure severe cold and suffers from intense heat, while it shares the horror its adopted people have always had for drafts. This meant that in northern or central France it could be raised only in closed rooms artificially heated and ventilated. Under such ideal conditions, provided by one or two men, such as Camille Beauvais, the productivity of the worm was increased enormously, and the causes and conditions of it were studied with admirable skill by Beauvais' distinguished chemist, d'Arcet, at the model silk farm of Sénart, near Paris, in the Department of Seine et Oise.[30] At this excellent establishment young growers were trained and sent out over a period of more than ten years to the districts where the production of worms and mulberries was most important. Such excellent work was highly appreciated and advertised by scientific organizations, such as the Société d'Encouragement pour l'Industrie Nationale, and by the government. Had its influence been really general, it might have prevented the disaster that came forty years later and might have made unnecessary the subsequent redemption of silk-growing by scientists like Louis Pasteur. But, despite encouragement by the government, work such as that promoted by Beauvais required both scientific care and financial resources that simply could not be found on a large scale in the France of the early nineteenth century, and particularly in the Midi.

Climatic conditions, then, were decisive in growing silkworms and mulberries, and the really significant expansion was confined to the south as it had been in earlier periods when growth was slow. In the middle valley of the Rhône, from a point near Rive de Gier

[30] Adrien, comte de Gasparin, "Considérations sur le progrès de l'éducation des vers à soie, depuis le commencement du siècle," *Mémoires de l'académie des sciences,* Série 2, v. 18 (1842), 518, 521. Charles Teissier du Cros, *La Production de la soie dans les Cévennes* (Paris, 1903), 59–60.

south to the vicinity of Avignon and extending some distance into the hills on either side, we find really intensive and significant production of silkworms. Here was much protection from the cold blasts of the north and considerable shelter from the intense heat of the Mediterranean plains, while, except in the bottom of the valley itself, there was fresh air that was absolutely essential. Within this area there might be occasional disasters from a sudden wave of heat during the period when the worm was spinning its cocoon, and protection for the eggs would be necessary in winter, but in general conditions were highly favorable. Expansion beyond this area, as into the districts close to Lyons, was rarely sufficiently profitable to have any permanent effect. Even mulberry trees, which, it was estimated, could have been grown successfully in fifty-seven French departments instead of fifteen,[31] did not produce enough leaves at the moment when they were needed in enormous quantities by the growing worms, or their leaves deteriorated in quality and thus became unsuitable to the very delicate digestion of the larvae. The department most productive in silkworms remained the Gard after 1815, as before, followed closely by the Drôme, Ardèche, Vaucluse, and Hèrault, and at some distance by the departments of Isère, Bouches-du-Rhône, and Rhône. Twenty-three more departments listed as growing worms did not produce altogether half as much as the Gard alone.[32]

---

[31] Charles Beaulieu, *Histoire du commerce, de l'industrie et des fabriques de Lyon* (Lyon, 1838), 166.

[32] Henri Bourdon, "Rapport sur l'état de l'industrie séricicole dans le midi de la France," *Mémoire de la société nationale et centrale de l'agriculture* (Paris, 1836), 8–22. Achille de Colmont, *Histoire des expositions des produits de l'industrie française* (Paris, 1855), 189. Paris, *Rapport du jury central sur les produits de l'industrie à l'exposition de 1834*, rédigé par le baron Charles Dupin, v. 2 (Paris, 1836), 102–3. Paris, *Rapport du jury central sur les produits de l'industrie française à l'exposition de 1823*, par Louis François Héricart-Ferrand, vicomte de Thury, et Pierre Henri Migneron (Paris, 1824), 57. François Félix de Lafarelle, "Etudes économiques sur l'industrie de la soie dans le midi de la France," *Journal des économistes*, Série 1, v. 32 (May, 1852), 30–31. Paris, *Exposition universelle internationale de 1889 à Paris: Rapports du jury international*, Classe 33: *Soies et tissus de soie*, par Marius Morand (Paris, 1891), 11; based on statements in *Annales de la société séricicole*, v. 1, 1837, and on reports of the exposition of 1834.

In addition to a favorable climate the region of the middle Rhône valley and the Cévennes hills had a population with a relatively simple standard of living which could grow the worms and reel the silk at low cost in wages. This seemed very advantageous, and it helped the farmers by providing remunerative employment for their wives and daughters at home. The growing of worms and mulberries was generally a secondary occupation supplementing ordinary farming, so that earnings from it, no matter how low, were pure gain to the farmer and his family. Furthermore, the work was relatively easy and quite healthful, while the morals of the workers, to which writers such as Audiganne and Villermé devoted so much attention, were safeguarded reasonably. To the manufacturer the cost of the silk thus obtained was gratifyingly low, but the quality was often poor, and the risks taken were ignored in the early nineteenth century because rapid expansion seemed to provide profits for everyone far into the future.

The defects of this application of the domestic system can be seen much more clearly now. Most peasant houses could provide no artificial ventilation and little, if any, artificial heat. They could not, therefore, guarantee a relatively constant temperature for the growing worms any more than they could give complete protection from drafts, much as they may have desired it. It was difficult also for the almost uneducated peasants to realize the vital importance of sanitation for the silkworm, when it seemed so unimportant for themselves. Accordingly, fresh air for the growing worms was not always provided, because in many cases that would have been impossible without expensive alterations to the family home; nor was there always sufficient space left between the worms when climbing to spin their cocoons. It is clear also that eggs were frequently selected carelessly, and cocoons were prepared for selling without proper precautions having been taken to ensure the death of the crysalis in a manner that would prevent putrefaction.

It is interesting to note that the best quality of silk came not from the Department of Gard, which produced the greatest quantity, but from that of the Ardèche,[33] which produced considerably

---

[33] Bourdon, *op. cit.*, 8–22. Ernest Pariset, *Les Industries de la soie* (Lyon, 1890), 169.

less. It is doubtful that the climate was more favorable in the Ardèche, but it is quite clear that the skill of the growers of both worms and mulberries was greater. At Annonay, near the important ribbon-manufacturing center of Saint-Etienne, we find a considerable production of worms of a species which the French called Sina, and which spun a silk that was pure white and remained so permanently, while the species of worms usually raised in France spun silk that was yellow and that, when bleached, was usually weakened and could not be relied upon to retain its whiteness permanently. It is not clear, from our scanty evidence, that the Sina was grown only in the Ardèche, but there is no description of its growth being important in any other department. We do know, however, that growing Sina worms was more expensive than growing the common breed that spun yellow silk, although the reason for the greater cost is not clear. The fact that this greater expense was borne successfully in the Ardèche, and probably was not in most other districts, gives us a clue to the greater skill and productivity of the growers of both worms and mulberries in that department. More capital appears to have been available there to the growers than in any other important department in the south, with the possible exception of Vaucluse. Also, we do not hear of the neglect of worms or mulberries for other crops, such as *garance* (madder), which we know was true in much of the best land near Avignon, which was the chief city in the Vaucluse. We know also that in the Ardèche many growers of worms and mulberries owned their own farms and, because of that, devoted more attention to the work, and were inclined to observe the practices of scientific investigators like Camille Beauvais. In most of the other important silk-producing districts farms were operated by tenants under the crop-sharing system known as *métayage*, where the tenant gave the owner of the land half of his crop in lieu of rent. This system of tenancy, whose bad effects are well known and which still exists in parts of France and in other countries, was certainly an important cause of carelessness in growing both worms and mulberries, because it emphasized the quantity rather than the quality of the crop.

Pulling silk from cocoons and reeling had always been done in the homes of the farmers who raised the cocoons, or in a small workshop owned by one farmer or a group of farmers who did all the pulling and reeling for themselves and their neighbors. The work was done by the same women who had grown the worms a few weeks before and for wages that were very low. Since heat was necessary to soften the gum that binds together the many fine threads in each cocoon, each woman put her cocoons in a basin of water heated by a small charcoal stove standing underneath, joined the threads from several cocoons into one and wound them on a reel which she kept turning by movements of her hand or foot. These simple methods were cheap and easy, but they varied in detail from one small workshop to another. The position of the woman who pulled, reeled and tended her stove was sometimes cramped, while the need of tending the stove prevented her from giving her undivided attention to pulling and reeling. The stove frequently gave out smoke that was bad for the delicate fibers of silk, and it often operated irregularly so that the temperature of the water in the basin was not uniform. Much of the silk reeled in these small workshops was, therefore, of poor quality, even if taken from the best cocoons; and most important of all, its quality was always uncertain.

The most important improvement in pulling and reeling of the first half of the nineteenth century was the application of steam, to both heating the basins and moving the reels, by Gensoul in 1805. This meant the elimination of the charcoal stove, with its smoke and irregular heat, and greatly simplified the work of the woman who pulled and reeled. A single boiler could heat almost any number of basins and keep the water at a uniform temperature, while a single motor could run with similar uniformity all the reels. Yet the Gensoul process, invented in 1805, spread very slowly indeed until about 1825. Even in 1848, although used in many large and important reeling mills, and in many more small ones, it had not driven out completely the small workshops which reeled without power and used charcoal stoves.[34] The Industrial Revolution had

---

[34] Paris, *Exposition universelle internationale de 1900 à Paris: Le Bilan d'un siècle,* par Alfred Picard, v. 4 (Paris, 1906), 222. Elie Reynier, *La soie en Vivarais* (Largentière, 1921), 92.

made headway, but it had not won a decisive victory. It is impossible to say how great the actual progress was, but it is significant that the only writers who try to give the impression that the use of steam was very extensive in the south are men from the north, like Charles Dupin, who did not know the south well and who wrote reports emphasizing progress for the national expositions at Paris. Villermé, who did visit the south on his famous tour of 1836–37, testified that all through the silk-producing departments of the south, even in the Ardèche, much reeling was still done by the old methods.[35]

The reasons for the very slow adoption of steam in the reeling mills are quite clear. The typical small workshop, owned by a farmer or groups of farmers, was operated only during the summer and early autumn and at very low cost. There was no need to accumulate any real supply of capital. But the use of steam meant buying a steam engine, installing a boiler and motor, and arranging for regular delivery of coal. In short, the small workshop run by a family or small group of families must be replaced by a factory serving a larger group. Even if this change was desired by the people concerned, and it frequently was not, it might be impossible to obtain the necessary capital or credit or to arrange for the regular delivery of coal, because mines were few and roads were both few and almost always bad. The violence of rains in the south and the general poverty of that part of France made it impossible to raise enough taxes locally to build and maintain a good network of highways.

Lack of good means of transportation and scarcity of credit made it difficult for a factory to market any large quantity of silk, although this difficulty was probably not a major obstacle to progress, since it is obvious that the production of raw silk in France increased enormously between 1815 and 1848. We know also that a number of fairly large reeling mills were built, especially at Annonay near the northern frontier of the Ardèche, where much white silk

---

[35] Louis René Villermé, *Tableau de l'état physique et moral des ouvriers employés dans les manufactures de coton, de laine et de soie,* v. 1 (Paris, 1840), 342–43.

was available. Yet we cannot say how many of these mills were built. It is clear only that the change to large-scale industry was not extensive, because in 1848 only one quarter of the silk workers were found in pulling and reeling mills. Finally, we must always bear in mind that pulling and reeling were a seasonal occupation, between July and November. This was a powerful deterrent to the development of factories, because at that season labor was needed in the fields, orchards, and vineyards, while there were not enough other factories in the south to which women could go during the longer season when the reeling mills were closed.

The finer spinning of raw silk, usually called milling or throwing, was generally done in a small workshop, which may have served to employ some of the women who had finished the preliminary pulling and reeling. But milling was not from necessity a seasonal occupation, nor was it confined to districts in or near which silkworms were raised, and it could also use raw silk imported from Italy or the Orient. In the period from 1815 to 1848, it is indicated, most of the large imports of raw silk came from Piedmont and other parts of Italy. Yet in practice a great part of the milling seems to have been done in those districts where the silk itself was produced and in establishments that belonged more to the domestic than to the factory system. There were factories erected, however, and while the essential processes were changed very little, the speed of throwing appears to have been doubled or trebled and the control of the movements of the machines made much more accurate. It seems probable also that in the Gard, which did a great deal of milling, most of the establishments were small workshops working slowly and with little power. In the Ardèche, which was nearer the great markets of Saint-Etienne and Lyons and which apparently possessed more available capital and certainly had far more water power, much of the milling was done in more up-to-date factories and with the fastest and most accurate reels and towers.

Finally, we must consider the production of waste silk, which was a relatively new industry in France and made immense progress under the Restoration and the July Monarchy, to the great benefit of textile manufacturers in many parts of the country. The silk threads from defective or stained cocoons, or the poorer threads from good cocoons, had formerly been thrown away in France, but with the advent of machinery for manufacturing cotton and wool and with the increasing use of those textiles for mixed cloths, waste silk came in great demand. Before 1848 it was used in mixed woolens and cottons, and even in some linens, in many shawls, in linings, in plush, and even in Mecklenburg velvets and imitation furs. The impetus towards the use of waste silk and the methods and machines for manufacturing it probably came to France first from England almost immediately after the Peace of Vienna, and some of them may have been smuggled in under the Empire. The introduction of this method from England was natural, as waste silk could be treated in almost the same way as cotton. Great efforts were made to naturalize it quickly in France, especially by the Société d'Encouragement pour l'Industrie Nationale, probably because of a wholesome respect for the rapid development in England, Rhenish Prussia, and Switzerland. The chief center for its manufacture was Lyons, but it was also made in considerable quantities in the Parisian area and in Nîmes. Its chief importance to us in this chapter lies, however, in its offering great encouragement and profit to the growers of worms and the reelers of southern France. It undoubtedly played an important part in the immense strides made in the production of silk in France between 1815 and 1848.

It is difficult to determine how adequate was the supply of silk produced in France in meeting the needs of her manufacturers. Figures given during the earlier nineteenth century are admitted guesses,[36] and we are forced to rely upon figures given by writers long after this period who were sufficiently well informed to make critical use of highly unsatisfactory statistics. It is possible to state that between 1815 and 1848 the production of raw silk in France increased about sixfold.[37] We know also that through use of steam and improvements in reeling, the quality of the raw silk was improved greatly. It seems apparent, however, that most of the increase

---

[36] Moreau de Jonnès, op. cit., 153–54.
[37] Morand, op. cit., 9, 11.

in the production of French silk was of the old yellow type and that
the white silk derived from the Sina worm was not produced in
large quantities before 1848. It is obvious from this fact alone that
much silk must still have been imported, and it is clear that imports
continued to increase greatly during the period from the Peace of
Vienna to the fall of the July Monarchy. Since the demand for silk
increased very greatly, not only in France but also in other continental countries, in England, and notably in the United States, a
steady increase in imports did no harm to the silk-growers of
France.

The sudden separation of Piedmont from France in 1815, and
the imposition of duties upon Piedmontese cocoons and silk, were
first a shock and then a stimulus to the French growers, reelers and
throwers. These duties were reduced greatly in 1833, and there is
no reason to believe that they did any serious injury to the manufacturers of silks.[38] There is every indication that raisers of worms
and both the reeling and throwing mills expanded and prospered
under the Restoration and the July Monarchy and that the silk industry in France was one of the few that was neither weakened nor
held back in its development by excessive protection. Prices of cocoons and raw or thrown silk varied considerably over short periods
because of uncertainties regarding each season's crop of cocoons.
The size and quality of each crop depended upon the health of the
worms, which might be affected by any sudden change in weather
or by the spread of disease. But prices were remarkably steady over
long periods.

On the whole, then, the period from 1815 to 1848 was one of
almost unbroken prosperity and expansion for the producers of silk
in France. Great increases in production and improvement in quality were balanced by ever-greater increases in demand, so that it
seemed as if the boom would have no end. This continued prosperity, however, was undoubtedly an important cause of the trouble
that came under the Second Empire at just the moment when the
production of cocoons reached its maximum. The growers of
worms, who had seldom taken enough precautions against the vari-

---

[38] A. Beauquis, *Histoire économique de la soie* (Lyon, 1910), 273.

ous diseases that were really endemic, now increased their production recklessly to meet the demand and seem to have taken no precautions at all in their eagerness to enjoy the almost unlimited profits that appeared to await them. Eventually the epidemic came, and the growers of worms and mulberries, and with them the reelers of silk, suffered a disaster that can justly be called a catastrophe.

CHAPTER EIGHT

Labor

CONSIDERATION OF UTOPIAN IDEALISM and agitation has been guiding the study of French labor. More interest has been shown in the labor movement than in labor itself. Such studies have their place and are both important and interesting. This chapter, however, is concerned with the conditions under which French workmen lived and labored in the earlier nineteenth century and the ways in which those conditions were modified by the gradual mechanization of several important industries and by the growth of cities which, in the case of manufacturing centers, was often more rapid than that of the population of the country as a whole. Acceptance of this new point of view requires the reinterpretation of some old sources of information, such as the very important book of Villermé,[1] and its comparison with the report of the socially obscure Dr. Thouvenin, who was not a member of a Parisian academy but a factory inspector at Lille.[2]

This new point of view would hardly be possible without the work of modern writers who did not witness the events they describe or interpret. Of these the most important is the late Henri Sée,

---

[1] Louis René Villermé, *Tableau de l'état physique et moral des ouvriers employés dans les manufactures de coton, de laine et de soie* (Paris, 1840); "Notes sur quelques monopoles usurpés par les ouvriers de certaines industries, suivis de quelques considérations sur la situation actuelle des ouvriers dans les bassins houillers," *Journal des économistes*, Série 1, v. 17 (1847), 157–68.

[2] Dr. Thouvenin, "De l'influence que l'industrie exerce sur la santé des populations dans les grands centres manufacturiers," *Annales d'hygiène publique et de médecine légale*, Série 1, v. 36 (1846), 16–46; v. 37 (1847), 83–111.

whose brilliantly illuminating books and articles appeared chiefly
between 1921 and 1937. In addition, we should mention the book
of Ernest Pariset on the silk industry of Lyons, which rises above
class prejudice and enables us to understand clearly the great revolts
of 1831 and 1834. We are indebted also to Professor Laufenburger,
who in a single brief article[3] has given us a remarkable interpretation of the industrial revolution in the cotton industry of upper
Alsace. Finally, a series of modern studies on Sismondi,[4] who wit-
nessed many of the events with which this chapter deals, has shown
that that rather conservative and aristocratic economist saw clearly
that machinery used in factories was producing industrial crises that
were already affecting disastrously the lives of numerous groups of
French workers.

THE LABOR SUPPLY

The supply of labor for industrial work in France in the period
1815–48 was adequate at most times and in most places. While we
have scarcely any accurate figures, we do know that the population
of the country increased from about 26,000,000 to nearly 36,000,-
000[5] through both decrease of deaths and increase of births. It
seems almost certain that, while the number of industrial workers
increased also, it did so strikingly only in a few manufacturing
centers, and that the proportion of such workers to the whole population changed rather slowly. We are justified in stating that
throughout this period the number of industrial workers was never

---

[3] Henri Laufenburger, "L'Industrie cotonnière du Haut-Rhin," *Revue
politique et parlementaire*, v. 125 (1925), 389–403.

[4] Jean Charles Simonde de Sismondi, *Nouveaux principes d'économie
politique; ou, De la richesse dans ses rapports avec la population*, 1st ed.
(Paris, 1819). Albert Aftalion, *L'Oeuvre économique de Sismondi* (Paris,
1899). Joseph Hitier, "Sismondi," *Revue d'économie politique*, v. 13 (1899),
529–82. Joseph Rambaud, *Histoire des doctrines économiques* (Paris:
Larose, 1902). Gaston Isambert, *Les Idées socialistes en France de 1815 à
1848* (Paris: Alcan, 1905). Mao-Lau Tuan, *Simonde de Sismondi as an
Economist* (New York: Columbia University Press, 1927).

[5] Henri Sée, *Französische Wirtschaftsgeschichte*, v. 2 (Jena: Brodnitz,
1936), 234.

more than 5,000,000[6] and that those in large-scale industries scarcely exceeded 1,300,000.[7] The number of workers in agriculture was approximately 14,000,000.[8]

It is clear that in the country existed a large reservoir of labor upon which the growing industries in the towns could draw throughout this period. There are indications that at times immigration into towns from the country was important, usually at times when industry was expanding rapidly. In most cases such workers were probably unskilled, but in some they were highly skilled from long experience in domestic spinning, carding, or weaving when not working in the fields. The rapid expansion of the cotton industry in upper Alsace shows clearly that both types of immigration were important: that skilled weavers came from Switzerland to train the Alsatian peasants and that great numbers of Germans and some Swiss came because they had been impoverished by the wars of the French Revolution and Napoleon and by the tariff policy of France. But if immigration from the country into towns was important in times of prosperity, there was also a movement in the reverse direction in times of depression.

It must be remembered also that, although the factory system grew, the domestic system certainly held its own with great tenacity. Thus in the region of Saint-Quentin the population of industrial workers in the country remained large throughout our period. In fact, this great reservoir of rural labor remained one of the greatest industrial assets of the region, which was a little remote from the main routes of trade and could not compete with near-by Alsace in water power. The work the laborers did might change from spinning flax to spinning cotton, or from spinning to weaving, but even the advent of the power loom did not seriously increase the number of urban workers at the expense of the rural. When the cotton in-

---

[6] Thouvenin, op. cit., 20.

[7] Henri Sée, "Quelques aperçus sur la condition de la classe ouvrière et sur le mouvement ouvrier en France de 1815 à 1848," Revue d'histoire économique, v. 12 (1924), 493.

[8] Pierre Quentin-Bauchart, La Crise sociale de 1848 (Paris: Hachette, 1920), 44.

dustry found it difficult to compete with the stronger industrial centers of the Nord, Alsace, and Normandy, rural weavers were employed on woolens and silks.

Another factor that counteracted the immigration from the country to the towns was the rising cost of labor for the manufacturers in the cities like Paris and Lyons. Many of those great metropolitan merchants, particularly in Paris, employed cheap rural labor for all processes that did not require close supervision or unusual skill, and they found such labor in abundance in Picardy and the Aisne and in many other districts. Even Rouen employed thousands of weavers in Picardy, and there is also the striking case of the migration of the cotton-muslin industry from the district of Alençon on the lower Loire to that of Tarare near Lyons because of the greater abundance of rural labor in the east.

Both Lyons and Saint-Etienne provide evidence of the immigration of rural labor and the emigration of urban labor, or the adaptation of agricultural labor to industrial work. Thus we hear of the emigration of urban weavers from Lyons into the country after 1819 and, to an even greater extent, after the revolts of 1831 and 1834. It is clear, however, that some of the increase of weavers in the villages came from the wives and daughters of farmers. We know also that when the cotton-muslin industry of the district of Tarare suffered from increasing competition from woolen muslins, some of the unemployed cotton weavers were utilized by the silk merchants of Lyons. On the other hand, we learn that in the later years of the Restoration there was such a large immigration of rural weavers into Lyons because of the rapid expansion of the silk industry that customs and standards were upset because the new workers refused to conform to traditions with which they were not familiar. Saint-Etienne, with its ribbon industry, had a similar experience with the immigration and emigraton of labor.

Another form of the constant movement of labor was the immigration of skilled foreigners into France, of which we have cited one example in the cotton industry of Alsace. We learn that about 1824 there were between 15,000 and 20,000 English workers in

France, most of them highly skilled artisans in iron work, cotton, or wool.[9] Many of them appear to have returned home for various reasons. They did not like French customs or food; the prohibition of the emigration of skilled labor from England was repealed in 1825; and English artisans had fulfilled their duties to their French employers by training the relatively unskilled French workers. We find also a smaller immigration of German metallurgists into the Tarn and Lorraine to train the French in making natural steel. Finally, there is evidence in hearings of the British government in 1841 that the emigration of skilled workers to France was still going on, although it seems almost certain that it was on a smaller scale than in the 1820's. An interesting explanation of this emigration given by Ure seems very plausible: [10] that English workers emigrated when there was serious unemployment at home, whether from strikes or from industrial depression. But here also there was a current in the opposite direction, even if a small one. We know that during some of the worst crises in the French silk industry skilled workers left Lyons for Rhenish Prussia or Switzerland, and that there was a very considerable emigration to Spitalfields about 1826 and for some years thereafter.

We can conclude, then, that the supply of labor in France in the period from 1815 to 1848 tended to approximate the demand and fluctuated between town and country, or between foreign countries and France, in response to the fluctuations of industrial production and the introduction of mechanical improvements. On the whole, the industries in the towns tended to absorb more labor than they lost, but in most cases the growth was slow enough not to create

---

[9] Great Britain, House of Commons, "First Report From the Select Committee Appointed to Inquire Into the State of the Law . . . Respecting the Exportation of Tools and Machinery," *Accounts and Papers*, v. 5 (London, 1825), 37. William Otto Henderson, *Britain and Industrial Europe, 1750–1870: Studies in British Influence on the Industrial Revolution in Western Europe* (Liverpool: University Press, 1954), 30; Henderson's estimate that there were less than 2,000 skilled English workers in France seems much nearer the truth than the estimate of 16,000 made before the Select Committee.

[10] Andrew Ure, *The Cotton Manufacture of Great Britain*, 1st ed., v. 1 (London, 1836), p. xix.

critical social or housing problems. If in a few cases such problems were created, they were generally solved in time by emigration or other means. When we hear of intolerable housing conditions persisting for a long period, it can usually be shown that this was not a result of a very rapid growth in the number of industrial workers.

The other side of the labor picture should not be passed over. Agriculture in France between 1815 and 1848 was prosperous on the whole and at times was very prosperous indeed. While there was a tendency for most of the profits to go to the large landowners, who were favored by the tariff policy of the government and by the fact that they could vote, there was also a tendency for the number of small landowners to increase. Not only was there no important enclosure movement, such as that in contemporary England, but the number of peasants who owned their farms was definitely increasing. In short, the owner of the soil was ever more frequently its actual cultivator. Hence, the condition of agriculture and the forms of land ownership not only did not force great numbers of laborers to seek employment in the towns but also tended to deter them from leaving the land. They induced them to work part of the time in mills and to return to their farms for the summer or for week ends. Since, then, the attractions of agriculture to the potential industrial workers increased rather than diminished, and since there was an almost constant demand for industrial labor that could be performed in the rural home, it is obvious that the emigration of labor to the towns must have been rather slow.

FRENCH MANUFACTURING TECHNIQUES

France, as we have seen, had a reasonably adequate supply of labor, willing to accept rather low wages because it retained its connection with agriculture. It either used industrial work to supplement agricultural wages or took to the farms in the summer to make up for inadequate earnings in the industrial towns. French manufacturers thus had a supply of cheap labor, but they paid a high price for it. Lack of proper training in more skilled forms of work obliged them to use far more labor than their English competitors for the production of goods equal in quantity, but distinctly inferior in quality. In this difficult situation we see the result of the long period of war from 1792 to 1815. We see also the results of the prohibitive tariff, which raised the cost of living and of production in France and kept her insulated, to a great extent, as had the wars, from the influence of British industrial and commercial progress. The situation was the result also of the ancient error of the French in seeking to dominate the Continent to the neglect of their colonial empire and its commercial possibilities. A vicious circle had been forged in France: industrial production was on a small scale with routine methods and the merchandizing practices of a pedlar because labor was largely unskilled; on the other hand, labor had not been given proper training, because the small scale of production seemed to make such training unnecessary and far too expensive.

Illustrations are at hand to prove the accuracy of these assertions. We have evidence that French engineers, admirably trained in the principles of their profession, lacked practical experience. Hence the number available for the construction of machines was far too small, and they had first to train their mechanics. The same situation had confronted Boulton and Watt, who had to spend years in training men to bore true cylinders before they could produce their steam engines on a large scale. We find the same difficulty in the manufacture of iron in France. Workers were ignorant, frequently even illiterate, and consequently most reluctant to learn new methods. So were their employers, in many cases, despite the advantage of literacy. Thus the great firm of Decazeville in southern France, with both iron and coal available, had to spend fifteen years, according to one able writer,[11] in training its 5,000 workmen. It should be added, however, in this case, that Decazeville was far from all possible markets and that the native population had had no experience either in mining or in manufacturing iron. In the basin of Valenciennes, where mining had long been practiced, there

---

[11] Adolphe Blaise, *Exposition des produits de l'industrie nationale de 1844* (Paris, 1844), 34–35.

was much less difficulty in training workers, as is proved by the histories of the establishments of both Anzin and Denain.

Another type of difficulty is shown in the hardware industry of Saint-Étienne. Here there was an abundance of coal and some iron, and the manufacture of firearms and hardware was almost venerable. But the commercial and industrial management were deplorable. The only justification—which seems very inadequate to us—was that the best workers of the community had gone into the ribbon industry, where the work was lighter and the wages higher, or into the foundries and forges, which were expanding rapidly and also paid well. The hardware workers were illiterate, isolated in near-by villages, and thoroughly exploited by the merchants of the city. It is hardly necessary to add that they refused to change their methods and adopt better tools. Clearly, the merchants were at fault. When the force of competition from other parts of France was felt and, very indirectly, that of England, the hardware merchants of Saint-Etienne did not start training a force of skilled workers; they met the competition by cutting both wages and prices. Inevitably, therefore, the quality of their hardware deteriorated still further. The example of this industry shows the dangerous power of provincialism and of the petty bourgeoisie in France.

Another example from still further south illustrates a very real difficulty confronting the employers of labor. At Nîmes many cheap cloths of silk, or of silk mixed with wool and cotton, were made very well, indeed, to the satisfaction of the public of the Midi. The workers were intelligent and friendly and reasonably contented in their homes, where they worked in very small groups, usually composed of one or two families. Then came the advent of the factory system, and these same laborers proved obstinate and undisciplined. It does not matter how the problem was solved, because the solution must have come after the period with which we are concerned, but the existence of the problem is important. It is simply one example of a situation that could be proved to have existed in many parts of France if an adequate body of evidence were available. Weavers of Nîmes had their vineyards and gardens and were as much attached to the land as were their fellow peasants of the north. An example from northeastern France shows this well, where the competition from the skilled embroiderers of Switzerland forced a typically French solution of a French problem. Experts were sent into the Vosges, and for years, and at great expense, a whole generation of peasant women was trained to embroider as well as the Swiss.

Michel Chevalier, the well-known economist who had been trained as a mining engineer, made a shrewd comment in 1838 which received little attention at the time. He said that France needed a whole system of industrial education and credit to train her workers to produce goods of the same quality as the English: and to give proper training to French merchants.[12]

Working and Living Conditions

How did this numerous and inadequately trained population of industrial workers live in the period 1815 to 1848, and under what conditions did they work? As usual, the evidence is scanty and often contradictory but does provide a certain amount of information. We must realize, however, that standards of hygiene and sanitation were very different then from those to which we are accustomed. Thus, one of our most reliable informants, Dr. Thouvenin of Lille, reports that the workers seldom washed and never bathed. Another fact that is particularly difficult for Americans to grasp is that in France most towns were old and grew slowly, if at all. When, therefore, an able writer, like Blanqui, tells us that the rush of workers to the towns was terrific and the towns were utterly unprepared to meet it, and when we have just found upon studying the demand and supply of labor that the rush could not have been overwhelming from our point of view, we must remember that the French had long been accustomed to static conditions utterly unlike those of the United States at any period in its brief history.

---

[12] Michel Chevalier, *Des intérêts matériels en France* (Paris, 1838), 18, 22, 25.

Housing in France in the early nineteenth century was frequently bad. The most striking cases of this among the industrial towns were Lille, Rouen, and Mulhouse. The first, Lille, was an ancient and fortified town, one of the most important in the old province of Flanders. We are told that because of the walls and the garrison the gates were closed at night, so that many workers were forced to live within the city because they could not get back to their homes after their long day of labor. Because of this, we are told, overcrowding was so great that Lille had the worst housing conditions in the whole of France. Many workers lived in enclosed courts or cellars that were damp, dirty, and badly ventilated. But let us consider the problem in the light of other evidence. Sedan also was a fortified town and was as important in the woolen industry as Lille was in cotton; yet all accounts agree that in Sedan housing was excellent. It is clear, then, even if we make allowance for the fact that the woolen industry was mechanized much more slowly than cotton, that the fortification of the town could not have been the main reason for overcrowding and the bad housing that resulted from it. The most important cause of the trouble was that Lille lay on a boggy island in the river Deule. It is interesting also to realize that when, under the pressure of public opinion, the government at the end of our period razed some of the worst houses in Lille and cut streets through some of the courts, the workers were not grateful but regretted their lost cellars. In other words, they cared little about cleanliness or fresh air and preferred to live in cellars rather than climb many flights of stairs.

The ancient city of Rouen was in a better position than Lille, yet it was close to the Seine and shut in partially between the river and the high chalk cliffs above, and because of the heavy rainfall it was almost as damp as Lille. But the housing problem was less serious. The city could and did grow to the northwest, where the cliffs were lower, and later still industrial suburbs appeared on the plain across the Seine. The workers who lived in the half-ruined houses of the old city were chiefly employed by small mills trying desperately to compete with larger and younger establishments with better equipment. In this struggle they cut wages below the level of subsistence, and workers were forced to accept the worst housing until competition had done its work. We hear also, however, of new quarters in Rouen that had fairly good houses with gardens, and we know also that the majority of workers in the cotton industry were domestic and lived in the suburbs or in villages that were sometimes as far away as Picardy.

In Mulhouse, the great cotton-manufacturing center of upper Alsace, we have an industrial town that suddenly after the beginning of the nineteenth century grew from what was hardly more than a village into a large, modern city. Here bad housing can be explained on other grounds. The rapidity of industrial expansion created an urgent demand for a large supply of unskilled labor, and the economic effects of the Napoleonic wars and of the prohibitive tariff policy of France created a supply in the impoverished workers and peasants of southwestern Germany and northern Switzerland. These people poured into the villages around Mulhouse and accepted housing that was appalling because their wages were incredibly small and their families incredibly large. It was many years before the rather unusually enlightened and public-spirited manufacturers and officials of Mulhouse were able to cope with their slums. Here, then, is one of the comparatively few cases in France, in our period, where we really do find a rush of workers that was overwhelming and a town that really did grow as rapidly as some of the industrial centers of contemporary England or as Lowell in Massachusetts.

We can say that, in general, the housing of industrial workers in France in the early nineteenth century was poor, but that they had seldom if ever known better homes, and that they were not shocked by the dampness and overcrowding and dirt, but took them for granted much as we take bathtubs and automobiles.

The factories in which many of these industrial workers labored were probably badly lighted and ventilated at first. Many were former church buildings confiscated during the Revolution, or were constructed hastily and carelessly to meet the sudden demand for housing the new spinning machines. But as time passed and the machines grew in number and value and as the application of power to them increased, larger and healthier mills were built. We are justified in accepting the verdict of contemporary observers that after 1840 newer factories were seldom dangerous to the health of workers. The real danger remained in their homes and in their own low standards of hygiene and sanitation, which were also those of their communities. Unfortunately, the growth of these new and healthy mills was very slow.

In general, industrial workers of the earlier nineteenth century were reasonably well fed and enjoyed more and better clothing than ever before. Only from Lille, where the housing conditions were worst, and from Mulhouse, with its large population of underpaid and unskilled workers, do we get clear indications that the food was quite unsatisfactory. Villermé noted a distinct improvement in the diet of most industrial workers. Those who had eaten buckwheat were now eating rye bread, and former consumers of rye were now enjoying wheat. The poorer workers were quite dependent upon the potato, but at least the terrible famines of the Old Regime did not recur. Meat was clearly too dear and tending to rise in price, so that most workers probably ate it seldom, and usually in soups. Villermé's one criticism is interesting: he tells us that the French people did not realize that industrial workers really need meat.[13] But this is not surprising, since the working classes of France never had had meat frequently. The workers of the early nineteenth century did have sugar and butter, which they had hardly known before the Revolution, and a very considerable supply of vegetables. It is interesting to note that Villermé found the food of the foremen among the silk weavers of Lyons very good indeed, including white bread, wine, fairly good meat, and vegetables. Even their helpers he describes as having simply less food and no wine. He then adds that these workers had been described as starving by the newspapers of Paris. Actually, he wrote, they had better food than the majority of workers in France, and that it was impossible to believe in the misery of workers who are so well fed.

Industrial workers were unquestionably far better clothed in the period from 1815 to 1848 than ever before. Cotton clothing became

[13] Villermé, op. cit., v. 2, p. 39.

common and cheap, far cheaper than linen ever had been or could be. Woolens also had greatly increased in quantity and decreased in price, so that probably all but the poorest workers had some woolen clothing. This was a great protection in the damp French winters, and a protection they had never enjoyed before. It seems clear, also, that the wearing of shoes by workers became common in this period. The picture is not idyllic, however. The general improvement in food and clothing in the earlier nineteenth century means a rise from frequent famine and misery to a standard of bare sufficiency like what we should now describe as the minimum necessary to maintain health. It is doubtful if any but the skilled workers had much more.

The character and hours of work tended to improve and to become less dangerous to laborers' health. When we read accounts of almost incredible misery, they can generally be traced to some dying domestic industry, such as the weaving of cotton by hand or the spinning of flax in Normandy and Brittany. Among the improvements we can record are the substitutions of mechanical beating of cotton for hand beating, which had filled the lungs with dust and caused tuberculosis and pneumonia. This came slowly, appearing first in Alsace, then in Normandy, and finally and very slowly indeed, because of the cost, in the Nord. The gradual replacement of the hand loom by the power loom, which began about 1826 and was general by 1848 in the cotton industry, meant work in a standing position in a fairly healthy mill instead of sitting bent over in a damp and badly ventilated cellar. Combing wool by hand, with the worker heating the comb over a charcoal fire that created gas fumes in many cases, was replaced just after 1848 by mechanical combing, which was quite safe. In other cases, however, there was little improvement. In some processes in the cotton industry, such as some finishing, mechanical dressing, and to a lesser extent fine spinning, a very high temperature was maintained, which was dangerous when the workers emerged. We know also that little or nothing was done to protect workers from the machinery, whose speed of motion was being steadily increased.

Finally, we should consider one of the most important of working conditions, the length of the day of labor. Unquestionably this was excessive. Among hand workers we hear of days as long as eighteen or nineteen hours, and in mills fourteen or even fifteen hours were common early in our period. At first this evil attracted little attention, but towards the end of the Restoration interest was aroused, with the result that hours were slowly shortened until by 1848 the prevalent working day in mills was probably thirteen hours and in many cases twelve.[14] The change seems to have begun about 1840 and appears to have been widespread.

In contrast to this important improvement of the shorter working day is the rather distressing picture of the labor of women and children. It has been said that this evil was far less serious in France than in contemporary England because the wages paid French men were so low that there was little need to employ children.[15] The evil probably was less in France, but it was more than sufficient, and any mitigation as compared to England was due to the very slow mechanization and concentration of industry. Where these changes occurred the level of wages did not prevent the widespread employment of women and children.

Women were used in French industry. They were very common in the cotton mills, as is well known, and also in spinning wool (which became a factory industry during this period), in some of the easier processes connected with the weaving of wool, in reeling and spinning silk, and in the weaving of silk ribbons. In the silk industry at Avignon nearly all the workers were women. They were numerous in the tulle industry and made all the braid, lace, and embroidery. In general their wages were so low that they could do little more than support themselves. But to contemporary observers in France the most serious problem raised by their employment was the mixture of the two sexes in the factories. This preoccupation

[14] Charles Rist, "La Durée du travail dans l'industrie française de 1820 à 1870," *Revue d'économie politique,* v. 3 (1897), 371–93.

[15] Great Britain, House of Commons, *Reports From Committees, 1824,* v. 2: "First Report From Select Committee Appointed to Inquire Into Law Respecting Artisans Residing Abroad" (London, 1824), 228.

with the morals of the lower classes was as widespread among the French bourgeoisie as in the middle class of contemporary England.

Conditions under which children were employed in France between 1815 and 1848 were termed by Villermé "too terrible to be endured."[16] Shortly before he made this comment in his well-known book, one of the great cotton manufacturers, who exercised considerable political influence, stated publicly that in his cotton mill at Lille half of all his workers were children, who entered employment usually at the age of eight and often at the age of six years. They worked the same hours as adults and had no schooling or protection whatever.[17] Mimerel clearly believed, as did many of his contemporaries in New England, that such employment was better for the children than some schooling with long intervals of idleness.

The problem of child labor in France is of interest to us chiefly because of two important statutes that were intended to mitigate its evils: first, Guizot's Law of 1833 on education and, second, the Child-Labor Law of 1841. Neither produced satisfactory results, but both were important. The Law of 1833 was enacted after a careful survey which showed that before the advent of Louis Philippe very few of the children of the working class received any education at all. In 1832 the 42,000 communes in France had 10,000 schools, which had, from a population of more than 30,000,000, only 1,300,000 pupils.[18] Guizot sought to have one school for every commune; but he did not make education compulsory, nor did he make it free, except to the indigent. The commune and the government were to co-operate in paying the teachers, but the salaries offered were below the minimum standard of living for common laborers and there were no guarantees of promotion or of allowances for retirement. Finally, there were neither sufficient funds nor sufficient pressure from public opinion to build the necessary schools, nor were there enough normal schools to train teachers. Yet, despite

16 Villermé, op. cit., 358.

17 France, Enquête relative à diverses prohibitions établies à l'entrée des produits étrangers, v. 3 (Paris, 1835), 194; testimony of Auguste Mimerel.

18 Amédée Villard, Histoire du prolétariat ancien et moderne (Paris, 1882), 436.

these difficulties, the number of schools and pupils increased very considerably and illiteracy was reduced notably before 1848.

The Law of 1841 had two main objects: first, the protection of children from labor in factories at too early an age or for too long hours and, second, their being taught to read and write before they entered upon their industrial careers. Neither object was attained, but the law was more than a gesture. It served to keep most children out of the factories until they were eight years old; it increased the number of pupils in the schools, and it helped to shorten the hours of labor for all workers. It did not accomplish more for several reasons. Workers were not in sympathy with it because they felt it would seriously decrease their incomes, and they were interested only in religious instruction for their children. The government made no serious effort to enforce the law and issued few of the regulations for which the statute gave it discretionary power. Inspectors were usually appointed by committees of manufacturers, although it was common knowledge that the great majority of the French manufacturers were opposed to the law, and they were to receive no compensation. Finally, the law gave no help at all to the children in small establishments who needed it most, for it was applicable only to establishments with twenty workers or more, and the average workshop that was officially classed as "large" employed ten.

WAGES

The wages received by the industrial workers in France between 1815 and 1848 are difficult to determine. There are no general tables of statistics that inspire confidence. Government statistics in this period are notoriously unreliable. Manufacturers who testified at government hearings usually gave their maximum wages as the average. Many important writers, like Blanqui, made statements regarding wages without giving their sources of information or any set of figures to support their conclusions. While most French writers on economic subjects have disliked statistics until recently, it also seems probable that there were few reliable figures they could use. It is also unfortunate that in many cases in which figures are given the date is not supplied. It may, therefore, be almost impossible to determine the significance of the figures, because we cannot determine the circumstances under which the wages named were paid.

Several other reasons for the confusion can be given in addition to the lack of reliable tables of statistics. One is that most workers in France in our period were paid by the piece rather than by the day, yet most writers naming specific wages give them by the day; they make a rough average of piece rates in order not to weary the reader with numerous contradictory rates. Piece rates are misleading also, because their reduction may lead to a statement that wages have been reduced. This may not be the case, for a reduction of the piece rate was often made because an improved machine had greatly increased the worker's production. Hence, the reduction in wages was usually small in such cases, and there might conceivably be an actual increase. Another reason is that little account has been taken of the effect of business crises upon wages, with the result that very erroneous interpretations can follow if figures from a year of depression, for instance, are compared with those from a year of prosperity. Our best course is to rely upon the four authors who seem thoroughly sound in their statements regarding wages: Duchâtellier, Villermé, Sée, and Simiand.

Sée gives us two brief sets of figures for wages: the first taken from Villermé, indicating that they were probably taken from 1836, a year of prosperity, and are probably as accurate as any we shall ever obtain; and the second from the very incomplete reports that have survived from the very thoroughly conducted *enquête* of 1848 —figures taken, therefore, in a year of revolution following severe crises in both industry and agriculture. Villermé, omitting workers whose pay was unusually low, such as handloom weavers of cotton, gave the average wage as follows: men 2 francs, women 1 franc, children 0.45–0.75 francs.[19] The figures from the *enquête* of 1848 were men 1.78 francs, women 0.77 francs, and children 0.50 francs.[20]

---

[19] Sée, "Quelques aperçus," 495.
[20] *Ibid.,* 498.

Since the year 1836 was prosperous and 1848 markedly adverse, we
are justified in assuming that there had been little change in wages
other than temporary fluctuations.

Duchâtellier states that wages had risen from 1790 to 1810 and
that the increase had continued until 1820, after which wages were
either stationary or declining until 1830.[21] Since we now know that
there was an industrial boom from 1819 until 1826, we can amend
Duchâtellier's statement to read that a rather sharp decline in
wages came in the later year, from which there was probably a slow
and incomplete recovery beginning in 1832. Both Sée and Simiand
agree that wages did not increase materially between 1815 and 1850
—that, on the contrary, they were stationary, with a tendency to
decline. This statement is supported not only by the exhaustive investigations which both authors made, but also by their statement
that on the whole the period 1820–50 was one of declining prices.[22]
It certainly must have been, since the period beginning with the
dangerously excessive issues of *assignats* about 1792 and characterized by continuous war for more than twenty years was markedly
inflationary, with a crisis attending the collapse of the First Empire,
and a second crisis coming with the severe crop failure of 1817–18.
These facts help us also to explain numerous statements that wages
between 1815 and 1848, or between various dates within that
period, were very much higher than those of the late eighteenth
century, or, more specifically, those of 1789. They seemed higher,
of course, and really were, if we ignore the inflationary period of
the later years of the Revolution and most of the First Empire.
Confusion from the failure to consider these financial facts was
probably the basis for the statements of several authors, including
one by Sée himself, that there was a general increase of wages during the Restoration and the July Monarchy.[23]

An important factor that served to depress wages during the
period from 1815 to 1848 was competition in various forms. Its

[21] Armand René Duchâtellier, *Essai sur les salaires et les prix de consommation de 1202 à 1830* (Paris, 1830), 19.
[22] Germain Martin, *Histoire économique et financière de la France,*
v. 10 of Hanotaux (ed.), *Histoire de la nation française* (Paris: Plon,
1927), 329.
[23] Sée, "Quelques aperçus," 497.

most significant form, perhaps, was that of the competition between laborers for work in industry. This was serious because of the great body of workers who retained some connection with the land and who accepted low wages because they could live comfortably because of their additional earnings from agriculture. This competition tended to lower wages for all industrial laborers. Other forms of competition were those between manufacturers in the same industry, some of whom adopted improvements quickly and others slowly. Those who found their difficulties increasing almost invariably cut wages. Foreign competition, which was felt keenly throughout our period in the silk industry at both Lyons and Saint-Etienne, was met, in many cases, by a reduction of wages. Other industries felt foreign competition at times, especially woolen and linen. In the main, however, internal competition was more important, because the struggle between different manufacturers, whether in the same or in different industries, for the highly protected French market was keen. The ferocity of this struggle and its hardships on the workers would probably have been mitigated somewhat if more foreign competition had been allowed.

France suffered not only from the exclusion of foreign goods but also from the absence or loss of foreign markets. This resulted from the low costs of production in England, from the loss of colonies in war, from the inadequate development of French shipping, and from retaliation by the British and other foreign competitors for their exclusion from the French market. Finally, there was the competition between workers using machines driven by power and those using machines run by hand. At the beginning of the period this occurred in cotton spinning, and it gradually spread to the spinning of wool. In weaving, it came in the cotton industry in the middle of the period and in the woolen at the end, while the effort to install better looms in the silk industry, forced directly by foreign competition, was an important cause of the critical condition of the weavers of both Lyons and Saint-Etienne between 1830 and 1840.

A final factor depressing wages in the period between Waterloo and the Revolution of 1848 was the frequent recurrence of industrial crises, which usually brought reduction of wages for all and unemployment, or no wages at all, for many. We can list the most important as coming from 1817–19, 1826–32, 1837–42, and the last beginning in 1846. The first and last were greatly aggravated by serious crop failures, while the longer depressions of 1826–32 and 1837–42 were mitigated by one or two brief periods of temporary recovery, but were intensified and prolonged in the first case by the Revolution of 1830 and in the second case by the danger of war in 1840 over the Eastern Question. The effects of these crises on wages were serious, first, because the reductions were usually rapid and the subsequent increases slow, and, second, because they caused frequent variations in the workers' earnings and constant uncertainty. These crises and their effects were noted by contemporary observers, such as Sismondi, Villermé, Blanqui, and even Baron Charles Dupin, and by Charles Picard, who wrote in 1867, and among modern writers have been stressed by Sée, Gossez, and Quentin-Bauchard. But their effect on wages needs prolonged and intensive investigation.

Before concluding our study of wages, let us throw what little light we can find on the subject of real as distinguished from nominal wages. The pessimistic view is expressed by Duchâtellier, who stated that, with the development of industry, wages remained below the increase in prices.[24] The worker, consequently, had to work harder for the same comparative income and grew ever weaker in the face of the capitalist. The optimistic view was expressed by Dupont-White, who pointed out that the French population had not increased beyond the natural resources of the country as had the English, but that national wealth had increased more than twice as fast as population in France. Wages were not decreasing steadily, and if general misery came, he concluded, it would be because of excessive procreation by the masses.[25] The verdict must, unfortunately, incline towards the pessimistic view. Little if any of the increase of national wealth ever reached the workers, because it was absorbed by the bourgeoisie. While it is true, apparently, that wages did not decrease steadily to any great extent, frequent industrial crises certainly prevented any marked improvement in the

---

[24] Duchâtellier, op. cit., 8–9.
[25] Charles Brook Dupont-White, Essai sur les relations du travail avec le capital (Paris, 1846), 149, 152.

standard of living of the industrial worker. During periods of industrial expansion, wages usually rose and many workers could live fairly comfortably; but during crises, with widespread unemployment, suffering was acute in many of the industrial towns, such as Lille, Rouen, Mulhouse, and Lyons. Sée tells us frankly that in the textile centers of the north, especially of the cotton industry, wages were at or below the minimum standard of living. This is shown more clearly if we translate a daily wage of 2 francs for a man and 1 franc for his wife into terms of an annual family income of approximately 900 francs. This would probably meet the minimum standard of living at Rouen and Mulhouse, but would probably be below it at Lille and possibly at Lyons, depending upon the number and age of the children.

We must also remember the masses of unskilled labor, sweated labor, such as the women making braid, and labor in declining industries, such as small hardware and the weaving of cotton by hand. Even in industries where wages were considered high, such as the iron industry, with its foundries and forges, the wage of a skilled French worker probably seldom exceeded 4 francs a day, although the work was hard and the number of workers not very great. This income would mean, however, something like comfort. In the rising woolen towns of Roubaix and Tourcoing, after 1830 wages were rather high and comfort undoubtedly existed. Industrial workers living in the country got low wages but had lower costs than urban workers. They may have had better food and better housing than the worst in the cities, but it is certain that their standard of living was low. Our conclusion is, therefore, that for the majority of industrial workers in France real wages were approximately at the minimum standard of living in times of prosperity and definitely below it in times of depression.

THE OFFICIAL ATTITUDE TOWARD LABOR

We must turn now from the laborers, who are our main interest, to the bourgeoisie, which employed them, and the bourgeois government, which ruled them as useful servants of their employers. What historians have called the philosophy of *laissez-faire* that was so prevalent in contemporary England was prevalent in France also, where it was dubbed by Louis Blanc *laissez-mourir*.[26] Yet any Frenchmen of the period, while busily trying to imitate English business methods, industrial inventions, and agricultural improvements, would have reminded the reader promptly that the very phrase *laissez-faire* was French and derived from a French school of philosophers. He might proceed to enrich himself just as his neighbor across the Channel was doing, but he would insist that he was doing it in a French way. And it is true that things were not the same in France as in England. The French are logical. Their government has long been highly centralized, first under an absolute monarchy, then under Napoleon, and after 1815 under an equally absolute bourgeoisie. The attitude of the government toward the working class was not changed fundamentally by the Revolution, any more than it was by the lesser revolutions of 1830 and 1848. The workers remained a useful mass of childlike, ignorant servants that must be strictly controlled to ensure the docility needed for their own welfare and the state's.

We must remember also that the government and the bourgeoisie not only had the same philosophy about labor but were closely connected under the Restoration and were virtually identical under the July Monarchy. While we can still usefully bear in mind the famous remark of Colbert's almost unknown uncle, Pussort, that France had the best laws in Europe and the worst law enforcement,[27] we must recognize that the bureaucracy had been made vastly more efficient by Napoleon. It was convinced of its own wisdom and was exceedingly jealous of its power, but it remained blind and ignorant in many important respects and this had significant consequences. There had been a certain tolerant understanding of the lower classes in the later years of the Old Regime and a certain efficiency in the handling of industrial and commercial matters as

[26] Isambert, *op. cit.*, 266.
[27] Ernest Lavisse, *Histoire de France illustrée*, v. 7, part 2 (Paris: Hachette, 1911), 294.

they were connected with labor that seems to have been swept away by the Revolution. The abolition of the guilds was a great gain, but the love of power and privilege remained, and, as the Industrial Revolution slowly got under way, the attitude of the bourgeoisie towards labor seemed to harden, as if there were a vague consciousness of clashing interests.

Boussinesq, the economic historian of Reims, has aptly described the government of the July Monarchy as "slow, stingy, and uneasily prudent." [28] It took no interest in the workers of the newly industrial town and their problems, which became increasingly urgent. There was no official investigation of the rising tide of pauperism; the government possessed no adequate information and, consequently, took no action. It originated nothing in charity, but continued to encourage its practice by individuals. There were numerous projects of model housing launched and successfully administered. These were near important industrial centers like Lille, Mulhouse, Reims, and Lyons, but they were sponsored by the municipalities or, perhaps more frequently, by charitable or unusually intelligent manufacturers. The government never intervened when a manufacturer cut wages below the minimum standard of living. Nor did it act when, at the beginning of an industrial crisis, he threw all his workers on the street without feeling any responsibility for their relief any more than he did when they were sick or too old to work.

There was nothing criminal in this official inaction, nor was there any legal obligation, and public opinion did not condemn either the government or the employer. Poverty was unfortunate, but it was as old as history, and for nearly two thousand years there had been the Church to deal with it. The government publicly stated its view that the worker was responsible for the wages he voluntarily accepted and for the conditions under which he agreed to work. The government not only did not wish to intervene but said that it had no right to. But the results were unfortunate, for

---

[28] Georges Boussinesq, *Reims à la fin de la monarchie de juillet et pendant la période révolutionnaire de 1848* (Angers: Société Française d'Imprimerie et de Publicité, 1923), 2.

the working class came to believe that the inactivity of the government was due to official hostility toward them. They saw that the government, in almost every case, supported their employers; and the bigger and richer the employing company, the stronger was that official support. Why, then, should they regard it as their government?

The laws and institutions intended to restrain the workers were numerous and, in most cases, were effective for some time; but in the end they contributed powerfully to strengthen in the mind of the working class the conviction of official hostility. There was no Ministry of Labor. Some questions concerning workers might be handled by the new Ministry of Commerce, but usually the body with jurisdiction was the Ministry of the Interior, which operated through the prefects and the police.

Among the institutions designed to control the workers, the one that has received most attention is the *livret*, a book in which the employer inscribed the record of service and the debts of the worker. According to the Law of 22 Germinal of the Year XI,[29] every worker must have one and show it to a new employer. Through it an employer could force a worker to accept wages or conditions of work against his will. He could also persuade him to borrow on the security of his future wages, in the knowledge that he could not leave without the employer's consent until the old debt had been paid or a new employer had agreed to assume it. The opponents of the *livret* described it as the instrument of industrial slavery; its supporters as the pride of every honest workman. Yet the *livret* has received far more attention than it deserved. As mills increased in size and the relationship of the worker to his employer became largely impersonal, the *livret* lost much of its importance. It should also be realized that, although the law required every workman to have a *livret*, it provided no penalty for his not having one. It was generally disliked. Many workers refused to acquire *livrets* and

---

[29] Honoré Antoine Frégier, *Des classes dangereuses de la population*, v. 1 (Paris, 1840), 18. Claude Anthelme, baron Costaz, *Mémoire sur les moyens qui ont amené le grand développement que l'industrie a pris depuis vingt ans* (Paris, 1816), 14.

when, in 1831, the prefect of police at Paris ordered the prosecution of workers without *livrets,* the courts refused.[30] Finally, in 1840, the investigations of Agricole Perdiguier showed that most holders of *livrets* were petty bourgeois or officials, domestic servants, and skilled workers with high wages.[31] It is clear, therefore, that the *livret* was not for long an effective instrument for the control of the mass of industrial workers.

Another institution that has received much attention was the Conseil des Prud'hommes, which originated at Lyons under the First Empire through the reconstruction of an old industrial court run by the guilds. It was a court of conciliation dealing with disputes between employers and workers where no large sum of money was involved. It dispensed with legal formalities. It operated successfully at Lyons because the workers there were, for some years, rather adequately represented by their foremen. But its efficiency depended upon the proper representation of the workers, who were supposed to have about half the judges. In most French cities where it was set up, the Conseil des Prud'hommes was somewhat ineffective. It proved impossible to find, or to induce to serve, men who had the interests of the workers at heart and who were at the same time acceptable to employers and government officials. Even at Lyons this court ceased to be really useful after the interests of the foremen and the workmen under them began to conflict following the revolt of 1831. The failure of the Conseil des Prud'hommes was due to the most fundamental defect in the whole of the official machinery for dealing with labor: labor was not properly represented, because it was not considered competent to deal with its own interests; nor was it felt that labor could be relied upon, if given even a little power, to show respect and obedience to its betters. No attempt was made to revise this court, or any other institution, to give better representation to the workers; no new institutions were created by the government, nor was anyone else allowed to create any.

France forbade all combination, as did England, whether by

---

[30] Frégier, *op. cit.,* 19.
[31] Martin, *op. cit.,* 344.

employers or workers and, as in England, provided heavier penalties for violations by employees than by employers. As in England, employers were never prosecuted and workers were. But the French legal system was more rigid than the English because it was embodied in the Civil and Criminal Codes of Napoleon, which could not be modified by judicial decisions. In addition, France had the Law of Le Chapelier of 1791 forbidding associations of more than twenty persons without authorization by the government. This, like the prohibition of combinations, was put into the Penal Code. The effect of these laws, administered by a bourgeois government indifferent to the welfare of the workers and suspicious of any action by them, was to make anything like the English trade-union movement impossible in France.

As economic difficulties increased with the progress of the Industrial Revolution, the workers necessarily became more active. Since they could not organize legally to defend their interests as employees, they developed mutual-aid societies, or, as they were called in England, friendly societies, to insure workers against sickness or old age. As pressure grew in centers like Lyons, these apparently innocent societies, organized in groups of less than twenty to comply with the law, came to be called *sociétés de résistance*. The leaders of the groups kept in touch with each other, and a large organization really interested in raising wages and improving working conditions was actually created in Lyons, although it had no formal or legal existence as a unit. When it was found, before the end of the crisis of 1826–32, that the new July Monarchy had not abolished any of the restraints on the workers and that it was even more the government of the employers than the Restoration had been, the stage was set for serious trouble. Thus, the labor movement in Lyons, as we shall see, came to be largely republican in 1834 and, to a considerable extent, socialistic in 1848. This was not so much from faith in any new form of government or social organization as from the realization that the monarchy of Louis Philippe was not the government of the French nation but of the employing bourgeoisie.

LABOR RELATIONS

It is doubtful if the development of economic thought in France between 1815 and 1848 had any appreciable influence on the labor movement. The rigid views of the classical school of Ricardo in England did not suit the French, who are emotional as well as logical. The thinkers whom we could call "Christian economists," like Villeneuve-Bargemont, or Utopians, like Sismondi or Louis Blanc, were more to French liking, provided they mixed with their idealism a strong dose of practicality. We must, therefore, combine these prominent French traits of romantic emotionalism on the one hand with logicality and shrewdness in daily life on the other. In this way we can reconcile the statement of Blanqui that in 1848 the textile centers of France were full of all sorts of different varieties of socialism which agreed only in their common hatred of existing society,[32] with the statement of Sée that no real socialist movement developed among the workers of France before 1848.[33] Sée states that neither Saint-Simonism nor Fourierism really appealed to them and that they understood few of the preachings and doctrines that were addressed to them under the July Monarchy.[34] At the same time he made the interesting observation that the beginnings of organization among the workers were not caused by industrial concentration, but by ideology. Sée's observations seem to the writer fundamentally true. The French workers sought and found their ideology, but they kept their feet on the ground. They might talk about a new society that could be created only by the destruction of the old, but they did not deliberately organize destruction.

If the development of economic thought had only a slight effect on the workers of France, it did influence some of the bourgeoisie. Sismondi showed as early as 1819 that crises from overproduction were causing great suffering among French workers and that one

---

[32] Jérôme Adolphe Blanqui, "Des classes ouvrières en France pendant l'année 1848," in *Petits traités publiés par l'académie royale des sciences morales et politiques,* v. 1 (Paris, 1849), 21.

[33] Sée, "Quelques aperçus," 518.

[34] *Ibid.*

of the causes of overproduction was the introduction of machinery. He believed that hours should be shortened and that employers should support their workers in sickness, unemployment, and old age. He may have been an aristocrat, a dilettante, and a Utopian who failed to think his problems through and to propose a single remedy that was practical at the time. He was too keenly aware of existing evils to see that in many respects they were temporary. In particular he was unable to see any benefits coming from the introduction of machinery, or any possible expansion of markets that could mitigate the crises of overproduction without arresting the progress of industry. Yet Sismondi was the first to analyze realistically the hardships caused by the Industrial Revolution in France in terms that appealed to some of the more thoughtful of his adopted countrymen. He greatly influenced many men who played a prominent part as investigators, teachers, and even as legislators. Among those whom he thus influenced we can name de Villeneuve-Bargemont, Eugène Buret, Blanqui, and Louis Blanc, while Villermé himself must have been impressed.

The value of these followers of Sismondi, however, was more in the field of action than of thought. De Villeneuve-Bargemont recommended developing agricultural colonies as the best means of relieving the distress of industrial workers; it was akin to the desire of Sismondi to arrest the progress of industry, but de Villeneuve-Bargemont was a singularly acute observer and helped greatly to make his countrymen aware of the actual economic distress. Buret, similarly, helped less by his rather Utopian socialism than by his accuracy as an investigator of social and economic conditions. Blanqui also was not important as an original thinker. He was influenced both by Sismondi and by Jean-Baptiste Say, whom he succeeded at the Conservatoire des Arts et Métiers. He was useful as an opponent of the prohibitive tariff and as a teacher in showing the progress of industry and trade. He was useful also as a reliable observer and investigator who reached very sound conclusions, and as an outspoken advocate of better housing. Louis Blanc, distinctly mediocre as a socialist thinker, and an unavowed follower of Babeuf, had some direct influence on the industrial workers through his *Organisation du travail,* which was the first real attempt to propose a definite program of action.

Finally, Villermé, a physician and member of the Academy of Moral and Political Sciences, did more than anyone else to bring before the public the actual distress of industrial workers. His investigations of industrial conditions were by far the most thorough and intelligent, and when he made them he had been known for twenty years as a courageous advocate of prison reform. He also worked hard for the Child Labor Law of 1841 and the mitigation of the abuse of the *livret.*

But the main contribution of all these men, including Sismondi, was to arouse public interest in the condition of industrial laborers and in its improvement. They did not change the attitude of the government in any important respect, nor did they do much to stimulate the organization of a labor movement; but about 1840 they did put an end to the smug satisfaction of many bourgeois in the pleasant pursuit of their own enrichment.

This sudden awakening to the distress of industrial workers was reinforced immediately by an epidemic of strikes that began because of the depression that had been weighing upon French industry since 1837 and continued for several years. There had been a similar development, although on a smaller scale, during the depression of 1826–32.

Of these numerous industrial strikes, the most important for a study of labor in relation to the progress of the Industrial Revolution were those in the coal and silk industries. It is unfortunate that we have so little information about the causes of the strikes in the coal industry. We know that that industry was growing rapidly after 1832. There is reason to believe that important improvements in mechanical appliances, the use of steam, and the methods of mining were being made that must have affected laborers. We know that the miners at Anzin struck in 1833 against a series of reductions of wages made by the most powerful coal-mining company in France, which had great political influence. The Anzin company had long been well known for its high prices and low wages, yet it yielded to the miners in this case and granted an increase in wages. We could say, perhaps on economic grounds, that the miners won because they struck after the end of a long depression when rapid industrial recovery was under way. Yet three strikes by miners in the coal basin of the Loire against a far less powerful company, which came in 1840, 1844, and 1846, all failed. We might explain the failure of the first of these by the economic depression which was still serious; but the two others came in a period of marked prosperity. If the national government used its troops to stop the greatest of these strikes in 1844, as it had used them to crush the revolt at Lyons in 1834, why did it allow the miners to win at Anzin in 1833? There is room for much investigation of labor in coal-mining in France if evidence can be found and the records of the Anzin company opened to inspection.

The revolt of the silk weavers at Lyons in November, 1831, is the one strike upon which we have a fairly adequate body of evidence. This enables us to state the main facts; it is possible also to name their causes and to show the relationship of both facts and causes to the progress of the Industrial Revolution as it affected French labor. While our various accounts are written from different points of view and sometimes contradict each other, it is possible to form a fairly accurate picture of what happened and why.

First we must consider the position of the manufacturers of silks at Lyons. Under the Restoration they had enjoyed such prosperity as they had not had since 1789. In the main it was a period of expansion for the silk industry and for the approximately 750 manufacturers[35] who directed it at Lyons. They were merchants and members of the bourgeoisie that controlled the government of the city as well as its trade. Their power was great, but their economic position was far from impregnable. Although the demand for silks was increasing greatly, on the whole, it was variable. Silks were expensive and fashions changed frequently. The merchants were handicapped by inadequate production of raw silk in France. They had to import considerable quantities, chiefly from Italy, upon which they had to pay duty, whereas foreign silks could enter France

[35] Ernest Pariset, *Histoire de la fabrique lyonnaise depuis le XVIe siècle* (Lyon: Rey, 1901), 277–78.

freely. They were faced with competition, such as they had seldom known before, from expanding industries in England, Rhenish Prussia, and Switzerland. They were also competing keenly with each other. Finally, they were faced with the competition of fine woolens and cottons and of woolens mixed with silk, all of which were cheaper than pure silks. Under these conditions they naturally took the opportunity which their economic and political power gave them to cut wages, increase hours when possible, and place the costs and risks of technical improvements upon the shoulders of their workmen. Under similar conditions manufacturers in every industrial country, including our own, have followed a similar policy.

The weavers on their side had only the power of their skill and numbers. They flocked into Lyons because of the rising demand for their services from 1819 to 1826 and ignored the warning afforded by the manufacturers' increasing use of cheap rural laborers. They worked in the homes of the foremen, each of whom usually owned from two to eight looms and gave out silk yarn and patterns ordered by the clerks of several different manufacturers. These foremen had had to buy their looms, for which they had frequently remained permanently in debt to the manufacturers. They also had to pay for the changing of all patterns. When business was good they prospered and ate and drank well, but they ran grave risks, had few or no personal contacts with their employers and no effective means of meeting adversity or injustice. They have been reproached for not saving in times of prosperity, but we cannot be sure that they had the means to do so to any appreciable extent. We have said that many of them were in debt to their employers for the original purchase of their looms. In addition, manufacturers were trying to introduce new and better looms, which foremen frequently could not buy because the whole of their capital was frozen in the old looms which were losing all their value. There were probably about 9,000 of these foremen and 27,000 to 30,000 helpers or *compagnons*,[36] some of whom were the wives and daughters of foremen.

The depression in the silk industry at Lyons seems to have reached its lowest depths soon after the Revolution of July, 1830.

---

[36] *Ibid.*

In the normal course of events, judging by the experience of other industries, recovery would have begun in 1832. But the government of Lyons, probably having lost a considerable amount of revenue through the depression, changed the method of assessment and collection of the personal-property tax and the taxes on furniture and on doors and windows, so that the burden of taxation upon the workers was increased about threefold. There is only one specific clue given by contemporary authorities as to why this very serious increase in taxes was made. The central jury of the Exposition of 1834 stated that the municipal government of Lyons had to have a great increase in revenue because it had embarked upon an extensive program of public works.[37] This may have been the case, but it is well to remember that such a jury was composed largely of manufacturers. We can presume that it was trying to explain the uprisings of both 1831 and 1834 in a way that would reflect credit on the bourgeoisie of Lyons. Whether this explanation be true or not, it seems certain that the increase in taxation occurred and was a very heavy burden on the working class of Lyons but a comparatively light one on the bourgeoisie.

In the meantime, the foremen among the silk weavers of Lyons had increased their mutual-aid societies until they had a membership of about 3,000, representing one third of the licensed foremen; their helpers had organized a somewhat similar group as *ferrandiniers* to the number of 15,000, or nearly half of the *compagnons*.[38] Both groups of societies hoped to keep wages fixed through pressure on both the manufacturers and the government. A committee of twenty-two manufacturers and twenty-two foremen met and with the approval of the prefect, Bouvier-Dumolard, drew up a scale of wages.[39] At this point we have again to choose between somewhat conflicting accounts. It seems probable that a part of the manufacturers refused to be bound by a fixed scale of wages at a time when the production of silks varied so greatly that they could not

[37] Achille de Colmont, *Histoire des expositions des produits de l'industrie française* (Paris, 1855), 194–95.
[38] Blanqui, *op. cit.*, 145.
[39] Isambert, *op. cit.*, 374.

tell whether to expect profits or losses in the near future. The weavers were divided as to their future course, some being satisfied with the apparent redress of one of the worst of their grievances, and some feeling that they were strong enough to seek still further advantages. The prefect, representing a thoroughly bourgeois government, took advantage of the vehement disapproval of many of the manufacturers and of the division of opinion among the weavers to withdraw his approval of the wage agreement. He did so either on his own responsibility or, as seems more probable, upon orders from the Minister of the Interior. In consequence, the weavers, bitterly resentful of the bad faith shown by both the government and the manufacturers, revolted.

This rather long explanation of the revolt of 1831 at Lyons has been made because it shows, first, the economic factors resulting from the development of the Industrial Revolution; second, the complete lack of wholesome relations between employers and employees; and, third, a government representing the employers only. These three factors were more important than the development of a republican or socialistic ideology, or than any labor movement in Lyons. It is clear also that the workers were almost bound to fail, because in trying to fix wages they were appealing to the dead past and repudiating the living present. English workers had done this when, early in the nineteenth century, they had appealed to the magistrates to enforce the Statute of Apprentices of 1563.

SUMMARY

Our survey of the industrial workers of France between 1815 and 1848 has shown that the number of workers in large-scale industries was very small in relation to the population as a whole and was only about a quarter of all the industrial workers. Because of this and of the power and vitality of the domestic system in France, industrial laborers in large-scale industries had little influence and no power. Their weakness was intensified by the close connection which we have noted between many industrial workers and agriculture. It took a long time for French factory workers to become a separate class and still longer for them to become conscious of their existence as a group. In view of these facts, it is not surprising that the bourgeoisie paid little attention to workers and continued to regard them as animated tools to be taken up or cast down according to the dictates of profit and loss. Even the earlier reformers sought not to mitigate through control or guidance the evils produced by the Industrial Revolution but to induce the factory workers to return to the land. It was not until about 1840 that they began to look forward instead of backward.

Since the factory system remained rather weak throughout the period and the domestic system rather strong, the labor movement scarcely grew beyond childish beginnings. The most powerful organization, *compagnonnage,* like the domestic system and the earlier reformers, looked backward. It was dying despite the attempted reforms of Agricole Perdiguier. It was strongest in the older professional occupations, such as those of the bakers, millers, and carpenters, and in the building industry. It is in these and similar occupations also that we find the first indications of leadership of the working class by its own members. Such leaders were printers, tailors, or carpenters, not spinners, weavers, or miners. The labor movement, then, remained in its infancy until 1848, primarily because France had made slow progress in industrialization. We have described the various legal and administrative restraints imposed upon industrial laborers in France. They were important, but they were less important than incomplete industrialization. We can see clearly that even if they had not existed, the time would not have been ripe for a really strong labor movement among the workers in large-scale industries.

Economic theory has received little attention in this chapter because it had little influence upon the bourgeoisie up to 1840 and scarcely any upon the workers in large-scale industries. It would require more attention if the period for our survey were longer, or more recent than 1848. Many economists in France had very interesting ideas. The Utopian socialists, in particular, such as Saint-Simon and Fourier, and even the bitterly destructive but brilliant

Proudhon, have an appeal for any scholar who knows and loves the France of a hundred years ago. Yet it is clear that little was accomplished by such theories in guiding or strengthening the labor movement until after 1848. It can be argued also that we have overemphasized such factors in studying French labor because the evidence upon them was abundant and available. In the same way economic historians have overemphasized the tariff because information was accessible. We should turn our faces forward now and seek to use sources of evidence that have been less available, or that have escaped our attention. Among these none seems more important for a study of the industrial workers of France than a series of careful investigations of the business cycle: of that series of booms and depressions that created distress among laborers then as now. They were less significant in France in the earlier nineteenth century than in contemporary England, yet their study does give us a new insight into the problems of French labor.

CHAPTER NINE

Capital

A STUDY OF the Industrial Revolution in France is necessarily closely concerned with the financial resources of the country and their utilization. Yet there is far too little information from which to paint a clear picture, and the greater part of what evidence is available is either of doubtful value or presented with prejudice. We have good accounts now of the financial policy of the national government[1] and of the official actions of the Bank of France,[2] but neither of these illuminate directly or clearly the problems of greatest interest to the economic historian. Was there enough capital to finance the growth and transformation of French industry in the period between 1815 and 1848? Was it readily available to entrepreneurs who needed it, and at reasonable rates? Many contradictory answers have been given to both questions, but it is possible to remove some of the doubts and refute some of the criticisms.[3]

We find first that the majority of writers, and especially those of French nationality, think that there was not enough capital in France for the reasonable expansion and transformation of industry, but the number of such writers and the intensity of their con-

---

[1] Marcel Marion, *Histoire financière de la France depuis 1715,* v. 5–6 (Paris: Rousseau, 1914–31).

[2] Gabriel Ramon, *Histoire de la Banque de France, d'après les sources originales* (Paris: Grasset, 1929).

[3] This chapter has been enriched by co-operation for several months in 1947–48 with Dr. Fritz Redlich, whose knowledge of French finance, and especially of banking during and after the Revolution, is exceedingly valuable. It owes much to Dr. Redlich's knowledge and relentless search for elusive facts. Much of this has been published in his article "Jacques Laffitte and the Beginnings of Investment Banking in France," *Bulletin of the Business Historical Society,* v. 22 (Boston, Dec., 1948), 137–61.

viction is much greater in periods of depression than in those of prosperity. Very few French writers, and not many foreign ones, have considered the supply of French capital in connection with the temporary degree of business activity, because economic and financial crises in France between 1815 and 1857 have received comparatively little attention. In reply to the second question, it could probably be said that in the majority of cases capital for entrepreneurs was not readily available, although much depended upon the place and the source from which they sought it, as well as upon their purpose. With regard to its cost, we should find some variation corresponding to the degree of business activity, but a great deal more due to the location of the place where the funds were sought.

Henri Sée, with his usual clarity of vision, has supplied us with a very valuable comment on the financial situation in France in the period between 1815 and 1848. He says that the marked increase in the centralization of government in France accomplished by the Revolution was accompanied by an accentuation of the previous decentralization of most economic activities.[4] In short, the great increase in efficiency of administration was felt chiefly in Paris, where, for the most part, it occurred; but as the means of communication and of transportation were not improved greatly, many parts of France remained isolated both from Paris and from each other, or found communication little easier than before the Revolution. Two illustrations will suffice to emphasize the importance of Sée's observation: first, in the crisis of 1846–47 grain imported from Russia to relieve the threatened famine in France was distributed with considerable difficulty and at comparatively high cost;[5] secondly, the notes issued by the Bank of France increasingly after 1815 were not fully utilized in circulation until 1845.[6] Both of these facts indicate that even at the close of our period France was neither economically nor financially well knit together.

---

[4] Henri Sée, *Französische Wirtschaftsgeschichte*, v. 2 (Jena: Brodnitz, 1936), 208.

[5] Marion, *op. cit.*, v. 5, p. 226.

[6] Ramon, *op. cit.*, 202.

When we consider the financial markets of France we become aware immediately of the overwhelming importance of Paris. It will be necessary to speak chiefly of that market in this chapter, but we must remember that there were some others, such as Lyons, with important international connections, and many more provincial markets without such connections and lacking adequate relations both with Paris and with each other. The development of the financial market of Paris was not necessarily, therefore, representative of the whole of France, nor was the rest of the country quite as dependent upon it as might be supposed.

A good illustration of the situation is afforded by the opening of the Bank of Bordeaux in 1819 and its activities until it became a branch of the Bank of France in 1848. Bordeaux was then a seaport trading chiefly with the remaining French colonies and with the countries of Latin America and possessing a small but important wine industry. It had few other industries and had suffered the loss of much shipping and many markets during the revolutionary wars. Its bank was founded by a small group of promoters, led by Balguerie-Stuttenberg, who had some knowledge of English business methods and who acted under pressure from the government in Paris.[7] It was opposed, by a majority of the leading businessmen of the city organized in the Chamber of Commerce, as likely to encourage speculation. It succeeded because of sound and conservative management and because it was able to get from near-by departments, through the Receivers-General, funds with which to finance the annual wine harvest. Its history shows both dependence upon Paris and the difficulty and high cost of financial operations which that dependence imposed. It shows that local supplies of capital were more considerable than had been supposed and were obtainable at a more reasonable and regular price, but that they were not sufficient to create a provincial market that could have promoted notable developments in industry or public works.

---

[7] Pierre de Joinville, *Le Réveil économique de Bordeaux sous la Restauration: L'Armateur Balguerie-Stuttenberg et son œuvre* (Paris: Champion, 1914). This book is the best source on the foundation of the Bank of Bordeaux.

Paris itself was a financial market of limited size but of real importance in 1815. The Bank of France was young and had dealt only with the abnormal conditions of war under a domineering emperor who was not interested in developing a system of public credit. The government was weak and faced with the pressing problems of raising revenue without the assurance of national support and of paying indemnities, individual claims, and the costs of the army of occupation. Banking in the capital was no longer dominated by the Swiss, who were usually the descendants of former French Huguenots. To the members of this group who had survived the Revolution, the Mallets, Delesserts, and Hottinguers, we should add Enfantin, the teacher of the well-known Saint-Simonians Sanlot and Bagenault, and François Seillère, who now turned from trade to banking, which was true also of the Hottinguers; and, last, but far from least, the old bank of Perrégaux was now under the vigorous leadership of the French Catholic Laffitte. Jewish bankers were not yet playing an important part. Influential also were the financial advisers of the government, Baron Louis, Count Roy, Corvetto, and Jacques Laffitte himself.[8]

The small size of the money market of Paris is made clear to us in various ways. The Law of 1816 creating the Bourse specified that it was to consist permanently of sixty brokers, all of whom, and their successors, must be approved by the government.[9] We know that they listed few securities other than the *rentes* of the French government for several years and that the volume of trading for some time was very small, so that the government itself was troubled, because it wanted a larger market for the negotiation of its *rentes*. But the number of holders of *rentes* remained small for several years. Finally, in 1819, Corvetto, as Minister of Finance, gave permission for the sale and transfer of *rentes* in the provinces and for the payment of interest there.[10] this proved very fruitful, because the formalities of purchase and transfer, with the commissions involved,

---

[8] Redlich, *op. cit.,* 138.

[9] Alphonse Courtois, *Opérations de bourse,* 3d ed. (Paris, 1859), 103. The reference is to the Law of 28 May, 1816.

[10] Gonsalve, baron de Nervo, *Etudes historiques: Les Finances françaises sous la Restauration,* v. 1 (Paris, 1865), 845.

had made the purchase of *rentes* by people of moderate means, or by anyone far from Paris, amazingly difficult. Savings banks did not accomplish nearly as much as their benevolent founders had hoped —first, because they spread very slowly, and, secondly, because they helped only skilled laborers and the bourgeoisie, since unskilled laborers received such low wages that they could not save.

Another step was probably even more important, because it made possible far more co-operation between the government and business. This was the organization in 1826 of the Syndicate of Receivers-General of Taxes by one of the bolder and abler Receivers, Bricogne. These Receivers had existed as individual officials since the fourteenth century, when they collected the produce of the king's lands. Under the Consulate they were used to assemble funds collected by various financial agencies of the government. They were tax officials, not contractors, yet their position was ambiguous, since as individuals they acted as entrepreneurs and almost as investment bankers. Each had to subscribe as a monthly obligation half of the tax roll of his department and was charged for this four months later, but, in the meantime, he could use the funds as he pleased. Mollien, in 1806, modified this obligation, directing each Receiver-General to pay all surplus funds into the Treasury as interest-bearing advances, but he was encouraged to raise funds on his own credit and received interest on them. Villèle, finding that the government was paying the Receivers approximately 30,000,000 francs a year as interest at 4 per cent on their advances, got them in 1826 to form a voluntary syndicate as a company under the Code of Commerce to provide capital to sustain the *rentes* on the Bourse and to support public stocks in general. The company's original capital of 30,000,000 francs appears to have been increased later. This organization as a company greatly increased the activity of the Receivers-General as entrepreneurs, as has been seen most clearly in the promotion of railroads described in Chapter IV.[11]

Jacques Laffitte (1767–1844), who was probably the most useful of all the big Parisian bankers to the entrepreneurs of France, was the son of a carpenter in Bordeaux; but he entered the bank of

---

[11] Redlich, *op. cit.*, 149–50.

Perrégaux, a Parisian banker of Swiss origin and one of the principal founders of the Bank of France. Thus, he joined the circle of conservative and wealthy bankers of the capital, but he was also sensitive about his birth, very vain, and keenly interested in politics. It was he who interested French private enterprise in the business possibilities resulting from the foundation of modern public credit in France. In the beginning his success was due to his ability to lure money out of hoards, which he then lent to industry, charging a high risk premium. In 1815 he received several millions from Napoleon, and he handled the fortunes of several of the imperial officials; yet he also dealt freely with the Bourbons on their return and was governor of the Bank of France from 1814 to 1820—that is, during the more liberal part of the reign of Louis XVIII. He saw clearly that the restoration of French public credit would depend on the favorable attitude of foreign investors and speculators. He realized the importance of lowering the rate of interest in France as a whole and openly supported Villèle in his attempt to convert the 5 per cent *rentes* in 1824. He was much interested in financing the development of industry and in the last years of his life did notable work and took great risks in that field.[12]

The nucleus of the *haute-banque* in Paris, a group referred to by nearly all writers on the financial history of the earlier nineteenth century, was formed by Laffitte, Bagenault, Greffulhe, of whom we shall hear more later in connection with his partner, the engineer Urbain Sartoris, and Hottinguer, a Swiss Protestant who now turned from commerce to banking. These men in 1817 helped the Barings and Hopes float a loan for the French government. Later in that year they were joined by the Delessert brothers, sons of the Calvinist Etienne Delessert (1735–1816). Benjamin, the

---

[12] The chief sources on Laffitte other than Marion, Ramon, and Redlich are Jean Baptiste Capefigue, *Histoire des grandes opérations financières,* v. 3 (Paris, 1858), 21, 51, 136–38, 164, 170, and 221; Marthe Camille Bachesson, comte de Montalivet, "Le Roi Louis-Philippe et sa liste civile," *Revue des deux mondes,* Nouvelle période, v. 8 (Oct., 1850), 112–45; Paul Duchon, "Les Mémoires de Jacques Laffitte," *Revue des deux mondes,* Septième période, v. 8 (July 15, 1930), 289–92; and André Liesse, *Portraits des financiers* (Paris: Alcan, 1908), 247.

elder (1773–1847) had been educated in Scotland and knew English industrial methods. He had great influence on the economic development of France through promoting the refining of beet sugar, the spinning of cotton, and the foundation of savings banks. He was also for many years a regent of the Bank of France, in which post he was succeeded by his brother François (1780–1868). In 1818 broke into the circle of the *haute-banque* James de Rothschild, who had come to Paris the year before and was the youngest of the famous brothers from Frankfort and a member of the well-known firm of bankers headed by his brother Nathan in London. He soon became the chief floater of government loans in France. He became also the principal financier of French railroads, as we have seen in studying transportation, but much earlier he was somewhat interested in canals and in various industrial undertakings. Yet he was always a financier rather than a merchant or a manufacturer. While probably the ablest financier in France, he was not a pioneer in developing either transportation or manufacturing on a large scale. More useful than he in the industrial field were the Périers: Jacques Constantin Périer (1742–1818), an industrialist, deviser of atmospheric engines, and builder of the foundry at Chaillot, and Scipio Périer (1776–1821), and his better-known brother, the liberal politician Casimir, who died in 1832 as prime minister of Louis Philippe. They founded a bank in 1801 in which Casmir was the leader, while Scipio was more interested in the development of manufacturing and the promotion of public utilities. Finally, we should add to the group of financial leaders in 1818 the Jewish bankers d'Fichthal, Cahen d'Anvers, and Fould.[13]

We turn now to a forgotten class of financiers, few of whose names are yet known and many of whom cannot be defined clearly in terms of their occupations. In many cases they were private bankers, in others capitalists—that is, according to the French terminology of the earlier nineteenth century, investors or holders of funds who were not technically bankers. In most cases they were really entrepreneurs or promoters. The majority of them seem to

---

[13] Redlich, *op. cit.*, 144–45, 148. John Reeves, *The Rothschilds* (London, 1887), 342.

220   THE INDUSTRIAL REVOLUTION IN FRANCE

have accumulated their capital in the troublous times of revolution
and war, some as army contractors, others as smugglers, and some
as both. Others made money through more legitimate commercial
operations, combined, perhaps, with sensible marriages. In most of
these respects they differed from the great majority of the regular
bankers.

Among the most successful promoters was Balguerie-Stuttenberg
of Bordeaux,[14] the first part of whose name was made famous by a
combination of trade and manufacturing, while the second half was
acquired by marrying the daughter of his employer. He learned
about English banking methods on frequent business trips and was
the principal founder of the Bank of Bordeaux in 1818. He also did
much to develop the port of Bordeaux and successfully organized
several companies to build bridges in southern France. His methods
impressed the government of the Restoration and are believed to
have influenced its decision to obtain from private sources the funds
for building a whole network of canals in 1821–22. The principal
figure in the canal loans was Urbain Sartoris, an able and excep-
tionally well-informed engineer who promoted many waterways. His
chief partner was Greffulhe,[15] a private banker in Paris who specialized in investments in urban real estate and mortgages. He was
also prominent in society in the capital, and was a close personal
friend of the royal family and of several prominent politicians as
well as financiers.

Another group of promoters was composed of three Alsatians:
Georges Humann,[16] Saglio, and Raynouard de Bussière. Of these,
Humann was the best known, because he became a specialist in
finance in the Chamber of Deputies and was twice Minister of
Finance under the July Monarchy. His fortune was begun in his
boyhood in Strasbourg through profits from the Napoleonic inva-

[14] Joinville, op. cit., 184.
[15] Ibid. Also Nervo, op. cit., v. 1, p. 500; v. 2, p. 195; Courtois, op. cit.,
321; Jacques Bresson, Histoire financière de la France, 1st ed., v. 2 (Paris,
1829), 349, 402; [Urbain Sartoris] Notes sur les canaux adjugés en 1822
(Paris, 1832); and Capefigue, op. cit., v. 3, pp. 73, 84.
[16] Félix Ponteil, "L'Alsacien Jean-Georges Humann," Revue d'histoire
moderne, v. 12 (1937), 227–45.

sions of Germany and the emperor's efforts to make the continent
a market for French goods while excluding the English by a rigor-
ous blockade. Humann in 1826 became one of the principal partners
of the Duc Decazes in founding the metallurgical establishment of
Decazeville in the south, one of the few big enterprises of that sort
under the Restoration, and one which followed the unusual procedure of reinvesting all profits in the business for no less than
fifteen years. Humann, with his two Alsatian friends, was interested
in several waterways, such as the canal from the Rhône to the
Rhine, in the enterprises of Urbain Sartoris in 1821, and in other
metallurgical establishments; he was also one of the organizers of a
company formed in 1838 to build a railroad from Paris to Rouen
across the plateaux instead of by the valley of the Seine.

Among the promoters we should mention also Seillère, a member
of the Haute Banque who made a fortune as an army contractor
during the revolutionary and Napoleonic wars and then, apparently,
became a private banker both in Lyons and in Paris. It was he,
together with the heirs of the metallurgist Louis Boigues, who
financed the purchase of Le Creusot by the Schneider brothers in
1836.[17] This was an event of great importance, because there had
been several bankruptcies in rapid succession that had hampered
the growth of this establishment, which under the Schneiders soon
became the most important in the iron industry of France.

Finally, there should be named Count Roy, who was Minister
of Finance for several years in the reign of Louis XVIII. In that
capacity his actions have been recorded by Professor Marion and
need no further mention here. But Roy was clearly important as a
capitalist, in the French sense, for he was a great owner of real
estate, especially forests, and he is said also to have held more than
1,000,000 francs of *rentes*.[18] He typifies the period of the Restoration, whose leaders were so often great landowners and whose companies were frequently launched by a small number of aristocrats,
each of whom held shares of very large denominations, such as
10,000 francs. It seems probable that Roy bought some of the forests

---

[17] Capefigue, *op. cit.,* v. 4, p. 161.
[18] Nervo, *op. cit.,* v. 2, p. xv.

222   THE INDUSTRIAL REVOLUTION IN FRANCE

that belonged to the nation in the period when the government was willing to sell almost anything to obtain cash; and it would be interesting to know where he obtained the cash to do this. He made large profits because the price of wood rose with the increasing demand for fuel from the growing iron industry. Finally, Roy appears as one of the shareholders in the Rouen railroad company of 1838, in which Humann also was prominent and whose leaders were described by Séguin as wealthy capitalists who knew nothing about railroads.[19]

We may now pause to survey the financial scene in 1830 in an effort to see what was accomplished under the Restoration and how and why it was done or left undone. Many writers criticize the Bank of France for refusing, or neglecting, to perform its greatest function of leading in the economic development of France. They have accused the bank on the ground that its monopoly of note issue not bearing interest and its close connection with the government gave it the necessary power and that it refused or failed to use it. They have said that it chose instead to make large profits for its directors, who were usually members of the *haute-banque* of Paris.[20] It is true that, on the whole, the Bank of France did not take the initiative in promoting the economic development of the country. It is also true that the country needed badly a more abun-

[19] Ternaux stands out in opposition to Roy as a self-made man and manufacturer interested chiefly in the woolen industry—a genius in promotion and organization. As such, he looked forward to the new age of large-scale industry and failed, under the July Monarchy, because of too many frozen assets.

[20] Charles Coquelin, "Les Crises commerciales et la liberté des banques," *Revue des deux mondes,* Nouvelle série, v. 24 (1848), 445–70. Léon Cahen, "L'Enrichissement de la France sous la Restauration," *Revue d'histoire moderne,* Nouvelle série, v. 5 (1930), 197. Emile Bères, *Causes du malaise industriel de la France et moyens d'y remédier* (Paris, 1832), 51. Michel Chevalier, *Lettres sur l'Amérique du nord* (Paris, 1836), v. 1, p. 374; v. 2, p. 484. Ferdinand, comte d'Esterno, *Des banques départementales en France* (Paris, 1838), 26. Jean Gustave Courcelle-Seneuil, *Le Crédit et la banque* (Paris, 1840), 62, 65–66. Paul Coq, *Le Sol et la haute-banque* (Paris, 1850), 137–38. Capefigue, *op. cit.,* v. 3, p. 228. Gustave Du Puynode, *De la monnaie, du crédit et de l'impôt,* 2d ed., v. 1 (Paris, 1863), 326, 328–29. Edmond Teisserenc de Bort, *Les Travaux publics en Belgique et les chemins de fer en France* (Paris, 1839), 163.

dant supply of credit. The error in the reasoning of the bank's accusers lies in their statement that the bank should have taken the initiative in leading economic expansion. Its chief duty was to inspire confidence through sound and conservative finance and, next to that, to maintain adequate reserves for its note issue, and, thirdly, to support the government whenever possible. The bank rate was very rigidly maintained, usually at 4 per cent, and occasionally at 5, as in the crisis of 1817–18. This may have been too rigid, but it was not unreasonably high at that time. The bank may have kept reserves that were unnecessarily large, and it certainly did not expand its note issue rapidly.

It has been stated that 1845 was the first year in which all the notes issued by the Bank of France were put into circulation.[21] We have testimony that under the Restoration its notes circulated freely only in the vicinity of Paris and were received elsewhere at a discount.[22] The shortage of credit, which was real enough, was not due to the selfishness or inefficiency of the Bank of France; there were several other causes. In the first place, the French people were suspicious of banks even if many of their writers urged the government to charter more of them, and the larger the bank and the further from their homes, the greater was their suspicion. In most cases they insisted on metallic money or on notes issued in their native cities by banks whose circulation was limited strictly to the locality, and which often paid interest. On the other hand, we must remember that the French people, despite their fear of paper and their thrift, had a strong inclination toward speculation. This was shown again and again on the Bourse and the Curb at Paris, and in other cities, as well as in the popular love of horse races and lotteries. Thus, the rigid policy followed by the Bank of France was only partly caused by an excessive amount of red tape because of the bureaucrats in the government. Even more, it resulted from the

---

[21] Ramon, *op. cit.*, 202.

[22] Alexandre Léon Joseph, comte de Laborde, *De l'esprit d'association dans tous les intérêts de la communauté*, 2d ed., v. 1 (Paris, 1821), 155. Esterno, *op. cit.*, 139. Courcelle-Seneuil, *op. cit.*, 70. Du Puynode, *op. cit.*, v. 1, pp. 329, 347. For similar situation in Belgium see Ben Serge Chlepner, *Le Marché financier belge depuis cent ans* (Brussels: Capenhout, 1930).

contradictory wishes of the French people, who on the one hand were suspicious of banks they did not know personally and on the other were eager to speculate. We are justified in believing that, under these conditions, the rigid policy of the Bank of France did more to inspire confidence and cause the ultimate expansion of credit than would have been accomplished by a more liberal policy.

The period of the Restoration was really the one when the foundations for the future expansion of both industry and credit were laid. The government had first to produce honest budgets on time, and then to show that it intended to honor both its own debts and those of its predecessor. It had also to pay an indemnity and the cost of an army of occupation. All this was accomplished quickly and with skill. The government issued considerable quantities of bonds, or *rentes,* first in order to pay the victorious allies and then on a large scale as a convenient form of credit, which was thoroughly under governmental control and which met some of the needs that the small number of banks could not supply.[23]

By 1823 the 5 per cent *rentes* had reached par, and their sale and payments of interest had been so simplified that they were becoming a popular investment for the bourgeoisie all over France. The organization of the Syndicate of Receivers-General greatly facilitated this nationalization of the French *rentes* while affording also an organization that could promote important enterprises, such as public utilities, either in its corporate capacity or through its members as individuals. The Receivers were thus, in a sense, acting simultaneously as officers of the Treasury, as bankers, and as entrepreneurs. Thus the French people were taught to invest rather than to hoard, and to extend their investments from land to the bonds, first of their own government and then of other governments. It may well be that the numerous issues of *rentes* locked up too large a part of the nation's capital, but we cannot assume that this capital would otherwise have gone into commerce and manufacturing. Almost certainly it would have been hoarded or invested in the land in the form of mortgages.

[23] Ernest Frignet, *Histoire de l'association commerciale* (Paris, 1868), 340.

Factors delaying the accumulation of capital under the Restoration were the time required for recovery from the long period of war which, it should be remembered, had been civil as well as foreign; the continued prevalence of agriculture as the occupation of the great majority of the French people; the hindrance to the flow of foreign capital into France by the prohibitive tariff; and the fact that most investors who had funds that were not frozen in real estate sought to place them only in government securities or, in a few cases, in public utilities. The period needed for recovery was not really very long, but it has not received enough attention. It was prolonged by the unpopularity of the restored Bourbons and their unfortunate political views. It was lengthened also by the short crisis of 1817–18 and the longer depression of 1827–32, which was itself made unnecessarily long by the Revolution of 1830, an event desirable from the political point of view but unfortunate from the economic. The prevalence of agriculture meant that few people were interested in or informed about manufacturing and that what manufacturing there was, was usually on a small scale and frequently dependent upon rural labor. Mills were commonly handicapped in the summer because many of their workers returned to their farms, and they had also to permit many absences over week ends. It is true that this situation made it easier to pay low wages and thus diminished the amount of capital needed, but this advantage was neutralized by the greater turnover of labor and by the greater difficulty of training skilled workers and of keeping them after they had been trained.

While there are numerous instances of foreign investments in French metallurgical establishments, machine shops, and cotton mills, they were not usually large or of long duration. One reason for this was that costs in France were high and the market very limited, while the tariff frequently made it difficult to get raw materials. Finally, French investors were inclined to regard industry as unprofitable and risky. Also, as so many French writers complained, they were neither willing to co-operate nor accustomed to co-operation. They were afraid of companies and inclined to regard the "spirit of association" as an exotic importation from perfidious

Albion. They often said that the government interfered too much
with business and allowed too little scope for individual initiative.
They protested against the power of the Bank of France and the
accumulation of capital in Paris under governmental control
through collection of taxes and issuance of *rentes*. Yet they themselves contributed to the difficulties of which they complained by
their distrust of other banks and means of credit and by their widespread and continued purchase of *rentes*.

It is clear also that under the Restoration the financial market
grew slowly. The Paris Bourse came to deal extensively in *rentes*,
even if not as extensively as the government desired. Its volume of
business increased, as is shown by the rise in the value of a seat
upon it between 1816 and 1830 from 30,000 francs to 850,000
francs.[24] But few, if any, industrial shares were listed on the Bourse.
They had to be dealt in, if at all, on the Curb, whose brokers were
not legally recognized, so that the risk of doing business with them
was much greater than with those on the legitimate exchange. The
Bourse remained small and its customers few.

The transition from the Restoration to the July Monarchy was
slow and painful. Whatever the causes of the Revolution of 1830
may have been, the results were serious for business, which suffered
far more than the Treasury or the Bank of France. Business was
apparently caught in the midst of liquidation. The depression which
had begun in 1827 was, in consequence, prolonged for another two
years. Business was as frightened by the ease with which the dynasty
had been changed as were the Great Powers, and none of the fears
were stilled until it was clear that the policy of Louis Philippe
would be sane and peaceful liberalism. Distress in France was so
great that the Chambers voted a subsidy of 30,000,000 francs for
relief to businessmen.[25]

Another step to relieve the financial crisis was the founding of
the Comptoir d'Escompte of Paris to supply credit on somewhat

[24] Courtois, *op. cit.*, 103.

[25] Alphonse Courtois, "Histoire des institutions de crédit en France depuis
1790: La Banque de France, 1836–48," *Journal des économistes*, Série 3, v.
34 (1874), 58; reference is to the law of 17 October, 1830.

easier terms than those offered by the Bank of France. The chief sponsor of the new bank was the city of Paris, which guaranteed its obligations to the Bank of France to the extent of 4,000,000 francs, while the government gave it 1,300,000 francs from the subsidy voted by the Chambers. Unfortunately, the only other information we have about this bank is that its doors were closed in September, 1832, and its affairs liquidated gradually. As there was no fresh financial crisis in 1832, it is not yet possible to give the causes of this bank's failure.

Similar banks were founded in several provincial centers of industry.[26] They apparently received shares of the subsidy of 30,-000,000 francs, as had the Comptoir of Paris; but we know no more about them, not even the dates of their failures. It would seem probable, therefore, that they failed within a few months of their foundation or they would have received new strength from the general economic recovery that began in 1833.

Some years later, five other banks were organized in Paris. The most important of these, the Caisse Laffitte, and apparently its four competitors also, tried to help business by discounting many kinds of paper, issuing notes, and participating in other financial operations, such as floating government loans, organization of railroads, and formation of industrial concerns. Since the Bank of France, which appears to have regarded these banks with hostility, had a monopoly of the issue of notes payable to the bearer on sight, the Laffitte firm issued notes either for a few days or a month with interest, or for three months without interest. In this, apparently, it was successful and met a great need, for in the first year its note circulation reached 15,000,000 francs. The Caisse Béchet-Dethomas appears also to have achieved great success. Apparently, however, both erred in attempting too many kinds of banking simultaneously at a period when such widespread activities were too novel and when neither the Bank of France nor the government appreciated

---

[26] *Ibid.*, 58–60. Amiens, Cholet, Condé-sur-Noireau, Limoges, Nantes, Rethel, Reims, and Troyes. Most of these were important centers of one or more of the textile industries, while Limoges and Nantes were more important in other industries or in commerce.

228   THE INDUSTRIAL REVOLUTION IN FRANCE

the importance of the services they were attempting to render. They were probably rash also in allowing too many liquid assets to become frozen in long-term investments. In short, the attempt to provide more credit for business at more reasonable terms was made a little too soon. It failed also because of the crisis of 1846–47, from which no substantial recovery was possible before the unexpected outbreak of the Revolution of February 24, 1848.[27]

Under the July Monarchy there was a great increase in the volume of business done on the Bourse in Paris as well as a great increase in the amount of speculation. As usual, there is little evidence, but the tendency is quite clear. One proof of the increase in the volume of business is the decrease in the par value of the average share dealt in from 1,500 or 1,000 francs, or, in a few cases, 10,000 francs, to small denominations such as 100 francs.[28] This, and the fact that promoters of companies were beginning to advertise in the press, shows that the number of investors was increasing greatly. A further indication of the increasing volume of business done is the rise in the value of a seat from 850,000 francs to 950,000,[29] although the increase was much greater than this rise in price would imply.

In addition to the increase in the volume of business done on the Bourse of Paris, we should note also the listing of many new types of securities. At first, as we have seen, the Bourse had dealt almost wholly in *rentes;* then it had added foreign *rentes* and at about the same time various types of insurance and a very few public utilities, such as the Messageries Royales and one or two companies producing gas. After 1830 we find a great increase in public utilities such as bridges and canals and, later, railroads, although

---

[27] *Ibid.*, 203–5. Capefigue, *op. cit.*, v. 3, pp. 221–22. Eugen Kaufmann, *Das französische Bankwesen,* 2d ed. (Tübingen: J. C. B. Mohr, 1923), 9–10. André Liesse, *Portraits,* 289–94; *Evolution of Credit and Banks in France, From the Founding of the Bank of France to the Present Time* (Washington: Government Printing Office, 1909), 73–75.

[28] Capefigue, *op. cit.*, v. 4, pp. 123–24.

[29] Courtois, *Opérations,* 103; *Tableaux des cours des principales valeurs négociées et côtées aux bourses des effets publics de Paris, Lyon et Marseille,* 2d ed. (Paris, 1873). Capefigue, *op. cit.*, v. 4, p. 152.

this increase appears to have been made rather gradually. Simultaneously, we find in 1837 listed the securities of numerous asphalt mines, both French and foreign, of many of the smaller coal mines, and of several different types of manufacturing companies, such as candles, soap, and beet sugar—with two important metallurgical establishments, one linen mill, one woolen mill, and one or two producers of leather. In 1842 nearly all the canal companies were listed, the large coal mines, several more metallurgical establishments and linen mills, and a large number of gas companies; but the securities of most of the asphalt mines had disappeared. Finally, in 1847, there were further increases in coal-mining, metallurgical, and insurance companies, the listing of most French railroads, and the disappearance of most gas companies. This last item seems surprising as gas lighting obviously did not decrease. It suggests the probability of the amalgamation of numerous small companies into a few large ones, a process that was occurring at that time on a considerable scale in other industries.[30]

A third change that occurred after the July Revolution was a marked increase in speculation. In 1836 it started in coal mines, driving the values of the shares of some of them to three times the previous figure. While there was some increase in mining at that time and a considerable increase of investment in mines, the greater part of this increase in value was clearly speculative. Then, suddenly, speculation shifted to asphalt, a movement which affected other countries also, and with startling rapidity. In 1836 also the *jouissance* shares of several French canal companies were suddenly forced up to five times their previous value without any sound economic reasons. These were the shares that represented the future earnings of the canal companies when their construction should have been completed. While we know now that these earnings were never to be substantial, this was not clear then, and one of the

[30] Courtois, *Opérations*, 120–34. Jacques Bresson, *Des fonds publics français et étrangers et des opérations de la Bourse de Paris*, 8th ed., v. 2 (Paris, 1843), 18–106. Emile Bères, *Manuel de l'actionnaire* (Paris, 1839), 139–45.

factors that prevented their ever becoming important—the irresistible competition of the railroads—was not foreseen. This particular wave of speculation was probably launched, as Michel Chevalier says,[31] by some of the promoters in the field.[32] We know that in 1836 the government was trying to force through uniformity of rates on the French canals, and there was much talk in the press of the need of the government's buying back the *jouissance* shares of the canal companies. It was natural, therefore, for the promoters to force up the value of the shares; it is surprising only to note their lack of finesse. Had they been less greedy they might have succeeded. Finally, after several years of depression, there was a new wave of speculation from 1842 to 1847 in railroad shares, a movement of considerable magnitude and significance which made even more obvious the fact that the cautious and thrifty French bourgeoisie loved to gamble.

We should note in the reign of Louis Philippe the marked acceleration of the increase in the supply of both French and foreign capital for investment in industrial enterprises as well as public utilities. It is clear also that company organization was increasing. Promoters were being replaced by unincorporated companies, while the size and capitalization of the individual firm was increasing notably, whether through original organization upon a larger scale or through the amalgamation of several smaller and older companies. There are striking examples of both these tendencies in coal-mining, metallurgy, and the linen industry, as well as in railroads. This is interesting, because throughout the July Monarchy the government showed that it still disliked large companies with great financial power, especially in the field of public utilities.

The policy of the government towards public utilities, which in France were generally called "public works," requires separate consideration largely because of the very considerable volume of litera-

---

[31] Eugène Flachat and Jules Burat, "Des canaux exécutés par le gouvernement," *Journal de l'industriel et du capitaliste*, v. 1 (May, 1836), 272. Chevalier, *op. cit.*, 512.

[32] The most important of these promoters were Greffulhe and Sartoris, to whom we should probably add Humann.

ture it brought forth. As has been shown in the chapter on railroads, the comments on this policy were as variable as the policy itself, and rarely was there a sound and reasoned discussion of government versus private ownership or construction. Writers and orators were influenced by their opinion of the ministry in power at the moment, or by their relationship to that ministry or to one of the leading bankers, or, even more frequently, to the Ecole des Ponts et Chaussées.[33] But the views of commentators depended also upon the degree of prosperity of the country at the moment of writing. Thus, between 1838 and 1840, a period of depression, nearly everyone thought that railroads could not be built without substantial help from the government, and the government itself agreed. But after the enactment of the Law of 1842 a period of great prosperity began, as we have seen, and capital flowed out freely. Hence, during the next five years it seemed obvious to almost everyone that the greater part of the cost of railroad construction could and should be borne by private companies.

The first action, or expression of policy, by the government that deserves consideration is the Law of 1821, which authorized the government of the Restoration to borrow from a company headed by Urbain Sartoris the funds for the construction of several waterways in northern France. The government paid approximately 8 per cent for these funds, but agreed also to the issuance of *jouissance* shares by the promoters—that is, shares that would secure for those promoters most of the profits from the operation of the waterways for a specified term of years that was never less than forty nor more than ninety-nine. After the waterways had proved to yield very moderate profits, the government was criticized for this transaction on two grounds: first, it had paid far too high a rate of interest; secondly, by letting the promoters issue *jouissance* shares it had lost the power to buy back those shares at a reasonable cost and thus

---

[33] Among these writers was Eugène Flachat, a former government engineer now in private employment. Others were Prosper Enfantin, Emile and Isaac Péreire, and Léon Faucher, all of whom had close business connections with James de Rothschild.

had rendered itself unable to ensure uniformity of rates on French waterways.[34] In 1821 the 5 per cent *rentes* had reached 90, so that the government could probably have borrowed at less than 8 per cent for the construction of these waterways. Yet 8 per cent was a rate commonly charged by merchants and other private bankers at that time for lending funds for which they had paid 5 per cent; in fact, such rates were common in the provinces under the July Monarchy. The government can be criticized justly only for not realizing sufficiently the soundness of its credit and for not using the power thus available for the benefit of the nation.

The government was influenced by other considerations also. Balguerie-Stuttenberg, a promoter at Bordeaux of singular ability and integrity, had built several bridges under terms resembling those of the contract with Sartoris for the canals and had done the work quickly and well. Then Sartoris had as his partner Greffulhe, a private banker in Paris who moved in the highest society and had been a close personal friend of the Duc de Berri, who had been murdered in 1820. There is also reason to believe that Greffulhe was supported by Genevese bankers in Paris who may have obtained some capital from Switzerland, and also by Jacques Laffitte and Lapanouze, and possibly by James de Rothschild as well. In view of the power held in the market of Paris by these bankers, it is difficult to find grounds for just criticism of the government for the terms on which it borrowed from the Sartoris company.[35]

In 1836, however, a change in the government's policy of financing public works became clearly apparent. The first indications of this had come in 1833, when two laws were enacted: the first to facilitate the condemnation of land,[36] and the second to direct and

---

[34] Alphonse Courtois, "Notices historiques et statistiques sur les canaux entrepris en vertu des lois de 1821 et 1822," *Journal des économistes,* v. 39 (1851), 214–15. Jacques Bresson, *Histoire financière de la France depuis l'origine de la monarchie jusqu'à l'année 1828,* 1st ed., v. 2 (Paris, 1829), 349. Sartoris, *op. cit.,* 8–10. Alphonse Toussenel, *Les Juifs, rois de l'époque: Histoire de la féodalité financière,* v. 1 (Paris, 1847), 32–34. *Statistique de la navigation intérieure,* France, Ministère des Travaux Publics, *Les Travaux publics de la France,* v. 3, par Henri Melchior-Lagréné (Paris, 1883), 7.

[35] Joinville, *op. cit.,* 130. Capefigue, *op. cit.,* 73, 86.

[36] Law of 21 May, 1836.

finance the study of a national network of railroads. Then in 1836 was enacted the excellent statute that was to endow France with a good system of local roads.[37] The government was now ready to act with energy and showed that it was fully aware that it possessed the funds and the credit to enable it to finance directly improvements in transportation. The government's energy at this time is not surprising. It felt confident of its political strength in 1833, and in that same year prosperity returned to the country. For the next four years business continued to expand and appropriations for public works became a regular part of every budget.

The government did not, however, finance the ever-increasing construction of waterways, roads, and railroads simply by including appropriations for it in each regular budget. It wished to avoid a drastic increase in taxation and also the frequent flotations of new loans, fearing that through those means it might lose some of its popularity. For several years, chiefly after 1837, it utilized two other financial resources. It financed improvements in transportation, first through the reserves of the amortization fund, which were ample and which could not then be used profitably to buy back for redemption the 5 per cent rentes, because these were then well above par and were expected to remain so.[38] It also used the large and steadily increasing deposits in the savings banks, which previous legislation had required to be invested in rentes.[39] These devices for financing permanent improvements for the benefit of the country from the nation's capital invested in government bonds seemed adequate for a time. The government was anxious to make these improvements slowly, because it realized with some anxiety that it was committed to developing all these forms of transportation simultaneously. The depression that began in 1837 and continued intermittently until 1842 gave the government the leisure it felt it needed for several years and gave it also the illusion that it would have plenty of time in the future.

---

[37] Law of 7 July, 1833. A second law was passed 3 May, 1841. See Marion, *Histoire financière,* v. 5, p. 154.

[38] *Ibid.,* 173–76.

[39] *Ibid.*

But in 1842 a change began that soon altered the situation completely. Two railroads that had been begun during the depression were opened in the spring of 1843 and proved highly profitable at once. Both these lines, which ran from Paris to Orléans and to Rouen, had received help from the French government, while the Rouen line received a large part of its capital from England. This flow of British capital soon grew rapidly and for several years helped to relieve the strain on the financial resources of the French government. Several French railroads were built by British engineers and contractors. It seems, doubtful, however, that the mania for railroad construction in England which reached its climax in 1845 was a potent factor in promoting the flow of British capital into France.[40] Financial promoters of railroads in Great Britain were seeking foreign markets which promised greater profits, as is shown by investments in American railroads as well as French. We shall probably never know how much French capital would have poured into French railroads had there been greater need of it. It is clear that the flow would have been grossly inadequate before 1843, but we cannot be so certain of that inadequacy between 1843 and 1846.

After 1842 France was swept by a wave of enthusiasm for railroads that became almost as much a speculative boom as in England, even if on a much smaller scale. The public desire for quick action and quick profits caused a great increase in the French government's program of construction, because the Chambers felt the enthusiasm of the public and forced action upon a slightly reluctant administration. The government stiffened in its attitude towards the companies. Concessions were made for ever-briefer terms and under ever-harsher conditions, but were accepted by the companies, because during the boom funds seemed to flow in increasingly. The effect of this increasing severity of the government towards the railroad companies, largely forced by the Chambers, was to make the launching of railroad companies ever more a matter of speculation with an ever-increasing emphasis on quick profits

---

[40] The best account of British investment in French railroads before 1848 is Leland Hamilton Jenks, *The Migration of British Capital to 1875,* 2d ed. (New York: Knopf, 1938), 126–53.

and the probability of their realization, rather than upon sound and long-term investing. The situation played directly into the hands of the most important and shrewdest of the Parisian bankers, James de Rothschild, who took part in the more-important mergers of railroad companies, as has been shown, forced up the prices of the stocks, and then sold out at the height of the boom, awaiting the opportunity to buy back his former holdings during the expected depression.

The government of the July Monarchy, it is true, condemned the wave of speculation that swept the financial market of Paris, but, as we have seen, its policy of ever-shorter concessions to the railroad companies on ever harsher terms served merely to intensify it. The Chambers undoubtedly forced the government to move faster and to treat the companies more harshly than it had intended to do; yet we hear little of any heroic resistance by any minister to unreasonable legislative demands. We must not, however, condemn the whole financial policy of the government in the field of public utilities because that government was unable to control the speculative boom of 1843–46 in France. The July Monarchy has been accused of recklessly increasing the public debt and thereby incurring an ever-increasing deficit.[41] It is true that the government did not prevent the crisis of 1846–47 or the Revolution of 1848, which probably did even more damage. But other governments proved unable to cope with that crisis, and the revolution is hardly within the province of this study because its causes were only partly economic. We must remember also that this monarchy which perished so suddenly and ingloriously has been an easy mark for critics ever since. It seems wisest to accept the conclusions of the late Professor Marion, the soundest authority available on the public finance of that period. He states that the borrowings of Louis Philippe's government for the promotion of public utilities did not exceed unreasonably the resources of the country, and that the pro-

---

[41] Léon Faucher, "Situation financière de la France," *Revue des deux mondes,* Nouvelle série, v. 5 (1843), 1051. Gaston de La Place de Chauvac, *La Crise des finances publiques en 1848* (Toulouse: Marqueste, 1916), 31–40.

gram of construction they made possible was indispensable to the prosperity of France at the time and to its healthy development in the future.[42]

Before concluding this study of the financial development of France we must consider the prevalent rates of interest and discount and their variations. Our study of the 5 per cent *rentes* has shown that a limited conversion to 4 per cent was achieved as early as 1825 and that financial conditions alone would have permitted a general conversion. It was largely the influence of *rentiers* who possessed political power, or controlled those who did, that prevented such a general lowering of the rate of interest, and it appears that the judgment of Villèle in desiring it was sound. The Bank of France continued to charge 4 per cent steadily, as it had for several years, except during financial crises, when it occasionally raised the discount rate to 5 per cent. The Bank of Bordeaux followed a similar policy. By 1824 good commercial paper could be obtained in Paris at 4 per cent, and this may have been possible as early as 1817;[43] by 1832 it was obtainable at between 2 and 3 per cent. We know also that the government charged 4 per cent for its loans to businessmen in 1830, and the same to the Orléans railroad company in 1840 and 3 per cent to the second Paris-Rouen company shortly afterwards.

These rates of interest show us, first, that Paris, even under the Restoration and in the early years of the July Monarchy, although in many ways a small and restricted market, was a really important financial center in which money could be obtained at a reasonable cost that varied little. When it did vary it changed because of economic factors primarily. The steadiness of the discount rate of the Bank of France is notable and stands in sharp contrast to the policy followed by the Bank of England, which has generally appealed to us as the more reasonable. But should we not ask ourselves if in France in the earlier nineteenth century it was desirable to allow the rate of discount of the national bank to vary in response to the

---

[42] Marion, *op. cit.*, v. 5, p. 226.

[43] Bères, *op. cit.*, 51. Esterno, *op. cit.*, p. vi. Capefigue, *op. cit.*, v. 3, p. 89. Liesse, *Portraits,* 275.

currents of business? The Bank of France has frequently been criticized for the rigid maintenance of its rate, and there are sound grounds for such criticism. But there are also reasons for approval which do not appear to have been considered frequently or carefully enough. In most of the provincial money markets, rates of discount and interest were usually higher than in Paris, frequently so high that they practically constituted usury; and they varied suddenly and often. We are told that at Marseilles, before the establishment of its government-sponsored bank in 1836, the rate of discount was between 1½ and 5 per cent, which was reasonable enough, but that it varied so frequently and so suddenly as to constitute a serious hazard to business.[44] At Bordeaux, before the foundation of its bank in 1819, a charge of 15 per cent for money at the season of the wine harvest was common, while during the rest of the year the usual rate was 5 per cent.[45] A similar situation seems to have prevailed at Nantes as late as 1839, and this is even more interesting, because a bank approved by the government had existed there for some time.[46] The prevalent rate of discount of the Bank of Nantes was 3.8 per cent, and this has frequently been cited with approval as the lowest in France. But Guépin, who published a history of Nantes in 1839, tells us that the Bank of Nantes[47] would discount only paper based on mortgages and that it raised its rate during the harvesting of grains and grapes and during the fairs of Anjou.[48] It is a pity that Guépin gives no figures, but he was a physician who lived in Nantes and was, therefore, well informed on local matters.

We must consider financial markets also in the light of another clearly demonstrated fact—that in the period between 1815 and 1848 France was still overwhelmingly agricultural. This goes far to explain the irregularity of the bank rate at Nantes, where there were

[44] Jules Julliany, *Essai sur le commerce de Marseille,* 2d ed., v. 1 (Paris, 1843), 373.

[45] Joinville, *op. cit.,* 64. The Bank of Bordeaux was authorized 23 November, 1818, and opened 1 July, 1819.

[46] The Bank of Nantes was authorized 11 March, 1818.

[47] Courtois, "Histoire des institutions de crédit . . . La Banque de France," 68.

[48] Ange Guépin, *Histoire de Nantes,* 2d ed. (Nantes, 1839), 561–62.

both commerce and industry which the bank was able to ignore. This was possible because the chief industry of Nantes was the refining of cane sugar, which was connected with the French colonial trade. This had suffered severely from the ever-increasing prosperity of the beet-sugar industry in France and the steady decline of the production of cane sugar in the French West Indies. Most other towns in France were dominated even more by agriculture than was Nantes, and their financial markets therefore had high rates, since their supply of liquid capital was very small. Ramon tells us that in 1836 the rate of interest at Châteauroux was between 6 and 8 per cent and that in the rest of the Department of Indre it was higher,[49] while d'Esterno says that in 1837 the rate at Châteauroux varied between 7 and 12 per cent.[50] A statement by the ardent Alphonse Toussenel in 1847 is interesting. He cannot be trusted when speaking of the Rothschilds, but as a journalist he did pick up much information. He tells us that in purely agricultural districts the usual rate of discount, presumably for landowners and well-established tenants, was 15 to 20 per cent, for laborers 20 to 30 per cent, and for manufacturers 4 per cent.[51] The rate for landowners and tenants was probably based on the value of their mortgages, for we know that most agricultural land was heavily mortgaged. That for laborers was probably based on the fact that they had little if any security to offer, other than chattel mortgages, and it is known that the rates on those were usurious. The rate of 4 per cent for manufacturers in agricultural districts is probably incorrect, since it would have been a normal rate only in the best financial markets. In agricultural districts, manufacturers probably paid at least 6 per cent at the best times and considerably more at the worst.

It is easy to understand why interest rates were high in most provincial towns in France in the earlier nineteenth century when we remember that large banks with adequate capital and governmental support were exceedingly scarce and that even the notes of

---

49 Ramon, *op. cit.*, 196.
50 Esterno, *op. cit.*, p. iv. He cites as his authority Damourette, banker and judge of the Tribunal of Commerce at Châteauroux.
51 Toussenel, *op. cit.*, 184.

the Bank of France did not circulate throughout the country at par much before the Revolution of 1848. In important cities that did not have banks, and even in some that did, there were private bankers, usually merchants still active in some branch of trade or industry, or recently retired from such a business. Stendhal describes them as still an important source of credit in Lyons in 1837,[52] and Ramon tells us that a small group of such men controlled the credit of Grenoble in 1840.[53] Such private bankers operated chiefly with cash and secured their funds generally at 4–5 per cent. They lent them usually at between 7 and 10 per cent, the rate depending upon the accessibility of their town, the soundness of their business, and the liquidity of their capital. In small towns the private banker was usually replaced by a notary, the type of lawyer who in France records contracts and property settlements and advises individuals on the legal aspects of their business affairs. Such a man might be the leading citizen of a small town or village, but at that period his resources were probably smaller and less fluid than those of the private banker in a larger town, and his horizon was probably much narrower.

The law in France in the earlier nineteenth century said that the legal rate of interest should not ordinarily exceed 5 per cent, but that merchants who acted as bankers might charge an additional 1 per cent as a commission.[54] Thus interest was not effectively limited to 5 per cent, except where the ordinary economic forces operating in a financial market forced it down to that level or below. Commissions could be charged on numerous occasions and for various services. Thus, many businessmen in Paris paid more than the usual discount rate of the Bank of France, which was 4 per cent. Unless they were financially well known Parisians, they would have to secure from some private banker in the capital the third signature required, and they would, of course, have to pay for it. Hence it is not surprising to the economic historian to find in the complaints of

[52] Stendhal (Henri Beyle), *Mémoires d'un touriste,* v. 2 (Paris, 1837), 135.
[53] Ramon, *op. cit.,* 181.
[54] Toussenel, *op. cit.,* 184. Esterno, *op. cit.,* 112.

manufacturers the statement that they commonly had to pay 6 per cent or more for funds.

It is impossible to say whether capital in France in the period 1815–48 was scarce or not. It seems clear that the amount of capital increased slowly after 1815, because of the effects of the Revolution and the Napoleonic wars both within the country and in the loss of colonies and foreign markets. The increase was slow also because the industrialization of the country proceeded slowly and the increase in both foreign and domestic trade was rather slow. But more important than the quantity of capital and its rate of increase, about which we may never be fully informed, is the question of the availability of the capital. Here the picture becomes clearer. We know that much of the capital was frozen in land, frequently in the form of mortgages on which an effective rate of interest of 10 per cent was common (obtained by charging a nominal rate of 5 per cent and declaring the value of the property mortgaged at half the proper figure).[55] The banker d'Esterno of Dijon tells us that in near-by Autun were many landowners receiving only 2 per cent from their real estate and eager to obtain more. So in 1836 he went to Paris as the representative of these landowners and of a group of businessmen of Dijon who lacked capital and proposed to the government the chartering of a bank with the power of note issue in a region including Dijon, Autun, and Gray-sur-Saône. When he had been referred to one ministry and committee after another in Paris for two years, he expressed his rage in a book whose footnotes and observations are valuable to the economic historian. We cannot agree that d'Esterno's scheme was rejected simply because of bureaucratic routine. Notes bearing interest, or issued for a term, could legally be issued by a bank receiving such authority from the government, but it is well to remember that d'Esterno himself tells us that in 1838 the notes of even the Bank of France were not accepted at par in Dijon. Furthermore, the proposed bank would have involved the co-operation of several towns, a situation most unusual, if not unknown, in French banking history. D'Esterno tells us also that notes such as those his bank could have issued were

---

[55] Toussenel, *loc. cit.*

little used in France, because people lacked confidence in them. The government, then, had sound reasons for believing that a bank such as that proposed by d'Esterno would fail because people would be afraid to use the credit it offered.

In general it can be said that France had few banks even in 1848, not simply, or even chiefly, because the government and the Bank of France were opposed to them, but primarily because the people were afraid of banks, just as they were afraid of notes even when issued by the Bank of France itself. D'Esterno, himself the eager promoter of a bank, says that France in 1838 had only eight or ten cities with a volume of business sufficient to support a bank.[56] The Péreires, writing towards the close of the Second Empire, tell us that even then France had few banks, and that the influence of each bank that the country did have was purely local. They tell us also that industry had money, but that it could not be used as readily as if notes had circulated freely.[57]

The problem of the monarchy in the field of finance between 1815 and 1848 was fourfold: first, it must establish a sound system of public credit; second, it must make that system known to the people and get them to use it; third, it must put an end to the isolation of provincial markets in France from the market of Paris and from each other; and, finally, it must overcome the popular fear of notes and banks. The Restoration solved the first two of these problems very well indeed. The third problem, that of knitting together the markets of France, it merely studied, as is shown by its plan for a system of waterways made in 1820. The July Monarchy carried on this work by building many of those waterways and by planning systems of highways and railroads, and by constructing many of them. It ran considerable risks in its last years of financing its huge program of public works, but those risks were more than justified in view of the desperate need of France for an adequate system of transportation. But the task was too great and was begun too late, so that the fruits were gathered in by the Second Empire and the

[56] Esterno, *op. cit.*, 100.
[57] Emile and Isaac Péreire, *Du systeme des banques,* in Conseil Superieur du Commerce, *Enquête sur la Banque de France* (Paris, 1866).

Third Republic. The July Monarchy also attacked the fourth problem by making the circulation of the notes of the Bank of France truly national, but it made only a little progress in developing a system of banks.

It is quite clear that in the earlier nineteenth century the financial system of France was inadequate for the full economic development of the country. But the improvements that had been begun during the Consulate were both broadened and strengthened under the Restoration and the July Monarchy. Progress between 1815 and 1848 was considerable. If the government did not lead with more vigor, the fault lay only partly in the love of routine and the arbitrariness of its great bureaucracy. It lay also in the need of protecting the people against the love of speculation on the one hand, and against the love of hoarding and thrift and the spirit of individualism on the other. It is very significant that many able contemporaries wrote of the "spirit of association," which we should call doing business through companies, sometimes as a danger, and sometimes as a sort of cure-all that could produce any miracle; but always as an importation from abroad. If the government sometimes encouraged companies, and sometimes treated them with suspicion, it was, then, representing only too well the public opinion of France.

CHAPTER TEN

Machinery

THE DEVELOPMENT OF the Industrial Revolution in France obviously depended upon the ability of the French to mechanize their iron and textile industries. The problems raised were serious and difficult to solve; England had already solved many of them, but France was cut off from most contacts with her by the wars of the French Revolution and the First Empire. The French iron industry was backward and, as we have seen, was handicapped by poor transportation and an inadequate supply of coal. It is true that, like the United States, France was not seriously short of wood, as was England, and that she had a potentially great supply of water power. She did develop, as has been noted, various good methods for using wood in metallurgy, and she produced some good hydraulic motors, as did the colonial ancestors in America. But these resources simply helped her to postpone the development of machinery made from iron smelted and refined with coal and driven by the power of steam. It was necessary for her iron industry and her textile mills to learn from their powerful and progressive competitor, who, unchecked, might have crushed them. The French were proud and obstinate. They were also devoted to small-scale production at a leisurely pace, and an abundant supply of cheap rural labor made the domestic system strong. But the French had some able and intelligent manufacturers who were willing to learn English methods and who, with the support of a government whose wisdom in economic matters has often been underestimated, were ready to study those methods across the Channel and even to smuggle in the machines. On the other hand, there were English manufacturers willing to break the laws of their country by bringing over skilled workers to teach the French and by smuggling out machines, all for the sake of high wages and substantial profits.

When peace was restored between England and France at the downfall of Napoleon, the French were weak, backward, and unorganized. They realized only dimly the seriousness of the problem of developing their own machines; while they had a few machine shops, these were all small and virtually without power or machine tools. We know that Calla and Cavé had machine shops in Paris in 1815, or soon afterwards, and that another was started in Paris by Pihet, probably in 1818, and that the Chaillot works begun in the eighteenth century by Jacques Constantin Périer and his brother were taken over in 1816 by Humphrey Edwards, his son Henry, and the Périer brothers, Scipio and Casimir, who belonged to a different family than Constantin. Hallette had a machine shop in Arras; an important firm was organized in Alsace by the Risler brothers and Dixon in 1817, and in the same year a shop was opened at Saint-Quentin by Cazalis and Cordier, two graduates of the French School of Arts and Crafts at Chalon-sur-Marne who were fortunate enough to win the support of the Duc de La Rochefoucauld-Liancourt. In addition to these truly French machine shops were others which were run wholly by Englishmen with English workers. Among these were the shop of John Collier in Paris and the great establishments of Charenton and Le Creusot run at that time by Manby and Wilson. In Normandy there was the workshop of Waddington at Saint-Rémy, that of J. C. Dyer and Sons at Blangy, which made cards for the textile industries, and at Rouen the highly successful firm of Barker, Roundcliffe, Sudds, and Atkins, whom French writers describe as making machines and tools as well as the English. These few facts show us, then, that by 1825 at least the French had several machine shops which were really their own and others operated in France which were really English.[1]

---

[1] Général Jean-Victor Poncelet, *Les Machines et outils spécialement employés à la fabrication des matières textiles,* v. 3 of Paris, *Exposition universelle de 1851 à Londres,* travaux de la Commission Française sur l'Industrie des Nations (Paris, 1858), Partie 1. Emile Eude, *Histoire documentaire de la mécanique française: [Fragments] d'après le musée central*

The first serious step in French progress was one which Englishmen often forget they had to take: substitution of iron for wood in building machines. English witnesses at the parliamentary investigation presided over by Hume in 1824 and 1825 testified that French spinning machines were frequently made of oak and were, in consequence, slow and difficult to operate. Yet it would appear that about the time this evidence was given French machine shops had already substituted iron machines in many cases, but had done so only very recently. It was possible, even if difficult, to get the iron cast properly, and even more difficult to get it in sufficient quantity, and complaints of the greater cost of iron machines were common. Yet the substitution continued and was probably completed by the end of the depression of 1827–32. The chief obstacles to be overcome were clearly lack of power in the machine shops, the scarcity and cost of well-cast iron, and the slight demand for machines. When we add to these difficulties scarcity of capital, we can understand why progress was slow. It is well to remember that two of the most energetic firms in France, Manby and Wilson, and Risler brothers and Dixon, both failed after some years of apparent suc-

de la mécanique à l'exposition universelle de 1900 (Paris: Dunod, 1902), 68, 79, 184, 232, 236, 256. France, Ministère du Commerce, Enquête faite par ordre du parlement d'Angleterre pour connaître et pour constater les progrès de l'industrie française et dans les autres pays du continent, conclusion de l'enquête traduit par L. Raymond Balthasar Maiseau (Paris, 1925); this is an accurate French translation of Great Britain, House of Commons, "Second Report From Select Committee Appointed to Inquire Into the Law Respecting Artisans Residing Abroad and Into That Respecting the Export of Machinery," in v. 5 of Accounts and Papers (London, 1824); there are six reports in v. 5. Société Industrielle de Mulhouse, Histoire documentaire de l'industrie de Mulhouse et de ses environs au XIXᵉ siècle, v. 1 (Moulhouse: Bader, 1902), 665–66. Andrew Ure, The Cotton Manufacture of Great Britain, 1st ed., v. 1 (London, 1836), p. lxxxix. Claude Gabriel Simon, Observations receuilles en Angleterre en 1835, v. 2 (Paris, 1836), 180. Paris, Rapport du jury central sur les produits de l'industrie française à l'exposition de 1823, rédigé par Louis Etienne François Héricart-Ferrand, vicomte de Thury, et Pierre Henri Migneron (Paris, 1824), 303; this shows that John Collier was a partner of Abraham and Poupart de Neuflize, manufacturers of woolens at Sedan. William Otto Henderson, Britain and Industrial Europe: Studies in British Influence on the Industrial Revolution in Western Europe (Liverpool: University Press, 1954), 29, 58.

cess.[2] The demand for machines grew, but so slowly at first that it seemed as if little progress was being made.

Stimulation to progress in making machinery in France came chiefly from England. We hear of one important machine that appears to have come from the United States, that for making cards. A French writer has claimed that this machine was seen in Boston by Calla and either brought to Paris by him or copied from memory; but it was used most extensively by J. C. Dyer of Normandy who, with his sons, made cards for many years, while there is no evidence that Calla made cards mechanically on an extensive scale. It seems clear that Dyer began making cards with this machine in France in 1821, but we cannot say whether he brought the machine directly from the United States or indirectly by way of England; nor can we be certain that the machine had not already been introduced by Calla. We can only express doubt that the machine came to France from England, because the making of cards by machinery seems to have been more common in France than in England for many years.[3]

We have seen that many of the leading machine makers in France were English and that some firms were wholly so. This meant that mechanical progress in Manchester or Leeds was certain to be known soon afterwards in France. Another case which could probably be duplicated if we had more evidence is that of André

---

[2] Société Industrielle de Mulhouse, *op. cit.*, v. 1, p. 665. Napoléon Vadot, *Le Creusot* (Le Creusot, 1875), 10. Henri Chazelle, *Le Creusot* (Dôle: Imprimerie Presse Jurassienne, 1936), 83. Henderson, *op. cit.*, 28, 33.

[3] France, *Enquête faite par ordre du parlement*. Louis Héricart-Ferrand, vicomte de Thury, "Rapport sur les procédés, inventions et perfectionnements introduits par M. Calla père dans la construction des machines," *Bulletin de la société d'encouragement pour l'industrie nationale,* v. 28 (June, 1829), 236. France, *Rapport du jury central sur les produits de l'industrie française à l'exposition de 1844,* rédigé par Jules Burat, v. 1 (Paris, 1845), 40. Great Britain, House of Commons, "First Report From Select Committee Appointed to Inquire Into the Operation of the Existing Laws Affecting the Exportation of Machinery," *Accounts and Papers,* v. 7 (London, 1841); session March 17, testimony of Mathew Curtis, wire-card manufacturer of Manchester, 112, 114; session March 10, testimony of Granville Withers, machinist of Liège, 64; session March 11, Withers, 72. Henderson, *op. cit.,* 33.

Koechlin and Company of Alsace, competitors and then successors of the firm of Risler brothers and Dixon, which failed in 1832. André Koechlin himself, who lived from 1789 to 1875, was a member of one of the best-known industrial families in Alsace and was related to most of the others. He started his firm in 1826, won the support of Jérémie Risler, who is described as an excellent mechanic, in 1830, and then persuaded Richard Roberts of the well-known firm of Sharp and Roberts of Manchester to come to Alsace to introduce English machines and to train French workmen. Roberts appears to have remained some time and to have done his work so well that the Alsatian firm found it very difficult to win its independence from English domination.[4] This is one of the clearest cases we have of direct English influence in a French machine shop, but there were many others. Most leading French machine makers made trips to England and brought back models of English machines and English workmen to copy them. We know that English machine makers added from 5 to 20 per cent to the price of their machines when they were to be exported to the Continent, because at least one of the workmen who went over to set up such a machine was likely to be bribed to remain abroad, or if this did not happen, the French would not know how to keep the strange machine in repair, and the English firm, to protect its reputation, would eventually have to send one of its men over.[5]

Actual smuggling was also common. English law forbade exportation of most textile machinery, but not of steam engines. The French, on the other hand, doubled the duty on steam engines in 1818 and were thus able to make most of their own, but they were eager to obtain spinning and preparatory machines, particularly in the cotton and linen industries. English machine makers were quite willing to smuggle them out, despite accounts of French manufacturers who went to England at risk of fine and imprisonment and bravely shipped out the parts of such machines in scattered shipments to be assembled on the Continent, and then returned to re-

---

[4] See Note 1.

[5] Charles Babbage, *On the Economy of Machinery and Manufacture,* 2d ed. (London, 1835), 371.

ceive the Legion of Honor from their grateful king. In general, smuggling was not very difficult. Since some machines could be legally exported and others could not, it was difficult for the British Customs Service to detect violations of the law. If they did succeed the fines imposed were not heavy and the machine, after confiscation by the government, could usually be bought back for a fraction of the cost of its manufacture and then smuggled out again. The chief limitations on smuggling were the very considerable expense, both of shipment and of insurance, the fear British manufacturers felt of foreign competition, and the increasing manufacture of machines in France. In general it can be said that machines were usually smuggled as models to be imitated by French machine makers or by English established in France. Only rarely, as when mechanical spinning of flax became important in France about 1834, do we hear of whole mills equipped with smuggled machines.

We have seen that the first great problem solved by French machine makers was the substitution of iron for wood and that this was well under way by 1825. About that time a few of the leaders among the French machinists became aware of the rapid progress being made in England in the use of machine tools. Here again our information is confusing, or even contradictory, and exact dates cannot be given. But it seems clear that mechanical files were introduced about the end of the depression that began in 1827 and that tools to dress and plane machines came into use in France at about the same time.[6] The spread of these tools was probably slow, for we are told that in 1837 several qualified French writers on technical subjects wrote about the use of machine tools in England with a view to stimulating their spread in France. By 1844 General Poncelet, who has written the nearest approach we have to a history of machine making in France in this period, tells us that towers and planing, cutting, and boring machines were to be seen in profusion, and ten years later machine tools were being made all over France, but could not be produced in quantities sufficient to

[6] Great Britain, "First Report," *loc. cit.;* testimony of Granville Withers, 66, and of Thomas Marsden, machinist of Salford, 84. Jules Burat, *op. cit.,* 37.

meet the demand.[7] While during the later years of the period 1815–48 use of coal in French metallurgy had spread and the casting and refining of iron had improved, most French machine shops probably remained small and few could have been able to specialize in a single type of machinery. They could not, therefore, cut their costs, greatly increase their skill, and improve their methods, as did the great machine makers in England. One estimate is that the French were fifty years behind the English in developing the division of labor. This is a British estimate made in 1824[8] and can be discounted a little since it is not confirmed by French estimates, but this applies only to the term of years mentioned. It is clear that the French were far behind the English in their use of the division of labor, not only in the making of machinery but in many other aspects of manufacturing. To this the French reply that the demand for machinery was not sufficient to justify the expense of drastic reorganization. This could hardly be denied. But were the French doing their best to stimulate the demand?

It will be remembered that de Girard's method of preparing and spinning flax was taken to England and developed there, chiefly in Leeds, by Marshall, the manufacturer, and his son and by Fairbairn, the machinist, beginning in 1824.[9] In ten years the production of mechanically spun yarn in Great Britain had become so great that the surplus could be exported on a scale sufficient to threaten the spinning of flax by hand in several districts of France. This threat produced a great investigation by the French government

---

[7] Adolph Blaise, *Exposition des produits de l'industrie nationale de 1844* (Paris, 1844), 67. D. L. Rodet, "De l'industrie manufacturière de la France de 1844," *Revue des deux mondes,* Nouvelle série, v. 7 (1844), 721. Poncelet, *op. cit.,* 33, 46, 48.

[8] Great Britain, *Reports from Committees, 1824,* Vol. 2, "Third Report of Select Committees to Inquire Into the Law Respecting Artisans Residing Abroad"; *Accounts and Papers,* v. 5 (London, 1824), 140; testimony of Peter Ewart, cotton spinner and former engineer of Boulton and Watt.

[9] Charles Coquelin, "De l'industrie linière en France et en Angleterre," *Revue des deux mondes,* Série 4, v. 19 (1839), 71. Great Britain, "First Report," 208; testimony of Peter Fairbairn; he began his work at Leeds in 1828.

in 1838, which is one of the best sources we have for a study of the French linen industry and will be discussed in detail when we study linen manufacturing.[10] It produced another and more-immediate result in the large-scale smuggling of preparatory and spinning machines from England by French manufacturers or by English manufacturers who went to France to take advantage of this unusual opportunity. Then it caused the manufacture of these machines in France, first in reckless and servile imitation of English models, then with more attention to the somewhat different problems of the linen industry and trade in France. Finally, it is desirable to contrast the methods of these smuggling manufacturers, whether French or English, with the methods of a Belgian machine maker who proved ultimately to be one of the great benefactors of both the linen industry and the machine-making industry of France.

The smugglers were led by Scrive, an important flax spinner of Lille, and Feray, a leading spinner and weaver of linens at Essonnes, near Paris. Both men went to England in 1834, studied the methods of the mills there and the machines used, and smuggled out sets of the machines which they sent to France in scattered shipments. On their return they were received with joy and honor as national heroes by the French government. Others who did likewise were Malo and Dickson, spinners at Dunkirk, and Vayson of Abbeville and Maberly of Amiens, both linen manufacturers.[11] In all cases they seem also to have brought over English workmen to set up and maintain the machines smuggled in, to train French workers, and, frequently, to make machines in France in imitation of English models. We know that Scrive and Feray made such machines themselves intensively and spent years in training French workmen during which they were often obliged to import or smuggle in parts of English machines in order to keep up with incessant

---

[10] France, Ministère des Travaux Publics, *Enquête sur les fils et tissus de lin et de chanvre par le conseil supérieur du commerce en novembre 1838* (Paris, 1838).

[11] France, *Enquête . . . en 1838,* testimony of Feray, spinner of Essonnes, 175, and Vayson, carpet manufacturer of Abbeville, 189. Coquelin, *op. cit.,* 204–5. Alfred Renouard, *Etudes sur le travail des lins,* 4th ed., v. 4 (Paris, 1879), 34–36.

mechanical improvements across the Channel. All this seems normal
enough in view of the prohibitive French tariff, the mechanical
backwardness of French industry, and English prohibition of the
exportation of textile machinery. What is surprising is that all these
smuggling heroes made these machines for preparing and spinning
flax according to the best English methods for themselves alone and
refused to sell the machines they made or to allow them to be
copied by other French manufacturers or even by the French government. In short, this group of linen manufacturers in France,
whose leaders, Scrive and Feray, were French, sought to profit
themselves at the expense of the French linen industry as a whole.
Their selfishness was clear to all.[12]

A more constructive policy in introducing these machines was
followed by Pierre André Decoster,[13] who was born in Belgium in
1806 and came to Paris as a young mechanic. He went to England
in 1834, ostensibly to sell a flax-comber he had developed from that
invented by de Girard. He returned towards the end of 1835, having
successfully smuggled out some English machines. He then opened
a machine shop with capital obtained partly from Liénard, a linen
manufacturer of Pont-Rémy in Normandy, and about eighty workmen, nearly all of whom were French. His source of power was
winches drawn by horses. By 1838 he had enlarged his shop, acquired a steam engine of 120 horsepower, and got rid of any
English workmen he may have had at the start. In the next year,
we are told, he had equipped no less than fourteen French linen
mills. A few years later André Koechlin and Company were making
similar machines, as were Debergue of Paris and Nicolas Schlumberger of Guebwiller in Alsace.[14] These machinists not only saved
the French linen industry but made machines for other textile
industries as well. But Decoster did even more for machine making
in France. Apparently as early as 1838 he began intensively to
manufacture machine tools, and did it so well that by 1844 he had

---

[12] France, *Enquête . . . en 1838.*
[13] Renouard, *op. cit.*, v. 4, p. 36. France, *Enquête . . . en 1838,* 204–12;
testimony of Decoster. Also Coquelin, *op. cit.*, 217–19.
[14] Renouard, *loc. cit.* France, *Enquête, loc. cit.* Coquelin, *loc. cit.*

met the needs of seventy French mills[15] and had acquired a reputation as a toolmaker that was even greater than the one he had acquired as a builder of machines.

In that same year of 1844 France had one of those expositions that were held every five years after 1819 and that have provided us with valuable evidence on the progress made by French industries. The local jury for the Department of Haut-Rhin, which contained most of the important mills of Alsace and the industrial and commercial center of Mulhouse, declared that, now that England permitted the exportation of textile machinery, the machine shops of Alsace, faced with the high price of fuel and iron and the high cost of cartage, would be quite unable to maintain their record of producing half the textile machinery of France.[16] As usual, we lack detailed evidence as to just what happened to the machine shops of France after England repealed the prohibition of the exportation of most textile machines in 1843. It is clear that this repeal was largely the result of the parliamentary investigation of 1841, which showed both the impossibility of enforcing prohibition and the very notable progress of the machine shops of France. The reports of the Exposition of 1844 indicate that French progress was maintained.[17] The real answer to the complaint of the Alsatian jury of 1844 is found, however, in the reports of the French Exposition of 1849, which are unusually full and reliable, and in those of the International Exposition held at London in 1851, where the French commission alone published reports filling no less than sixteen volumes, which include the *History of French Machinery* by General Poncelet.[18] Widespread ruin of French machine shops because

---

[15] Blaise, *op. cit.*, 71, 76.

[16] "Rapport du jury départemental du Haut-Rhin pour l'exposition de 1844," *Bulletin de la société industrielle de Mulhouse*, v. 17 (1843), 174–76.

[17] To these should be added the excellent volumes by Jules Burat and Adolphe Blaise already cited.

[18] The report of the Exposition of 1849 as published at Paris in 1850 in 3 volumes is in the library of the Chamber of Commerce of Paris. That of the French commission to the Exposition of 1851 in London is at the University of Michigan. Both are difficult to find in France because they are not prepared by individual editors and, therefore, are not cross-indexed by many French librarians. Yet they are probably the most important sources on the industrial history of France for 1815–48.

of the flooding of the French market with English machines as a result of the repeal of prohibition in 1843 could not have been concealed. It need only be said that the reports of neither exposition mention even a serious increase in the competition of British machines with French in any part of France. We must conclude, therefore, that the progress of the French in making both machines and machine tools continued through 1848 and beyond. It seems obvious that maintenance of French duties on iron and machinery, plus the demonstrated strength of the French machine-building industry, more than balanced the decrease in the cost of shipping machines from England. The French paid a high price for their machines and owed much of their success to British machinists in France, but they did succeed.

Before closing this brief chapter on the general development of machinery in France, which was essential to the growth of the Industrial Revolution, we must mention a great French invention which played a vital part in the growth of all the textile industries and which, unlike de Girard's great invention for spinning flax, received its full development and its practical application in France itself. All through the eighteenth century the French were trying to solve the problem of weaving patterned silks well and cheaply. Vaucanson, one of the greatest of their inventors, perhaps the greatest of them in the textile industries, came close to success and left a loom which was forgotten in the Conservatoire des Arts et Métiers in Paris. Not many years afterwards Joseph-Marie Jacquard, who had been first a helper in his father's weaving shop in Lyons and then a weaver and manufacturer, conceived the idea of a loom that would accomplish this purpose. He did this without any direct knowledge of Vaucanson's machine and finally built his own in 1800 and exhibited it in Paris the next year. Then he studied the loom of Vaucanson, which he found in the Conservatoire. He apparently combined its best features with those of his own in 1804; this is the date usually given for the invention of the Jacquard loom. Its importance was appreciated almost immediately in Lyons, where its use threatened such widespread unemployment that serious riots of the silk workers broke out and Jacquard's life was in danger. The Jacquard loom made unnecessary the work of a whole army of helpers who had pulled the cords operating the many lifts necessary in weaving a pattern, a work that required great precision and concentration and was so arduous that it had greatly injured the health of Jacquard himself.[19]

Jacquard lived for thirty years after 1804 and received numerous honors, a pension from the government, and royalties from the sale of his looms, but there is no record of any active part played by him in the improvement of his loom. Ideas for this, and probably money also, for Jacquard himself never profited greatly from his invention, were supplied by Depouilly,[20] a silk manufacturer of Lyons. We do not know what he persuaded Jacquard to do, but there is evidence that the loom did not run smoothly and did not produce good cloth until Breton, one of the mechanics who had worked under Jacquard, made changes that caused the carriage under the cylinder to run smoothly and eliminated many of the levers, pulleys, and weights.[21] There followed many more improvements before the Jacquard loom achieved its full usefulness. One of the ablest writers on the silk industry, Pariset, tells us that the process of developing these improvements constituted a costly and radical revolution so difficult that it was not completed until 1853.[22] Among the most important was making interchangeable the cards which passed before the loom in an endless chain so that the pattern could be changed without taking down the loom, to accomplish which had required from a week to nearly a month. Lighter cards were also developed, and the use of more needles made possible, so that ever-richer patterns could be woven at even-lower cost.[23] In

---

[19] *Grande encyclopédie,* "Jacquard." *Hutchinson's Technical and Scientific Encyclopedia,* v. 3 (New York: Macmillan, 1935), 1505–16.

[20] Paris, *Exposition universelle de 1851 à Londres,* travaux de la Commission Française sur l'Industrie des Nations, v. 4 (Paris, 1854): "Industrie des laines foulées," par M. Bernoville, 180–82.

[21] Paris, *Exposition universelle de 1851,* v. 3, Partie 2 (Poncelet), 366. Ernest Pariset, *Les Industries de la soie* (Lyon, 1890), 278–79.

[22] Paris, *Exposition universelle de 1851, loc. cit.* Henri Reboul, *L'Industrie nîmoise du tissage au XIXe siècle* (Montpellier: Firmin et Montane, 1914).

[23] Paris, *Exposition nationale des produits de l'industrie agricole et manufacturière de 1849: Rapport du jury central,* v. 2, sect. 7 (Paris, 1850), 92; report of Kuhlmann, of the Jury Départemental du Nord. Hector Rivoire, *Statistique du département du Gard,* v. 2 (Nîmes, 1842), 24–27.

the meantime, the mechanical improvement of the loom itself by
Breton made possible a great increase in the speed of its operation
and even, in some cases, a mechanical motor.[24] There is no evidence, however, that Jacquard looms were generally operated as
power looms before 1848. It would appear that power was used
only for some looms weaving the plainer silks and some other textiles, just as we know that power was applied to looms weaving
plush in 1836, but was not used for weaving all plush and did not
spread to the silk industry as a whole for many years.

The effects of the Jacquard loom on all the textile industries
of France can hardly be exaggerated, nor, of course, could they be
confined to the country of its origin. In France the new loom began
to transform the manufacture of fancy silks as early as 1817. It was
introduced at Nîmes in 1816 and within three years had made
possible there the imitation of the fancy silks of Lyons and Paris.[25]
It was adapted to making hosiery at Nîmes and thus transformed
two of the most important industries of that southern textile center.
During the depression of 1827–32 it was introduced at Roubaix for
stuffs, and this led to the development of the richer satins: it was
then introduced at Rouen, where it helped one of the best of the
cotton printers to change to manufacturing smooth woolens. A few
years later we find it used to change the production of one of the
greatest firms of Sedan, Bonjean, from the plain black cloths, which
had been traditional for many years, to fancy woolens of mixed
colors, designs, and shades. The Jacquard loom saved the very life
of the cashmere-shawl industry by reducing its cost of production
40 per cent in seven years between 1827 and 1834.[26] In the next
depression, in 1837, it was introduced at Reims and Mulhouse.

Finally, we must mention what seems to have been the most
important application of the Jacquard loom outside the silk industry itself, that to the manufacture of mixed cloths, developed

---

[24] Jules Séguier, "Rapport sur les perfectionnements apportés au métier
à tisser de Jacquart par MM. Dhomme et Romagny Jr. de Paris," *Bulletin
de la société d'encouragement pour l'industrie nationale,* v. 36 (June, 1837),
206.

[25] Rivoire, *loc. cit.* Reboul, *op. cit.,* 42.

[26] Paris, *Exposition universelle de 1851,* v. 4 (Paris, 1854): "Industrie
des châles et des tissus mélangés," par Maxime Gaussen.

extensively and brilliantly by Jacquard's professional friend Depouilly, who moved from Lyons to Paris for the purpose in 1818
and was the leader of the new work there and in Picardy, where
much simpler weaving was done until 1830. This manufacture of
mixed cloths is of the greatest importance to the progress of the
Industrial Revolution in France. It provided a new market for silk,
especially waste silk which could be spun by machinery more like
cotton than like ordinary silk; it provided also new markets for
cotton and linen; but it did most for the development of the woolen
industry, which it strengthened immeasurably in its difficult struggle
with the more powerful and more highly mechanized industry of
cotton. The Jacquard loom was not, of course, the only factor in
creating the manufacture of mixed cloths, but it was the most
important. Finally, it was like a gift from heaven to the artistic
French, with their talent for color, design, and good taste. The
enthusiasm with which this talent was expressed is contagious and
was so intense that few seemed to realize that the endless changes
involved were important causes of sudden and disastrous overproduction, crises, and unemployment.

CHAPTER ELEVEN

The Cotton Industry

THE YOUNGEST OF THE TEXTILE INDUSTRIES in France grew so rapidly in the period from 1815 to 1848 that it soon became more
powerful than any of the others. From the start it received the
machines which brought it such amazing strength from England, in
the order in which they were invented and perfected across the
Channel. The spinning jenny appears to have been introduced as
early as 1773 and to have been fairly common by 1780. It was in
general use by the beginning of the Revolution, certainly in the
more important industrial regions of Normandy and Picardy. The
men who brought it over and who manufactured it in France were,
in most cases, Englishmen who settled in France for a few years
and were subsidized partially, or wholly, by the French government.
The jenny made possible the manufacturing of pure cottons on a
considerable scale in France. It frequently caused the erection of
mills, but did not necessarily do so, as it was well adapted to use
in the home and could be run without the application of power.
For these reasons it aroused little opposition, for it caused little
unemployment, and it could be used without any serious expenditure of capital. Finally, it was being used widely before the economic
crisis that began shortly before the outbreak of the Revolution.[1]

---

[1] Charles, baron Dupin, *Forces productives et commerciales de la France*
(Paris, 1827), v. 1, p. 206; v. 2, pp. 52–54, 104. Pierre Siméon Lelong.
"Aperçus historiques et statistiques sur l'industrie cotonnière dans le département de la Seine-Inférieure," *Bulletin de la société libre d'émulation de
Rouen* (1834), 222–25. Natalis Briavoinne, *Sur les inventions et perfectionnements de l'industrie depuis la fin du XVIII° siècle jusqu'à nos jours*,
in *Mémoires couronnés par l'académie royale de Belgique*, v. 13 (Brussels,

The water frame, or throstle, followed the jenny shortly before the Revolution. It was scarcely known in France before the crisis that began in 1787. It spread slowly, therefore, during the long period of civil and foreign war during which France was almost completely cut off from industrial and commercial contacts with England. This was a serious disadvantage; but there were others which were even more formidable. The throstle was a large and heavy machine requiring housing in mills and a very considerable expenditure of capital. Also, it produced a strong, hard yarn which, while it was better for warps than that spun by the jenny, was not liked by the French. While it spread, especially under the Empire, and was even used in the mill of the Duc de La Rochefoucauld at Liancourt in the Department of Oise in 1800, it never became popular in France, and we may well wonder if it would ever have sufficed to mechanize the spinning of cotton.[2]

The throstle was followed quickly by Crompton's mule, a smaller and lighter machine which also required housing in mills, but a smaller expenditure of capital. Also, it produced a softer yarn which appealed more to French manufacturers. But the mule, or mule jenny, as French writers usually call it, spread slowly, chiefly during the Empire when civil war in France had been stopped and Napoleon was eager both to ruin England and to make the Continent a market for French goods. We have not enough accurate descriptions of the machines and mills of that period to describe the spread of the newest and best of the spinning machines. This may account for the strange statement of Chaptal in 1819 that the cotton mills of France used jennies and water frames. He does not mention mules, but it is possible that he meant to include mules under the term

---

1838), 69. Charles Schmidt, "Les Débuts de l'industrie cotonnière en France, 1760–1806," *Revue d'histoire des doctrines économiques et sociales,* v. 7 (1914), 26–27. Jules Sion, *Les Paysans de la Normandie orientale* (Paris: Colin, 1909), 301–3. Charles Picard, *Saint-Quentin: De son commerce et de ses industries,* v. 2 (Saint-Quentin, 1867), 13–15. An excellent account of the early introduction of spinning machines is given by Charles Ballot, *L'Introduction du machinisme dans l'industrie française* (Paris: Rieder, 1923), chap. II; this account does not go beyond the early years of the Revolution.

[2] See Note 1.

"jenny." It is surprising that he did not dwell on the increasing use of the mule, if we assume that he omitted to mention it intentionally, because his general tendency was to exaggerate rather than minimize the progress of French industry. But whatever the distinguished Minister of the Interior under Napoleon intended to say, we know from other accounts that hand spinning had almost disappeared in France when peace came in 1815 and that the machine most widely used was the mule.[3]

We must not, however, ourselves exaggerate the progress of French industry. France had just emerged from a long period of war in which, while she had tried to ruin England by blockade, England had retaliated by using the same weapon. Cotton had, therefore, been scarce, very expensive, and usually very bad in quality. What there was could be sold as yarn or cloth at high prices and there was no foreign competition. Furthermore, the French were not yet thoroughly familiar with cotton goods, and what they used chiefly were coarse and cheap prints. It is not surprising, then, to find that the quality of the yarn spun was not good, as Chaptal says, but bad. Witnesses at the great *enquête* of 1834 said that really fine yarn was scarcely spun in France at all and that manufacturers who needed it, such as the producers of muslins and tulle, were obliged to obtain it by smuggling from England; that meant that they could not keep large supplies and often suffered severe losses from delays in shipments. The important spinners, who generally wove and printed also, were few in number and were reaping such large profits from their monopoly under the prohibitive tariff that to them changes in equipment hardly seemed necessary. The market also was small, and so many different qualities of yarn were wanted that specialization by any spinner was difficult. All yarn was dear, but this caused little complaint, partly because the spinners usually wove their own yarn, and partly because other consumers were accustomed to high prices because they had never known any that were reasonable. But they did complain of the poor quality of the yarn. One of the most critical witnesses, Leutner of Tarare, however, said

[3] Jean Antoine, comte Chaptal, *De l'industrie française,* v. 2 (Paris, 1819), 4–7.

that one man in France could spin fine yarn well.[4] This was Nicolas Schlumberger of Guebwiller, who had built in 1819 the first mill in Alsace devoted to spinning alone and had equipped it in 1826 to spin fine yarn.[5] As Nicolas Koechlin, president of the Chamber of Commerce of Mulhouse, remarked, no man should try to produce fine yarn unless he specialized in spinning and had a thorough knowledge of mechanics.[6] Schlumberger had met these standards, had studied spinning in England, and, like many distinguished manufacturers in Alsace, kept in touch with mechanical improvements in England. Finally, we should mention the fact that in 1834 the French government issued an ordinance repealing the prohibition of the importation of fine yarn.

The situation of the cotton industry in France had actually begun to improve as early as 1818. The first promoters of change were undoubtedly the machinists mentioned in the preceding chapter. Many of them were keenly interested in textile machinery, and some of them, like Risler brothers and Dixon, tried hard to specialize in it. We know that this firm introduced the English mechanical beater in 1825 and improved it. Yet we know also that this machine had not wholly replaced hand beating even in 1844. It appears to have torn long staple cotton, to have injured less seriously other cotton, to have filled the lungs of workers with its clouds of down, and to have caused fires by overheating itself and the cotton. The workers could have been protected from inflammation of the lungs and the cotton from fire by the use of ventilators, as in England, but they would have required the application of power, which was considered too costly in France.[7]

Another machine, about which we know far too little, appears to have contributed far more to the better preparation of cotton for

[4] France, *Enquête relative à diverses prohibitions établies à l'entrée des produits étrangers,* v. 3 (Paris, 1835); testimony of Leutner, manufacturer of muslins, Tarare, 297–300, 306–11; of Ernest Feray, spinner of Essonnes, 507–16; of Auguste Mimerel, spinner of Lille, 590–91; and of Nicholas Koechlin, 610–13.

[5] *Op. cit.*

[6] *Op. cit.*

[7] F. Bresson, "Rapport de la commission des prix en 1844," *Bulletin de la société libre d'émulation de Rouen* (1844), 101–2. Achille Penot (ed.), *Statistique générale du départment du Haut-Rhin* (Mulhouse, 1831), 321.

spinning. This was the fly roving frame, which Laborde tells us was both used and manufactured in France in 1826. It did the coarse or preliminary spinning. The first type used had been invented in England by Cocker and Higgins and was introduced at Ourscamp in Picardy, a mill whose management was keenly interested in mechanical improvements. In 1829 a new and better type of roving frame, invented by Houldsworth in England, was introduced by André Koechlin and subsequently improved. But by 1840 its possibilities had been exhausted, and a third type came into use that allowed three times as much cotton on the spools and was operated with gears.[8] We know no more about it, except that it is spoken of first in Alsace. These developments in coarse spinning were of great importance to spinners, weavers, and printers and served as a foundation upon which other and more spectacular improvements could be built. They show as well that the Alsatians were in constant touch with mechanical improvements in England and frequently made others themselves; they also show that long before 1840, and even before the *enquête* of 1834, the pace of progress had become rapid. Even if this rapidity was greater in Alsace than elsewhere, it was an example that other parts of France must soon follow if they were to continue to compete

It is difficult to trace in detail and with dates progress in the improvement of spinning in France, but we do know that it occurred. In Alsace the number of spindles producing fine yarn trebled between 1828 and 1846, and a writer from the district of Lille tells that between 1827 and 1844 the fineness of the yarn spun was doubled; that is, it rose from No. 200 to No. 400[9] and possibly even more. It is impossible to be sure of the exact degree of fineness, because even in 1839 the metric system was not in general use in France,[10] so that we may well feel some doubt as to the unit of measurement used. But it does appear that the improvement was

---

[8] Société Industrielle de Mulhouse, *Histoire documentaire de l'industrie de Mulhouse et de ses environs au XIXᵉ siècle*, v. 1 (Mulhouse: Bader, 1902), 232.

[9] Penot, *op. cit.*, 321. Victor Derode, *Quelques documents pour servir à l'histoire de l'industrie à Lille* (Lille, 1868), 38.

[10] Adolphe Blaise, *Exposition des produits de l'industrie nationale en 1839* (Paris, 1839), 113, 125.

great and was actually realized, for the reporters of the expositions after 1839 do not refer, as did those of 1823 and 1827, to what could be spun but to what was spun. We can say also that each of the great crises of 1827, 1837, and 1847 had an important influence on progress. We know that the first crisis, following several years of speculation and rapidly rising prices in cotton and most of its products, was very severe in the cotton industry in both Alsace and Normandy. Nicolas Schlumberger began intensive production of fine yarn in 1826, a year when prices had begun to fall, and André Koechlin introduced Houldsworth's fly roving frame in 1829. Ure, who wrote in 1836, said that for two years French yarn had been spun as well as English and that the recent crisis, which we know lasted as a depression until 1832, had forced better spinning at lower cost.[11] He probably referred chiefly, if not wholly, to Alsace, but we should expect that region to lead in most mechanical improvements. The second crisis, that of 1837, whose effects were felt until 1842, was the period when the use of gears on spinning machines first became important; and the crisis that began in 1847 was the time when the self-acting machine first became significant in French spinning. Five years after the *enquête* of 1834 it had become possible for Nicolas Schlumberger alone to supply half of the fine yarn needed by the muslin manufacturers of Tarare,[12] and a decade later it was clear that the production of fine yarn had saved the tulle industry, whose existence had been highly precarious fifteen years before.

A few figures and other scraps of evidence indicate that in the period from 1815 to 1848 production of each French spindle was increased between three- and fivefold[13] and the cost of production cut 60 per cent or more.[14] It seems probable, also, that the size of

---

[11] *Ibid.*

[12] *Ibid.*

[13] Société Industrielle de Mulhouse, *Histoire,* v. 1, 220–21. Emile Dollfus, "Notes pour servir à l'histoire de l'industrie cotonnière dans les départements de l'est," *Bulletin de la société industrielle de Mulhouse,* v. 27 (1857), 439–40.

[14] Paris, *Exposition des produits de l'industrie française de 1844: Rapport du jury central,* rédigé par Jules Burat, v. 1 (Paris, 1845), 30.

the mule was doubled, that the number of mills increased greatly, and the size of each mill also increased. We do know that between 1816 and 1842 the number of spindles in the district of Lille increased from 81,000 to 400,000, while those of the Department of Haut-Rhin increased from 530,000 to 780,000 between 1834 and 1846 and the size of the average mill from 12,000 to 16,000 spindles. We cannot say how rapidly the size of the average mill increased in other parts of France, but we know that in Normandy that average in 1834 was approximately 3,600 and at Lille 4,000 spindles. There were, of course, notable exceptions, Normandy having one mill of 44,000 spindles and Alsace one mill of 100,000 spindles and several of 50,000. How great the increase was in the number of cotton spindles for France as a whole seems highly uncertain at present.[15] That there was such an increase seems probable, but we cannot measure it. Much of the increase in production, which we know was great, came through better and larger machines in better and larger mills and also through concentration of spinning in certain regions only.

Finally, we must consider as the last item in the improvement of cotton spinning in our period the introduction of the self-acting mule. This was invented in England in 1826,[16] when the power loom was first becoming important. It was common there as early as 1832, but was still spoken of as unknown in France in 1840, and for some years after that as unsuited to the needs of French spinners. Actually, Nicolas Schlumberger and André Koechlin had models of it in 1836,[17] but for some time they made copies only for

---

[15] France, *Enquête relative à diverses prohibitions*, v. 3 (Paris, 1835), 183; testimony of Auguste Mimerel. "Exposition de 1839: Rapport du jury du Haut-Rhin," *Bulletin de la société industrielle de Mulhouse*, v. 12 (1839), 566. Dollfus, *op. cit.*, 439. Lelong, *op. cit.*, 231. Derode, *op. cit.*, 38. "Rapport du jury du Haut-Rhin sur l'exposition de 1844," *Bulletin de la société industrielle de Mulhouse*, v. 18 (1844), 180.

[16] Paris, *Exposition universelle internationale de 1900 à Paris: Le Bilan d'un siècle* (1801–1900), par Alfred Picard (Paris: République Française, Ministère du Commerce, de l'Industrie et du Travail, 1906), 200. Paris, *Exposition . . . de 1844*, 30.

[17] Achille Penot, "Histoire de l'industrie cotonnière dans l'est," *Bulletin de la société industrielle de Mulhouse*, v. 44 (1874), 203.

Normandy or for foreign countries. It was costly to install, caused much unemployment, and gave the greatest economy in coarse rather than fine yarn. Its requirement of more power was a real handicap in France, and its immense saving of labor was less significant where labor was still cheap. Its use in Alsace began only in 1844, and not until the crisis of 1847 brought down prices and intensified both regional and international competition did its use in France spread on any considerable scale.[18]

Much of the yarn spun in two of the three great regions where cotton was manufactured, Normandy and Alsace, was used for prints. In fact, in Alsace printing was really older as an industry than spinning or weaving, and for many years the cloth needed was obtained largely from Normandy or other sources outside Alsace. But the mechanization of printing did not begin in either Alsace or Normandy. Continuous printing with a copper cylinder was invented by the Scotsman Bell in 1783 and used successfully at Manchester in 1785.[19] There the cylinder was seen and smuggled out in 1800, either by Oberkampf himself or by his English mechanic Hardriss, and set up at the Oberkampf mill at Jouy not far from Paris.[20] With this machine Oberkampf achieved an immediate and striking success, but he does not seem to have been active in spreading the use of the cylinder in France. This was done by two other men: Ebingre, a printer of cottons at Saint-Denis, who had worked for Oberkampf, and by Lefèvre, a locksmith of Paris, who appears to have obtained the information he needed for duplicating Oberkampf's cylinder from old friends of his who were still working at

---

[18] Paris, *Exposition nationale des produits de l'industrie agricole et manufacturière de 1849: Rapport du jury central*, v. 2, sec. 7: Kuhmann, "Rapport du jury départemental du nord" (Paris, 1850), 28–92. William Otto Henderson, *Britain and Industrial Europe, 1750–1870: Studies in British Influence on the Industrial Revolution in Western Europe* (Liverpool: University Press, 1954). Richard Roberts, inventor of the self-actor, came to Alsace to help the new firm headed by André Koechlin about 1832 and remained for two years.

[19] Ernest Jules Lamé-Fleury, "Les Arts industriels: De l'impression des tissus," *Revue des deux mondes,* v. 22 (1847), 140.

[20] *Ibid.*

Jouy.[21] The cylinder thus made had a bulky and heavy wooden frame and it was both painful and dangerous to move it. Yet it produced better prints than the smaller English machine, which had an iron frame and was easier to operate.[22] The French had evidently failed again to copy exactly an English machine, or else they intentionally modified it in order to improve the quality of its printing, to which they attached greater importance than to the convenience and cost of operating the machine.

It is known that several cylinders were made by Lefèvre for important printers in Alsace. One was delivered to Gros, Davillier, Roman and Company of Wesserling in 1803; a second to Dollfus-Mieg and Nicolas Koechlin in 1804; a third to the Daniel Schlumberger Company at Lutterbach in 1810; and a fourth to Robert, Bovet and Company of Thann in 1818. All these were made by Lefèvre in Paris and had wooden frames.[23] The only action we hear of as being taken by Oberkampf himself is the improvement of his cylinder by the addition of boards applied by hand, so that it could print two or three colors simultaneously. Soon afterwards he, or his rival Lefèvre, must have lost their Alsatian business, for cylinders were being made with iron frames by Risler brothers and Dixon, a firm founded in Alsace in 1817. But the method of printing remained the same, for in 1819 the Zuber Company[24] of Alsace was using boards that could print several additional colors simultaneously, just as Oberkampf had done, probably in the effort to meet English competition.

We know little about progress in other parts of France. There is no evidence regarding early printing from either Picardy or the Nord. In Normandy, while printing by hand was probably as old as in Alsace, we are told that the use of the cylinder began in 1818. Baron Dupin goes on to say that when he wrote in 1827 the Department of Seine-Inférieure alone had seventy mills using water power.

---

[21] Société Industrielle de Mulhouse, *op. cit.*, v. 1, p. 367.

[22] Paris, *Exposition . . . de 1844*, 45. Henri Laufenburger and Pierre Pflimlin, *Cours d'économie alsacienne*, v. 2 (Paris: Sirey, 1932), 7.

[23] Paris, *Exposition . . . de 1844*, 45. Laufenburger and Pflimlin, *loc. cit.*

[24] Achille Penot (ed.), *Statistique du Haut-Rhin*, 357.

He does not say that they all used cylinders, or how many did, so that it is impossible to draw useful inferences from his statement regarding the origin of cylindrical printing in Normandy or the rapidity of its increase.[25] But as Normandy was much nearer Paris than Alsace and had long been printing by hand, we may well wonder if one or more of Oberkampf's cylinders was not sent there by Lefèvre or someone else. There are other possibilities. There are numerous cases where English machines were imported or smuggled directly into Alsace, but, again, Normandy is nearer to England and like Alsace had long been importing other machines across the Channel. It is hard to believe that the intelligent Normans sat by idly for fifteen years while their Alsatian rivals used cylinders. We know that the cylinder was used in Belgium as early as 1807.

There were, however, many real difficulties in using the cylinder. As late as 1839 copper cylinders were costly and difficult both to make and to use. No further explanation is given by the Société d'Encouragement pour l'Industrie Nationale, but at the Exposition of 1844 two different and highly reliable reporters mention the casting of copper cylinders in France as if it were a novelty or, at least, a notable thing to have them cast really well. Jules Burat said that as early as 1841 the firm of Hugenin and Ducommun was making copper cylinders for Dollfus-Mieg and Company that combined the merits of the French and English machines, that they were casting the copper in their own foundry, and that they were the only firm in France able to do so. Adolphe Blaise stated that Thiébault, dean of copper founders, had removed the great handicap to the development of printing in France by making copper cylinders as well as in England. Unfortunately he gave neither date nor place. One thing only seems to be clear: that casting really good copper cylinders in France was difficult and expensive until after 1840.[26]

Another problem that was difficult was the engraving of the cylinders, yet this seems to have been solved much more quickly than the problem of making well and on a large scale the cylinders

---

[25] Dupin, op. cit., v. 2, pp. 59–60.

[26] Paris, Exposition . . . de 1844, 43–46. Adolph Blaise, Exposition des produits de l'industrie nationale en 1844 (Paris, 1844), 104.

themselves. Until 1820 English engravers did far better work than French. About that time, said the reporter to the Exposition of 1851, a French engineer went to England, studied the method of engraving there, and then opened a school for engravers in Paris with funds obtained from French manufacturers. This may be the true explanation of how engraving in France was improved. We know that there were excellent designers of the most delicate and expensive prints in Paris at that time and that there were others in Alsace and, we can assume, in Normandy as well. But Vicomte de Thury, who reported on the Exposition of 1827, said that a heavily capitalized firm of Saint-Denis, Juval and Company, had recently brought over an entire engraving mill from England. He added that this firm had been one of the first to introduce the use of the cylinder into France.[27] It may well be that this was the firm that sent the engineer to England to study engraving and also the same firm, or the successor of the firm, that first employed Lefèvre to copy Oberkampf's cylinders in 1802.

Soon after the rapid improvement of engraving began in France, an engineer in Rouen started to experiment with engraving wooden boards instead of cylinders for printing. Normandy was then the region where the cheaper prints were produced, just as the better ones were usually made in Alsace, and the best and most expensive usually in Paris. It was obvious that cylinders were few and costly, while hand printing was slow and, therefore, also costly. Burat tells us that the perrotine was invented in 1821, but other accounts mention 1834 as the time when the invention was really successful, and as the date of its introduction into Alsace. Colonel Perrot had solved the printing problem cleverly. His boards could make most of the impressions made by hand with perfect precision. After being engraved they were filled with colors and pressed successively against the cloth as it passed before them, much as it would pass before

---

[27] Paris, *Rapport du jury central sur les produits de l'industrie française à l'exposition de 1827,* rédigé par Louis Etienne François Héricart-Ferrand, vicomte de Thury, et Pierre Henri Migneron (Paris, 1828), 172. See also Jean François Persoz, "Impressions et teintures," in Paris, *Exposition universelle de 1851 à Londres,* travaux de la Commission Française sur l'Industrie des Nations, v. 5 (Paris, 1855).

cylinders. The amount of the color and the degree of pressure of the board on the cloth were regulated. Successive improvements were made by the inventor and other mechanics until the perrotine could print from four to six colors simultaneously and produce as much in a day as fifty hand printers. That the machine was cheap to make and use and was fought bitterly by the hand printers indicates that it hurt them more than the cylinders did. It was adapted to printing wool and silk and reproduced designs more sharply and with brighter colors than the cylinder. But part of its success was due to the expense of getting good copper cylinders, a problem that appears to have been solved in 1841, or soon afterwards. The cylinder also worked faster, so that it was more practicable for printing on a large scale, and it reproduced delicate shades better. Finally, the perrotine required better engraving. As cylinders improved and increased in number the perrotine came to be used only for special products, such as foulards and handkerchiefs. Its brief period of great influence had certainly ended before 1848.[28]

In the meantime, the English had evidently improved their engraving, for we hear that in 1851 their cylinders were small, simply built, and easy to use and that they were both cheaper and better than the French. Our French informant says that they could print as many as twelve colors simultaneously, when the French cylinders could use only five.[29] It is not possible to refute this account of French tardiness in progress, but it can be assumed that the French, with their gifts for design and color, did not let their printing remain inferior long. We know that in Alsace, at least, integration was proceeding rapidly, as shown by the decrease in both the number of mills and the number of workers, while production was increasing. Since at the end of the period 1815–48 the French were improving their machinery rapidly, we can safely believe that their printing of cotton continued to prosper.

[28] Paris, *Exposition . . . de 1844,* 45. Lamé-Fleury, *op. cit.,* 140. Persoz, *op. cit.,* v. 5, 18–19. "Description d'une machine à imprimer inventée par M. Perrot," *Bulletin de la société d'encouragement pour l'industrie nationale,* v. 38 (Nov., 1839).

[29] Paris, *Exposition . . . de 1844,* 45. Lamé-Fleury, *loc. cit.* "Description d'une machine."

The first step in the improvement of the weaving of cottons in France was probably the introduction of the flying shuttle, which had been invented in England for weaving wool in 1733 and adapted to cotton in 1758. Briavoinne, one of our best sources for Belgium, says that Bauwens brought it there in 1798 and that it was introduced by Jérémie Meyer in the later eighteenth century.[30] As this Jérémie Meyer was an Alsatian who was a skilled mechanic in the firm of Risler brothers and Dixon, founded in 1817, and later a partner in André Koechlin and Company, this would mean that it was introduced into Alsace at or before the date of its importation into Belgium. We do not know, however, when it was introduced into Normandy or the Nord; but as weaving in the eighteenth century was more widespread in Normandy than in Alsace, it would seem probable that it was brought into that region before the end of that century. In Alsace, at least, the flying shuttle did not produce immediately a decisive improvement in weaving. Manufacturers there at the beginning of the nineteenth century were more interested in printing than in weaving fine cloths. An early attempt to weave them made by Martin Ziegler failed. Later attempts by one of the Schlumberger family in 1818–19 succeeded, and the smuggling of fine cloths was stopped. A large supply of native weavers was trained so rapidly that a crisis from overproduction resulted in 1822.[31]

Another improvement which was no more important than the flying shuttle, but about which we have more information, was the dressing machine which prepared the warp for weaving, invented at Bradbury in 1803 by Thomas Johnson. Immediately it became possible for one woman to run two Cartwright looms instead of one, thus enabling her to produce three times as much as the best hand weaver. The dressing machine was used by one of the Koechlins at Mulhouse as early as 1811, but it spread slowly because its operation was slow. On the other hand, it saved much labor and required little beyond the starch obtained from potatoes. It would appear

---

[30] Briavoinne, *op. cit.*, 78. Achille Penot (ed.), *Statistique du Haut-Rhin*, 325.

[31] Penot, *op. cit.*, 326–27.

that the real reason why the dressing machine was not used universally even in Alsace before 1850 was that it was really useful only in preparing warp for the power loom.[32] There was probably little advantage derived from its use for the slower process of weaving by hand.

The belated development of the power loom in France was not due simply to mechanical or industrial backwardness in France itself. Even in England, where the loom was invented, it required approximately forty years to make it a practical success. Construction of iron instead of wood, dressing of the warp by machinery, improvements in metallurgy, and the use of machine tools were all needed. This work in England was begun in 1796 and was not completed until after 1820. Thus, in 1818 Manchester had only 2,000 power looms and in 1820 the whole of England had only 14,000. In 1828 Manchester alone had 45,000 and in 1835 England had 116,000. We can say, therefore, that the power loom in England was not a complete success before 1825; in fact, Gilroy said in 1834 that it did not weave light, fancy goods with small patterns well before 1830 and was not successfully adapted to other textiles before 1834.[33]

In France, improvement of Cartwright's loom of 1785 began in 1804, the same year in which it was imported into Belgium, but progress was much slower than in England. As early as 1826 Josué Heilmann began to work on the problem and had some success. His looms were used in the mill of the Koechlins, his relatives by marriage, at Willer in that year, but there is no evidence that their use spread rapidly to other mills, and Emile Dollfus, one of the great cotton manufacturers in Alsace, said that the power loom was not a success in Alsace before 1830. A similar effort made at Ghent in 1824 seems to have had similar results. In Normandy the first

---

[32] Emile Dollfus, "De l'industrie cotonnière," *Bulletin de la société industrielle de Mulhouse*, v. 27 (1857), 446–47. Société Industrielle de Mulhouse, *op. cit.*, 249–51. Penot, *op. cit.*, 325. Briavoinne, *op. cit.*, 79.

[33] Clinton G. Gilroy, *Treatise on the Art of Weaving* (New York, 1844), 345. Marcel Gras, *Du machinisme et de ses conséquences économiques et sociales dans l'industrie moderne* (Paris: Rousseau, 1911), 27–28. Briavoinne, *op. cit.*, 79.

power loom is mentioned in 1825. It seems probable that the greater delay in France was due to the slower growth of machine shops and the use of machine tools, to the poor quality of the French yarn, and to the cheapness of labor. The power loom does not seem to have spread rapidly in either Alsace or Normandy until the depression that began in 1837.[34]

Tulle was in many ways a special product rather than one typical of the cotton industry as a whole, but the development of its manufacture is an integral part of the growth of the Industrial Revolution in France. It was conditioned primarily by mechanization, but it was affected profoundly also by international competition, despite the high French tariff, as well as by competition between different French industries in which the tulle manufacturers played an active part. Finally, it was rescued from an almost chronic crisis by means that were characteristically French.

The tulle industry started in England in the neighborhood of Nottingham with the invention of Heathcoat's machine in 1808. There followed almost immediately with extraordinary rapidity a series of improvements. Heathcoat's loom was changed from wood to iron and patented within a year; in 1812 it was largely superseded by the Pusher loom, in 1814 by the Leaver, and in 1817 by the circular bolt. Then, in 1822, it became, through the application of steam, a power loom. In addition to these major inventions there were incessant improvements and changes of fashion. Tulle was easy to make, profits were low, and if cost decreased rapidly so did prices. In short, the tulle industry in England was in a condition of depression, or even crisis, most of the time and it sought salvation by characteristic means such as dumping in France its older machines that could no longer be used profitably at home, and by smuggling both yarn and the tulle itself. All this remained easy until 1834. But there seems to have been some retaliation about which the French have naturally been reticent. Ferguson, a British citizen long resident in France, tells us in his very interesting book on the tulle industry in that country that the French customs service was so much more efficient than the British that in 1835 French tulle

---

[34] Penot, *op. cit.*, 326. Briavoinne, *loc. cit.* Emile Dollfus, *op. cit.*, 446.

could be smuggled into England for a fee of only 7 per cent, whereas British tulle shipped illegally into France had to pay 50 per cent. The latter figure is probably a great exaggeration. Other sources indicate that the smuggling fee was rarely more than 30 per cent and that, after the French repealed the prohibition of the importation of fine cotton yarn in 1834, the usual fee for smuggling fell to 10 per cent. Nevertheless, the essential fact remains unchallenged, that French tulle was smuggled into England. When we consider England's advantages in large-scale production of cotton yarn, her mechanization, and her development of the division of labor, the French exportation of tulle across the Channel is significant.[35]

The tulle industry was introduced into France by British manufacturers within a few years, probably as early as 1816. The chief center from the beginning was Calais, or rather its independent suburb of Saint-Pierre-lès-Calais, but the manufacturing of tulle was soon established also at Saint-Quentin, Douai, and Lille. From the start, life for the new industry was difficult. It was easy to smuggle cotton yarn and even the tulle itself into France, and French machinists could not make machines as cheaply as the English. It really seems as if in this case the French derived no benefit from their high tariff as compensation for its many disadvantages. This condition of permanently acute competition soon brought prices down 60 per cent, producing loud complaints from the French manufacturers, although at Nottingham at the same time they fell 92 per cent. The year given is 1825, but this is probably a slight error, as the speculative boom in the French cotton industry did not collapse until the following year. Despite this complaint, we know that the tulle industry was solidly established at Calais and that it was strong enough to reduce the wages of its workmen from 15 or 20 francs a day to 1.50–3 francs. This meant, of course, the dis-

---

[35] William Felkin, *History of Hosiery and Machine-Wrought Lace Manufacture*, 3d ed. (Cambridge, Eng., 1867). S. Ferguson, Jr., *Histoire du tulle et des dentelles mécaniques en Angleterre et en France* (Paris, 1862), 53–63, 72–85, 92–97. France, *Enquête sur diverses prohibitions*, v. 3; testimony of Smith, manufacturer of tulle, Calais, 318–21; of Robert Belin, delegate of tulle manufacturers of Saint-Quentin, 534.

missal of most of the English workmen who had had to be bribed
by high wages to remain in France and payment to their successors
of wages normal for workers in textile industries in France.[36]

French manufacturers were helped by the repeal of the prohibition of the importation of fine yarn in 1834, which has been mentioned. In time this proved an important factor in the improvement
of French spinning, so that by 1849 tulle manufacturers could obtain
an adequate supply of the yarn they needed in their own country.
But they were helped more by other things. The English used better
and wider looms than the French, but in their zeal to use all their
advantages to the utmost they destroyed more looms for producing
narrow tulle than was necessary. If the French suffered from overproduction of tulle until 1838 at least, and from the low prices
resulting, the English suffered even more. Conditions in England
were so bad that many English workers remained permanently in
France; that meant accepting French wages, French citizenship,
and, hardest of all for an Englishman, French food. Finally, the
English, in their emphasis on speed, neglected the quality of their
tulle and the perfection of its finish. The French saw their opportunity and used it. Hitherto they had made plain tulle and lost their
wealthier customers, who returned to the purchase of real lace.
Now the French began to manufacture fancy tulle in imitation of
real lace, and they did this with silk as well as cotton. They had
used the Jacquard loom for making silk tulle at Lyons and Nîmes
as early as 1823. Beginning in 1836–37, they adapted the Jacquard
loom to the production of cotton tulle by using it as an attachment
to the Leaver loom. Then they added embroidery until they were
able to drive out muslin curtains, and finally, they applied steam to
the running of the Leaver loom, as the English had done in 1822.
Most of these steps were taken, or developed on a considerable
scale, during the depression that lasted from 1837 to 1842. The
French had again saved one of their industries less by imitating the

[36] Paris, *Exposition nationale des produits de l'industrie agricole et
manufacturière de 1849: Rapport du jury central* ["Report on Tulle Industry," by Félix Aubry], v. 3 (Paris, 1850), 291, 298.

English than by utilizing fully their talent for design and their inherent good taste in the production of fancy goods.[37]

---

[37] Paris, *Exposition universelle de 1851 à Londres,* "Dentelles, blondes, tulles et broderies," par Félix Aubry, v. 5 (Paris, 1865), 30. Henri Hénon, *L'Industrie des tulles et des dentelles mécaniques dans le Pas-de-Calais, 1815–1900* (Paris and Calais, 1900), 22–23, 74, 76, 105. Paris, *Exposition . . . de 1849* (Aubry), v. 3, pp. 28–29. Paris, *Rapport du jury central sur les produits de l'industrie française à l'exposition de 1839,* v. 3 (Paris, 1839), 259; report of Nicolas Koechlin and Charles Legentil on cotton.

CHAPTER TWELVE

The Woolen Industry

THE COTTON INDUSTRY, as we have seen, grew rapidly in France and was mechanized rapidly, partly because the fiber of cotton is easier to manipulate than that of any other textile, and partly because of the enormous expansion of the industry in England. In the woolen industry, mechanization was much less rapid, yet the industry grew fast and adapted itself to new conditions with remarkable skill, showing great vitality. We miss here the constant sense of fear felt by the small French cotton industry for its mighty rival across the Channel, a fear kept alive by the fact that even by the great efforts made the French industry could never grow beyond a third the size of the British. In the woolen industry there was confidence from the start of the expansion in the early nineteenth century, and there was far less adherence to routine than could reasonably have been expected.

One very important branch of the woolen industry, the worsted, was confronted from the beginning with two very difficult problems. The supply of long, shiny wool in France was greatly inadequate, and as we saw in the earlier chapter on raw materials, efforts to increase it were not really successful. This helped to produce the second problem of combing short French wool at a reasonable cost. The difficulty of this second problem is proved by the fact that the English, who generally led in mechanical progress, did not produce a mechanical comber that was a practical success until the French did so. Both countries tried to solve the problem for years. Demaurey invented a mechanical comber in France in 1809, but we are told that it was a failure because the demand for combed yarn was not yet sufficient.[1]

Some years later, in 1824, Godard invented a second machine at Amiens. This also was very imperfect, but it was good enough to be bought by the English machinist John Collier, who had been established for many years at Paris.[2] He improved it, and by 1841 it was being manufactured on a large scale by Risler, Schwartz and Company of Alsace. This comber was able to comb really fine wool and removed the prejudice against mechanical combers. It was widely used at Reims in 1844.[3] We are told also that it cut the cost of combing in half. Yet it did not really replace hand combing, even if the Société Industrielle of Mulhouse predicted that it soon would. Even this Godard-Collier comber, then, was merely a palliative that alleviated but did not solve the problem of combing wool cheaply.[4]

In the meantime, Josué Heilmann had been working as a skilled mechanic and inventor in Alsace for many years. He seems to have had real ability, since he did much to improve the power loom, and he was well connected, as he had married a Koechlin. In 1843 the Bourcart prize was offered for a substitute for heating and combing by hand long-staple cotton from Georgia. Heilmann won the prize and patented his machine in France in 1845 and in England in 1846. Then it gradually became apparent that the new comber was a really remarkable invention. It proved to be the first such machine that could be used for cotton, wool, tow, and waste silk, because it acted independent of the nature of the fiber. It really did arrange the fibers parallel and separate the long from the short. But before this recognition came Heilmann had died in 1848. Nicolas Schlum-

---

[1] Paris, *Exposition universelle internationale de 1900 à Paris: Le Bilan d'un siècle (1801–1900)*, par Alfred Picard, v. 4 (Paris: Imprimerie Nationale, 1906), 187.

[2] Julien François Turgan, *Les Grandes usines,* v. 8 (Paris, 1868), 64. Paris, *Exposition des produits de l'industrie nationale de 1844: Rapport du jury central,* rédigé par Jules Burat, v. 1 (Paris, 1844), 7–14. Adolphe Blaise, *Exposition des produits de l'industrie nationale en 1839* (Paris, 1839), 47.

[3] Turgan, *loc. cit.* Paris, *Exposition . . . de 1844, loc. cit.* Blaise, *loc. cit.*

[4] Société Industrielle de Mulhouse, *Histoire documentaire de l'industrie de Mulhouse et de ses environs au XIXe siècle,* v. 1 (Mulhouse: Bader, 1902), 506–8.

berger, the noted spinner and constructor, then took over the Heilmann comber, improved it, and showed that it could comb successfully short and fine merino wool. It was adopted at Reims and,
finally, in 1852, was generally recognized as a notable invention.
There is only one criticism of it that can be made, and that is not
a serious one. It never succeeded in driving out in England the
Lister-Donisthorpe comber invented there about 1842, despite the
winning of a lawsuit by Heilmann's representatives. This would
indicate that Heilmann's comber was not an unqualified success in
combing long and shiny wool.[5]

The problem of carding wool by machinery was as difficult as
that of combing and was not solved fully during the period from
1815 to 1848. Machines for carding and for spinning carded wool
were devised by Douglas and Cockerill as early as 1803 and were
manufactured in Paris, at Verviers, and at Liège. Later they were
used at Reims, and they seemed to have been improved by various
machinists.[6] But there is no evidence that these early carding machines were good enough actually to eliminate carding by hand.
Some years later Mercier, the great machine builder of the woolen
industry in France, who had begun his career at Louviers in 1814,
applied power to the billy, a machine with 50–60 spindles, which
was the equivalent of the fly roving frame in the cotton industry.
In that same year of 1826 Mercier began making frames, carding
machines, and spinning machines of iron instead of wood.[7] Yet,
despite the recognized ability of Mercier, his power-driven billy was
evidently not a practical success, for in 1837 a spinner at Elbeuf

---

[5] Paris, Exposition . . . de 1900 (Picard), v. 4, pp. 204–5. Général
Jean-Victor Poncelet, Les Machines spécialement employées à la fabrication
des matières textiles, in Paris, Exposition universelle de 1851 à Londres,
travaux de la Commission Française, v. 3, Partie 2 (Paris, 1855), 16–18,
266–74. James Burnley, History of Wool and Woolcombing (London,
1889), 211–52. Lister played a much more important part in woolcombing
in both England and France than had been realized; William Otto Henderson, Britain and Industrial Europe, 1750–1870: Studies in British Influence
on the Industrial Revolution in Western Europe (Liverpool: University
Press, 1954), 79–91.

[6] Paris, Rapport du jury central sur les produits de l'industrie française
à l'exposition de 1819, rédigé par Baron Louis Costaz (Paris, 1919), 5.

[7] Turgan, op. cit., v. 5, pp. 410–13.

imported from the United States at great cost a set of three carding machines[8] which are reported to have eliminated the old hand-
run billy and greatly facilitated production of really fine yarn. It is
obvious that if the power-run billy had been a success there would
have been no need a decade later to eliminate the one run by hand.
This indicates also that the carding machine for cotton imported
from the United States some years earlier had not been, or could
not be, adapted to carding wool.

Spinning carded yarn, on the other hand, seems to have been
mechanized more rapidly and the adaptation to wool of machines
for spinning cotton to have been easy. Douglas and Cockerill began
to spin carded wool by machinery in France in 1811. While they
could thus spin only yarn for plain and heavy woolens, it required
only twenty years to improve the machine sufficiently to spin really
fine yarn. The Exposition of 1823 stated that carded wool was spun
by hand only in backward regions, but there must have been many
of those, for one of our very best informants on the woolen industry
tells us that the mechanical spinning of carded wool was not really
prevalent until after 1830. This would put the woolen industry in
France about twenty years behind the cotton in its mechanization,
as seems reasonable. We find the usual beneficial results in more
regular yarn which not only cost only half as much as the poorer
yarn spun by hand but also cut the cost of weaving from 3 to 4
francs per metre to one franc.[9]

Mechanization of spinning combed wool also began in 1811, the
same year as that of carded wool. A machine invented by Dobo of
Paris was set up in one of Ternaux's mills near Reims. While it did
not put a stop to spinning combed wool by hand, it did produce
better yarn and showed that the future of the worsted industry in
France would depend on the use of the short French wool grown
chiefly by the merino sheep and breeds crossed with them. The next
step forward is not quite clear. Moreau de Jonnès, a useful but not

---

[8] *Ibid.*

[9] Alexandre Moreau de Jonnès, *Statistique de l'industrie de France*
(Paris, 1856), 28–29. Paris, *Rapport du jury central sur les produits de
l'industrie française à l'exposition de 1823,* rédigé par Louis Etienne
François Héricart-Ferrand, vicomte de Thury, et Pierre Henri Migneron
(Paris, 1824), 13. Paris, *Exposition . . . de 1900* (Picard), v. 4, p. 203.

always reliable statistician, says that in 1815 there was invented or
worked out in France a method for spinning combed wool dry
which was more successful than any method then in use for carded
wool. He says further that this French system was copied by Saxony,
Prussia, Spain, and England, and he gives the names of two Scots-
men, Cochrane and Flint, who, he says, brought the French system
to Scotland and built a mill for it at Glasgow. We lack nearly all
the details we could wish for, but the progress of the spinning of
combed wool in France was sufficiently rapid to make the Jonnès
story seem plausible, and it fits in also with the known fact that the
progress in the spinning of carded wool, although notable, was
slower.[10]

In 1824 there came to Paris from Sommières in the Gard a
skilled spinner of combed wool who had trained workers for years
in mills in the south and was to continue the work at Reims. He
soon became one of the leaders in the worsted industry. Griolet spun
only the short and fine wools of France and used French machines
in most cases because he found that they were usually better than
English ones, since England used chiefly long and shiny wool. The
English themselves testified some years later to the excellence of
French combed yarn and to the superiority of the preparatory machines used by the French, which, they said, were very different
from their own. For actual spinning the French used mules only,
never the throstle, which the English liked so well. By 1844 we even
hear of self-actings being used at Reims, a date which would have
been highly creditable in the cotton industry.[11]

The struggle to obtain an adequate supply of combed wool at a
reasonable cost was evidently severe, even if we do not know the

---

[10] Paris, *Exposition universelle de 1851 à Londres,* travaux de la Commission Française sur l'Industrie des Nations, v. 4: F. Bernoville, "Industrie
des laines peignées" (Paris, 1854), 194–95. Turgan, *op. cit.,* v. 8, pp. 59–
61. Paris, *Exposition . . . de 1844* (Burat) 10–11.

[11] France, Ministère du Commerce, *Enquête sur les fils de laine longue
peignée, tordus, du cordonnet, et grillée (décembre, 1836)* (Paris, 1836),
28; testimony of Griolet. Great Britain, House of Commons, "First Report
From the Select Committee Appointed to Inquire Into the Operation of the
Existing Laws Affecting the Exportation of Machinery," *Parliamentary
Papers, 1841,* v. 7: *Reports From Committees,* v. 4 (London, 1841), 64–65;
testimony of Grenville Withers. Turgan, *op. cit.,* v. 8, p. 78.

details. The cause of the struggle is clear enough: the rapid invention of various kinds of light cloths developed after the introduction of merinos between 1801 and 1804. We know also that the production of combed wool spun by hand had increased tenfold by 1827. As the jury of the Exposition reported in 1819 that it knew of no machine for spinning combed wool on a large scale, and the jury of 1827 said that, although much progress had been made, most combed wool was still spun by hand, it is clear that the great increase in the production of combed-wool yarn was made by the hand spinners. Despite our ignorance of most of the facts we should like to know, it can be stated that the great struggle for spinning combed wool by machinery opened at the beginning of the depression that started in 1827. Bernoville, who wrote our best account of the growth of the French worsted industry for the Exposition of 1851, says that spinning combed wool was established in the region of Amiens after 1825. He goes on to tell that the struggle to produce it was caused by merino cloths and the development of novelties, and that it began in 1826 when Legrand and Billiot founded the worsted industry of Fourmies. This is confirmed by the recent study of Falleur, who shows that the Legrand family, who had had what we should call a small cotton mill for some years, changed to spinning combed wool at about that time. This was also the period when mules that spun wool were being doubled in size and built of iron instead of wood. Finally, Burat reports that the tenfold increase in the production of combed wool occurred between 1827 and 1834.[12]

Poupart de Neuflize in 1827 had in his family's well-known mill at Sedan 9,000 spindles working on spinning combed yarn from short French wool that was much more difficult to comb and spin than the longer and silkier wool of England. In that same year we hear of seven mills in Paris with 10,000 spindles of combed wool; by 1839 this number had increased to 60,000. There were also great increases at Reims and at Rethel in the Ardennes, which worked

---

[12] Paris, *Exposition universelle de 1851* (Bernoville), v. 4, pp. 152, 203–8. Paris, *Exposition . . . de 1844* (Burat), v. 1, p. 10. Adrien Falleur, *L'Industrie lainière dans la région de Fourmies* (Paris: Université de Paris, 1930), 18–21.

for both Reims and Sedan; in Picardy, which did much spinning and hand weaving for Parisian manufacturers of novelties; and, above all, at Roubaix. As early as 1834 France had an assured superiority in such light worsteds as merinos, serges, cashmeres, bombazines (*alépines*), and thibets.[13]

Alsace followed the other regions of France that have been mentioned in the production of worsteds, because her chief interest was still in printing. But when she began, she worked vigorously and displayed her usual propensity for being in the vanguard of mechanical progress. The reason for taking up the new form of production also was typical: it was too costly to get woolen muslins for printing from Saint-Quentin. The firm of Risler, Schwartz and Company was anxious to meet the increasing demand for woolen prints. In 1838 they founded the first mill in Alsace for the spinning of combed wool; they soon organized a corporation with a capitalization of 605,000 francs which built a mill for 3,000 spindles and employed as an expert Jérémie Risler-Dollfus, who had studied combing both at Reims and in the Nord. They had to get combs and preparatory machines from Reims to sort and comb the wool. This firm produced mules with 300 spindles such as they were already using for cotton. The experiment was clearly a success, for in 1839 a second mill for spinning combed wool was built and in 1845 a third. Yet, while noting these interesting facts, we must remember that the greatest increase in the spinning of combed wool did not occur in Alsace, or even at Reims, but in the region of Roubaix, of which Fourmies was still a small dependency. Perhaps the greatest contribution of the Alsatians was their irrepressible interest in the problem of combing wool by machinery, which they never forgot until they won their outstanding victory in the mechanical comber of Josué Heilmann.[14]

Improvement in the spinning of combed wool was rapid after

[13] Paris, *Rapport du jury central sur les produits de l'industrie française à l'exposition de 1834,* rédigé par Baron Charles Dupin, v. 2 (Paris, 1836), 15. Paris, *Exposition . . . de 1844* (Burat), v. 1, p. 11.

[14] Emile Dollfus, "Exposition de 1841," *Bulletin de la société industrielle de Mulhouse,* v. 15 (1841), 199–200; André Koechlin et Cie. had become Koechlin, Risler et Cie. in 1838, and then Risler, Schwartz et Cie. Société Industrielle de Mulhouse, *op. cit.,* 505.

1827. Every exposition seemed able to report increasing fineness and decreasing prices and wages. As early as 1836 Dr. Ure reported that the French could spin fine wool better than the English, although still not as well as the Saxons. While the highest number spun in 1824 was 60, a decade later it was 120. By 1834 the price of combed yarn had fallen 30 per cent, and by 1844 it had been cut another 20 per cent, while the number of combed-wool spindles had increased to 550,000 or more. Much of the improvement in spinning seems to have been secured simply by adapting the rapidly improving mules used for cotton to the spinning of wool, as was done by modifying the pressure of the cylinders, the spacing, and the speed of stretching. By 1843 the Nord alone had 220,000 spindles making worsted yarn and Roubaix had outdistanced all other French centers. In less than twenty years the French worsted industry had grown to equal the British in its production of yarn, and it did this before the commercial success of Heilmann's mechanical comber.[15]

There is much evidence of improvement in weaving woolens and worsteds in the period from 1815 to 1848, but it is important to view the problem as it actually was and to realize both the achievements and the failures of the ancient industry in the past. For this purpose we should turn to the report of the Vicomte Héricart de Thury on the Exposition of 1827, which says that the jury tended to reward the largest mills and that it was interested only in the finest cloths.[16] It considered the color and finish of those cloths far more important than the use of machinery. This shows that the jury expressed accurately views that, to a great extent, prevailed in

---

[15] Paris, *Exposition . . . de 1900* (Picard), v. 4, p. 203. Paris, *Exposition . . . de 1844* (Burat), v. 1, p. 11. Jean Pierre Hachette, "Mémoire sur les diverses modes de numérotage employés dans les filatures et dans les tréfileries," *Bulletin de la société d'encouragement pour l'industrie nationale,* v. 23 (Dec., 1824), 354. Paris, *Exposition . . . de 1834* (Dupin), v. 2, pp. 16–17. Paris, *Rapport du jury central sur les produits de l'industrie française de l'exposition de 1839* ["Report on Fulled Cloths," by Charles Legentil], v. 3 (Paris, 1839), 45. Paris, *Exposition . . . de 1851* (Bernoville) v. 4, p. 155.

[16] Paris, *Rapport du jury central sur les produits de l'industrie française de l'exposition de 1827,* rédigé par Louis Etienne François Héricart-Ferrand, le vicomte de Thury (Paris, 1828), 34.

all the textile industries. It expressed also the old tradition so greatly strengthened by Colbert which had glorified the production of fine cloths for the wealthy and ignored the needs of people of moderate means and of the poor. Because of the scarcity of evidence it is difficult for us not to do the same, but we can point out that cheap and coarse woolens were made for the masses from native wool, although this was not considered important or even interesting. The jury looked back, not forward. It did not see that already industrial improvements and a slowly rising standard of living were forcing down prices and making provision of woolen clothing for plain people a matter of the greatest importance to both merchants and manufacturers.

It is clear that during the first half of the nineteenth century the quality of woolens improved greatly, chiefly because of better spinning of the yarn used as well as to improvement in the quality of French wool. French manufacturers liked to point this out and to add that the improvement in the quality of the cloth was real and permanent and not due to an attractive finish such as that given by the English through the use of steam. One would suppose that there was no improvement in the quality of English yarn in this period, which is inconceivable to any historian aware of the constant improvement of machinery across the Channel; and one would suppose also that the French never used steam. The improvement of French woolens was accompanied by a marked decrease in price, in spite of the fact that the price of wool did not fall but tended to rise. The fall in cloth prices was due, then, chiefly to the same progress in spinning that caused the improvement in quality. It appears to have been gradual and steady through the period from 1815 to 1848, despite minor variations during booms or depressions.

There is little evidence of value or interest regarding the increasing production of woolens of medium quality, yet we know that it occurred. It is obvious that a decrease in prices of from 25 to 50 per cent would have forced it, since the price of wool was not falling, while the improvements in machinery were not being made with startling rapidity. We have only one case to cite of the new point of view, but it is an interesting one. Louviers had long reigned supreme in Normandy in the manufacture of fine woolens. But in the early nineteenth century a rival center with a better situation grew up a few miles away on the Seine. At first, apparently, Elbeuf did not produce the finest woolens in great quantity, although in the course of time it proved that it could do so. Several manufacturers from Elbeuf testified at the *enquête* of 1834, and all spoke of the rising price of wool, the falling price of cloth, and the improvement in the quality of the cloth. One manufacturer from Louviers, Jourdain-Ribouleau, gave exactly the same testimony. But in 1839 we have a different picture, and the change cannot have been caused wholly by the depression that had begun in 1837. Now we hear that Louviers had been ruined by keeping up the manufacture of the finest woolens too long and by the loss of its valuable markets in Spain and Italy. But the shrewd observer Adolphe Blaise, who gives us this information, adds that the ruin was not complete and that recovery seemed possible. Jourdain-Ribouleau had cut the production of the finest woolens to only one sixth of the total. He had also introduced the best machines available in all processes, had cut prices one third or more, and had greatly increased the variety of cloths manufactured, emphasizing particularly those of medium quality.[17]

Another fact that must have had influence is that the great Ternaux, who died in 1832, and was one of the most notable of all French entrepreneurs, had a distinguished rival in Depouilly, who came from Lyons to Paris in 1818, where he was, perhaps, the greatest of all creators of mixed cloths and one of the greatest creators of novelties as well as one of the chief supporters of the new Jacquard loom, on which many of the novelties were woven. Depouilly also was a great organizer who developed the weaving of his cloths all through Picardy and the Nord and who worked hard and steadily to improve the methods of manufacturing.[18]

There is evidence also that the weaving of worsteds responded

---

[17] France, Ministère du Commerce, *Enquête relative à diverses prohibitions établies à l'entrée des produits étrangers,* v. 3 (Paris, 1835), 50, 68, 98, 454–55, 557. Blaise, *op. cit.,* 145–46.

[18] Paris, *Exposition . . . de 1851* (Bernoville), v. 4, pp. 181–83.

to the enormous increase in the production of combed yarn. Even Reims, which had been held back by inadequate means of transporting fuel, had increased its production of worsteds fivefold between 1808 and 1848; and if figures were available, we could probably show an even greater increase at Roubaix. But weaving lagged far behind spinning. It was held back for a time because the flying shuttle was not generally used in the woolen industry until 1817. Attempts to use the power loom in weaving woolens and worsteds began soon afterwards, but all failed, probably for the same reasons that had caused delay in the cotton industry. Hand weaving of woolens was a much more ancient occupation among the peasantry than that of cotton, and the fiber of wool made mechanical spinning and weaving more difficult. Finally, after trying for eight years, Croutelle, who had a woolen mill near Reims, succeeded in weaving woolens on a power loom in 1844. By 1847 he was producing cloth of excellent quality and of amazing cheapness. But the next year his mill was burned to the ground. This may have been merely an episode in the revolution of that year, but in view of the reception of other inventions by the peasant laborers in France, it seems probable that the destruction of the mill was a protest against prospective unemployment. The result was a further delay in the development of the use of the power loom in the woolen industry, so that in 1856 Audiganne described it as an unexpected novelty.[19]

Among the improvements that helped to bring down the price of woolens was the introduction of the mechanical shearer. A similar machine had been invented in England as early as 1758 and was in general use there early in the nineteenth century. Yet attempts to introduce it into France accomplished little because the human shearers in the chief textile centers were sufficiently well organized

[19] Paris, *Exposition nationale des produits de l'industrie agricole et manufacturière de 1849: Rapport du jury central*, "Laines peignées et filées," par Tibaut et Dumas [and on yarns of Roubaix and Lille], Partie 1, Sect. 1 (Paris, 1850), 66–68. Paris, *Exposition . . . de 1851* (Bernoville), v. 4, pp. 186, 198–99. Armand Audiganne, *L'Industrie contemporaine, ses caractères et ses progrès chez les différents peuples du monde* (Paris, 1856), 287.

to terrorize the manufacturers. This is the explanation of Manuel, who has written an excellent article on the introduction of the shearer into France, but we may wonder if there were not defects in the English machine either as introduced or as copied by machinists in France.

In the meantime, a mechanized shearer had been invented at Boston and was brought to France by Jonathan Ellis in 1812. This was bought and improved by John Collier, the English machinist established in Paris. Whatever Collier's own contribution may have been, he secured proper financial support from the de Neuflize brothers of Sedan, who generally resided in Paris and had great influence with the Minister of the Interior. The machine, now bearing Collier's name, at first cut only lengthwise, but in 1819 it was improved so that it could cut transversely as well and, finally, was given a movable blade that could cut coming and going. It could be run by any motor; that was important in France, where steam engines were scarce and water power was comparatively abundant. In its improved form Collier's mechanical shearer seems to have been generally adopted in French woolen and worsted mills without undue difficulty or great delay.[20]

Another improvement made towards the end of the period 1815–48 was the fulling mill. John Hall's rotary fulling mill is reported to have been used at Louviers in 1838 with success and subsequently to have been replaced at Elbeuf by a better machine giving pressure by springs rather than weights. This account is given, however, by Colmont in his *History of Expositions*. It may be correct, but Colmont is inclined to accept evidence without much criticism, and he may not have been able to resist the temptation to minimize the contribution of England. The date he gives may be accurate, for Burat speaks of fulling by machinery as a general practice in 1839. Dupérier, reporting on the Exposition of 1849, says that fulling had been greatly improved by 1844 and that this

---

[20] Frank E. Manuel, "The Luddite Movement in France," *Journal of Modern History,* v. 10 (1938), 189–93, 196. Paris, *Exposition . . . de 1900* (Picard), v. 4, p. 294. *Exposition . . . de 1823* (vicomte de Thury), 303–4. Great Britain, "First Report . . ." *Parliamentary Papers,* v. 7, p. 112.

improvement was continued by the introduction of the English fulling mill, which was easy to set up and to run under supervision. It seems clear, then, that the fulling mill was introduced from England before 1839 and greatly improved thereafter, but it would seem probable that improvements were made in England as well as France, and we are not warranted in saying that a French fulling mill replaced one imported from England.[21]

When we consider the cloths manufactured in France we are impressed by their endless variety. Jonnès shows this in his figures for the year 1850: 1,038 mills made heavy woolens and hosiery; 652 merinos, shawls, stuffs, muslins, and other light cloths; 516 made mixed cloths in which wool was an important element.[22] His classification does not seem of great importance or value, but it does show how the woolen industry of France had changed. We can add that that change had begun early in the period from 1815 to 1848.

Another prevalent tendency was the ever-increasing production of cloths of medium quality. A few centers like Sedan and Aubusson held out for the production of the specialties for which they had long been famous, but even Sedan succumbed before the end of the period, and Aubusson found it ever more difficult to sell its costly tapestries and velvet carpets. Foreign markets and the domestic market were all changing. Other countries were developing their own textile industries and discriminating increasingly against France because of her prohibitive tariff. At home the nobility and a few very wealthy bourgeois still existed, but the number of middle-class consumers of reasonably priced woolens had grown so large that no sensible merchant could ignore their demands. All through this period the creation of every fancy cloth led promptly to the creation of one or more cheaper substitutes. Finally, the woolen industry showed most clearly that an era of intense competition between the different textile industries of France had opened. The woolen industry demonstrated also the fact that it could compete forcefully

---

[21] Turgan, op. cit., v. 5, p. 44. Paris, Exposition . . . de 1844 (Burat), v. 1, p. 14. Paris, Exposition . . . de 1849, v. 3, p. 20; report of Kuhlmann.
[22] Moreau de Jonnès, op. cit., 36.

with its young and powerful rival, the cotton industry, as well as with the older industries of silk and linen. In all the textile centers of conservative France, even in the south, we find change. Beauty of form and color were still admired and created, but price became ever more important and fashions now changed frequently because the demand for endless variety was insatiable.

Louviers, as we have seen, had cut the finest woolens on which her reputation had rested to one sixth of her production. But even so, she was outdistanced increasingly by Elbeuf. First Elbeuf dropped the label "Louviers" which she had formerly put on all her cloths. Then she increased steadily her production of woolens of medium quality. Rouen, which had long been the center for the production of cheap cotton prints, suddenly started to produce woolens for women's gowns and cloaks. Reims, formerly known chiefly as the site of one of France's most beautiful and venerated cathedrals, quickly rose to become one of the chief centers for the production of an almost endless variety of woolens and worsteds. Roubaix, which had been for a brief period a minor center for cottons, now grew into the greatest of all centers for the making of mixed cloths and novelties. Even Paris, the capital, used its leadership in skill and design to produce such an endless number of novelties in prints, shawls, waistcoats, and other cloths that towns like Roubaix could have devoted all their energies to their imitation at a lower price. We must not be deceived by complaints that long and shiny wool could not be obtained in sufficient quantity, or at a reasonable cost, or that cheap and medium qualities of wool could not be imported over the French tariff. Both of these complaints were based on fact, but the increase in production and in its endless variation continued in spite of them.[23]

Paris had long been the home of Morin, a leading designer of novelties whose work was so good that most of the Nord either worked for him or in imitation of him. He remained, however, a

---

[23] Paris, *Exposition . . . de 1839* (Legentil), v. 3, pp. 48, 52–55. Paris, *Exposition . . . de 1834* (Dupin), v. 2, p. 69. France, *Enquête relative [1834]*, v. 3, pp. 398–403; testimony of Henriot, manufacturer of woolens, Reims. Paris, *Exposition . . . de 1849* (Thibaut and Dumas), v. 3, pp. 70–83, 86. Paris, *Exposition . . . de 1851* (Bernoville), v. 4, pp. 205–7.

strategist, interested in displaying his skill and ingenuity, but indifferent to the development of business on a large scale. Yet we know that he employed hundreds of rural weavers in Picardy as well as in the Nord.[24] He had rivals in Paris, of course, such as Pagès-Baligot, a specialist in novelties for waistcoats who founded his firm in 1832.[25] Even more dramatic must have been the struggle between Depouilly, who came to Paris from Lyons in 1818, as the one who did most to spread the Jacquard loom and the production of mixed cloths, and Jourdan,[26] a designer of great skill, an energetic entrepreneur, and a protégé of the great Ternaux. Jourdan came to Paris in 1826, almost immediately bought a mill there that had belonged to Depouilly, and began to devise new kinds of woolens and mixed cloths. It is a pity that we cannot trace the history of what was already a bitter struggle and may have been a long one, for Depouilly was still flourishing in 1834.

The novelties produced by the skilled designers of Paris, usually at high cost and on a small scale, were promptly imitated by Roubaix, which made them the next year on a very large scale and at a much lower cost. The greater volume of sales was not, however, the only explanation of the success of Roubaix, for mixture with cheaper textiles was a favorite weapon. Roubaix seemed able to imitate anyone, usually at a lower price, but not always, for she produced rich cloths, too. When Aubert introduced English stuffs at Rouen, Roubaix promptly copied them and did it so well that she kept them and later developed from them the richer satins. Her volume of business soon became as great as that of Reims, and she grew faster than any other center in France; yet most of her firms remained partnerships and her mills were usually small. All these facts make the performance of Roubaix seem remarkable, but we must add to them the purchase or importation over the high tariff of an endless variety of wools, whether long and shiny or short, whether fine or coarse, as well as all kinds of cotton, flax, silk, waste silk, goat's hair, and alpaca. When we realize that all this was done by

---

[24] See Note 23.
[25] See Note 23.
[26] Paris, *Exposition . . . de 1851* (Bernoville), v. 4, pp. 175, 186.

a considerable number of small firms all competing bitterly with each other, the achievement seems almost miraculous.

In sharp contrast to Roubaix in the north stood Nîmes in the south. Where the northern center had suddenly emerged from an obscure village into an important city, Nîmes had been a center of importance in the days of Rome. Later still she had been important as a stronghold of Protestantism. Now, in the earlier nineteenth century, she was trying to imitate the products of Lyons and Paris, just as Roubaix was, and she made a particular effort to do so in her shawls. Where Paris made pure cashmere shawls of rare beauty and great price, Lyons produced the thibet shawl, in which wool of French sheep was mixed with that of the Asiatic goat that even Ternaux had been unable to acclimatize in France. Nîmes in her turn produced the Hindu shawl at a still lower price. She reduced the size, the number of threads, the amount of wool, and the number of colors. She had great skill and ingenuity in her Protestant manufacturers and a large supply of cheap labor which was almost wholly Catholic. For a time Nîmes seemed highly successful. The production of Hindu shawls there reached its height in 1838, when Nîmes made 110,000 on 5,000 looms. Then, with the depression of 1846, came the collapse of the industry. The Hindu shawls were driven from the Levant by the competition of Glasgow and Vienna. They were excluded from Spain by an anti-French tariff which discriminated against cloth containing cotton. The laborers of Nîmes grew restive and refused to accept further reductions in wages. The industrial plants of the southern center had outgrown the limited supply of water. As means of communication improved, Nîmes suffered more from the products of Paris and Roubaix. The ingenuity of her manufacturers could not overcome these obstacles, and their judgment had been faulty in carrying cheapness too far. It could be argued, of course, that Nîmes suffered from an inadequate supply of cheap wool; but this should not be emphasized, because we find the same evidence of decadence in numerous parts of the silk industry at Nîmes.[27]

---

[27] Henri Reboul, *L'Industrie nîmoise du tissage au XIX° siècle* (Montpellier: Firmin et Montane, 1914), 61–64. Paris, *Exposition . . . de 1839*, v. 3, pp. 137–40; report of Griolet.

One curious industry should be mentioned which flourished for a quarter of a century when it would seem as if it should have succumbed early. This was the manufacture of pure cashmere shawls in or for Paris. These shawls had been known in France before Napoleon's expedition to Egypt; they had been imitated first in silk and linen, and later in silk and wool. Then Ternaux brought in a flock of the goats that grow the wool. While, as we have seen, he failed ultimately to make them increase in France, he did succeed in starting the manufacture of pure cashmere shawls about 1820. Their beauty was great, but their cost was greater. Cashmere wool was too soft, the amount of waste very great, and the threads frequently broke in weaving. But spinning was improved by the development of better machines and by 1827 the cost had been cut 30 per cent. Curiously enough, this industry held its own against many cheaper imitations until 1840. It employed four thousand persons for the preparation and spinning of the wool and several hundred looms. There were, of course, many changes in manufacturing methods, of which the most important was the application of the Jacquard loom, and it was probably only through these that the industry survived at all.[28] But its prosperity for so long a period is not only a proof of the innate French love of luxurious beauty; it is also a tribute to French ingenuity.

---

[28] Paris, *Exposition . . . de 1839*, v. 3, pp. 130–43. Jean Rey, *Etudes pour servir à l'histoire des châles* (Paris, 1823), 192, 207. Paris, *Exposition . . . de 1834* (Dupin), v. 2, p. 78. Paris, *Exposition . . . de 1851* (Bernoville), v. 4, pp. 161–62: "Industrie des châles et des tissus mélanges," par Maxime Gausseu, v. 4, p. 2.

CHAPTER THIRTEEN

The Linen Industry

THE PREPARATION OF FLAX and its manufacture into cloth is probably the oldest of all the textile industries in France. Like the woolen industry, it was thoroughly indigenous. Many parts of France, such as Flanders, Brittany, and southern Normandy and Anjou, grew flax on a large scale, and it was often of excellent quality. It was then spun and woven by the peasants who had grown it in their spare time when they could not work in the fields. It is well to remember that even in the period from 1815 to 1848 the peasants formed the largest single class in the French population and that their industry and thrift as well as their love of the land were of vital importance to the French nation in the nineteenth century, as they had been throughout its history. We have, then, an occupation associated intimately with both agriculture and industry and appealing strongly to the French government and people as promoting the welfare of the peasantry and, with it, the maintenance of the life of the family, with all the moral implications that were frequently discussed by the middle class in both France and England.

No industry could have been more deserving of protection by the government, and yet none was so gravely endangered. The flax of France, as we have seen, was threatened by the flax of Russia, which, while admittedly inferior in quality, could be grown in enormous quantities and at amazingly low cost because land was so cheap and abundant in the Muscovite empire. In the second place, the linen industry of France was threatened both by the commercial power of England, which made it easy for her to import Russian flax cheaply, and by her genius for the use of machinery and of large-scale production, which enabled her to spin the cheap Russian flax into yarn at a cost far below that paid by the French and of a quality that only her best hand spinners could equal. Finally, and most dangerous of all, the French linen industry was threatened by cotton both at home and abroad, for the cotton industry could provide easily and cheaply very satisfactory substitutes for most linens. This last danger was realized only dimly in the period of which we write, but to the historian it is the gravest of all—so grave that the very existence of the linen industry was threatened.

The fact that most flax was grown and prepared by the peasants led to serious results in the nineteenth century. Wherever commercial spinning or weaving was involved—in short, where the flax was not spun and woven by the same peasants who had grown and prepared it, and for their own use—the questions of uniformity and quality of yarn and cloth were raised. In one case, it is true, the flax was so good and so well prepared that it was used for the manufacture of batistes without ever being sold in important markets. But this flax was grown only in the best soil in and near Flanders.[1] In Brittany, on the other hand, where the soil and climate were also favourable, the flax was prepared so carelessly by an illiterate peasantry that it could be used only for the coarsest yarn and cloth.

This close connection of the linen industry with the soil of France and the peasantry that tilled it was the chief cause of the marked reluctance to use mechanical improvements that is more striking than in any other of the textile industries. It was tragic that the inventive genius who pointed out the road to salvation, and who was himself a Frenchman, was not appreciated by his countrymen until after foreigners had developed his ideas into a great mechanized industry. It is true that Philippe de Girard was not a good entrepreneur and that he made his great invention when the wars of Napoleon were at their height. Nevertheless, his countrymen

---

[1] Paris, *Exposition nationale de produits de l'industrie agricole et manufacturière de 1849* ["Report on Linen," by Desportes], v. 3 (Paris, 1850), 235. Auguste Chérot, *Etudes sur la culture, l'industrie et le commerce du lin et du chanvre en France,* v. 2 (Paris, 1845), 14–15.

cannot absolve themselves of blame for failing to listen to him by dwelling upon British perfidy. De Girard may have tried to do too much, and he was not actually very successful in the development of the mechanical spinning of flax, but he did realize some of the essential steps and he was very good indeed in preparing flax for spinning. Charles Ballot[2] expresses a common French attitude when he condemns Decoster, with whose work on machinery we are already familiar, as a mechanic disloyal to the master who trained him. General Poncelet, on the contrary, wrote as an unimpassioned historian, although he composed his history of French machinery only a few years after de Girard's death.[3]

Attempts to ret and scutch flax mechanically were made as early as 1789 in both France and England,[4] but failed because the machines were too complex and expensive to compete with cheap rural labor. Their real success in France would have destroyed one of her most important rural industries. Less than a quarter of a century later de Girard showed how to soften the fibers of flax by using a soap or some other alkaline solution with hot water. This was not, strictly speaking, a mechanical invention, but it was essential to the success of the machines that were developed later. It produced fibers that made the yarn four times as fine as that obtained from flax spun by hand that had not been soaked in this way, and de Girard used it himself for some time in France before it was known in England. Even the great English spinner and entrepreneur John Marshall, who went to France in 1824 and lured one of de Girard's former partners to England, failed to produce really good yarn until

---

[2] Charles Ballot, "Philippe de Girard et l'invention de la filature mécanique du lin," *Revue d'histoire des doctrines économiques et sociales,* v. 7 (1914–19), 136–91.

[3] Général Jean-Victor Poncelet, *Les Machines spécialement employées à la fabrication des matières textiles,* in Paris, *Exposition universelle de 1851 à Londres,* travaux de la Commission Française sur l'Industrie des Nations, v. 3, Partie 2 (Paris, 1855), 171–248. Charles Coquelin, "De l'industrie linière en France et en Angleterre," *Revue des deux mondes,* Série 4, v. 14 (1839), 70–73; *Nouveau traité complet de la filature mécanique du lin et du chanvre* (Paris, 1846), 150–55. Coquelin was the best informed and least prejudiced of all the writers on the French linen industry.

[4] See Note 3.

he soaked his flax as de Girard had directed. Another Englishman, Kay, had meanwhile patented the process in England in 1826. The English, with their keen sense of justice, annulled Kay's patent when it was shown that it rested wholly upon de Girard's idea, but this did not prevent English manufacturers from continuing to use it without paying royalties to its real inventor.[5]

De Girard made another invention useful in the preparation of flax—a mechanical comber which was adopted at Leeds in 1826. Like many important inventions, it was not very successful at first. Perhaps the most important idea supplied by de Girard for the comber was that of combing simultaneously both sides of the mesh. Another was the progressive and regular decrease in the size and spacing of the needles or combs, beginning with the entrance of the mesh into the machine. The comber is estimated to have eliminated four fifths of the labor needed to comb by hand. These conceptions of the French inventor are important, but it is perfectly clear that the Girard comber did not run smoothly. It had to be improved and then imported into France in 1832, where, as we have noted, it was seen and used by Decoster, who after further improvements began making it on a commercial scale in Paris in 1835. Even then it could not prepare flax properly for the finest yarn, but it was considered the best comber available until 1842, at least. It would seem as if it were difficult enough for the French to have their own invention brought back to them from England, even if it had been improved there. But there was even more trouble in store, for this Girard-Decoster comber proved much more successful in treating the strong flax of Russia than the tender flax of France. It thus added directly to the difficulties of the peasants growing flax in both France and Belgium, and probably to those of northern Ireland as well.[6]

At the great *enquête* of 1838, called by the French government to discuss means of meeting the crisis in the linen industry, all the witnesses agreed that the spinning of flax by hand was doomed, but they disagreed as to the time of its demise. Some were so impressed

---

[5] See Note 3.
[6] See Note 3.

by the flood of British yarn that had been pouring into France for several years that they thought the demise of hand spinning would come very soon. Others, more familiar with French agriculture and the doggedness of the peasantry, and more willing to admit the power of tradition and routine, felt that hand spinning would die very slowly indeed. The latter view was expressed by Charles Legentil, a Parisian merchant who remained for many years one of the shrewdest and most honest observers of French industrial progress, and by Charles Coquelin, who was probably the ablest of all the writers on the French linen industry. Coquelin predicted that hand spinning would die out very gradually, because it was so widespread and because the French used linen far more than the English did and cotton far less. Yet he realized as clearly as the other observers of the time that the menace of mechanically spun yarn from England must be met, and that this should be done not so much by raising the tariff on yarn as by developing mechanical spinning in France.[7]

The first years of the period 1815–48 had shown that little progress was being made in the mechanization of the French linen industry. Not only had de Girard failed to solve fully the problem of spinning flax by machinery, but he had failed completely to impress the importance of his ideas on his government and his countrymen. He had received the prize offered by the government for the mechanical spinning of flax in its decree of 1810, but even that decree had had an unfortunate feature that helped to make de Girard's invention ineffective. The government had emphasized the need for fine yarn, so that manufacturers neglected coarse yarn and tow, with which it would have been easier to solve many of the practical problems of mechanization. In addition, de Girard's workshop was called upon for many different kinds of yarn, so that the machines used had constantly to be adjusted. This made it much more difficult to spin well with machines that were already imper-

[7] France, *Enquête sur les fils et tissus de lin et de chanvre,* par le Conseil Supérieur du Commerce (Paris, 1838), 1–8, 10–18, 22–27, 32–38, 41–49, 54–59, 108–28, 130–35, 136–43, 144–49, 157–69, 173–83, 189–93, 218–27, 235–54; the sessions were held in June, 1838. Coquelin, *Nouveau traité,* 211.

fect. There were other difficulties, such as commercial and industrial crises and the downfall of the Napoleonic government. It is not surprising, then, that de Girard's work was neither understood nor appreciated in France and that, since he was not a good manager, his invention was sold by his partners to Horace Hall in November, 1814. It is true that in 1815 de Girard received an English patent for his invention, but this was largely ignored and in 1830 his spinning machine was brought back to France under a French importation patent granted to the firm of Viau, Houdoy and Lenty of Lille. Few French writers seem to realize that his own countrymen treated de Girard with quite as much treachery as had the alien English.[8]

Up to about 1834 there seems to have been little progress in France in the mechanization of the spinning of flax. The machines used after 1815 chiefly spun coarse yarn, so badly that they did not compete effectively with the hand spinners. They had been introduced by men lacking proper technical and business experience. In 1821 a spinning mill had been established at Nogent near Creil and three years later its manager Breidt introduced more than a hundred machines for the spinning of coarse yarn. This experiment was constructive in that a man who was technically competent attempted what had been tried before by others unfitted for the task. It is interesting also because the machines introduced were throstles, which the French did not like for spinning either cotton or wool. Finally, we may note that the real owners of the firm were two members of the Schlumberger family. It may well be that one of them was Nicolas Schlumberger, the famous spinner of Guebwiller, who was keenly interested in the construction and improvement of textile machinery. We do know that at the Exposition of 1851 Nicolas Schlumberger exhibited a throstle for spinning flax which was highly commended. But if he was personally interested in the mill at Nogent he failed there, for we hear that in 1828 the mill was offered to the government by its owners for the training of managers and foremen in the spinning of flax. This offer may have been sincere, for it was endorsed by the Société d'Encouragement pour l'Industrie Nationale, but it may also have been

---

[8] Poncelet, *op. cit.*, 171–78.

caused by the failure of the firm in the depression that had begun in 1827. There seem to have been other experiments with mechanical spinning of coarse yarn in both Picardy and Normandy, but there is no indication that any of them was successful, or even made any important improvement.[9] Little was known about the improvements being made at Leeds by Marshall after his visit to France in 1824.

The effective mechanization of the spinning mills in France was the direct result of the enormous increase in the production of mechanically spun yarn in England, which resulted about 1830 in a flood of exports to France. The change in France began slowly because it was dependent upon the importation of preparatory and spinning machines, most of which had to be smuggled across the Channel. In 1832 Malo and Dickson began the construction of a mill for spinning tow equipped completely with machines smuggled from England, but they were not able to open it until 1837. In the meantime, the Scrive brothers had opened a large mill of 10,000 spindles at Lille in 1834, wholly equipped with English machines, and Feray opened a similar but much smaller mill in 1835. Both the Scrives and Feray, it will be recalled, began immediately to copy English machines for their own use exclusively and seem to have been successful, although their machines were expensive. Other mechanized mills that were started early were that of Colin and Company at Boulogne, opened in 1834, and the Liénard mill at Pont Rémy in Normandy, opened in 1835. We do not know where Colin obtained his new machines, but we do know that he had been nearly ruined by the prolonged use of old machines. The increase of foreign competition forced him to renew his equipment completely. He was a linen merchant and his capital appears to have been French. Liénard has been mentioned before as the manufacturer who financed Decoster when he built his enlarged machine shop in Paris in 1835, but his mill does not seem to have grown

---

[9] Coquelin, "Industrie linière," 70–73. Louis François Etienne Héricart-Ferrand, vicomte de Thury, "Rapport au nom du comité des arts mécaniques sur la filature du lin et du chanvre par mécanique, de MM. Schlumberger père et fils et compagnie, à Nogent-lès-Vierges, Oise," *Bulletin de la société d'encouragement pour l'industrie nationale,* v. 27 (1828), 33–36. Poncelet, *op. cit.,* 185.

beyond 6,000 spindles, whereas the Colin mill had more than 10,000 and was the largest spinning mill in France at that comparatively early date.[10]

The construction of new mills continued through the depression that began in 1837 and the boom that followed from 1842 to 1847. The largest and best mill in France, that of the Société Anonyme de la Filature de Lin at Amiens, was opened in 1838 and had 10,360 spindles before 1849. It may have had all these spindles at or soon after its opening, for it was described as early as 1844 as the best mill for the spinning of flax in France. The three very incomplete sets of figures we have giving the mechanized spindles in France after 1840 indicate rapid expansion from 1840 to 1845 at least, then slow growth until 1849, and thereafter resumption of rapid expansion. From these figures, incomplete as they are, and from other sources, it is clear that the mechanization of spinning was not checked seriously by the depression of 1837–42. Yet we know that there were grave difficulties to surmount because of rapidly falling prices and because of injudicious and even reckless imitation of English machinery without regard to the different needs of French industry. The crisis of 1847, followed by the revolution, appears to have been more serious, but recovery seems to have begun in or soon after 1849, and to have continued unchecked until after 1856, for during those seven years the number of mechanical spindles in France was almost doubled.[11]

Our information regarding the size of the new mills for mechan-

[10] France, *Enquête [de 1838]*, 10–12, 41–46. Coquelin, "Industrie linière," 213–14. Emile Dollfus, "Exposition des produits de l'industrie alsacienne de 1841; Rapport général," *Bulletin de la société industrielle de Mulhouse*, v. 15 (1841), 203–5. Paris, *Exposition . . . de 1849*, v. 3, pp. 237–39; report on linen by Desportes. Paris, *Rapport du jury central des produits de l'industrie française à l'exposition de 1844*, rédigé par Jules Burat, v. 1 (Paris, 1845), 34–38.

[11] Paris, *Exposition universelle de 1851 à Londres*, travaux de la Commission Française sur l'Industrie des Nations, "Industrie du chanvre et du lin," par Charles Legentil, v. 4 (Paris, 1854), 9–13. Alfred J. Renouard, *Etudes sur le travail des lins*, 4th ed., v. 4 (Paris, 1879), 42–43. Guillaume Jacquemyns, "Histoire de la crise économique des Flandres, 1845–50," *Mémoires, lettres, etc., de l'académie royale de Belgique*, v. 26 (Brussels, 1929), 87–88. Conseil Général des Manufactures, *Traité belge*, "Session de janvier, 1846" (Paris, 1846), 19–20.

ized spinning in France is scanty, as usual, but it shows not only that most of the mills were very small, as we have seen, but that they were positively puny in comparison with the great Marshall mill at Leeds with its 60,000 spindles and several other English mills with 40,000, while even Ghent had a mill with 36,000. The largest mill in France mentioned by Audiganne had only 16,000. It is clear also that the spinning machines used in the French mills were small, that very few were run by steam, and that those that were had about half as much power as was available for running comparable machines in England. As usual the French were reluctant to use power because of the high cost resulting from inadequate means of transportation and insufficient or excessively costly supplies of coal. The few records available show also that the new mills for mechanized spinning were arising chiefly in French Flanders and Picardy, with only a few in Normandy, and virtually none in Brittany.[12]

The achievements of French spinners in the last years of the period from 1815 to 1848 were not, then, brilliant, but they were important and show that risks were taken and great determination shown. This should be stated, for it might be supposed from some French writers themselves that French spinners were saved wholly by their high tariff on flax yarn and linens.[13] The tariff was clearly a great help, but the manufacturers did not rely upon it alone. It is clear that prices of both yarn and cloth were much too high between 1835 and 1837, and that then they fell suddenly. This was due to the crisis of 1837, which was felt severely in France, even if French writers called it a British and American crisis. We must remember

[12] Armand Audiganne, *L'Industrie contemporaine, ses caractères et ses progrès chez les différents peuples du monde* (Paris, 1856), 395–97. Paris, *Exposition universelle de 1851* (Legentil), v. 4, pp. 9–13. Alexandre Moreau de Jonnès, *Statistique de l'industrie de France* (Paris, 1856), 173. Paris, *Exposition . . . de 1844* (Burat), v. 1, pp 34–38.

[13] Most of the witnesses at the *enquête* of 1838 were ardent protectionists and consistently overemphasized the importance of the tariff. Ernest Feray was one of the worst offenders in this, although eager to have his own ability and energy recognized, as they deserved to be; for despite his vanity and prejudices, he was one of the ablest manufacturers of both linens and cottons in France. Renouard, despite his great knowledge of the manufacture of linens and the fact that he wrote as late as 1879, was influenced in most of his judgments by his ardent protectionism.

this crisis, as well as the flood of mechanically spun yarn from England in the years before it, if we are to understand the gloom of so many of the witnesses at the great *enquête* of 1838. After the crisis was over, the increased mechanization of spinning kept the price of yarn down. It is the estimate of Legentil, an excellent observer, that mechanization brought the price of French yarn down one third and a similar conclusion was reached somewhat earlier by Jules Burat. We cannot say, of course, how much of the fall was due to the depression, and how much to mechanization, but it is clear that the boom of 1842–47 did not bring the price of yarn back to its former level. It is clear also that by 1849 French spinners had recovered control of their home market and had done so in great part by their own efforts.[14]

It is interesting to compare with the French mechanization of spinning the experience of Belgium, where conditions of production resembled those of northern France, except that coal and iron were rather more abundant and cheap. Belgium had been alarmed by the rapid increase in the exports of British yarn to France, which affected Belgium in 1830. The Belgians met the new danger, as the French did in the Nord, by building mills, presumably with new and improved machines, between 1834 and 1838, causing a bitter struggle with hand spinners during the ensuing decade. This was prolonged and embittered as the Association pour le Progrès de l'Industrie Linière, organized mainly by political interests in 1838, tried to help the hand spinners by providing better wheels and mechanical combers and by granting subsidies. It attempted to assist the hand weavers also with flying shuttles, Jacquard looms, and the creation of schools of weaving. The effort to help the spinners failed and was given up by the government in 1842. By the time of the depression of 1847, the mills had won a complete victory, and their 14,000 spinners with 295,000 spindles were producing as much yarn as 200,000 hand spinners had been able to make. There were still

---

[14] Paris, *Exposition . . . de 1844* (Burat) *loc. cit.; . . . de 1851* (Legentil), *loc. cit.* Moreau de Jonnès, *loc. cit.* [Charles Schlumberger] "Exposition de 1839: Rapport du Jury du Haut-Rhin," *Bulletin de la société industrielle de Mulhouse,* v. 12 (1839), 285. Of these commentators on prices the one with the soundest judgment was Legentil.

nearly 70,000 hand spinners of flax in Belgium, but their wages were below the minimum standard of living, which was even lower than in France. Hand weaving survived much longer, but it is impossible to say how much this was due to the help provided by the association. We know that hand weaving survived for many years in France also, where it was not given organized assistance with governmental approval.[15]

The effects of increasing mechanization of spinning upon the weaving of linens in France were good. Even as early as the *enquête* held in the summer of 1838 two important witnesses testified that the price of cloth had been reduced 20 per cent and the production of it increased.[16] Several witnesses said also that the production of linens at both Cholet and Alençon in central France north of the Loire had been revived by the use of this yarn. It should be remembered that in the summer of 1838 France was approaching the bottom of a deep depression. Evidence of increasing production was, therefore, of great importance. While at that time most of the mechanized yarn used was probably British in origin, we know that it was largely replaced by French yarn during the following decade. Great benefits were felt also at Lisieux, described by several merchants in 1838 as the most important center of the linen industry in France. It is interesting to note also that they spoke of Belgian competition as the only one which they regarded as serious.

Weavers of linen in France were not troubled by the competition of British cloth in 1838 as were the spinners because, in the main, the two countries did not manufacture the same kinds of

---

[15] Ernest Dubois, *L'Industrie du tissage du lin dans les Flandres* in v. 2, Royaume de Belgique, Ministère de l'Industrie, *Les Industries à domicile en Belgique* (Brussels, 1900), 119. Louis Varlez, *Les Salaires dans l'industrie gantoise,* v. 2 (Brussels: Royaume de Belgique, Ministère de l'Industrie, 1904), pp. xxxv–xlv. Jacquemyns, *op. cit.,* 44–89. The victory of mechanical spinning in Belgium was certainly secured more rapidly than in France. One reason was that the depression which began in France in 1837 and lasted until 1842 began a few months later in Belgium but was so much more severe that Belgium never really experienced the French boom of 1842–47.

[16] France, *Enquête [de 1838]*, testimony of Delloye, 22–27. Paris, *Exposition . . . de 1839,* 285.

linens and because the mechanization of weaving in England had not proceeded very far. There is ample evidence that most British linens that reached France were of coarse or medium quality and that those woven on power looms were distinctly inferior. One of the abler witnesses at the *enquête* of 1838, the merchant-manufacturer Colin, said that the English had returned to hand weaving, although it cost 10 per cent more, because it enabled them to weave wider cloth and cloth that could be washed and bleached better. This does not mean, of course, that the English really abandoned the power loom, but rather that it took them many years to improve it to the point where it could produce cloth as good as that woven by hand. This had been their experience with both cotton and wool earlier, and linen is a much more difficult textile to weave mechanically. Legentil tells us that between 1839 and 1851 the number of power looms in England had increased only from 300 to 1,000 and that most of those were in Scotland. The French in 1851 had 600 power looms, of which 300 were in the Nord, 150 in Calvados, of which the commercial center was Lisieux, and the rest scattered. These figures indicate that France was following England in the mechanization of linen weaving almost as rapidly as in that of combed wool and rather more rapidly than in cotton. Yet it shows that at the end of the period, in 1848, the power loom had not yet begun to threaten the hand weaver seriously, if we consider the country as a whole. Nor have we reason to believe that the situation changed rapidly in the first years of the Second Empire.[17]

Some of the most marked characteristics of French textile manufacturing are well illustrated, in the period from 1815 to 1848, by weaving forms of fine linen for which France was famous, damasks and batistes. Damasks had been brought to France from Silesia after the Napoleonic conquest of Germany and developed at Saint-Quentin in Picardy, where there had long been an adequate supply of spinners and weavers of flax. They were exhibited first at the Exposition of 1819 at Paris. Later they were manufactured at Saint-Quentin by Dollé, who sought to drive out the older batistes and

---

[17] France, *Enquête* [*de 1838*], testimony of Colin of Paris, 110. Paris, *Exposition de 1851* (Legentil), v. 4, pp. 15–16.

is said, for this purpose, to have adapted the Jacquard loom to weaving damasks. There is truth in this, for it was about 1820 that the adaptation of the Jacquard loom to the manufacture of mixed cloths was made and the rapid increase in novelties began, as we saw in our study of the woolen industry. But Dollé does not seem to have succeeded in his competition with the batistes woven not far away in the north, for we continue to hear of their manufacture and we do not hear again of Dollé or the manufacture of damasks at Saint-Quentin. It would appear that the whole linen industry of Saint-Quentin succumbed to the competition of cotton which, as we have seen, was growing rapidly there after 1820, largely through taking over spinners and weavers of flax. After 1840 we hear of the manufacture of damasks by the firm of Schlumberger and Schwartz in Alsace, and by Ernest Feray, whose mill was near Paris; and finally, their manufacture had been established at Roubaix in 1834. There are indications also that Dollé, in his adaptation of the Jacquard loom to weaving damasks, followed by several years Feray himself. The error was probably not made intentionally by Dollé, but is more likely to have been the result of ignorance and pride on the part of a provincial historian of Picardy.[18]

Batistes were a cloth first woven near Cambrai in 1309 and, therefore, usually called "cambric" by English writers. In the earlier nineteenth century they were woven chiefly in the districts of Valenciennes, Cambrai, Bapaume, and Vervins because of the unusually fine flax grown in that part of France. The cloth was so fine that only the best quality of flax could be used, and French pride in it was so great that flax was reserved for batistes and grown for them exclusively without ever being sold in the larger markets. Humidity also was necessary for the production of true batistes, so they were

---

[18] Pajot Descharmes, "Report in Name of Comité des Arts Mécaniques on Damasked Linen Mill of Dollé Jr. at Saint-Quentin, Aisne," *Bulletin de la société d'encouragement pour l'industrie nationale,* v. 21 (Jan., 1822), 13–15. François Emmanuel Molard, Jr., "Report on Damasked Linen," *Bulletin de la société d'encouragement pour l'industrie nationale,* v. 23 (Aug., 1824), 229–30. Jean Baptiste Brayer de Beauregard, *Statistique de l'Aisne,* v. 2 (Saint-Quentin, 1826), 294. Dollfus, *op. cit.,* 224–26. Paris, *Exposition . . . de 1849* (Burat), *loc. cit.* Adolphe Blaise, *Exposition des produits de l'industrie nationale en 1839* (Paris, 1839), 191–92.

woven in rural homes or small workshops and frequently in the cellar. But fine as the batistes were, they suffered from the prevailing desire for cheaper cloth, and their makers were forced to use some mechanically spun yarn before 1848. As early as 1834, also, it was noted that the number of weavers of batistes was declining and, a few years later, that they could be found only in the country. Then it was recorded that their production had fallen from the 350,000 pieces produced early in the Restoration to 90,000 pieces towards the end of the July Monarchy. They had apparently competed successfully against the printed calicoes of Normandy and Alsace, probably because of the fine quality of their cloth, but when they tried printing themselves they found they could not compete with the artistic though costly prints of Paris. It is probable also that they suffered from the increasing perfection of tulle, especially after the adaptation to the manufacture of tulle of the Jacquard loom. And, finally, the manufacturers of batistes suffered from the excessive domesticity of their manufacturing and probably also from defective organization of selling.[19]

We know that in making batistes the spinners, weavers, and bleachers had no direct contacts with each other, but were entirely dependent upon brokers who may have been competent but were certainly expensive in both time and fees. The economic historian may well suspect that this system was characteristic of many parts of the linen industry and, perhaps, of all parts in some regions. Jules Burat, one of the most intelligent and imaginative of French writers on industrial development, wrote in his book on the Exposition of 1044 that manufacturers were complaining of the quality of the cloth woven by the peasants, whose deficiencies they attributed to their isolation, which prevented them from getting the best yarn. Legentil added in 1851 that France was divided into

---

[19] Paris, *Rapport du jury central sur les produits de l'industrie française à l'exposition de 1827*, rédigé par Louis Etienne François Héricart-Ferrand, vicomte de Thury, et Pierre Henri Migneron (Paris, 1828), 95–97. Arthur Malotet, "L'Industrie et le commerce des toiles fines à Valenciennes pendant l'époque contemporaine," *Revue du nord*, v. 3 (1912), 340–81. Paris, *Exposition . . . de 1849* (Burat) ["Report on Batistes," par Félix Aubry], v. 3, p. 256. Audiganne, *loc. cit.*

zones, each of which produced its own local linens exclusively. The remedy which they sought to apply was not the use of the power loom but bringing hand weavers into mills, where they could be given better yarn and where their weaving could be supervised. This interesting attempt was being made in the Nord, where, Burat said, there were already two such mills while a few existed in other parts of France. It is interesting to remember that at the *enquête* of 1838 a manufacturer from Alençon had testified that any attempt to bring the peasants into a mill would cause a revolution, because of the 45,000 he used only 3,000 lived in the town. This shows that resistance to the spread of the factory system in France was a real obstacle, even if that resistance seldom took the form of violence. The universal love of the land and its cultivation which gave France so much stability were not conducive to the best methods of manufacturing, and in no industry was this felt more keenly than in linen.[20]

---

[20] Paris, *Exposition . . . de 1849* (Burat), *loc. cit.;* . . . *de 1827* (vicomte de Thury), *loc. cit.;* . . . *de 1851* (Legentil), *loc. cit.*

The Silk Industry

IN THE OTHER TEXTILE INDUSTRIES we have dealt with fibers that were sometimes difficult to manipulate but were usually tough enough to endure mechanical treatment. As a rule, also, they were not very costly to obtain, whether by domestic production or by importation. In silk we have a fiber of great delicacy and great cost that required gentle and regular manipulation. These facts help to explain the very different kinds of material with which the historian must deal. Writers on the silk industry show an interest in mechanical problems and they give a somewhat clearer picture of the growth of their industry and a much clearer picture of its organization. It is much easier to see both domestic and foreign competition at work and to appreciate the effects produced. Some of these differences may be due to the fact that the silk industry of France was the only one of the textile industries that was definitely superior to its foreign rivals in most fields of production; it inspired as much respect in England as the British cotton industry did in France. But little sense of superiority is found in French writers on silk manufacturing; they simply show less fear of foreign competition and a greater willingness to tell us quietly how and why they were able to meet it. Yet in numerous cases they demanded and received protection through the tariff, which rendered their sales abroad somewhat more difficult and certainly raised the prices of some silks at home. Finally, our sources on ribbons in France are unusually rich, so that the manufacture of ribbons will receive somewhat more emphasis than its position in the silk industry as a whole deserves. Louis Joseph Gras, who wrote some useful books on the transportation and the iron industries of the Loire, has written also a history of the ribbon industry in the region of Saint-Etienne. He writes more in the spirit of an archivist than in that of a historian and shows too little understanding of the economic problems of France as a whole, but he is useful and rather unusually accurate, except in handling figures. Another unusual source is a series of pamphlets called *L'Indicateur*, issued at intervals between 1828 and 1842 by Philippe Hedde, one of the more important silk manufacturers of Saint-Etienne, prominent in its Chamber of Commerce, and director of its Industrial Museum. While neither modest nor national in his point of view, he was unusually shrewd and intelligent in his observations and criticisms.[1]

General Poncelet, in his *History of Machinery*, criticizes the French silk industry severely. He mentions the large number of patents taken out for the manufacture of silk under both the Restoration and the July Monarchy, but says that they were not written about because of slight interest in machinery. He regrets also that these French patents covered silk only and not textiles in general, as was customary in England. Then, he says, his countrymen are sunk in routine in the development of machinery for milling silk. He adds that French machines were of wood, even in the larger mills. This he contrasts with England's active improvement of machines for milling or working silk, but he comforts his countrymen by remarking that the English made cheaper silks than the French and sought mass production and speed, so that they did not fully appreciate

---

[1] Louis Joseph Gras, *Histoire de la rubanerie et des industries de la soie à Saint-Etienne et dans la région stéphanoise* (Saint-Etienne: Thomas, 1906). Philippe Hedde, "Aperçu sur l'état actuel des fabriques de rubans de Saint-Etienne et de Saint-Chamond en 1828," *Bulletin de la société industrielle de Saint-Etienne,* v. 6 (1828), 201–7; *Indicateur du commerce, des arts et des manufactures de Saint-Etienne* (Saint-Etienne, 1831, 1836–38), 4 vols.; the first issue of the *Bulletin* has a historical sketch of the ribbon industry and is the most important; later volumes are largely repetitions of the first, but give a few new details. Hedde, "Notice sur la fabrication de rubans de Saint-Etienne, suivie de la description des métiers mécaniques dits à la barre," *Bulletin de la société industrielle de Saint-Etienne,* v. 6 (1828), 123–40; this contains valuable comments on the manufacturing and trading methods of the ribbon industry of Saint-Etienne with a discussion of the danger of foreign competition.

the delicacy of fine silks. After criticizing the French for having wooden machines, he quotes Vaucanson to the effect that wooden gears were better than iron unless tools and methods used permitted the shaping of iron with perfect precision. On the basis of this judgment of the old master, Poncelet concludes that the French should not yet use iron gears for silk warps.

Our information is too scanty to permit a detailed study of Poncelet's criticism. It is even difficult to know to what French machines and processes he referred. We can only assume that he was concerned chiefly with milling. We may wonder, however, if his criticism was not too harsh. He said that French machines were not made by machinists but by local carpenters; manufacturers should learn to make them in their own shops and to adapt to silk machines already in use for cotton, wool, and hemp. This is what the English had done. We know from other sources that they were busy between 1830 and 1838 improving and changing their old wooden spinning machines for silk, which they had copied from those of Piedmont, to machines of cast or wrought iron imitating closely the water frame, or throstle, in cotton. This was being done by Lillie and Fairbairn of Leeds, who were excellent machinists. Poncelet said that silk manufactures of the south had enough capital to build their own machines, but lacked the interest that would induce them to make the effort.

We cannot definitely refute these criticisms of General Poncelet, but there are interesting possibilities which future research may be able to develop. Thus Gras says that Saint-Etienne was building its own looms as early as 1791 and that it had replaced carpenters by specialized mechanics, although he does not tell us when. He adds that Lyons replaced combs of rush or cane by steel as early as 1810, although it made them badly, and Saint-Etienne followed suit in 1820. Gras tells us also of a gifted mechanic named Boivin, who was born in 1794 and seems to have worked for many years in Saint-Etienne. He replaced toothed wheels able to change rotary motion to perpendicular, or vice versa, that were made of iron and copper, and he is described as using gears of both copper and leather. There is no further explanation, and no other writer has yet been found

who mentions this work of Boivin, although there is evidence to
confirm his existence and his skill as a mechanic. The economic
historian may well wonder, therefore, if in the leading centers of the
silk industry, such as Lyons and Saint-Etienne, and possibly Nîmes
also, there was not active improvement of most machines used in
the manufacture of silk in the period from 1815 to 1848. We know
that there was such improvement in weaving, brocading, and embroidering. Even the power loom was understood as well by French
silk manufacturers as by those of woolens and linens.[2]

One of the notably progressive steps that the French did take
was in making crepe. About the year 1818 they succeeded in imitating the crepe of both China and India so well that French crepe
was preferred to that of Bologna. This seems to have been accomplished partly by producing a new and better strain of unusually
white silk, the sina, and by the invention of a machine in 1818
which made the crepe by simply twisting silk to increase its strength
by diminishing the length of the thread by 5 per cent. This machine,
oval or round in shape, usually carried 216 spindles, used only one
horsepower per hundred spindles, and cut the cost of creping to
one third. The description of the machine indicates that it was used
for making ribbons. But we know that at the same time, or shortly
afterwards, many kinds of crepe were produced at Lyons and
elsewhere.[3]

---

[2] Général Jean-Victor Poncelet, *Les Machines et outils spécialement
employés à la fabrication des matières textiles,* in Paris, *Exposition univer-
selle de 1851 à Londres,* travaux de la Commission Française, v. 3, Partie 2
(Paris, 1855), 141; in discussing English progress, 1830–38, Poncelet quotes
Dr. Ure's *Philosophy of Manufactures* (London, 1836) and his English
Dictionary (1843). Paris, *Exposition universelle internationale de 1900 à
Paris: Le Bilan d'un siècle* (1801–1900), par Alfred Picard, v. 4 (Paris,
1906), 224. Gras, *op. cit.,* 293, 295–96.

[3] Alphonse Peyret, *Statistique industrielle du département de la Loire*
(Saint-Etienne, 1835), 14–16. Joseph Duplessy, *Essai statistique sur le
département de la Loire* (Montbrison, 1818). Paris, *Rapport du jury central
sur les produits de l'industrie française à l'exposition de 1819,* rédigé par
Louis, baron Costaz (Paris, 1819). Paris, *Rapport du jury central sur les
produits de l'industrie française à l'exposition de 1823,* rédigé par Louis
Etienne François Héricart-Ferrand, vicomte de Thury, et Pierre Henri
Migneron (Paris, 1824), 66. Baron Charles Dupin, *Progrès de l'industrie*

The improvement of weaving in the silk-ribbon industry, on which alone we have sufficient information for discussion, presents a confusing picture. There were two old types of loom used, both of which were clearly utilized for cloth as well as ribbons, the *haute lisse* and the *basse lisse*. In the former, part of the warp was above the other, the two being connected with vertical threads kept at uniform tension by the worker, who used them to trace an outline of his design and pulled them with his hands. The advantage of this form of loom was that the weaver could see readily at all times the progress he was making toward the realization of his pattern. The advantage of the loom *à haute lisse* was obviously greatest in very fancy silks, whether cloths or ribbons. The loom *à basse lisse* was low and run by the foot of the weaver on pedals. Originally the pattern appeared on the under side, so that the weaver could not easily note with accuracy the progress of his work. This was improved by making the two planes of the nap oscillate so as to show the work done up to that moment. In the period from 1815 to 1848 the *haute lisse* was used little and tended steadily to disappear. Nearly all looms came to be of the *basse-lisse* type. This did not mean that ribbons became plainer and simpler to weave. We know that, on the contrary, the proportion of fancy ribbons became steadily greater and the number of varieties almost endless. The explanation lies in the development of new types of looms and of various attachments added to them. Obviously the term *basse lisse* in the period 1815 to 1848 becomes applicable to different kinds of looms.

Towards the end of the eighteenth century there had been imported at Saint-Etienne from Switzerland the bar loom or, as it was sometimes called to indicate the place of origin, the Zurich loom. No source gives any date for this importation and this fact, together with the kind of references to the new loom, suggests that the importation was gradual over a considerable period of time and that numerous improvements were made in France, although we have

française depuis le commencement du XIX⁰ siècle (*Discours et leçons sur l'industrie* [pamphlets], v. 2, no. 11; Paris, 1825), 104; speech of November 23, 1823. Charles Beaulieu, *Histoire du commerce, de l'industrie et des fabriques de Lyon* (Lyon, 1838), 156. Ernest Pariset, *Histoire de la fabrique lyonnaise depuis le XVI⁰ siècle* (Lyon: Rey, 1901), 302.

no clear description of any or any discussion of their possible significance. The raising of the bar appears to have required strength on the part of the weaver, but it is difficult to believe one description late in our period, which states that once the bar had been raised the action of the loom was automatic—unless, in the meantime, it had become a power loom, of which fact there is no evidence. Gras says that the bar loom was transformed between 1799 and 1850, the planes of the nap, or *lisses,* being increased from two to eight for very wide ribbons. He adds that the Jacquard loom was adapted to ribbons about 1815, the date when improvements had first made it run smoothly and well; but he says also that on the Jacquard loom the weaver could make from ten to thirty ribbons simultaneously of different designs and types, as long as they were all narrow. There seems to have been much confusion in terminology on the part of French writers on the silk industry, so that we cannot always be sure what they mean by a Jacquard loom for weaving ribbons. In most cases it would appear that the bar loom was the one actually meant, but that in the course of time this older loom was improved and greatly changed and that in the process of modification it borrowed many of the features of the Jacquard loom, although in the later years the Jacquard loom seems to have been used most frequently in the form of an attachment to the bar loom. In this work one mechanic, Burgin, who was employed at Saint-Etienne from 1798 to 1852, seems to have been the most active. In other forms of silks the Jacquard loom itself seems to have been used far more. We are told that at Lyons the great mill of La Sauvagère used no less than 200, and as many as one third of the looms of Lyons in 1830 may have been of the Jacquard type. It appears to have been used at Nîmes more as an attachment to other looms or to knitting machines, for Nîmes was always a great producer of silk hosiery.[4]

Another improvement in the weaving of ribbons which could be

[4] Hedde, *Indicateur* (1831, 1836), *loc. cit.* Louis René Villermé, *Tableau de l'état physique et moral des ouvriers employés dans les manufactures de coton, de laine et de soie,* v. 1 (Paris, 1840), 402–3. Gras, *op. cit.,* 587–88. Duplessy, *op. cit.,* 391, 397–98. Beaulieu, *op. cit.,* 123.

attached to the Jacquard loom but was more frequently used on the bar loom was the brocading drum. This was invented about 1818 by the mechanic Boivin. The problem of brocading ribbons quickly and cheaply was one that must have faced many ribbon manufacturers at that time. Hedde wrote in 1842 that he had called attention in 1828 to the brocading drums used in England and Switzerland and pointed out how they could improve the weaving of ribbons by the Jacquard method and how they could reduce the cost by saving time. It may be that Boivin borrowed ideas from drums used in other countries; or it may be that he knew of them and failed to use them. We cannot say. We do know that despite the immediate adoption of his drum at Saint-Etienne and the rapid increase of its use, it required improvement before it gave really satisfactory results. The brocading drum as an invention may be like the braiding machine which was invented in Germany in 1750 and in Normandy in 1782. Whether the later French inventor in that case borrowed from the earlier one in Germany is not clear, but we do know that both machines were used in both countries when they were united under Napoleon and that each machine was used to improve the other. We cannot determine at present the actual originality of Boivin, but of the success and importance of his drum in the ribbon industry at Saint-Etienne there is ample evidence. Boivin learned much from observing the Jacquard loom, just as Jacquard had learned much from the looms of Vaucanson which he found at the Conservatoire des Arts et Métiers in Paris. We know that Boivin worked at Saint-Etienne at the time of his invention, and there does not seem to be reason to doubt that he was the inventor; but two important writers, Blaise in 1839, and Villermé in 1840, mention the firm of Godmar and Meynier of Lyons as the inventor. This suggests a relationship like that between the inventor Jacquard and the manufacturer Depouilly. The drum sent at one stroke ten to twelve threads of different colors through as many points in the warp by means of little shuttles, each with its own color, which were arranged in a row before the drum and each of which operated within a determined area of the piece of cloth. Godmar and Meynier may have been manufacturers of ribbons, for very fancy ones were made at Lyons, or they may have used the drum for brocading other silks.[5]

Another problem that faced the ribbon manufacturers was that of embroidering their ribbons while they were being woven on the loom. Philippe Hedde is the only writer who discusses the question fully, and he does so for the purpose of proving that he invented a process for accomplishing the desired end with the help of his partner Barthélemy Thimonnier, Sr. There are reasons for suspecting that Hedde was neither accurate nor modest. He says that the invention was made chiefly by Thimonnier, but on machines used in his mill in 1829. Then Thimonnier went to Paris during the revolution of 1830, where he disappeared forever. This seems a strange fate for an important manufacturer, particularly as the revolution lasted only a few days and caused very little loss of life. In 1831, Hedde continues, he published his method in a book, but he gives not the title of the book, nor the name of the publisher, nor the place of publication. Other facts that add to our doubts of Hedde's veracity are that a mechanism for embroidering with needles to be attached to the knitting machine was invented at Nîmes by Grégoire and Lombard in 1827, introduced at Saint-Etienne in 1829 and improved there in 1841–42 at the very time Hedde wrote the account, which we are using, in his *Indicateur*. Finally, Hedde describes the visit to Saint-Etienne in 1832 by Dr. John Bowring, who told him that he was surprised to find embroidery of ribbons on the loom still in the experimental stage at Saint-Etienne, because manufacturers at Paisley, in Scotland, had perfected a method for doing this and had described it in a *Treatise on Weaving* in 1831, the

---

[5] Philippe Hedde, *Rubans brodés sur le métier pendant le tissage au moyen des battants brodeurs à aiguilles* (Saint-Etienne, 1842), 5. Adolphe Blaise, *Exposition des produits de l'industrie nationale de 1839* (Paris, 1839), 54–55. Paris, *Rapport du jury central sur les produits de l'industrie française à l'exposition de 1844*, rédigé par Jules Burat, v. 1 (Paris, 1845), 27. M. Faure-Lacroze, "Notice sur les progrès obtenus ou possibles de la fabrique des rubans à Saint-Etienne," *Bulletin de la société industrielle de Saint-Etienne*, v. 17 (1840), 156. Paris, *Rapport du jury central sur les produits de l'industrie française à l'exposition de 1839* ["Report on Silk Ribbons," by Caez et Petit], v. 3 (Paris, 1840), 217. Gras, *op. cit.*, 293. Villermé, *op. cit.*, v. 1, p. 351.

very year in which Hedde claims to have published his method. The odds would seem to favor strongly the priority of the Scottish invention.[6]

One final improvement in weaving ribbons on hand looms should be mentioned, that of a regulator to make the strokes more even. The Vicomte de Thury in his book on the Exposition of 1823 describes a loom invented by Maisiat which revolutionized the silk industry. As no other writer mentions it, one can only be doubtful and wonder if it was not simply one of the numerous forms of improved Jacquard looms. What is really interesting is that the position of the regulator was changed. It had formerly been attached to the shuttle, making it difficult to raise the shuttle when the weaver wished to make repairs; now the regulator was not attached to the shuttle, so that a new precision in patterns could be achieved. Other regulators are mentioned both by de Thury and Gras, so that it seems safe to assume that a really important improvement in this part of the weaving process was made early in the period from 1815 to 1848. But the conclusion seems inescapable that this improvement was simply one more derivative from the really remarkable invention of Jacquard.[7]

The possibility of applying power to weaving silk was considered in the period 1815–48, and practical successes are recorded much as in the woolen and linen industries. Accounts of looms making laces and run by steam or hydraulic motors at Saint-Chamond, a village near Saint-Etienne, early in the nineteenth century are only misleading. Nearly all writers from Saint-Etienne include the production of these laces in their accounts of the silk ribbon industry. Actually, they were shoe laces made chiefly of cotton and woven on very small machines. Because the chief ingredient used was cotton,

---

[6] Hedde, *Rubans brodés;* these two small pamphlets bound together both deal with this machine for embroidering ribbons on the loom.

[7] Paris, *Exposition . . . de 1923* (vicomte de Thury), 66. Gras, *op. cit.,* 293. Jérôme Adolphe Blanqui, *Histoire de l'exposition des produits de l'industrie* (Paris, 1827), 114–16. Louis Etienne François Héricart-Ferrand, vicomte de Thury, "Rapport sur les nouveaux procédés introduits dans les métiers à fabriquer les étoffes de soie par M. Etienne Maisiat," *Bulletin de la société d'encouragement pour l'industrie nationale,* v. 27 (1828), 68–73.

not silk, and because the machines were small, no real light was thrown on the problem of weaving silk by a power loom.

The *Bulletin* of the Société Industrielle de Mulhouse remarked in 1838 that silk is hard to weave on a power loom because its elasticity is so great that it is difficult to secure uniformity of tension, especially in the weft. This distinguished journal was not simply enunciating an obvious truth but discussing a problem that had been solved. It is curious that the adaptation of the power loom to the weaving of silk should not have been made at one of the great centers of the silk industry, like Lyons or Saint-Etienne, but in Alsace, which we generally associate with the manufacture of cotton, and by an inventor who is generally regarded as the great benefactor of the worsted industry. In 1835 Josué Heilmann and Charles Webber produced a single power loom. In the next year work was started on a large scale with the help of Nicholas Koechlin; steam was used to supply the power, and sixty looms were built. These were tested in the weaving of some plainer silks, especially those woven at Avignon, and proved successful in all cases but one. A reporter of the Exposition of 1839 tells us that already some manufacturers at Lyons were investing heavily in power looms, although none was exhibited. He added that this investment was being made in order to meet the rising cost of French labor, but that another remedy existed in the spreading of hand looms through the country. Ten years later we hear of the extensive use of the power loom in the manufacture of silk plush for hats at Tarare, where one firm used 200 and another 100. Both firms worked for main offices in Lyons and in an industry that was comparatively new in France and had grown with startling rapidity. They did not weave the best plush, which was made by hand in the Moselle. But the plush industry of Tarare was a brilliant exception in the use of the power loom for weaving silk. Even hydraulic motors do not appear to have been used extensively. An attempt to do so at Bourg-Argental near Saint-Etienne had failed in 1831 for causes that are not clear, although hostility of the workmen is known to have been one. Another attempt was being made in 1848. The real reason why the power loom was not extensively used in the silk industry appears to have been economic. There seems to be no doubt that the mechanical problem had been solved with reasonable success by Heilmann and Webber in 1835.

But the power loom required large mills, and both manufacturers and workers were accustomed to small workshops or even to work in the homes. High costs both at Lyons and Saint-Etienne were met in most cases by an extension of silk weaving through the villages of the countryside, with the emigration of some urban weavers to escape heavy urban expenses, such as the *octroi,* and the employment of an ever-increasing number of peasants willing to accept low wages.[8]

The growth of the French silk industry in the period from 1815 to 1848 cannot be discussed in detail, because available figures are inadequate in number and are too frequently demonstrably inaccurate; but certain general tendencies can be noted, and one period of rapid growth and glorious achievement. Errors in figures were inevitable, for the careful preparation of accurate statistics was probably not common in any country at that time. In France we have first the figures of Comte Chaptal, published in his book in 1819. These were based partly on the *Exposé de la situation de l'Empire,* which was prepared hastily and arbitrarily on the order of Napoleon by his prefects. Chaptal himself, despite his experience as a manufacturer and his keen intelligence, loved to swell figures; all figures for the production of silks from the beginning of the Revolution to 1815 must therefore be scrutinized with care. Then, in 1826, the government established the values to be given in its statistics of imports and exports according to the prices then current, and it maintained those values unchanged until 1850. Moreau

<hr>

[8] "Rapport, Exposition du 13 juin, 1838," *Bulletin de la société industrielle de Mulhouse,* v. 12 (1838), 71–74. Paris, *Exposition . . . de 1839* (Caez et Petit), 194; *Exposition nationale des produits de l'industrie agricole et manufacturière de 1849: Rapport du jury central* ["Report on Silks," by Arlès-Dufour], v. 3, Partie 2, Sect. 2 (Paris, 1850), 119. Germain Martin, *Le Tissage du ruban à domicile dans les campagnes du Velay* (Paris: Sirey, 1913), 64. Armand Audiganne, *Les Populations ouvrières et les industries de la France dans le mouvement social du XIXe siècle,* v. 1 (Paris, 1854), 309. A. Beauquis, *Histoire économique de la soie* (Paris, 1910), 154.

de Jonnès has estimated that by 1850 this had caused a considerable error in the case of silks because through improvements in manufacturing they had grown lighter in weight. But even writers with expert knowledge of the silk industry, such as Philippe Hedde and Louis Joseph Gras of Saint-Etienne, do not give figures that are either abundant or accurate.

Writers on the silk industry of Lyons, Pariset and Beauquis, provide us with a few statistics that can safely be used. Pariset rejects the figures supplied by Chaptal and, for the earlier years, relies on Beaulieu, who wrote in 1838. According to him the number of looms in the Lyons region was as follows: 1810, 12,000; 1824, 20,000; 1832, 42,000; 1845, 50,000; 1853, 60,000. Beauquis gives us interesting figures on the spread of looms through the countryside beyond Lyons, chiefly villages in the Department of Isère: 1819, 11,000 for the Isère alone; 1834, 19,000; 1848, 25,000; 1883, 70,000. Figures given by various good authors for Saint-Etienne, Nîmes, and Avignon are not sufficiently numerous to be useful.

The figures of Pariset on the increase of looms in the region of Lyons show that the greatest increase was in the period between 1824 and 1832. This agrees with our information that the period after the crisis of 1818 was one of rapid development and brilliant achievement in the silk industry. It does not seem to have been checked seriously or for any length of time by the depression that began in 1826–27, but did suffer severely from the great strikes of 1831 and 1834 and from the depression that began in 1837 with the crisis in the United States, perhaps the largest single market for the fancy silks and ribbons of Lyons and Saint-Etienne. We find a similar period of brilliant development in the ribbon industry of Saint-Etienne between approximately 1817 and 1834. The figures of Beauquis indicate that ruralization in the silk industry began as early as 1819, caused probably by foreign competition and by the rising cost of living in the city of Lyons. It is Pariset's opinion that this ruralization did not check the increase of looms within the city of Lyons for many years. Movement of weavers into the country was intensified, of course, by the great strikes of 1831 and 1834, and probably also by the depression that began in 1837, as it would have been by any serious depression; but we do seem justified in stating that a marked increase in the rural weaving of silks began in the Isère before the strikes of the early years of the July Monarchy.

Beaulieu, whom Pariset considers one of the most reliable of the authors who wrote in the period from 1815 to 1848, gives us a set of figures for the period 1824–30 which breaks up the production of silks in a very interesting way: he says that 14,965 looms made plain silks, 1,756 tulle, 964 gauze and crepe, and 964 velvet. We have no comparable set of figures for any other period within the scope of this study, or for the ribbon industry of Saint-Etienne. But Beaulieu shows us graphically that within that period of years at least the production of plain silks was of overwhelming importance, despite keen competition from England, Switzerland, and Rhenish Prussia. We know also that at that time fashion favored plain silks, which were often decorated with knots or ribbons. In the ribbon industry the production of plain silks was also of great importance, since there was a production of fancy ribbons that was excessive because a large part of it could only be sold abroad. The ribbon industry was becoming dependent to a dangerous degree on sales in foreign markets, while, at the same time, the competition of Switzerland made it increasingly difficult to sell plain ribbons at home. It was essential, therefore, to increase the production of plain ribbons, but there is reason to believe that this increase was not achieved.[9]

The growth of the ribbon industry of Saint-Etienne became extraordinarily rapid between 1817 and 1819. It may be that one reason why the growth did not begin before was the one brought forward by Gras, that the price of silk was too high until 1818. We cannot say, as we lack information to confirm or disprove the statement of Gras, although we believe it to be justified. Other factors causing the increase are clearer. In December, 1817, Bancel invented the gauze ribbon which was the basis for nearly all the fancy ribbons developed later. A second cause was the adaptation of the Jacquard loom to the weaving of ribbons, in which we should

---

[9] Alexandre Moreau de Jonnès, *Statistique de l'industrie de la France* (Paris, 1856), 153, 158. Ernest Pariset, *Les Industries de la soie* (Lyon, 1890), 367. Beauquis, *op. cit.*, 244. Beaulieu, *op. cit.*, 123.

include various improvements to the bar loom imported from Switzerland and the older type of loom known as the *basse lisse*. We must always remember that the ideas of Jacquard were used by many mechanics and were often embodied in attachments to other looms. A third cause was the perfection of the process for making crepe in 1818, which, as we have seen, was connected with improvements in spinning and with the production of the new and white sina silk. Finally, there was the invention of the brocading drum in 1818, which, as we have stated, was of the greatest importance in the production of fancy ribbons and which would appear to have been derived in part from some of the ideas of Jacquard. Peyret, who described this boom in 1835, when it had apparently run its course, added that two thirds of the ribbons made at Saint-Etienne were fancy.[10]

A curious episode in the period 1815 to 1848 is the collapse of the silk industry at Saint-Chamond in 1840. This appears to have come suddenly in that year upon the failure of two of the most important firms there, Dugas-Vialis and Bancel, who were the leading manufacturers of silk ribbons. The causes given by Gras are these: (1) Saint-Chamond had had gilds before the Revolution, as Saint-Etienne had not, and this tradition was felt after the Revolution. (2) The railroad between Saint-Etienne and Lyons, which was opened in 1832, did not pass through the center of the village of Saint-Chamond. This was a great disadvantage, thought Gras, because merchants now used the railroad in going to Saint-Etienne and no longer troubled to stop at Saint-Chamond, as they had when they traveled on the highway. (3) After 1833 the mail of Saint-Etienne came by stage from Paris by a road which did not pass through Saint-Chamond, while the inhabitants of that village received their Parisian mail by way of Lyons. (4) Saint-Etienne had commission merchants in ribbons and Saint-Chamond did not. And (5) Saint-Etienne had had a school of design since 1804.[11]

Economic historians can hardly accept all these causes for the collapse of the ribbon industry at Saint-Chamond. We should agree

---

[10] Peyret, *op. cit.*, 10, 14. Gras, *op. cit.*, 585–87, 674–75.
[11] Gras, *op. cit.*, 674–75.

that its desertion by the modern and improved means of communication, or rather the inadequate service given it by them, was important. It seems clear to us also that the smaller industrial center handled both its labor and mercantile problems in a less progressive spirit than did Saint-Etienne. But we should be inclined to say that if Saint-Chamond had been an industrial center of great importance and, above all, one with a promising future, the new means of communication would have been designed to serve it directly and efficiently. It would seem to us that there must have been geographical disadvantages in the position of Saint-Chamond which Gras, as a local historian, does not explain because he assumes all his readers already know them. We can assume also that the manufacturers of Saint-Chamond suffered from the crisis of 1837 and the ensuing depression and, being in a very small industrial center, were unable to survive the strain as did the manufacturers in the larger center of Saint-Etienne. It would seem that Saint-Chamond had carried the production of fancy ribbons too far and, as in the case of the depression just mentioned, suffered more from this strategical error than did her stronger rival. Finally, the collapse of the ribbon industry indicates that there were very grave disadvantages in excessive decentralization of industrial production which neither Saint-Etienne nor the ribbon industry as a whole understood; in short, the real lesson that the disaster of Saint-Chamond should have driven home was not learned.

Some aspects of the development of the silk industry in France are illustrated by the manufacture of certain cloths. First we should mention the apparently new industry of mixed cloths, which was not really new, but which, in the period following the Napoleonic wars grew so rapidly that it seemed to contemporaries a new creation. We have seen that wool had played a very important part in these cloths. Now we must remind ourselves that silk and cotton were quite as important. Lyons during the continental blockade had been the chief center in France for the importation of cotton from the Levant. As the commercial and industrial capital of the silk industry in France, she was also the leading center for the utilization of waste silk which improvements in reeling and spinning made economical to use. It was these two materials, cotton and waste silk, that formed the foundation for the great development of the manufacture of mixed cloths which was said to have occupied half the looms of Lyons in 1819. This was one of the most striking developments of the Restoration in the silk industry, but it was not an entirely healthy one, because it depended upon novelty and the whims of fashion. In a few years mixed cloths were dropped, only to be revived again later. The frequent readjustments and unemployment caused by such changes of fashion were a characteristic feature of the silk industry.[12]

The manufacture of plush for hats has already been touched upon in discussing the adaptation of the power loom to the weaving of silk. It is interesting also for other reasons. Dupin asserts that the attempt to fix wages at Lyons in this new and rapidly growing industry was the chief cause of the great strike of 1834. This is a statement that deserves further investigation, for, although the judgment of Baron Charles Dupin was not always sound, his position and his many investigations gave him an unusually large amount of information. Plush was also one of the mixed cloths, chiefly a combination of cotton and waste silk, although in the manufacture of hats it profited from the high price of felt and the ability to provide a new finish through the use of steam. This profitable use of steam was in turn one of the factors that made the power loom pay in the manufacture of plush.[13]

The manufacture of tulle became an important part of the silk industry in the period from 1815 to 1848. Bonnard helped make this possible by his improvement of spinning and by giving silk yarn

---

[12] Paris, *Exposition universelle internationale de 1889 à Paris: Rapports du jury international,* v. 5, Classe 33: "Rapport sur les soies et tissus de soie," par Marius Morand (Paris, 1891); *Exposition . . . de 1819* (Costaz), 43. Dupin, *op. cit.,* 103.

[13] Paris, *Rapport du jury central sur les produits de l'industrie française à l'exposition de 1834,* rédigé par Baron Charles Dupin, v. 2 (Paris, 1836), 116. Adolph Blaise, *Exposition des produits de l'industrie nationale en 1839* (Paris, 1839), 230; describes firm of Massing et Huber, Puttelange, Moselle. Paris, *Exposition . . . de 1844* (Burat), v. 1, p. 28. *Statistique de l'industrie à Paris, résultant de l'enquête par la chambre de commerce de Paris pour les années 1847–49* (Paris, 1851), 124.

the necessary finish in the same operation that pulled the threads
from the cocoon. The industry was important at Lyons as early as
1819 because it found there a large supply of skilled labor receiving
low wages. It is said to have occupied in that year as many as 2,000
looms. Dognin made a further contribution by bringing to Lyons
the English bobbin loom, although it is uncertain whether he made
a direct importation. It would seem more probable that he simply
brought to Lyons looms he found in use at Calais. At any rate, the
development of the tulle industry at Lyons was on different lines
from those followed at Calais. Dognin himself developed the strong
grenadine silk in black and white which drove out knotted and
embroidered tulle at Lyons. Then he made tulle so delicate that it
was positively diaphanous and was given the name *illusion*. This
form of tulle was so successful that it reigned supreme at Lyons
for a decade.[14]

While the production of silk tulle was important in the silk
industry as a whole early in the period, as was the manufacture of
mixed cloths, it was slowly supplanted in time by printing on silks.
Fashion appears to a great extent to have deserted mixed cloths
and, to a lesser extent, tulle in favor of prints, because people grew
tired of plain silks decorated with ribbons. This change in fashion
seems to provide the chief explanation of the sudden failure of the
ribbon industry to continue after 1833–34 the rapid growth it had
maintained since 1818–19. Other factors favored the rise of prints,
such as the use of steam in finishing silks as well as woolens, and the
perfection of printing itself, which we have considered in our study
of the cotton industry. For a time after 1820, it is true, printing was
used successfully to increase the richness and variety of fancy ribbons. At Saint-Etienne, it is said to have given life to a great mass
of ribbons abandoned after the crisis of 1825 in the ribbon industry
when prices rose excessively. But this gain was canceled by the
change in fashion, and after 1834 the public demanded printed silks

---

[14] Paris, *Exposition . . . de 1819* (Costaz). Paris, *Exposition internationale de 1851 à Londres,* "Rapport sur les dentelles, blondes, tulles, et
broderies," par Félix Aubry, v. 5 (Paris, 1854), 138–40. Pariset, *Industries
de la soie,* 360.

rather than plain silks decorated with ribbons, whether the ribbons were printed or not. This change was a great blow to Saint-Etienne, but a blessing to Lyons, where ribbons formed only a small proportion of the silks manufactured, and to Nîmes, which scarcely produced ribbons at all, but rather great quantities of shawls, scarves, and handkerchiefs.[15]

In concluding our study of the development of the French silk industry from 1815 to 1848, we must emphasize again the prevalence of small-scale manufacturing. In Saint-Etienne there is no mention at any time of a really large mill. Many workshops are known to have been very small, even when in the town itself. The number of manufacturers in Nîmes appears to have been about the same in proportion to the number of looms as at Saint-Etienne, and we hear of only one large mill, at the very end of our period. In Lyons there was one very large mill, that of La Sauvagère, early in our period, and if we include the manufacture of plush, there may have been three or four at the end. This serves simply to emphasize the existence of a very large number of small manufacturers. In Lyons, it is true, there was a kind of silken aristocracy composed of a small number of wealthy merchants who were well trained, broad-minded, and well informed—men like Arlès-Dufour, who did much for his city and his country as merchant and financier. But, while these merchants developed foreign markets with great skill and success, they did not change the organization of manufacturing, nor do we have reason to believe that they even tried seriously to do so. We hear of no great merchants at Saint-Etienne; Hedde states definitely that no manufacturer even thought of selling his ribbons to a foreigner, but Peyret, who wrote in 1835, states that there were twelve commission merchants in Saint-Etienne who possessed a combined capital of 3,000,000–4,000,000 francs. The manufacturers dealt with them through six brokers who charged a fee of ¼ of one per cent.[16]

---

[15] *Bulletin de la société industrielle de Saint-Etienne,* v. 16 (1838), 169–71. Paris, *Exposition . . . de 1834* (Dupin), 116. Pariset, *Histoire de la fabrique lyonnaise,* 302.

[16] Peyret, *op. cit.,* 16.

The increasing ruralization of the silk industry in the regions of both Lyons and Saint-Etienne does not seem to have cut down the number of manufacturers. It would seem that a large company with a well-developed organization of clerks, foremen, and horses would have been more efficient than many small organizations. We can only repeat that such large organizations did not arise. The inability or unwillingness to co-operate seems to have been ingrained. This may not be surprising in Saint-Etienne, which was comparatively small and provincial, but it is surprising in Lyons, which had been for centuries a great center of international trade. The result of such a situation was, of course, narrow, selfish, and bitter competition between the manufacturers. The pressure of foreign competition, which was felt strongly at Lyons in plain silks and at Saint-Etienne in both plain and fancy ribbons, caused increasing ruralization, as we have seen, but had no effect on other aspects of the organization of manufacturing. Many were forced to reduce wages and even, for a time, to sell without profit or below the cost of production. Many of the smaller manufacturers must have been eliminated by this ruthless warfare; yet, if they were, they seem to have been replaced. The social effects were deplorable. It was this struggle which, combined with the *laissez-faire* philosophy of the time, really caused the great strikes at Lyons in 1831 and 1834. We have every reason to believe that social conditions were almost as bad at Saint-Etienne.

The bitterness of this struggle among silk manufacturers was denounced eloquently by Beaulieu in his useful book published in 1838 in Lyons. It was denounced also by Hedde at Saint-Etienne in his *Indicateur* and was clearly described and condemned by Faure-Lacroze in the *Bulletin* of the Société Industrielle.[17] It was recognized that the frequency and intensity of crises was increased and that work frequently stopped when there was no decrease in demand. The temptation to create ever more new designs and thus embarrass rival manufacturers was irresistible. New types of ribbons were created and more ribbons were woven on each loom, but there was little time to improve methods in more constructive ways, some-

[17] Beaulieu, *op. cit.*, 173–74. Faure-Lacroze, *op. cit.*, 157.

times hardly enough to repair the machines as they existed. Critics pointed out clearly the better organization of the silk industry abroad. In England, of course, this was explained by the usual French excuses that capital was abundant on the wrong side of the Channel and that the English cared only for mass production and speed and made only those silks for which a steady and great demand was assured. It was said that they did not appreciate the beauty of the most artistic goods. While there was truth in these allegations, the French could have learned much from copying some of the English methods instead of merely stating that their own goods were better, even if that was often true. There was certainly capital in Lyons that could have been used to organize large companies, and there was probably enough in Saint-Etienne also. Mass production and speed could have been applied to the manufacture of plain silks and ribbons in France with beneficial results, as they applied successfully to the manufacture of plush at Tarare. Even Switzerland, which was certainly not a rich country then, had far fewer manufacturers of ribbons and plain silks in proportion to the number of looms than the French. It is interesting to recall that a manufacturer of Saint-Etienne declared that the standard of sobriety there was lower than abroad, that apprentices were not trained adequately, and that the capital of the ribbon industry had a bad reputation for dishonest weighing.[18]

Faure-Lacroze of Saint-Etienne spoke clearly in 1838. He said that Saint-Etienne could easily continue to dominate international markets for ribbons of taste, but that the sale of these was not sufficient to sustain the ribbon industry. Saint-Etienne must learn, therefore, to produce plain ribbons as cheaply as her foreign rivals in Switzerland, England, and Rhenish Prussia. To do this she must simplify her manufacturing methods and decrease the cost of labor. Workers must be trained more carefully and with stricter discipline. They must be taught to have better taste and keener imaginations by studying design and geometry in conjunction with practical labor.[19] All this was excellent advice, but it is difficult to see how

---

[18] Philippe Hedde, "Notice sur la fabrication de rubans," 132.
[19] Faure-Lacroze, *loc. cit.*

the desired results could be obtained by spreading weaving through the countryside and by continuing to reduce wages. No one seemed to realize that in breaking the great strikes of 1831 and 1834 and in dealing similarly with less dramatic situations at Saint-Etienne, the manufacturers actually lost heavily and delayed for years the healthy progress of the silk industry in France.

CHAPTER FIFTEEN

Industrial and Regional Competition
Within France

IN GENERAL, we have considered hitherto the development of each of the textile industries separately, and we have studied each chiefly as it was stimulated by the increasing use of machinery. We have observed the development of transportation and the increasing supply of capital as well as the growing supply of coal, whether produced in France or imported. We have seen also that the French market was protected by high tariff barriers and that, at the beginning of the period from 1815 to 1848, it seemed to be split up into a series of local or provincial markets which had to be brought into closer contact with each other. Now we must consider how these local markets reacted upon each other; that is not easy, because local and provincial conservatism were not readily overcome. We must also consider the subject of industrial competition. It is obvious that, despite the high tariff, imports were an important factor in French industrial growth. But the question that concerns us in this chapter is whether the artificially limited amount of foreign competition was compensated for by an adequate amount of domestic competition, whether between the different textile industries or between the different regions of France, or both. The conclusion must be that both industrial and regional competition were increasingly important, with a very slow increase up to about 1825 and a progressively rapid increase thereafter.

We have seen that the development of the cotton industry was so great and rapid as to seem almost overwhelming. Not only were the spinners moved into mills, but many of the weavers were also; the volume of production soon increased far beyond the ability of the French market to consume the cloth manufactured, despite the stimulation of demand by falling prices and by the ambitions and desires aroused by the Revolution. This element of overproduction was emphasized as early as 1834 by Bigot de Morogues, who thought the remedy lay in the removal of pauperized urban workers to agricultural colonies, just as the economist Sismondi, considering the problem somewhat earlier, had advocated a return to the gilds as the best means of checking overproduction and the inevitable crises which it produced. A few years later one of the Koechlins, an Alsation entrepreneur, and Legentil, a merchant of Paris, wrote that the cotton industry was suffering severely from the competition of woolens and linens, and five years after this rather startling statement Jules Burat, who is already well known to us as a writer and observer of unusual intelligence, said that the cotton industry was then going through a crisis caused by the competition of the woolen and linen industries to the extent that the existence of both domestic and foreign markets was threatened. We can dismiss Bigot de Morogues and Sismondi as idealists or theorists who sought to escape from the tragic difficulties of their time by returning to what they fondly thought of as a simpler and more wholesome civilization in the past. But we cannot say this of men like Koechlin, Legentil, or Jules Burat, who were practical leaders in business or engineering, just as Bigot himself, some years earlier, had been a practical administrator. Another view of the situation was expressed by Adolphe Blaise, another writer on industrial progress with whom we are familiar. He said that behind the tariff wall which had long given them security the manufacturers, with their monopoly of the home market, had earned such great profits that they had created keen competition within the country. The great increase in production that had produced these profits had not been accompanied by a parallel increase in consumption, but had merely caused an increased investment of capital and a condition where everyone wanted machines, money, metals, and mechanics simultaneously and in numbers or quantities that France could not possibly supply.

The statement of Jules Burat, that the crisis through which the cotton industry was passing was caused by the competition of other textiles, can neither be wholly accepted nor completely refuted. We know already that there was a severe depression from approximately 1837 to 1842 and that he made this statement in 1839. But we should differ from him by saying that the cotton industry itself was responsible for this crisis by its own overproduction, and we should add that the competition of the woolen industry was felt more in the earlier depression of 1827–32, and that of the linen industry was never felt seriously at any time, except possibly during the American Civil War. We should agree with Blaise that French textile manufacturers had a substantial monopoly of the home market, but we could not accept without qualification the statement that it was the great profits that created the keen competition which he noted in 1844.

It would seem to the economic historian looking back a century or more that the competition was caused even more by the steady decline of textile prices caused by improvements in machinery and industrial organization and by an increasing demand for more adequate, cheaper, and more attractive clothing. Thus, women were demanding woolen dresses for summer as well as winter, and we have seen in our study of the woolen industry that production for the middle class through decreasing prices was becoming a necessity for most progressive manufacturers. Finally, this reasoning leads us to the bewildering variety of mixed cloths devised by many ingenious and competing manufacturers because pure silks, pure woolens, and pure linens were in many cases far too costly.

Consumption sometimes tended to exceed production, as Blaise had noted in 1844—what we should call a boom or inflationary year —but it sometimes lagged behind production, as in 1828, when the cotton manufacturers of Roubaix turned to woolens because they could not sell their cottons at all. The simultaneous demand for machinery, capital, and skilled workers, which was so intense that it could not be met, was only partly the result of a national market restricted by a high tariff. It was a condition that could be found in any country where the Industrial Revolution was really getting under way. We should find similar conditions in England, which was moving with exaltation towards free trade in the year in which Blaise wrote.[1]

We can best begin our study of the growth of competition, both industrial and regional, by considering the experiences of the town of Saint-Quentin, in the department of Aisne, and the districts around it. In terms of the old provinces, which most French writers use in preference to the departmental terminology devised by the Revolution, which they find as unreal as Americans find postal zones, Saint-Quentin would be a city of Picardy, not far from Champagne, the Vosges, and Alsace. It was the capital of a region with a fairly numerous and prosperous peasantry, where agriculture was diversified and only moderately profitable, so that supplementary work on textiles was welcome. Saint Quentin was not far from many more important industrial centers, yet apart from them and, on the whole, not on the most important arteries of trade. It is not surprising, then, to find that despite the efforts of entrepreneurs from Paris and Lyons, and of some of its own leading citizens, to put it in the front rank of industrial progress, it remained, even in the eyes of its own loyal historian, Charles Picard, rather conservative and backward.

The region of Saint-Quentin is described by the late Professor Demangeon, one of the most distinguished of the French writers on regional geography, as the home of the woolen industry until the sixteenth century, then of the linen industry until late in the eighteenth, and finally of the cotton industry.[2] But when the triumph of

---

[1] Pierre Marie, baron Bigot de Morogues, *Recherches des causes de la richesse et de la misère des peuples civilisés* (Paris, 1834); this is a lithographed copy of the author's manuscript, of which 100 were made. Jean Charles Simonde de Sismondi, *Nouveaux principes d'économie politique; ou, De la richesse dans ses rapports avec la population* [1st ed.], 2 vols. (Paris, 1819). Paris, *Rapport du jury central sur les produits de l'industrie française de l'exposition de 1839* ["Report on Cotton," by Nicolas Koechlin and Charles Legentil] (Paris, 1840), 250; *Rapport du jury central sur les produits de l'industrie française à l'exposition de 1844*, rédigé par Jules Burat, v. 2 (Paris, 1845), 30. Adolphe Blaise, *Exposition des produits de l'industrie nationale en 1844* (Paris, 1844), 77.

[2] Albert Demangeon, *La Plaine picarde* (Paris: Colin, 1905), 269–71.

cotton seemed almost complete, it was discovered that the woolen
industry had been growing again since about 1822. The manufacture of woolen muslins that had a warp of cotton became important
in 1833. At about the same time the Dufour brothers of Lyons
established there a mill to weave mixed cloths of wool and silk.
This shows us that versatility was a prominent characteristic of
Saint-Quentin, but it was a versatility based on weakness rather
than strength. The industry did not develop spontaneously at Saint-
Quentin through the intiative of its native sons, but under the
direction of men who were seeking a rural outpost for the great silk
industry of Lyons. A similar development occurred in the late eighteenth century when a Parisian manufacturer named Santerre established in the district of the same name near Saint-Quentin, from
which his family had probably come, the manufacture of a gauze
made of silk and linen. This again was not a spontaneous creation
of the locality, but was ordered from Paris and remained dependent
upon merchants of the capital.

Saint-Quentin had difficulty in maintaining all its textile manufacturers. In cotton spinning it developed mills and the use of both
water power and steam, but could spin only fine yarn because that
alone could bear the cost of transportation. It found it difficult to
compete with Alsace, which had higher waterfalls, even cheaper
labor, and industrial leaders who displayed initiative and imagination such as these Picards could not equal. Later, as transportation
improved, they felt the competition of Lille and Rouen as well. For
many years Saint-Quentin prospered tolerably by changing her
products frequently. For a decade she wove fine cottons with great
success, only to lose them to the Alsatians. For a time she was successful with cotton muslins, only to have the finest taken away by
Tarare, southwest of Lyons; then, when she began to embroider
these same muslins, she was defeated by a new manufacturer at
Nancy in Lorraine who used power looms.[3] Even in the tulle in-

---

[3] Adolph Blaise, *Exposition des produits de l'industrie nationale en 1839*
(Paris, 1839), 131; the manufacturer referred to was Bompard, who started
his mill in 1834.

dustry Saint-Quentin never showed the strength of Calais. Her cotton spinners were hit so hard by the depression that began in 1827 that they never recovered fully, as did those of Alsace, nor did they show the ingenuity of the manufacturers of Roubaix, who suffered quite as much. The same was true of woolen muslins, which Saint-Quentin claimed to have invented in 1833. A decade later its Chamber of Commerce reported to the government that only two local mills were still making these cloths, which seem to have had a considerably longer life elsewhere.[4]

Saint-Quentin seems to have succumbed to her competitors in each case chiefly because they had greater natural advantages or were on more important trade routes. Yet her manufacturers seem to have lacked the qualities that would have made them great entrepreneurs, like those of Alsace, who had many grave difficulties to overcome, such as the high cost of transportation of cotton, dyestuffs, and fuel. Finally, it should be remembered that Saint-Quentin, and the districts around it, were exploited continuously by the great manufacturers and merchants of Paris, Lyons, and even Rouen.

Competition on a larger scale is illustrated by Normandy, with the manufacturing centers of Rouen and Elbeuf, and Alsace, with the centers of Mulhouse and Sainte-Marie-aux-Mines. Here we run into the usual difficulty of inadequate information. Most of our evidence comes from Rouen and Mulhouse, which were prone to write about their industrial activities, while we have scarcely any information about Elbeuf, the chief Norman center in the woolen industry, and Sainte-Marie-aux-Mines, one of the most active centers of France in the manufacture of mixed cloths. Yet Elbeuf and Sainte-Marie, for the needs of this chapter, are much more important. We must also note the minor fact that Sainte-Marie is not, strictly speaking, in Alsace, but on the edge of that province in the Vosges. From the industrial point of view the closest relations of Sainte-Marie were with its Alsatian friends and rivals, and the

---

[4] Charles Picard, *Saint-Quentin: De son commerce et de ses industries,* v. 2 (Saint-Quentin, 1867), 212.

ingenuity of its manufacturers resembles that displayed in Mulhouse more closely than that of any other place in France, with the exception of Roubaix.

Rouen was well known as the capital of the cotton industry in Normandy and had the singular advantage of being an ancient port and the nearest one to Paris. It may be that because of its access to the sea, which enabled it to obtain American cotton through England and coal from Wales cheaply, Rouen had always been noted for its coarse and cheap products. By 1815 the custom had become fixed and, despite occasional evidences of versatility and originality, remained typical. Yet, despite its limitations, Rouen remained important and powerful as an industrial center.

In the period from 1815 to 1848 Rouen was notable first for its production of *rouenneries,* defined as any cotton cloth woven from dyed yarn, but which, in practice, were usually rather plain, colored cloths noted for neither designs nor patterns. When we compare the position and habits of Rouen with those of Alsace the contrast is striking. Alsace, although it had the Rhine, did not have its industrial capital of Mulhouse on that river and, because it was an integral part of the French customs system, must import its cotton through a French port. In practice this meant that Alsace must use Le Havre and transport its cotton in carts across the whole of northern France. Alsace, therefore, had to spin fine yarn and make as many fine cloths as it could because of the high cost of its raw material. Similarly, its dyes and coal were expensive.

The complexity of competition is shown by the fact that while Alsace and Rouen competed in *rouenneries,* cotton prints or *indiennes,* and, if we add Elbeuf, in woolen muslins and other mixed cloths, these cloths also competed with each other, sometimes because of warmth, lightness, or other intrinsic qualities and sometimes because of the unpredictable whims of fashion. We find, as we should expect, that soon after *rouenneries* became important it was customary for Rouen to make the coarser and medium qualities and Alsace the finer. The differentiation grew ever more marked. We find the same tendency in prints. But when we find Norman merchants or manufacturers complaining that their manufacture of

rouenneries was being ruined by the Alsatians, it becomes clear that
it was suffering far more from the competition of the gayer and
more varied prints in Normandy itself. And when we have established that fact, we discover that wool and silk are being introduced
into these prints and that Sainte-Marie-aux-Mines, which seemed
to have a genius for mixing textiles and colors and for making them
well, and usually cheaply, became a formidable competitor of the
Normans.

Rouen exhibits a kind of constitutional reluctance to vary products or mix colors. It competed best in plain and coarse goods.
Furthermore, since it was more skilled in spinning than in weaving,
it sent its yarn far into Picardy to be woven in the homes of
peasants. Thus Brayer, writing in 1826,[5] says that *rouenneries,* in
the district of Saint-Simon near Saint Quentin, had already replaced
coarse linens. The manufacturers of Rouen had found in this district
a large number of weavers who were highly skilled but willing to
accept low wages, presumably because they supported themselves
in part by farming. The region used by these Norman manufacturers
evidently spread until it included over one hundred villages in the
departments of Aisne, Oise, and Somme. Brayer says there were
5,000 weavers who had the assistance of 3,000 helpers. The manufacturers of Rouen had a foreman in each village with whom they
corresponded, and they sent carts three times a week full of yarn,
which were returned full of cloth. We have no further description
of this very extensive application of the domestic system, but it
seems safe to assume that it was used for other cloths later, such as
prints, and possibly for woolen muslins; and it seems probable that
this system described so carefully by Brayer was essentially the same
as that used by numerous merchant manufacturers of Paris and by
some from Lyons.[6]

Rouen competed vigorously with Saint-Quentin and Sainte-
Marie in ginghams, but this appears to have lasted only a few years,
because ginghams could be varied only with stripes and checks,

[5] Jean Baptiste Brayer de Beauregard, *Statistique de l'Aisne,* v. 2 (Saint-
Quentin, 1826), 304.
[6] *Ibid.*

whereas the number of variations of prints was infinite. As the public demanded bright, varied and cheap cottons, ginghams were soon driven out by prints, as *rouenneries* were checked from time to time for the same reason. Thus, in 1847, we hear of a printer at Rouen who learned to print on a large scale and by machinery muslins and jaconas, which had previously been printed mostly at Paris, Mulhouse, and Saint-Quentin. He also printed enormous quantities of handkerchiefs of Scotch batiste, a mixed cloth of cotton and linen, more cheaply than his competitors in other cities. Finally, this printer, who was most appropriately named Bataille, learned to imitate the shiny Scotch finish given to cloths at Saint-Quentin and applied it to a mixture of cotton and linen called *toile du Nord,* which was thus made to resemble pure linen. The splendid write-up given this enterprising citizen by the society of emulation of his city[7] indicates that he achieved a spectacular success there, because both Scotch batistes and *toiles du Nord* were then well known in northern France. There is good reason to believe that most mills in the region of Rouen were moderate in size, with the exception of a few that spun cotton. It seems clear also that most of the manufacturers were conservative, relying on established methods, reluctant to change their machines or to substitute steam for water power, and even more reluctant to co-operate to form large and powerful enterprises.

The role played by Elbeuf was quite different. This center of the woolen industry was on the Seine some miles above Rouen, but it was never a real port and never became a great city. It was not even on the railroad that was built from Paris to Rouen in 1840. Yet it may well be that its comparative youth and obscurity gave its manufacturers the incentive they needed to make it the capital of the woolen industry in Normandy. By 1819 it was already important, and by 1834 it was defeating its ancient neighbor and rival Louviers. Other and smaller centers of woolen manufacture, such as Déville and Darnétal near Rouen, declined, and writers from Rouen give the impression that the woolen industry in Normandy as a

---

[7] *Bulletin de la société d'emulation de la Seine-Inférieure,* 1847, pp. 34–35.

whole was declining, whereas, in reality, it was being concentrated in Elbeuf.

Other reasons why Elbeuf became the leader in the woolen industry are that several of its manufacturers had initiative and imagination, were not handicapped by tradition as much as those of Louviers, and were, therefore, willing to use steam and new machines and to make the new and cheaper cloths that the public demanded. It is a pity that the manufacturers of Elbeuf did not write more about their city and did not develop an industrial society like Mulhouse, Saint-Etienne, or Reims, or even a less modest society of emulation like Rouen. We are forced to rely solely, in this chapter, on the evidence of Turgan.[8] He tells us that up to 1815 fashion had been based on color alone; then new colors increased rapidly; after 1831 there were added checks, dots, and little figures. All these came into general consumption and caused a real revolution at Elbeuf. The number of novelties increased rapidly and came to constitute 90 per cent of the production of Elbeuf. Jacquard looms were introduced and workers brought from Lyons to demonstrate their use. When it was found that they were too high to be used in the homes of the peasants, the ceilings of the homes were not raised, as had been done in Picardy, but a new mill was built to house these machines, without which attractive novelties could not be made. Before 1848 the growth and enterprise of Elbeuf were causing anxiety in Sedan and Reims and respect in Roubaix.

It is interesting to turn next to the one center in southern France about which we have information available, thanks to two books written by witnesses of the events they describe and to one written in 1914. This is the city of Nîmes, which was important in the days of Rome, was prominent again in the medieval period, and again at the time of the Reformation as a center of Protestantism. In economic terms Nîmes had been more important as a center of trade rather than industry, but it shared in the decline of most of the commercial centers of Mediterranean France, which suffered partly from the rising of the land along the coast and partly from the

---

[8] Julien François Turgan, *Les Grandes usines*, v. 5 (Paris, 1866), 69–70, 119–20.

increasing size of ships. Both factors rendered the smaller ports almost useless. The religious struggle weakened Nîmes by leaving her with a Protestant aristocracy of manufacturers and a mass of Catholic workers.[9]

Despite these handicaps, Nîmes, in the earlier nineteenth century, was an industrial center of real importance. It was in a region that had access to considerable supplies of native-grown silk and wool and to cotton from the Levant. Its manufacturers showed skill and ingenuity, but were not on the whole great manufacturers. They were tacticians rather than strategists. They were faced with serious problems, however. It is almost certain that their supply of capital was inadequate. Their silk was produced by peasants in their homes; their wool was neither very cheap nor very good, and the same can be said of the cotton they received. Better silk was produced further up the Rhône Valley, and much better wool and cotton were available in northern France, while in silk manufacturing they were competing with Lyons, which, to them, must have seemed the colossus of the north. They lacked an adequate supply of coal until the opening of the railroad to the mines of the Grande Combe late in the period 1815–48. They suffered also from an increasingly serious shortage of water. In addition, they were troubled by the French war with Spain, the rising influence of England in the Mediterranean, the West Indies, and Latin America, influence that was important commercially as well as politically, and by the prohibitions of France, which caused serious reprisals.

If the manufacturers of Nîmes were not very wise, they were ingenious and clever and, in many respects, skillful. They introduced the Jacquard loom in 1819 and adapted it to hosiery in 1827. We are told that as early as 1824 half the looms of Nîmes, or about 2,000, were Jacquards. They were used to imitate the richer and dearer silks and mixed cloths of Lyons, to produce fancy silk hosiery so good that it was definitely superior to the products of all other

[9] François Félix de Lafarelle, "Etudes économiques sur l'industrie de la soie dans le midi de la France," *Journal des économistes,* Série 2, v. 1 (1854), 62–85, 191–204. Hector Rivoire, *Statistique du département du Gard,* 2 vols. (Nîmes, 1842). Henri Reboul, *L'Industrie nîmoise du tissage au XIXe siècle* (Montpellier: Firmin et Montane, 1914).

centers in France, to make cheap prints beginning about 1827, and, a little later, to develop on a large scale the production of shawls. When the men of France showed a preference for trousers and the women for cheaper cotton stockings, they abandoned their silk stockings. When they lost the markets of Spain and the colonies, they found others in southern France. They developed their woolen industry and produced gloves, stockings, caps, and, finally, carpets. From necessity their goods had to be cheap. They displayed great ingenuity in keeping their prices down, but they did it with too great a sacrifice of quality and too great a decrease in wages, which had always been low. They were consistently unable to use machinery run by power and to put their workers into mills because the economic and social obstacles to these necessary improvements, which were felt in most parts of France, were irresistible in the Gard.

The odds were against the manufacturers of Nîmes from the beginning, and it could be said that they should not have attempted the struggle. Lyons had a great supply of capital, far more Jacquard looms, a far better supply of silk and wool, and particularly of waste silk, with which machinery was used with great profit. Lyons also attracted workers from the whole of the Rhône Valley and not just from the northern part. In cotton Rouen, the Nord, and Alsace had resources that Nîmes could not match, and the same can be said of woolen centers such as Elbeuf, Reims, and Roubaix. Finally, Lyons had merchants and designers unequaled anywhere else in France, except in Paris and Roubaix. The struggle of Nîmes was, therefore, hopeless, but it was bravely and cleverly led. There was no reluctance to try new products and new methods, and there were few traces of that conservatism and devotion to tradition that were so common in France and so unusually strong in most parts of the Midi.

We can now consider the three great centers of the north that played so vital a part in the manufacture of textiles and their sale in France and abroad: Paris, Reims, and Roubaix. Paris was, first of all, the capital of the kingdom. Because the centralization of administration was based upon sound geographical facts, it was also the center of trade, finance, and transportation. These facts went far in determining the role of Paris in industry. The workshops of the capital produced shawls, waistcoats, and trousers that were the admiration of all beholders, although their price was almost as great as their beauty. Paris was too expensive a city for very large workshops or factories, although in its suburbs it had concentrated some of the largest and most efficient dyeing establishments for woolens because it could attract the most skilled dyers and have them trained by some of the most distinguished chemists in Europe. Nearly every French firm had an agent, warehouse, or shop in Paris, or made use of a selling house to dispose of most of its cloth. Because it was the center of the country's means of communication and its greatest financial market, Paris offered the best facilities for credit and the sale of goods. It also provided the largest single group of consumers who had the means to gratify every whim of taste and fashion. It was, therefore, the seat of what we could call the general staff of the textile industries.

As Bernoville, the Picard, wrote in 1851,[10] it was Paris that made the patterns and decided colors and fashions for the whole of France. This worthy son of Amiens even goes so far as to say that Paris supplied practically all the ideas used. This is too much. When we study the greatest designers of our period, we are struck by the fact that scarcely any of them were native Parisians, nor, after admitting to being born elsewhere, did they leave all provincial ties behind them. Ternaux, perhaps the greatest entrepreneur in France in the earlier nineteenth century, kept up close connections with Reims and other textile centers. Santerre, the originator of mixed cloths in the late eighteenth century, shows by his name that he probably came from the neighborhood of Saint-Quentin, and he certainly did much of his best work in Picardy. Even more important is the fact that Charles Depouilly, Camille Beauvais, and Jourdan, who are called the greatest designers of the period and the best trainers of other designers, all came from Lyons. It is known also that Depouilly, at least, kept up carefully his business connections

---

[10] Paris, *Exposition universelle de 1851 à Londres,* travaux de la Commission Française, v. 4: "Industrie des laines peignées," par F. Bernoville (Paris, 1854), 141.

with Lyons, and it is possible that Beauvais did also. If silks and linens were the first mixed cloths, according to Bernoville, who forgets the much older *siamoises* of Normandy, which were made of linen and cotton, silks and cottons came first from Lyons; so did silks and woolens, which, according to various sources, were invented by the Dufour brothers, J. B. Charles, or Villefranche, all manufacturers of Lyons. We recall also that the Dufour brothers founded a mill for the manufacture of silks and woolens at Saint-Quentin from Lyons, not Paris, and it is quite possible that other manufacturers of Lyons used freely the cheap, abundant, and frequently skillful labor of the peasants of northern France. We have seen how numerous cotton manufacturers of Rouen did the same thing; and it is certain that Paturle-Lupin, who from Paris directed the manufacture of merinos at Le Cateau near Cambrai, was not the only great entrepreneur in that industry. If we could only find sufficient evidence it would almost certainly be possible to prove that the Jacquard loom, probably the greatest of all the many French inventions in the textile industries, was spread from Lyons quite as much as from Paris.

Charles Depouilly started a great silk firm at Lyons in 1805. Later he is said to have shut up Jacquard in a mill with plenty of locksmiths and carpenters until he had made his loom run smoothly. This story may be apocryphal, but it comes from Bernoville, who is usually reliable. We know also from our study of the silk industry that Depouilly knew Jacquard personally and probably supported him financially, if not in improving his loom, then certainly in spreading it. In 1817 Depouilly started the mill of La Sauvagère at Lyons, using various materials that his workmen did not want to use at home. This is the mill which we saw in an earlier chapter was probably the only very large mill in the silk industry at Lyons soon after 1815, and which was certainly one of a small number of large mills in 1848. We do not know how long Depouilly remained at the head of it, but we do know that he retained an active interest in it after going to Paris to develop novelties soon after 1815. In the capital he had a workshop with 300 looms, while he controlled mills at Walincourt and Trois Villes in the Department of Nord by 1824, if not earlier. He is described as the leader in the development of mixed cloths throughout the decade from 1820 to 1830, and we hear of him in 1834 as starting a mill at Puteaux, one of the suburbs of Paris, for printing worsted on warp, in which he was sufficiently successful to make it the dominant method.[11]

Camille Beauvais, whom we have encountered in earlier chapters as a scientific grower of silk worms, an inventor of crêpe de Chine, and a promoter of English sheep in France, founded a silk mill in Lyons in 1805, the same year as Depouilly. We do not know what became of this mill, but we are informed that when Beauvais moved to Paris he became manager of the royal mill of La Savonnerie until it was ruined by the revolution of 1830. We know that Beauvais was in Paris in 1826, when he started a new type of novelties known as *articles forts* to distinguish them from the light cloths, such as gauze, that had been used before. He invented swansdown, a kind of plush, introduced English machines for making poplins at La Savonnerie, and later developed the cloth called *pondicherry,* a derivative from the older *alépine* of Amiens, which was a hand-spun worsted containing silk. Beauvais dyed this and used it on the silk instead of the woolen side. In the meantime Paturle-Lupin had been directing from Paris for some years the weaving of merinos at Le Cateau. He met Beauvais' invention of *pondicherry* by producing foulards.

These developments in Paris and the north, and the success of Depouilly in training designers, and probably that of Beauvais as well, challenged the power of Ternaux, who was a great promoter of the manufacture and sale of textiles until his bankruptcy in 1832. He was the creator of the cashmere shawl in France, whose manufacture had become a Parisian industry primarily, even if the spinning was usually done elsewhere, and possibly much of the weaving as well. In 1826 Ternaux accepted as a partner Théophile Jourdan, a manufacturer of Lyons, who came to Paris and became immediately a formidable rival of Depouilly, and probably of Beauvais and Paturle-Lupin also. Jourdan developed woolen muslins on a considerable scale after 1830, by which time he had taken away from Depouilly control of the mill at Trois Villes in the Nord. Finally,

---

[11] *Ibid.,* 180–89.

in 1838, Jourdan began selling woolen muslins in the United States. The competition in the production of these muslins brought down the price from 12 francs an ell to 1.50. Jourdan also took Scottish cashmeres, started at Paris by Lacanière in 1830, and developed them rapidly until by 1833 they were being sold in the United States as well as Europe. These few facts suggest that Jourdan may have been a promoter rather than a distinguished designer in his own right, or a trainer of other designers.

How much this struggle between industrial leaders helped the industrial development of Paris is uncertain. It is quite clear that most of the actual manufacturing was done, under the direction of these leaders, in the rural districts of northern France, which their capital and their artistic and mercantile experience enabled them to exploit profitably. Paris did become important as a center for shawls, such as pure cashmeres, for fancy waistcoats, for prints of the finest and most costly type, and for some of the more expensive mixed cloths. But it was primarily a city of merchants. In manufacturing it simply competed in certain limited fields. Even in dyeing it was merely one of the most important centers.[12]

Paris occupied a unique position with regard to both regional and industrial competition. As the commercial and financial center of the kingdom it served all regions, or was served by them. In the same way it served all industries and did not aid one at the expense of others. In developing manufacturing in the rural districts of northern and northeastern France, its designers and entrepreneurs promoted chiefly mixed cloths, each of which contained at least two different textiles. In contrast to it we find the almost equally ancient city of Reims, which had always been a center for wool manufacture and became during the period from 1815 to 1848 the chief center for the production of lightly fulled or unfulled woolens or worsteds. As the capital of the ancient province of Champagne, and the place where for centuries the kings of France had been crowned, it was associated with strong commercial and national traditions. In the early nineteenth century, therefore, we find it somewhat conservative, willing to meet the demands of the new age after careful

12 *Ibid.,* 141.

deliberation, but seldom, if ever, provincial. It had great advantages for the manufacture of woolens, because it was the natural market for many of the districts that produced the best wool in France. It was well served by roads, but was not on one of the great rivers of France and was not well served by the network of canals or by the first railroads. It was handicapped further by having no great local supply of fuel, so that it was forced to pay a high price for bringing fuel from a distance in carts.

Reims was the first great center to develop merinos, which were patented there in 1804 and owed much to the ability and energy of Ternaux. They were made with a warp of combed and a weft of carded wool. At first both types of yarn were spun by hand and various types of badly sorted wool were used. For some time manufacturers could not be sure of the permanence of dyes or shadings. But before 1827 it became possible to spin carded wool by machinery, and it will be recalled that the invention of the Godard-Collier comber in 1825 greatly improved and cheapened the production of combed wool. Reims may not have been a pioneer in such mechanical improvements in many cases, but she adopted them quickly and developed them with skill and energy. She was thus in an excellent position to lead in the production of worsteds, which increased very rapidly after 1826. She continued to produce merinos on a great scale; she became supreme in fine flannels, and a leading manufacturer of coarse flannels for underwear. To them she added *napolitaines,* which were made of merino wool, but with both warp and weft of carded wool, and were frequently printed. Later she developed *circassians,* a cloth for use in spring, made with a warp of cotton and a weft of carded wool. The consumption of these increased steadily and permanently and did not vary appreciably with the whims of fashion. Finally, she became, about 1834, a great producer of woolen muslins, which were usually printed and might be mixed with silk or cotton. Her volume of production was great, and its variety also great, so that Reims suffered less from the depression that began in 1837 than did most other textile centers.

At the end of 1832 there was organized at Reims a *société industrielle* much like the existing ones at Mulhouse and Saint-

Etienne, which were only a few years older. This was important, for few industrial and commercial centers had such societies, as we know from the early efforts of the society at Mulhouse to find a group with whom it could correspond. Even more important was the selection as its president of Croutelle, who, in 1848, after prolonged experiments, produced the first French power loom for the weaving of wool. The Société Industrielle obtained first a wool market for the city; then it brought in the Jacquard loom in 1835, taught the weavers how to use it, and worked so hard to spread its use that within a year Reims possessed 300. In that same year, 1836, Reims began on a considerable scale to produce shawls and novelties and started printing flannels. These last developments were greatly stimulated by the rapidly rising northern center of Roubaix, with which Reims now competed vigorously but in her own way. She showed originality in her novelties; she used her own capital without borrowing, and she did not form large companies, such as corporations. Audiganne described her policy as one of wisdom and restrained ambition. We may wonder if there was not too much restraint and too little ambition, yet we must admit that Reims, as an industrial center, remained both great and progressive.[13]

As Reims stood for dignity in the textile arts, so Roubaix stood for impudence. It had long existed, together with its near neighbor Tourcoing, as an obscure village, manufacturing coarse woolens or linens, and, about the end of the eighteenth century, changed, like so many other French centers, to cottons, which it made coarsely and cheaply until about 1825. Then, says the local historian of Roubaix, Leuridan, there came the terrible crisis of 1830–31, when cottons simply could not be sold and Roubaix imported stuffs from England.[14] Even these did not do well, for the French found them too rough and insisted that they be softened. They were. Soon they became one of the most extensively produced cloths in France, and from them were developed the richer satins and light woolen damasks for upholstery.

[13] Georges Boussinesq and G. Laurent, *Histoire de Reims depuis les origines jusqu'à nos jours*, v. 2 (Paris: Matol-Brainé, 1933), 520.

[14] Théodore Leuridan, *Histoire de Roubaix*, v. 5 (Paris, 1864), 141.

This account makes it appear that after some six years of appalling stagnation Roubaix suddenly changed from the manufacture
of cottons to that of woolens. We cannot accept this version of
industrial history. We must note, first, that the Jacquard loom was
introduced at Roubaix in 1828 by two different manufacturers,
Prus-Grimonprez and Jean Casse, and that Casse alone had 120.
This interesting piece of evidence comes from Leuridan himself.[15]
He adds that both Roubaix and Tourcoing built machine shops for
the construction of these looms. Unfortunately, he does not tell us
whether the new looms were used in mills or in the houses of peasant
weavers. As we know that at that time most spinning was done in
mills at Roubaix and most weaving was not, and as there is no
suggestion in any source of the application of power to weaving at
Roubaix, we can assume that they were used in the homes.

Other facts show that there could not have been a sudden
change from cottons to woolens at Roubaix in 1830 or 1831. We
have seen in earlier chapters that there was serious speculation in
cotton, with fantastically high prices for yarn and cloth in 1825,
followed by a serious depression in 1827, which lasted, with brief
exceptions, until 1832. We have ample evidence of the severity of
this crisis in both Alsace and Normandy, and there is no reason to
believe that it was not equally severe in the Nord. While it was
certainly prolonged by the revolution of July, 1830, it began long
before that revolution and was clearly produced by economic causes.

The rise to greatness of Roubaix, which began during this depression, was not based upon the manufacture of pure woolens, but
upon that of a great variety of mixed cloths. This is why the introduction of the Jacquard loom in 1828 is very significant. It must
have been very expensive, and it would not have been needed for
the making of plain but coarse cloths, whether of cotton or wool.
The later history of Roubaix shows that cottons were not abandoned
wholly, or even on a large scale. While there was evidently a decline
in the manufacture of pure cottons, it was neither great nor sudden,
and it was accompanied by a striking increase in the production of
cottons mixed with wool. Finally, the situation of Roubaix would

---

[15] *Ibid.*, 143.

naturally have encouraged the manufacture of mixed cloths. Through the ancient wool market of Tourcoing, which was only two miles away, Roubaix could get an abundant supply of the long wools of Flanders, or a similar type of wool could be imported from England, Holland, or Germany. Roubaix was not as well placed for securing the short wools of France that were so extensively used by Reims. She was, however, near Lille, a great center of the manufacture of linen as well as cotton, and near the regions where the best flax was grown. She was also near the port of Dunkirk, through which flax could be imported from Russia or yarn from England. It is not surprising, then, to find writers speaking of the introduction of linen into the products of Roubaix in 1834. This does not mean the production of pure linens, which never became important at Roubaix, but of linens mixed with cotton.

Roubaix naturally had many contacts with England, where stuffs had long been manufactured. The rising center in northern France knew and liked the long, shiny wools of England and Flanders, which were well suited to the cloths she now wished to manufacture. Mixed woolens and cottons were well known in England when Roubaix began to make them, and they could easily be woven by machinery, as we know England did in 1849, and probably much earlier. Of course, we know also that mixed cloths had been made in some form in France as early as 1780 and were well known in the form of mixtures of wool with both cotton and silk before 1825; the inspiration to develop them at Roubaix therefore probably came from both English and French sources. The whole history of Roubaix since 1825 shows that she was constantly imitating the cloths of other towns, whether French, English, Belgian, or German. At first she tended to economize on her materials in order to undersell her competitors, but she does not seem to have acquired a reputation for bad workmanship as did Nîmes, but rather to have shown in every recorded case a really remarkable ingenuity. She not only mixed wool and cotton, but also linen and cotton, and she clearly used some silk, although it appears never to have been used on the same scale as the other textiles. It is clear also that after Roubaix had learned to use long and shiny wools well she took up the manufacture of the short and curly French wools, and that, after underselling both French and English rivals by copying their goods in cheaper forms, she learned to make cloths as rich and fine as anyone.

The economic historian would be glad to know where Roubaix obtained the capital to make these incessant changes, some of which involved altering drastically well-established methods of manufacturing. She must have used credit widely and have borrowed extensively, if not recklessly, in great contrast to the financial practices of Reims. We know that she won many cloths away from Reims by her boldness, her ingenuity, and the risks she was willing to take; that by about 1848 she employed approximately the same number of workers as Reims and that she paid them better because she produced more fancy goods. At the end of the period from 1815 to 1848 the value of her production appears to have been equal to that of Reims, and she appears to have adopted the power loom for weaving plain cloths soon after her more ancient rival.

Even in dyeing and finishing, Roubaix rose to the top in a very few years. Usually this work on pure or mixed woolens had been done at Reims or Paris. A former workman at Roubaix, Descat, organized in 1843 his own firm, became one of the chief promoters of novelties, and also one of the two most important finishers and dyers. By 1848 Roubaix was able to finish and dye her own cloths and many of those of Reims and Paris as well. She sold cloths to the rich, the middle classes, and the poor. We cannot agree with Audiganne that every case of striking progress at Roubaix was the result of an industrial crisis, or an apparently disastrous change of fashion, although many were; but we do admit that no crisis or change of fashion could stop the progress of Roubaix long, and we do agree heartliy with Audiganne's statement that in no other manufacturing center in France was the spirit as bold and daring and as adjustable to change.[16]

The examples given in this chapter show that both regional and

---

[16] Armand Audiganne, *L'Industrie contemporaine, ses caractères et ses progrès chez les différents peuples du monde* (Paris, 1856), 303.

industrial competition were increasingly important in France in the period of 1815–48. We cannot say how much of it was due to the exclusion of many foreign textiles by the tariff, but we can say that it seems on the whole to have been healthy competition justified by a rising demand from an increasing population. From the regional point of view, we can see an increasing tendency for certain large centers to absorb or control the production of smaller ones. An example of this is the decline of several small wool-manufacturing towns in Normandy, while Louviers maintained its high rank with some difficulty and Elbeuf rose to the highest rank. Saint-Quentin and Amiens declined in importance in the former case because of irresistible competition from centers with greater vigor and greater natural resources, and in the latter from excessive conservatism. We should probably class Nîmes with Saint-Quentin. Rouen and Sedan maintained ably the high rank they held at the beginning of our period, while Reims built splendidly on the foundation of a glorious past, and Mulhouse and Roubaix rose from small beginnings to be the equals of the greatest textile centers in France.

Certain conclusions can be drawn also regarding industrial competition. The cotton industry grew rapidly and greatly for reasons that are well known, and sold its goods at prices that became amazingly low. Its progress was probably retarded by excessive protection, but on the other hand, the English industry was so large and grew so rapidly that without the tariff barrier it might have overwhelmed its French rival. The woolen industry in France probably needed little or no protection and was, therefore, also checked in its growth, but its record is excellent. Before 1848 it was certainly a powerful competitor of cotton, but there was room for both and there is no evidence that the widespread consumption of woolens by the French people decreased appreciably their demand for cottons. In most cases where the industries competed, it was in the production of mixed cloths from which both gained. The silk industry may have suffered a little from the powerful growth of cheaper cottons and linens, but its increasing production of waste silk and its share in the production of mixed cloths protected it from severe harm. It was in greater danger from foreign competition, the whims of fashion, and its stupid handling of labor than from competing textile industries within France.

In the case of linen, the competition of cotton was almost disastrous. It seemed as if cotton could replace almost any form of linen at a lower price. Linen was the only textile industry that did not increase its production at a rate faster than the rise of population in France. But the comparative shrinking of the linen industry was inevitable and, therefore, does not require further explanation. With the exception of the linen industry, which gained little and lost much, competition between the different textile industries of France from 1815 to 1848 was chiefly in mixed cloths, from which, as we have seen, all gained. What is of greatest interest to us is that, as financial facilities and transportation improved, competition among the textile industries and among different parts of the same textile industry increased rapidly. The vicissitudes of booms, crises, and changes of fashion did no permanent harm, and the drastic fall in the price of clothing was a precious boon to the underfed and underpaid workers of France.

CHAPTER SIXTEEN

Foreign Influences and Crises Which Affected French Industrial Growth

OF FRANCE'S NUMEROUS NEIGHBORS we have sufficient information on two to discuss their influence on the development of French industry and trade. The first, Belgium, is divided from France by a land frontier that is largely artificial, while the linguistic and racial ties are close and important. The great coal basin of Valenciennes in northern France, as well as the richer basin of Pas de Calais, discovered near the close of the period 1815–48, is simply a continuation of the great coal veins of Belgium. The parts of Belgium near the French frontier for centuries have grown flax as fine as any to be found in northern France or Ireland, while in Belgian Flanders, as in France, the cotton and linen industries were important. Political connections had often been close. For twenty years Belgium was a part of France, and during the later years of the July Monarchy a serious attempt was made to establish a Franco-Belgian customs union.

But there were also important differences between the two countries which, with the interest of England in maintaining a balance of power on the Continent, were strong enough to prevent any effective union for any great length of time. If many Belgians were related to the French, many others were not. Belgian connections with Holland were quite as close, and the union of these two countries from 1815 to 1830 was no more unnatural than the French conquest of her immediate neighbor in 1793. If the two greatest Belgian rivers, the Meuse and the Scheldt, or Escaut, ran through France in their upper courses, their mouths were controlled by the

Dutch. If French capital played an important part in the development of Belgian industry and transportation, it is probable that Dutch, English, and German capital were even more influential. If the veins of coal in the basins of Mons and Valenciennes were not sharply separated, the quality of the coal and the cost of mining it were very different. If the cotton and linen industries of France and Belgium resembled each other closely, national feeling was sufficiently strong to make them rivals.

Belgium was a small country and quite unable to defend her independence against France unaided, and during most of her history she had been a group of somewhat autonomous provinces rather than a national state. Yet her people showed unmistakably that they resented the domination of both France and Holland as they had that of Spain. Belgium also had important natural resources. Much of her soil was exceedingly fertile, and her people had practiced agriculture with skill for as many centuries as the French. Her linen and woolen industries were probably as old as any in Europe, and she had taught valuable lessons in manufacturing to both the French and the English. Her coal was abundant, easy to mine, and unusually good for coke, whereas French coal was scattered through many basins, was usually difficult to mine, and was frequently unsuitable for coke. Because of these favorable characteristics of Belgian coal and the nearness of several important French rivers to the waterways of southern Belgium, coal from the basin of Mons was an important resource to the industries of northern France and the city of Paris, as was English coal to the industrial development of Normandy and its capital of Rouen.

Belgium had a very large farming population, as did France, and most of her industries used this labor through the domestic system, as did the French. We find the same reluctance to adopt machinery run by power and the same distrust of large industrial companies. The new technical methods evolved by England in the late eighteenth century were brought to Belgium at almost exactly the same time that they were introduced into France.[1] Yet the Belgians seem to have learned more rapidly than most of the French,

---

[1] Ben Serge Chlepner, *Le Marché financier belge depuis cent ans* (Brussels: Capenhout, 1930), 5.

and in spirit they appear to have resembled the manufacturers of Alsace rather than those of Normandy. They had excellent mills in metallurgy, in the spinning and weaving of cotton, and in the spinning of flax. Yet they were not numerous. The domestic system remained dominant in Belgium, and wages and the standard of living were apparently somewhat lower than in most industrial districts in France in the period 1815–48. Steam power should have been much cheaper in Belgium because of the greater abundance and the lower cost of coal, yet, in general, it does not seem to have been used much more in proportion to the amount of industry to which it could have been applied than in the more progressive parts of France.[2] We hear much of large and well-organized coal-mining companies in Belgium beginning about 1835, but that is only three years before the start of the movement to organize the great coal trust in the basin of the Loire, and the Belgian development seems to have been checked for some years after 1838, while the French development continued despite the depression.[3]

The Belgians do seem to have developed their system of transportation sooner than the French. While it is obvious that their task was easier because their country was small and most of it comparatively flat, and because their industries were somewhat more concentrated than in most parts of France, these obvious factors were probably not the most important causes of the early growth of the railroad network, even if they were the most important in the cases of the roads and waterways. The compelling reason for the rather early beginning of the railroads in Belgium was the separation of Belgium from Holland after the revolution of 1830 and the virtual closing of the mouth of the Scheldt by the Dutch, who owned both banks near the sea.[4] This was a terrible blow to Antwerp, the greatest port of Belgium, as were the loss of the Dutch merchant marine and the Dutch colonial markets for Belgian cloth. The Dutch

[2] *Ibid.*, 7. Prosper Alexis de La Nourais, *De l'association douanière entre la France et la Belgique* (Paris, 1842), 105.

[3] Chlepner, *op. cit.*, 20, 35. Pierre Edmond Teisserenc de Bort, *Les Travaux publics en Belgique et les chemins de fer en France* (Paris, 1839), 171.

[4] Leland Hamilton Jenks, *The Migration of British Capital to 1875*, 2d ed. (New York: Knopf, 1938), 139.

were able also to close the Meuse in the same way, and this was the main outlet for the great metallurgical district of Liège. Hence, George Stephenson made plans for the Belgian railroads with the financial support of the Rothschilds in 1836. In that same year Bowring, that indefatigable agent of the British government in France, organized in Belgium the International Railway Company to build railroads from Antwerp and Brussels to Calais and Paris.[5] He may well have been supported by both the Rothschilds and John Cockerill, whose family had done much for metallurgy and machinery in Belgium, but he did not get the necessary co-operation of the French government. This first railroad boom in Belgium was checked by the crises of 1838–39 and possibly also by the death of John Cockerill in 1840. A second boom, corresponding to that in France, began about 1845, during which some ten railroad companies were organized in Belgium. Speculation in their stocks seems to have been conducted almost wholly by English investors on the Exchange in London, for the Belgian government refused to allow the shares to be listed on the Exchange at Antwerp until 1847.[6]

The woolen industry in Belgium was very old, as has been said, but was not a dangerous rival to the industry in France. In the period from 1815 to 1848 it was represented chiefly by the great center of Verviers in eastern Belgium, which manufactured considerable quantities of woolens of medium quality. These do not seem to have been imported into France to any great extent, probably because of the French tariff and the manufacture of similar cloths in France, and they did not interfere seriously with French exports in most cases. The industry of Verviers did have an advantage over its French rivals in the much greater cheapness of wool. Belgium no longer produced much wool, because of the prevalence of small landholdings, a condition that affected the French somewhat later, but she did import wool extensively from both England and Germany, and she admitted it free, whether it was to be manufactured in Belgium or was to be sent on to France. It was through Belgium

---

[5] Raymond Guyot, *La Première entente cordiale* (Paris: Rieder, 1926), 141.

[6] Teisserenc, *op. cit.*, 173.

that France obtained much of the fine wool of Saxony and the long, shiny wool of England.[7]

Despite numerous complaints by French manufacturers, especially those in the linen industry, there seems no reason to believe that any Belgian industry seriously endangered the prosperity of that industry in France. There was evidently some healthy competition, but France was so much larger and stronger that the danger would appear to have been rather that she would injure the industries of her little neighbor. France learned something from Belgian machine makers and manufacturers; she found Belgium a useful market for capital and for many manufactured goods, and a valuable source of skilled labor which emigrated readily into French Flanders and settled in centers like Lille and Roubaix. Belgium helped also in sending some fine flax, of which France scarcely produced enough, and in transmitting considerable quantities of wool.

The influence of England on the growth of French industry was very different from that of Belgium. It could best be described as all-pervasive and ever-present. It was grossly misrepresented by many writers and witnesses, both French and British, who were usually inspired by national prejudice. French writers frequently showed fear of the power of British industry and finance, or contempt for British materialism as expressed in large-scale production at low prices and in the continuous development of the search for foreign markets. Such prejudice and misunderstanding has governed Franco-British relations for the most part since the days of the Hundred Years' War. They had been intensified by the long and bitter struggle during the French Revolution and the First Empire, when warfare was both military and economic.

British influence on French industry, trade, finance, and transportation has been discussed in almost every chapter of this study, and every effort has been made to show it as it was and not as it was said to be. Thus, in transportation the French supplied a great highway engineer in Trésaguet, from whom British engineers like MacAdam learned much. The error of the French was that they

[7] La Nourais, op. cit., 141–42.

failed to appreciate Trésaguet and were, therefore, forced to follow MacAdam. One is reminded forcibly of the ability of de Girard and of the inability of his countrymen to appreciate it until it had been utilized by the British. In the development of waterways and railroads the French were well informed regarding British developments, but they had different problems and had able engineers of their own to solve them. In metallurgy, as we have seen, they borrowed heavily from England and were a little slow to develop leaders able to use the new methods and to train their workmen. But the period of French dependence was not long, and we have seen that after 1825 the French began rapidly to produce metallurgists, machinists, and workmen of reasonable skill although inadequate in numbers. Before 1848 it was clear that the French could make many of their own machines and tools very well indeed.

But we must not think wholly in mechanical terms. Dupont-White pointed out in 1846 that the great stimulus to the English cotton industry had not been machinery but the monopoly of colonial and other markets outside England obtained by war.[8] He added that the French cotton industry grew fast not through the use of machinery but through the increase of its consumers from 24,000,000 to 40,000,000 as the result of the conquests of the French Revolution. We cannot agree with this opinion wholly, for the adoption of British machines by the French cotton industry was essential to its growth. Yet Dupont-White did well to point out the commercial problem. The European market did greatly stimulate the French cotton industry under the First Empire, and not all of it was lost in 1815. It is well to remind ourselves that England did not acquire colonial and other markets simply through war, but even more through her excellent merchant marine and her fine ports. France had lost many of her colonies to England because she had not utilized them fully, had neglected her merchant marine before she lost it, and had not developed fully the ports which she possessed, inferior as they were, on the whole, to the best ports of England. She had made her greatest error in the seventeenth century when

---

[8] Charles Brook Dupont-White, *Essai sur les relations du travail avec le capital* (Paris, 1846), 50.

she chose to follow Louis XIV in his effort to dominate Europe, and turned her back on Colbert, who, despite many errors and prejudices, was right in urging her to develop her colonial empire. The leaders of the French Revolution, of whom Napoleon was simply the last and greatest, only repeated on a greater scale the error of the most famous of the Bourbons.

The French erred also in their tendency to despise the English for their large-scale production of textiles at low prices. Rodet pointed out that at the Exposition of 1834 cheaper cloths, such as those used in the Orient and in the French provinces, were not featured. He said also that France could not yet compete with England in flannels or in hosiery, although he admitted that much hosiery had been exported to England as well as to the United States in 1831–32. He concluded by noting that stockings of medium quality and low price were hard to find.[9] It is clear that here, as in the case of most textiles, France both admired and excelled in the finest qualities. In cheaper hosiery French manufacturers found it difficult to compete with the British in many cases because of their adoption of machinery run by steam between 1820 and 1830, while competition with Saxony was difficult because of her unusually low wages and her skill in selling goods abroad. Rodet's criticism of French expositions and their emphasis on luxury goods is justified and should have received more attention.[10]

A more valuable and constructive observation on French industry was made by an Englishman, Wyatt, after viewing the Exposition of 1849. He said: "France could compete very well if she would concentrate on developing her mechanical resources while retaining her artistic ability."[11] The seriousness of the problem is shown clearly in the case of the silk industries of the two countries. Camille Beauvais, who was one of the most distinguished leaders in France, felt that British competition was the most dangerous of all because of England's skill in the use of steam, her wealth, and her system of

[9] D. L. Rodet, "De l'industrie manufacturière en France," *Revue des deux mondes,* Série 3, v. 3 (1834), 647.
[10] *Ibid.*
[11] Matthew D. Wyatt, *A Report on the Eleventh French Exposition of the Products of Industry* (London, 1849), 8.

credit. She could manufacture some silks at one third the cost of producing the same article at Lyons; her silk looms were increasing rapidly, and she was considering seriously applying steam to the running of her Jacquard looms. Beauvais made these observations in 1825.[12] Thirteen years later, we learn, the Jacquard looms in England were being run by steam, and most of the secrets of dyeing at Lyons had been revealed to the English by French dyers who had emigrated.[13] Apparently English competition was felt severely in plain silks and in many ribbons, just as it was felt in most mixed cloths, in coarser cotton prints, and in many ribbons, just as it was felt in most mixed cloths, in coarser cotton prints, and in many woolens and worsteds.

It is surprising to find, as late as 1844, as shrewd an observer as Jules Burat saying that France could compete well with England in the weaving of cottons because of her cheap labor, but not in spinning, which had been thoroughly mechanized in England.[14] At that date much of English weaving had already been mechanized, while French spinning was mechanized and the use of the power loom was common in the cotton industry and had begun in the silk industry. The French cotton industry may have been in great danger early in the nineteenth century, but it was strong, healthy, and progressive in 1844. Competition in silks was keen between England and France through most of the period from 1815 to 1848 and seems to have grown keener with the progress of time, yet it is quite clear that France was able to meet British improvements in one way or another. Even although she did not apply steam to the Jacquard loom before 1848, there is no reason to believe that the French silk industry was ever endangered by British competition. French ingenuity and artistry were able to compensate for any serious deficiencies in mechanization.

---

[12] Camille Beauvais, *Essai sur quelques branches de l'industrie française* (Paris, 1825), 6–7.

[13] Charles Beaulieu, *Histoire du commerce, de l'industrie et des fabriques de Lyon* (Lyon, 1838), 148, 158, 160.

[14] Paris, *Rapport du jury central sur les produits de l'industrie française à l'exposition de 1844,* rédigé par Jules Burat ["Report on Tissus"] v. 3 (Paris, 1845), 3.

In the field of finance we find constant references to British wealth, low rates of interest, and widespread use of credit to aid industrial development. Much English capital, as we have seen, was invested in French *rentes,* in French ironworks and machine shops, in cotton and linen mills, and in railroads. Yet there is no reason to believe that there was serious danger of any important French industry or of the French railroad system passing under British control. France was neither poor nor helpless, and her government was vigilant and well informed. Even the withdrawal of a considerable part of the English capital from French railroads in 1845 and 1847 was not fatal to those enterprises. We are justified in concluding that in no important case, whether in the form of capital or of goods, was British competition really dangerous to any great French industry for any great length of time. We may even question whether the high French tariff was needed to save even the iron and cotton industries from British competition.

We must turn now to the crises which affected the French economy more seriously than has generally been realized and which, in most cases, were partly due to influences from abroad. No attempt will be made to deal here with the crisis of 1817–18, about which we still know very little, but we must consider those that began in 1825, 1837, and 1846. Even about these crises we have not enough information to state positively all the causes and results, but we can say that the crisis that began in 1826 in France, and which grew worse until 1829 at least, had an important influence upon the outbreak of the Revolution of July, 1830, and that the crisis which began in 1846 and grew rapidly worse in 1847 was a factor in producing the Revolution of February, 1848.

French writers have studied these crises but have seldom done so thoroughly, and have tended, as did contemporary observers, to subordinate those of 1826–27 and 1846–47 to the revolutions which followed and did not precede them. Thus, they frequently speak incorrectly of the economic crises of 1830 and 1848, although these crises were simply prolongations or intensifications of crises already underway. Other writers, who have usually been economists, have discussed the more obvious economic causes and developments but have seldom gone far enough. Horace Say, a leading merchant in Paris, and son of the well-known economist Jean-Baptiste Say, said that in France commercial crises were less frequent and their effects less serious than anywhere else. Usually, he said, they were the effects of crises in the United States or England diminished by distance; the home affairs of France were rarely affected except through speculation in *rentes* and in other securities.[15] We can accept any of the statements but the last. The textile industries in all cases and the iron industry in most were profoundly affected, although not always at the same time or in the same way. The effects on the various French industries discussed in this book have been touched upon in the chapters concernnig them or in those on labor, capital, and the railroads and cannot be considered in detail here. The subject has been mentioned here only because Horace Say dismissed it too lightly.

Germain Martin, in his important and interesting economic history of France, says that the theory of cycles has been only partly proved by events in the early nineteenth century. Crises, he found, generally started in England, especially early in the century, because industry had developed further there. The crisis that began in 1826 in France was felt much more severely in England in 1825 and affected the United States even before it was felt in France. The fear of dumping English goods, says Martin, produced the protectionist movement of 1826. We agree with the opinions of this distinguished author and wish only that he had said more. His last observation on the protectionist movement of 1826 is particularly interesting. It should lead to careful investigation with results that would be valuable to the economic historian in the future. In the light of the evidence now available, its accuracy cannot be proved, but it should be possible to do so in time.[16]

---

[15] Horace Say, "La Crise financière et la Banque de France," *Journal des économistes,* v. 16 (Feb., 1847), 193.

[16] Germain Martin, *Histoire économique et financière de la France,* in v. 10 of Gabriel Hanotaux (ed.), *Histoire de la nation française* (Paris: Plon, 1927), 398–99.

Juglar had written in 1889 that periodic crises had come in France, England, and the United States every six or seven years since 1800. It is probably this statement that Germain Martin had in mind forty years later when he said that the theory of cycles in France in the early nineteenth century had only been partly proved. But Juglar says further that no matter where the crisis starts it spreads to all places having business relations with the place of origin, although this may be delayed. The maximum price of wheat precedes and nearly always brings on the crisis between 1800 and 1848. Finally, Juglar perceived what many later writers have ignored: that these crises were not caused by riots or revolts, but by the extent of speculation, rising prices, and overstocked warehouses. This does not mean that movements like the revolutions of 1830 and 1848 did not have political causes, but it does indicate, as economic historians now believe, that they may have had economic causes as well and not simply economic results.[17]

The latest writer on these crises in France, Professor Labrousse, takes up the statement of Juglar that the maximum price of wheat precedes and nearly always brings on the crisis and says: *"Les crises de l'ancien type qui se suivront en France jusqu'en 1873 . . . sont caracterisées par le rôle capitale du secteur agricole. C'est la que naît la crise, qui gagne ensuite par contagion le secteur industriel et commercial."*[18] This is a significant statement of great utility by a scholar of great distinction well versed in the economic history of his country. (Labrousse made it in a paper on the crisis of 1847 in France in which he does not discuss earlier crises in detail. It has been given here a wider application than its author probably intended.)

The first crisis we shall consider began in England in 1825.

---

[17] Clément Juglar, *Des crises commerciales et de leur retour périodique en France, en Angleterre, et aux Etats-Unis,* 2d ed. (Paris, 1889), xvi–xvii, 403.

[18] Charles Labrousse, "Crise économique et crises politiques en France de 1847 à 1851," *Communication aux journées franco-anglaises d'histoire* (28 septembre, 1946), p. 1 *bis*. Sent to me in manuscript by Professor Labrousse.

Trade had become very active in 1823, and this resulted in an attempt to launch no less than 624 joint-stock companies before the end of the year 1825. Another cause of trouble lay in the loans sought in London by the new states of Latin America, which sold mining stocks in payment. Some 74 mining companies were organized between 1824 and 1825, although they were probably included among the 624 already mentioned. This development reached its peak in February, 1825, and subsided rapidly in May and June. Most of the companies collapsed, and the loans granted by England proved a total loss. If Dickens only used dates, it could be proved that it was at this time that Mrs. Pipchin acquired her bitter aversion to the Peruvian mines. There was a brief panic on the cotton market at Liverpool from January to March, 1825, and another from June to August in the same year. Then, at the end of November, 1825, numerous banks failed, and this brought on a general panic. The money market was prostrate through the years 1826 and 1827 and prices were still poor in 1829. The first half of 1830 was a period of recovery in England, but this was followed by the revolutions in France and Belgium, and later still there was a serious outbreak of cholera on the Continent. It will be recalled that there was a period of tension and war in the Near East that began in 1827.[19]

In France we note a rapid expansion of the cotton industry from 1825 to 1827, accompanied by a notable rise in prices that is generally described as speculative. There was also a rapid and speculative rise in the price of wool, although the exact time of it is not yet clear. In iron, prices rose from 1824 to 1826, chiefly because of a speculative mania in building. We know also that the French invested in many of the Latin-American mining companies

---

[19] Bishop Carleton Hunt, *The Development of the Business Corporation in England, 1800–1867* ("Harvard Economic Studies," v. 52; Cambridge, Mass.: Harvard University Press, 1936), 45. Sir John Harold Clapham, *An Economic History of Modern Britain*, v. 1 (Cambridge: Cambridge University Press, 1930), 272. Jenks, *op. cit.*, 57. Charles Kenneth Hobson, *The Export of Capital* (London: Constable, 1914), 102–3. Thomas Ellison, "History of Cotton Prices and Supply, 1790–1862," *Exchange Magazine*, v. 1 (Aug., 1862), 313–15; v. 2 (Oct., 1863), 45.

organized in England, probably in as many as forty, and that they obtained most of their American cotton in the market of Liverpool. In the silk industry there was great prosperity in 1825 and crisis all through 1826 because of the effect of the English crisis on the markets of both Great Britain and the United States. The dates of crisis or depression vary somewhat in the different industries, but, in general, it can be said that 1827 and 1828 were years of marked deflation in France. There appears to have been some recovery in 1829 and the first part of 1830, but the crops were bad for three years beginning in 1828. The price of wheat, which had begun to rise in 1827, remained high through 1832. While we know far too few facts, it does seem clear that a largely speculative crisis came in England in 1825 and soon affected both France and the United States, and that the resulting depression was prolonged, first by bad crops in both England and France, and then by revolutions in both France and Belgium. The position has been taken here, therefore, that there was a depression in France from 1827 to 1832. This seems to cover most of the French industries as well as we now can, even if one or two were affected earlier, as we know the silk industry was, in 1826.[20]

[20] *Mémoire général et récapitulatif des travaux de la sous-commission d'enquête pour l'industrie du coton* (Rouen, 1829), 28–32. Charles, baron Dupin, *De l'influence de la classe ouvrière sur les progrès de l'industrie* (discours d'ouverture du cours de géométrie et de mécanique appliquées aux arts et métiers et beaux arts, 30 novembre, 1834; Paris, 1835), 10. France, *Enquête sur les fers de 1828*, par une commission formée sous la présidence du Ministre du Commerce (Paris, 1829), 313. Phillippe Hedde, "Aperçu sur l'état actuel des fabriques de rubans de Saint-Etienne et de Saint-Chamond en 1828," *Bulletin de la société industrielle de Saint-Etienne*, v. 6 (1828), 201–7. Hector Rivoire, *Statistique du département du Gard*, v. 2 (Nîmes, 1842), 30. Ernest Pariset, *Histoire de la fabrique lyonnaise* (Lyon: Rey, 1901), 299–301, 303–4. France, *Enquête relative à diverses prohibitions établies à l'entrée des produits étrangers*, v. 3 (Paris, 1835), 183, 439–42, 453, 632. Andrew Ure, *The Cotton Manufacture of Great Britain* (London, 1836), p. xxx. Société Industrielle de Mulhouse, *Histoire documentaire de l'industrie de Mulhouse au XIXᵉ siècle*, v. 2 (Mulhouse: Bader, 1902), 221. Paris, *Exposition universelle internationale de 1900 à Paris: Le Bilan d'un siècle (1801–1900)*, par Alfred Picard, v. 4 (Paris, 1906), 313. Achille Penot (ed.), *Statistique générale du département du Haut-Rhin* (Mulhouse, 1831), 327.

The crisis of 1837, like the earlier one that began in England in 1825, had its origin abroad, but differed in being much more notably American. Crops failed in the United States in 1835, which meant more in a young and predominantly agricultural country than in more industrialized states of western Europe such as England and France. Railroad and land booms were flourishing and the number of banks was increasing rapidly, while at the same time the federal government was trying to reduce the volume of bank notes in circulation and increase that of specie. Cotton prices were rising rapidly, and the Second Bank of the United States was raising a considerable loan in London to facilitate settlements on the expiration of its charter in 1836.[21] As the late Sir John Clapham said: "the immediate cause of the monetary trouble in England was the close and dominant commercial and financial relations now existing between Great Britain and the United States. The United States which supplied the cotton for Britain's chief industry were absorbing British capital and playing with it as a young country with a continent in reserve is tempted to play with any tool or toy and they were operating on the gold to which the economic life of Britain was hitched."[22]

England herself had been indulging in a speculative boom since 1834. By 1836 too much specie was being sent to the United States, and the Bank of England raised its rate of discount. In November of that year an important bank in Manchester with thirty-nine branches failed, and three large merchant banking houses of Liverpool, despite help from the Bank of England, failed in June, 1837. There was no general panic in England when the banks in New York closed in May, 1837, but a severe depression began that continued until 1844. There are indications of some recovery in 1838, but the crops in the United States failed in both 1837 and 1838, while in England there was a series of crop failures from 1838 until 1842. The railroads, almost alone, survived the depression without serious losses, and they finally broke the depression and started a

---

[21] Clapham, *op. cit.*, 514.
[22] *Ibid.*, 513.

general business revival that soon turned into a colossal railroad boom.[23]

We have very little information regarding the crisis in France, so that it is very difficult to make general statements regarding its course. We know that there was a financial crisis in Paris in the spring of 1837, and sharp crises in the silk manufacturing centers of Lyons and Saint-Etienne, and probably in Nîmes as well. The cotton industry suffered early and severely in Alsace, Normandy, and the Nord. The woolen and linen industries probably suffered less, since mechanization had not progressed as far as in the cotton industry and they were not dependent upon large sales in the United States and England, as was the silk industry. We have no evidence of poor crops until 1838, although the price of wheat began to rise slowly in 1836 and reached its maximum in 1839, declining very slightly in 1840, because the crop of 1839 also was poor, and declining much more in 1841. It would appear that bad crops in France did not last as long as in England and that the financial stringency was not as great, and, therefore, did not last as long. In general we can say that there was a depression from 1837 to 1842 which affected the textile industries considerably and the iron industry much less, and which probably delayed for two or three years planning a general network of railroads and launching individual railroad companies. The year 1837 could probably be described as one of crisis in France, and 1838 as one showing a slight recovery, while a relapse came in 1839 because of bad crops and incomplete liquidation after the crisis of 1837. We know that the Bank of Belgium, in which much French capital was invested, failed in December, 1838, and that Belgium then went through some years of depression, although there is not yet general agreement as to its actual duration. There is need for research into the details of this industrial depression in France; it would be interesting to trace the vicissitudes of many French industries and to know at what

---

[23] Hunt, *op. cit.*, 58, 101. Clapham, op. cit., 517. Davis R. Dewey, *Financial History of the United States,* 9th ed. (New York: Longmans, 1924), 228–30.

times and for how long wages were reduced and mills closed. As yet the data are too few to permit general statements of real value or comparisons that might be interesting and instructive.[24]

The crisis of 1846–47 in France, which was prolonged by the revolution that broke out in February, 1848, was undoubtedly more serious than either of its predecessors that we have considered. Its origins in England have been touched upon in the chapters on capital and on railroads; the French origins also are clearer. France had very bad crops of cereals in both 1845 and 1846. Even in 1845 the price of wheat was higher than in 1838, and it rose to far greater heights in 1846 and 1847 than at any time during any previous crisis since that of 1817. France suffered also from the potato disease, although probably not as severely as Ireland or Belgium. She felt the effects of the financial crisis of England in 1846, and in 1847 she went through a crisis that affected far more French industries and injured them far more seriously than either of the preceding crises that we have considered here. Unemployment was widespread, certainly in the textile industries, and in the midst of it, when the prices of cereals were still high, came the Revolution. It did not break out when conditions were worst but, as in 1830, when it seemed as if recovery had begun. It soon made industrial and commercial conditions far worse than they had been at any time in 1847, although there was some relief through a notable decline in the price of wheat. It would appear that speculation, overproduction of textiles, and disastrous crop failures in France itself would have been sufficient to produce a crisis and depression about 1847, but it is even clearer that these same factors operated quite as strongly in Belgium and even more strongly in England. These countries were also impoverished temporarily by the too-rapid construction of

[24] Martin, *op. cit.*, 399. Alphonse Courtois, "Histoire des institutions de crédit en France depuis 1790: La Banque de France, 1836–1848," *Journal des économistes,* Série 3, v. 34 (1874), 218. Louis Joseph Gras, *Histoire de la rubanerie et des industries de la soie à Saint-Etienne et dans la region stéphanoise* (Sainte-Etienne: Thomas, 1906), 596. Charles Picard, *Saint-Quentin: De son commerce et de ses industries,* v. 2 (Saint-Quentin, 1867), 198. M. Mauguin, *Etudes historiques sur l'administration de l'agriculture en France,* v. 2 (Paris, 1876), 375. Noël Beaurieux, *Les Prix du blé en France au XIX⁰ siècle* (Paris, 1909), 101. Chlepner, *op. cit.,* 197.

railroads. Crop failures seem to have been almost universal throughout western Europe, which was obliged to obtain relief from the United States or Russia at a cost which it could ill afford. It is interesting to recall, also, that 1848 was a year of revolution in most of the countries of western Europe and that even England was anxious.[25]

Our conclusion must be, then, that whereas industrial factors alone in France might not have sufficed to produce a crisis in 1826–27, or in 1837, they would have sufficed to produce a crisis in 1847. It is also clear that foreign influences produced industrial strain within France in 1825 and 1836–37 and that they would have produced a crisis in France in 1847 if conditions in France itself had not sufficed to do so. Finally, we must recall that in the first crisis we have considered crop failures in France were not influential until from 1828 to 1830; in short, they did not produce this crisis but they did prolong it or revive it. In 1837 crop failures again did not start the crisis in France, but they did have a profound influence in causing the financial crisis in the United States as well as in prolonging it there. Then they affected grievously industrial and financial conditions in England through the United States, and the failure of the English crops prolonged the depression there after 1838 as did industrial conditions in England itself. They had some direct influence on industrial conditions in France, especially in the silk and cotton industries, and they had a much greater indirect influence because of the close industrial and financial connections of France with England. In 1846–47 crop failures were clearly the primary cause of financial and industrial crisis in England, France, and Belgium.[26]

---

[25] Mauguin, op. cit., v. 2, pp. 460–77. Beaurieux, op. cit., 41, 101. Henri Sée, La Vie économique de la France sous la monarchie censitaire (1815–1848) (Paris: Alcan, 1927), 42. Guillaume Jacquemyns, "Histoire de la crise économique des Flandres (1845–1850)," Mémoires, lettres, etc., de l'académie royale de Belgique, v. 26 (Brussels, 1929), 248, 253, 256. Juglar, op. cit., 415. Hobson, op. cit., 118. Gabriel Ramon, Histoire de la Banque de France, d'après les sources originales (Paris: Grasset, 1929), 202–10.

[26] See Note 25.

CHAPTER SEVENTEEN

Foreign Markets
for French Manufactures

WE HAVE STUDIED COMPETITION within France, whether between different industries or between different manufacturing centers, and we have also noted the influence of British and Belgian industries upon the French. It is now time to see how well France was able to compete with her rivals abroad, of whom England was almost always the most formidable. The period 1815–48 was, in many ways, a difficult one for French industry. French domination over the continent of Europe, which had been a highly profitable reality under Napoleon, had ended in 1814. Now French manufacturers must compete with those of England and of the other continental countries themselves on equal terms, except for the advantage France enjoyed in being, on the whole, more industrialized than any except England and Belgium. But there were also many markets outside the European continent which must be reached by sea, such as the United States, Latin America, the Levant, and the Orient. To reach these, France needed ships to carry her goods, ports from which to send them, inland transportation to carry them to the ports, and diplomatic and financial facilities for selling them on favorable terms. In all these cases the obstacles encountered were very serious indeed, and the success achieved considerably less than in the domestic field.

France was not fortunate in the number of good harbors on her coasts. On the Mediterranean the only really important one in the earlier nineteenth century was Marseilles, through which passed

most of the trade for the Levant and Africa and much of that with
the Orient. But Marseilles was not in a really important industrial
region. While minor centers, such as Nîmes, Montpellier, and
Avignon were not far away, the great manufacturing and commercial city of Lyons was far up the torrential Rhône and was not
connected with Marseilles by a railroad during the period with
which we deal. On the Atlantic the most important ports were
Bordeaux and Le Havre, the former a few miles from the sea on
the Gironde, and the latter at the mouth of the Seine. Bordeaux had
vineyards near by, while there were pine forests not far away, and
the country producing cognac was not far to the north; but Bordeaux was not really the center of an industrial region, except for
wine, spirits, the refining of sugar, and shipbuilding. Le Havre was
not nearly so far from numerous industrial centers as either Bordeaux or Marseilles and was connected with many of them by the
Seine, which, while difficult to navigate, was still much less difficult
than either the Rhône or the Garonne. Furthermore, some sixty
miles up the Seine was Rouen, a manufacturing and commercial
center of real importance, a port in its own right, and only ninety
miles from Paris, with which it was connected by a railroad in 1843.
It is curious that even as late as 1837 the possibilities of Rouen as
a really good port were not understood, and no one seems to have
imagined that in the twentieth century it would be the best-equipped
and most useful port in France.[1] There were minor ports also, such
as Calais, Boulogne, and Dunkirk on the Channel, Saint-Valéry at
the mouth of the Somme, and Nantes at the head of ocean navigation on the Loire. None of these was capable of playing a decisive
part in the development of foreign trade. Saint-Valéry would hardly
seem to us now useful for anything but fishing boats, but in the
period from 1815 to 1848 it was used as the port of Amiens and
Abbeville, and we are told that whole shiploads of goods were imported through it.[2] The channel ports were probably useful to the

[1] Jérôme Adolphe Blanqui, *Cours d'économie industrielle* (Conservatoire
des Arts et Métiers), v. 2 (Paris, 1838), 491.
[2] Albéric, baron de Calonne d'Avesnes, *Histoire de la ville d'Amiens au
XIX* siècle* (Amiens: Piteux Frères, 1906), 148; the reference is to shipments for the year 1835.

most northerly textile centers, but all had small harbors. Cotton was imported chiefly through Le Havre and sugar through Bordeaux and Nantes.

These seaports were sometimes badly connected with the interior. Boats could go down the Rhône, but could seldom go up unless moved by steam engines of unusual power, so that goods imported through Marseilles were usually sent up to Lyons by road until the latter part of the period from 1815 to 1848. The Garonne was not much better, and its largest tributary, the Dordogne, was not very useful and did much harm because, when its mouth was widened, it brought down so much silt that long and expensive dredging of the Gironde became necessary.[3] Since the government of the Restoration was compelled to practice rigid economy in order to pay war debts and repair damage done by years of neglect to roads and rivers, it became necessary to organize a company and finance the dredging through navigation dues collected by the port of Bordeaux.[4] Nantes could send goods, such as the sugar it refined, to Paris by the Loire and the canals of Orléans and Loing, but that meant the use of small barges. Only the Seine was really satisfactory as a waterway, and it connected with the Oise, through which many northern centers of industry could be reached.

On the whole more and better roads were needed to carry many goods to the seaports or to bear imports into the interior. What this meant is shown by the case of Mulhouse, the industrial capital of Alsace, mentioned in the chapter on raw materials. Because the tariff required that a French city obtain its cotton through a French port, Mulhouse had to send carts across northern France to Le Havre, a journey which took six days each way in good weather and added greatly to the cost of the cotton. Even by water the cost of inland transportation was heavy in those days, for uniformity of rates and dues and the policy of operating the waterways at or below cost came later. It has been shown that because of the cost

[3] Pierre de Joinville, *Le Réveil économique de Bordeaux sous la Restauration: L'Armateur Balguerie-Stuttenberg et son œuvre* (Paris: Champion, 1914), 104.
[4] *Ibid.*

of transportation the price of coal in Paris was often ten times the price at the mine. While France did not export any appreciable amount of coal, and while the manufacture of cotton prints at Mulhouse did not have to export through Le Havre, we know that in many cases they did. These examples are useful as reminders that exportation was difficult and expensive in France, first, because the good ports available were few and, second, because most manufacturing centers were far from any port. France suffered from her size, her many mountains, and her rather straight coast line. She suffered also, as Henri Sée pointed out,[5] from economic decentralization, based apparently upon the methods by which she had achieved political unity, but fundamentally upon the extraordinary number of geographical and geological variations of her many regions, or *pays*.

Le Havre, together with Rouen, was undoubtedly the most important seaport of France in the influence it exercised upon industrial development in the period 1815 to 1848 because it was the nearest good port to Paris, the greatest center of trade in France. Le Havre was near more industrial regions than any other port, at the mouth of the most useful of French rivers, and was itself the most important cotton market in France. Yet we lack information about the facts of its growth, and we have such information about Bordeaux, which also illustrates some of the important commercial problems of our period. We have seen that Bordeaux, while near the sea, was not in or near a really important industrial region. One of its leading historians wrote that the region of Bordeaux lacked industries to manufacture the products that its foreign trade should bring in and that the government, therefore, ought to encourage the development of such industries and did not.[6] This lack of local initiative was natural in a country accustomed to a prohibitive tariff combined with administrative control of local activities by the national government. Bordeaux in the eighteenth century had been

<hr />

[5] Henri Sée, *Französische Wirtschaftsgeschichte,* v. 2 (Jena: Brodnitz, 1936), 208.
[6] Louis Bachelier, *Histoire du commerce de Bordeaux* (Bordeaux, 1862), 276.

the chief port in the colonial trade, especially that with the French West Indies, and she had expected to resume that role in the nineteenth century. But she found great changes in the markets for wine, her chief export, in the demand for ships, the building of which constituted her chief industry, and in the supply and price of sugar, the most significant article sent to the mother country by Martinique and Guadeloupe. The wines of Bordeaux were as good as ever, and they had long been among the best in the world, as they still are; yet the French colonies did not take as many as before the Revolution and foreign countries levied new duties upon them and learned to like strange wines, such as port, Madeira, and Marsala; or they went so far as to prefer whiskey and beer. The most important reason for this unfortunate change was undoubtedly the prohibitive French tariff, against whose lofty barrier to their exports the excluded nations naturally took reprisals. The wines of Bordeaux were valuable and, therefore, easy to tax, and they were not indispensable to their potential consumers. Finally, the ability to build ships, if not the demand for them, seems to have grown less, probably as a result of the long period of war and the ensuing decline in the colonial trade of France. This seems to have lasted for some years, for we are told that about 1824 scarcely any ships were built in either Bordeaux or Nantes.[7]

The production of cane sugar in the French islands of Martinique and Gaudeloupe was peculiarly important in its influence on French trade and shipping in the period from 1815 to 1848. During the long period of warfare between 1793 and 1815 the French West Indies were occupied by the British and their trade with France cut off. At the same time a large part of the French merchant marine was captured or destroyed. The British kept order in Martinique

---

[7] Michel Chevalier, *Lettres sur l'Amérique du Nord,* v. 1 (Paris, 1836), 357. Bachelier, *op. cit.,* 250–76. Joinville, *op. cit.,* 231–85. Charles Coquelin, "Du commerce extérieur de la France en 1846," *Revue des deux mondes,* Nouvelle série, v. 13 (March 15, 1846), 1086. Vincent Marie, comte de Vaublanc, *Du commerce de la France: Examen des états de M. le directeur général des douanes* (Paris, 1824), 88. Vaublanc says: *"Nos chantiers sont abandonnés; il n'y a pas un seul navire en construction dans le port de Bordeaux; et plusieurs, construits depuis longtemps y pourissent faute d'emploi."*

and Gaudaloupe, but were naturally more interested in the prosperity of their own sugar-producing islands than in that of the possessions of their ancient foe. As a result, the planters of the French islands in 1815 were in financial distress and crushed by debts. The French government of the Restoration tried to revive fully the old colonial system under which the islands sent all their sugar to France and bought all their supplies in the mother country. Bordeaux and Nantes were keenly interested in the maintenance of this system, as shipbuilders who must carry cargoes to and from the colonies and as refiners of sugar. But the colonies no longer appreciated the old system. They had grown accustomed to selling sugar elsewhere and to obtaining their food and manufactures from other sources that were nearer and cheaper. Because of losses during the long period of war, there were no longer enough French ships to carry on the colonial trade.

The French government tried to meet this situation by increasing the bounty on colonial sugar. The result was that by 1822 the price of sugar began to rise and its cultivation in Martinique and Guadeloupe became so profitable that too much capital was invested in it. Other crops were neglected, and few improvements in methods of cultivation or extraction were thought necessary. The abolition of slavery by Great Britain in 1833 seemed to make slave labor in the French West Indies even more restless and unsatisfactory. To these difficulties were added a sudden drop in the price of sugar in 1828 and then a bewildering series of changes in the taxes, duties, and bounties on sugar. Shipping interests and refiners of sugar were interested in the welfare of the planters of the West Indies, and like the planters, they were interested also in selling refined sugar abroad. The French government was interested in the planters and in shipping too, but was anxious to obtain a plentiful supply of sugar for its people in France at a low price, and also in raising as large a revenue as possible from duties and taxes while keeping bounties down to a minimum. It had to consider a factor ignored by the planters of Martinique and Guadeloupe until about 1840, the rising production of beet sugar in France. The government wavered between these conflicting interests and at one time actually considered seriously the destruction of the beet-sugar industry; but after a long struggle the beet-sugar industry won and its victory over colonial cane sugar was consolidated by the abolition of slavery by the Second French Republic in 1848.[8]

The many variations in the prosperity of the French West Indies and in their treatment by the French government meant a decline in their value as markets for French manufacturers. The importance of this has been exaggerated, however, because both the government of the Restoration and the merchants of Bordeaux looked back towards the eighteenth century, which obviously could not be restored to life. There seems little doubt that the French colonies of the West Indies were not important as markets for the products of French industry and that French merchants would have been wise to have looked for other markets more quickly. But they were hampered by the French tariff, as we have seen, and by other evidences of looking backward rather than forward. It was natural for the restored Bourbons of France to rescue their beleaguered relative in Spain in 1823, and this may have been the only means of preventing Austrian or Russian troops from doing so. Yet the results for French trade were unfortunate both in Spain itself, where bitter resentment was felt against the French as the actual invaders, and in the Spanish colonies in central and South America, who revolted successfully at that time with the moral and economic support of England and the sympathy of the United States.

An economic struggle between France and Spain was probably inevitable, but it was certainly intensified by the political situation,

---

[8] Jules Hélot, *Le Sucre de betterave en France de 1800 à 1900* (Cambrai: Deligne, 1900), 44–45; *Histoire centenaire du sucre de betterave* (Cambrai: Deligne, 1912), 26–28. Emile Boizard, *Histoire de la législation des sucres, 1664–1891* (Paris, 1891), 38–41, 81–82. France, Ministère du Commerce et des Manufactures, *Enquête sur les sucres* (Paris, 1829), 225, 258, 262. Amédée Burat, "De la fabrication du sucre indigène," *Journal de l'industriel et du capitaliste,* v. 1 (May, 1836), 319–23. Charles Louis Gaston, marquis d'Audiffret, *Système financier de la France,* 3d ed., v. 2 (Paris, 1866), 116–20. M. Mauguin, *Etudes historiques sur l'administration de l'agriculture en France,* v. 2 (Paris, 1876), 365. Paul Chemin-Dupontès, *Les Petites Antilles* (Paris: Guilmoto, 1909), 195–98. Georges Lerat, *Etude sur les origines, le développement et l'avenir des raffineries nantaises* (Paris: Rousseau, 1911), 77–90.

and England seemed always ready to fish to her commercial profit in troubled waters. The prohibitive tariff of France inevitably caused reprisals by Spain, yet we cannot blame the French in this case, because the Spaniards had a prohibitive tariff of their own. They were trying to develop their textile industries, as were the French, and were much less successful. The French also should bear no responsibility for the continuance of the civil war in Spain, which, like the tariffs of the two countries, interfered seriously with French exports to her southern neighbor. They can, perhaps, be blamed for their rising duties on wool, against which Spain retaliated by levying higher duties on French *escots* (serge) than on the same woolens when imported from England. It was unfortunate also that Spain, about 1825, ceased to be an important source of supply of wool for France. This was probably due, however, to the fact that France herself now produced enough merino wool and needed to import chiefly long wool, which she obtained from England and Saxony. The French did sell some textile machinery to Spain, although the English probably sold a great deal more. French woolens, silks, and corduroy continued to be liked by the Spaniards, as were, to a lesser extent, the linens of Brittany, but the sales of all these seemed to decrease steadily.[9] The tariff war also increased enormously the smuggling of textiles into Spain, for which the Pyrenees seemed to have been expressly created. It is interesting to note that this smuggling by the French was extensive and successful, in view of their complaints of so much smuggling by the English, Belgians, and Swiss. Yet this method of exporting goods must have been far more

[9] M. Saint-Ferréol, *Exposition du système des douanes en France depuis 1791 jusqu'en 1834, précédé de quelques réflexions sur les modifications à apporter au tarif actuel des douanes* (Marseille, 1835), 17–20. France, *Enquête relative à diverses prohibitions établies à l'entrée des produits étrangers*, v. 3 (Paris, 1835); testimony of Victor Randoing, manufacturer of Abbeville, 80; of Mallet, merchant of Amiens, 421. France, *Enquête sur les fils et tissus de lin et de chanvre* (Paris, 1838), testimony of Charles Homon, merchant and manufacturer of Laval, Mayenne, 82. Guillaume Jacquemyns, "Histoire de la crise économique des Flandres (1845–50), *Mémoires, lettres, etc., de l'académie royale de Belgique*, v. 26 (Brussels, 1929), 127–28. Paris, *Exposition universelle de 1851 à Londres*, travaux de la Commission Française, v. 4: *Industrie du chanvre et du lin*, par Charles Legentil (Paris, 1854), 47–49.

expensive and far less profitable to the country than legitimate trade would have been.

France failed to retain her former position in the markets of the former Spanish colonies across the Atlantic. There are many reasons for this failure, although the political ones, together with the usual jealousy of England's commercial astuteness and wealth, are stressed most frequently. France was certainly slow to recognize the independence of the new republics of Latin America, as she was slow to recognize that of her former possession of Haiti. It may be that the English were very crafty in securing favorable commercial treaties in Central and South America, yet they can hardly be blamed for using the opportunities given them by their well-developed textile industries, their merchant marine, and their banking facilities. They undoubtedly had more numerous and efficient consuls, but it would have been possible for the French to have had them also if they had wished to. The French textile industries were smaller than the English in most cases, their merchant marine was much smaller, and their banking facilities were certainly less. Yet these were far from being wholly the most decisive factors. The French merchant marine could certainly have been larger if the French had been determined to have it so, and French banks could have been less cautious and conservative if that also had been keenly desired. French textile industries did not suffer in Latin America because they were small. If most were smaller than the English, silk was not, and all were larger than any of the textile industries of Switzerland, of whose competition in these markets the French complained almost as much as they did of the British. The real difficulty was that French textile manufacturers seldom led except in fine goods distinguished for their beauty and design and also notable for their high prices. The number of people who could buy such goods in Latin America must have been small, although French customers were often loyal to French standards and continued to welcome the best French prints, percales, batistes, and fancy silk ribbons. A few cheap French cloths from Normandy, such as *rouenneries,* and the ginghams made in various parts of France had some success in Latin America, but it was probably of brief duration. The French did not export cheap textiles on a large scale and so could not compete with the English in that field. They also were inclined to assume that a foreigner would, if really intelligent, prefer French goods because of their excellence and would seek them out. They seldom, therefore, tried to find out what foreigners wanted, and in nearly all cases they scorned to produce unusually cheap goods for foreign markets. Foreigners might value cheapness above all other qualities, and the English might encourage this depravity, but the French would not lower their standards. There is certainly something to be admired in the French attitude, which we often find in Belgium also, when the standards they upheld really were high. But we know that the linen industry of Brittany lost some of its best markets in Central and South America, not simply because English linens were cheaper or more attractively finished, folded, and wrapped, but even more because Breton flax was often carelessly grown, badly prepared, and spun and woven unevenly by peasants who were often ignorant and illiterate. That Breton merchants found it difficult to sell their goods elsewhere after their losses in Latin America indicates that the source of their trouble lay less in British perfidy than in Breton negligence.[10]

Various continental customers of France outside Spain should be mentioned briefly. We have little information about French exports to any of the states of Italy in the period 1815–48. French woolens appear to have suffered in Italy from the competition of woolens from Saxony and Belgium, while the French duty on silks was resented by Piedmont and that on wool by both Piedmont, which included the island of Sardinia, a producer of wool, and Naples, which was then also a producer of wool.[11] The Russian market is described as closed to France by the Russian tariff as early

---

[10] France, *Enquête relative à diverses prohibitions,* v. 3; testimony of Horace Say, commission merchant and member of Chamber of Commerce of Paris, 572; of Izam, commission merchant, Rouen, 248; of Nicolas Koechlin of Mulhouse, 626–27; of Bertèche, merchant of Paris, 168–69; of Chauviteau, merchant of Paris, 158.

[11] Saint-Ferréol, *loc. cit.* France, *Enquête relative à diverses prohibitions,* v. 3, pp. 80, 177, 637. Ernest Pariset, *Histoire de la fabrique lyonnaise* (Lyon: Rey, 1901), 291–92.

as 1824, partly in reprisal for the French tariff, and partly from Russian love of isolation. We should probably add to these explanations the greater cheapness and convenience of English goods imported by sea. Belgium was, of course, much more important as a market for French goods, although she was able to meet many of her needs from her own production. The French exclusion of Belgian linens by raising duties sharply late in our period was met by Belgian reprisals on French woolens. Concessions were made by Belgium through reduction of the duty on French wine, but to the great surprise of the French this helped little, because most Belgians persisted in their preference for beer. In other markets Belgian woolens made at Verviers competed successfully with all but the finest quality of woolens at Sedan. It is interesting to record the observation of Cunin-Gridaine, an able manufacturer of Sedan, that his city could greatly increase her exports under free trade. This would indicate that in his opinion the cloths of Sedan could have been sold much more widely abroad if their prices had been more moderate.[12]

More distant markets which should be discussed are the United States, the Orient, and the Levant. It is clear that by 1836 the American market was important to both Lyons and Saint-Etienne for its consumption of silks and ribbons. It seems also to have taken French muslins and batistes. But there were also difficulties. American ships brought considerable quantities of silks to the United States from China at prices which the French could not meet, while they also distributed goods to former French markets in Europe, especially those in the Baltic area. It seems doubtful if the United States was an important market for French woolens and worsteds, and towards the end of the period from 1815 to 1848 there was noted a tendency towards a higher tariff on imports and towards more manufacturing in the United States. At that period also there seemed to be few goods sent by the United States to France except

---

[12] France, *Enquête relative à diverses prohibitions*, v. 3; testimony of Cunin-Gridaine, 141; of Alexis Hamelin, export merchant and delegate, Chamber of Commerce, Paris, 476–80. Hamelin strongly denounced the existing tariff.

cotton, which was usually sent by way of England. More cannot be said, because French writers of the period frequently fail to distinguish between the United States and the countries of Latin America.

The Orient was an area in which the French showed some interest, but it is clear that they won few markets there. They attributed their failure partly to English imperialism and partly to American ability to trade there without military or naval pressure. One French firm, that of Bertèche, Chesnon, and Bonjean of Sedan, which had a remarkably efficient selling house run by Bertèche in Paris, was highly successful in China. It appears that other French firms could have had equal success in the Orient if they had shown sufficient interest and energy and had been willing to send cloths that Orientals wanted.[13]

On the Levant we have more definite information, but it indicates that France was steadily losing ground there between 1815 and 1848. There was evidently carelessness in sending to the Near East woolens and prints that the natives did not want because of their weight, quality, or design. More important explanations of French failure are (1) the substitution in France of cotton from the United States for that from the Levant because it was cleaner and of better quality and lower price, (2) the decline of French purchases of Levantine wheat caused by the improvement of agriculture in France, (3) the shipment to the Levant from Belgium and Saxony of better and cheaper woolens than any the French supplied and of cheaper silks from England, (4) the rise in the price of French wool, which was an important cause of the high

---

[13] Armand Audiganne, "L'Industrie française depuis la révolution de février," *Revue des deux mondes,* Nouvelle période, v. 2 (1849), 979–1006; a severe criticism of the tariff and the commercial policy of the July Monarchy probably motivated in part by the advent of the Second Republic. Alexandre Moreau de Jonnès, *Le Commerce au XIXᵉ siècle* (Paris, 1825), 141–42, 149. Charles Beaulieu, *Histoire du commerce, de l'industrie et des fabriques de Lyon* (Lyon, 1838), 163–64. France, *Enquête relative à diverses prohibitions,* v. 3; testimony of Grandin, manufacturer of Elbeuf, 65, 70. Paris, *Exposition nationale de produits de l'industrie agricole et manufacturière de 1849: Rapport du jury central,* v. 3 (Paris, 1850), 25; notice of Bertèche, Chesnon et Cie. of Sedan.

price of French woolens in the export trade, (5) direct steamship lines to the Levant from England and some other European countries in which the French did not share, and (6) the Greek war that began in 1827. The French failed in the Levant, then, because they took fewer of the commodities that that region could supply, because French costs of manufacture were too high from small-scale production and a high tariff, and because they did not develop direct and rapid transportation to the Levant, since they could not meet British competition in that important respect. The French were much interested in the market of the Levant, and its shrinkage was a severe blow to the woolen manufacturers of the Midi and to some of those of the north.[14]

English competition was the most formidable that France had to meet abroad, as we have seen that it was at home. It was encountered everywhere and was particularly strong in cottons, linens, and silks. England's success rested upon the factors with which we are already familiar: her large supply of cheap cotton, her large merchant marine, her system of mass production, and her extension of credit for long terms. In linens England again had the advantage of extensive use of machinery and importation of cheap flax from Russia, while she catered to the wishes of her foreign customers in the quality, finish, folding, and packaging of cloths. These all constituted obstacles that were very difficult for the French to overcome, but it seems clear that they did not attempt to concentrate on overcoming them. They continued to export goods of fine quality and high price in whose production they excelled, but they were never willing to admit that this meant inevitably frequent periods of unemployment at home and scanty sales abroad. They found it difficult to understand why foreigners should prefer cheapness to quality, and they tried hard to ignore the increase of such depravity

[14] Jean Antoine, comte Chaptal, *De l'industrie française*, v. 2 (Paris, 1819), 225. Moreau de Jonnès, *op. cit.*, 141, 149. Hector Rivoire, *Statistique du Département du Gard*, v. 2 (Nîmes, 1842), 30–32. Paris, *Exposition . . . de 1851*, v. 4 (F. Bernoville), 171–72. France, *Enquête relative à diverses prohibitions*, v. 3, pp. 441, 638. Christophe, comte de Villeneuve-Bargemon, *Statistique du département des Bouches-du-Rhône*, v. 4 (Marseille, 1829), 917. Camille Beauvais, *Essai sur quelques branches de l'industrie française* (Paris, 1825), 34–36. Ernest Jules Lamé-Fleury, "Les Arts industriels: De l'impression des tissus," *Revue des deux mondes*, v. 22 (1847), 142.

in their own country. They erred also in supporting the conservative government of Spain, where the English encouraged colonial revolts and the proclamation of the Monroe Doctrine. While the political and diplomatic historians can say that France did not err in her Spanish policy, the economic historian cannot, because of the unfortunate effects of that policy on the foreign trade of France.

But England did not have quite everything her own way in foreign trade, for her own island was an important market for French goods. She did, through her tariff, largely exclude wines and spirits, and she legally excluded French silks until 1826, and then levied a high duty upon them. Legitimate exports were smaller because of the duty, but many people in England liked French wines and brandy, and many more wanted French silks. French smugglers were, therefore, as successful in crossing the Channel as we have seen they were in penetrating the Pyrenees. It is clear that French exports to England of silk cloths and ribbons were very large in spite of the English duty. England took also considerable quantities of batistes and of French merino worsteds and woolens, as well as fine cotton prints and muslins, and she also imported silk hosiery, in which France was supreme, as England was in most grades of cotton hosiery and in many of woolen. At times the French sent England considerable quantities of tulle, but these shipments would appear to have been made almost wholly during economic depressions when France indulged in dumping wherever she could, exactly as England did. It seems probable that dumping by France was far more widespread than most French writers have been willing to admit and that it determined the amount of exports of numerous other cloths to England besides tulle.[15]

---

[15] For customs purposes the French government fixed the values of imports and exports which were taxed by weight in 1826 and did not change them until 1850. This meant that for most textiles the official tables of exports giving their full value in francs were too high and indicated an excessive volume of foreign trade, while on silks, whose weight was reduced by improvements in manufacturing, the exports were undervalued. Since bounties were given on the exportation of manufactures upon whose constituent raw materials import duties had been paid, manufacturers tended to overvalue their exports in order to get larger bounties. For these reasons it is difficult to use either the official statistics of the French customs service between 1826 and 1850 or the figures supplied by manufacturers.

Vidal wrote in 1846: "Industry is now caught in a vicious circle. It used long to count on foreign trade to sell its goods, but the brightest illusions are now gone. The colonial market is now as glutted as the home market. Manufacturers used to turn to foreign markets while keeping the monopoly of the home market, but now every nation wants to sell without buying. Periodic crises will soon become permanent."[16] There was much truth in these observations, even if the writer was clearly emotional and pessimistic and wrote in a year when a most formidable crisis was developing. It should have become obvious early in this chapter that France was having difficulty in selling her goods abroad and that that difficulty was apparently increasing. Vidal would have been more convincing if he had said clearly what he apparently had in mind: that the high tariff of France made exportation exceedingly difficult.

Bernoville, in his useful reports on the Exposition of 1851, called attention to still other reasons for the poor showing of French exports. He felt that the French genius in trade was far inferior to that in art and manufacturing. One is tempted to remark at this point that French conduct of foreign trade in this period does not exhibit genius at all. There is no evidence of general enthusiasm for it, or even of general interest. Rather is it clear that the French manufacturer dealt with foreigners on the principle of "take it or leave it." Bernoville did not, of course, express himself so crudely. He said that his countrymen did not know how to study foreign markets as the English and Americans did, nor how to get regular markets for French goods, nor how to develop the reputation of French goods. We must agree that between 1815 and 1848 the French did not know how to do these things, with a few notable exceptions such as Bertèche; but they did not know how because they had not tried to learn, and they had not tried because they saw no reason why they should make the effort. No one who knows the French people and their singularly keen and lucid intelligence can doubt that they could easily have learned these things if they had wished to. Had not several great manufacturers in Alsace learned them? Bernoville concludes by saying that, as in the eighteenth cen-

---

[16] François Vidal, *De la répartition des richesses* (Paris, 1846), 295.

tury, France did not study the objects suited to each foreign country and, therefore, sent them bargains they did not want.[17]

Penot, the highly efficient secretary of the Société Industrielle de Mulhouse, remarked in 1831 that for full success the French export trade must grow larger and more stable.[18] It may have grown larger; it is difficult to say on the basis of our scanty information, but it certainly did not grow more stable. French textiles were, in general, too expensive to be sold abroad except during crises when prices crashed, and French manufacturers did not generally produce goods with a view to exportation. In other words, they waited until a crisis came and then tried to dump their goods abroad. This is what Vidal meant by his "vicious circle" in which French industry found itself caught. Every other country that could was trying to dump its goods abroad at the same time. As long as most French manufacturers regarded export simply as a means of disposing of a surplus that could not be sold at home, there was no hope of building a sound foundation for the development of French foreign trade. Other reasons could be added, such as the English practice of using uniform yardage for pieces of the same type of cloth, which guaranteed the evenness of the cloth and, therefore, made it easier to sell abroad. Dupin, who knew England well, called attention to this in 1834 and, by implication, condemned his countrymen.[19] There is evidence that he was right in the fact which was brought out in the chapter on the cotton industry, that the metric system was not generally used in the sale of textiles until about 1840. We return, then, to the conclusion that French foreign trade in the period from 1815 to 1848 was a disappointment because the French did not really care enough about it to learn how to carry it on successfully. To conceal this lack of real interest, which they did not wish to admit, they dwelt upon the immense natural advantages and the shrewdness of the English.

---

[17] Paris, *Exposition . . . de 1851* (Bernoville), v. 4, p. 171.

[18] Achille Penot (ed.), *Statistique générale du département du Haut-Rhin* (Mulhouse, 1831), 369.

[19] Paris, *Rapport du jury central sur les produits de l'industrie française à l'exposition de 1834,* rédigé par Baron Charles Dupin, v. 2 (Paris, 1836), 170.

Several French writers under the July Monarchy criticized the government for not helping sufficiently the development of foreign trade, and they referred to various acts or policies of that government and of its predecessor, the monarchy of the Restoration.[20] One of the most frequent grounds of complaint was the tariff, but on this point there is good reason to believe that the Restoration was forced by the great landowners and their friends the manufacturers to accept and administer a far higher tariff than it thought advisable. Other complaints were that the government did not appoint enough consuls and that those it did appoint were purely political officials who knew little about trade and, therefore, showed little interest in its development. These complaints would appear to have been well founded, but the government could at least have pleaded *nolo contendere,* and an irresponsible and impartial commentator could say that it was a case of the pot calling the kettle black. The Restoration came to power through a foreign invasion of France after a period of many years of costly international and civil war. Under suspicion both at home and abroad and heavily burdened with indemnities and the task of restoring normal economic activity within France, it could hardly have been expected to embark promptly on a vigorous development of foreign trade. It was keenly interested in restoring the government's credit on a sound financial basis, and it succeeded in doing this through rigid economy. There is also every indication that the great majority of French manufacturers and many merchants took little interest in foreign trade, and that these later writers are trying to blame the government for not doing something which they or their predecessors should have urged at the time. A striking example of this kind of belated censure arising from a half-concealed sense of personal inadequacy is Bachelier's statement that the government did not encourage the development of industries in the region of Bordeaux that could manufacture the raw materials imported through

---

[20] Saint-Ferréol, *loc. cit.* Paris, *Exposition . . . de 1851* (Bernoville), *loc. cit.* Vaublanc, *loc. cit.* André Cochut, "La Politique du libre-échange: III, Le Régime économique de la France de 1815 à 1860," *Revue des deux mondes,* v. 36 (Nov. 15, 1861), 316–30.

that port.[21] To this it can only be replied that the days of privileged companies founded by the monarch, his ministers, and his court were over and that the industrial development of the Bordeaux region could have been promoted effectively only by its manufacturers and merchants with the assistance of the government. It has been shown that Balguerie-Stuttenberg, the founder of the Bank of Bordeaux, and an ardent builder of bridges and dredger of the Gironde, received much support from the national government and much opposition from his fellow citizens at home.

Sounder criticisms were made by Nicholas Koechlin in 1834, as president of the Chamber of Commerce of Mulhouse,[22] who said, first, that French foreign trade suffered because French consuls were political agents only, and then added that if French exports were to grow the government must drop prohibitions and duties on raw materials and reduce those on coal and iron. The government, said Koechlin, should also put an end to port privileges that prevented French manufacturers from using the nearest port and created markets controlled by monopoly and speculation. These are things that the government could and probably would have done if there had been a widespread demand for such action, but there was no such demand. The port referred to was Le Havre, through which cotton was supposed to be imported. Another equally sound criticism had been made a few years earlier by Camille Beauvais, whom we have encountered often as a singularly able and intelligent leader of French industry. He wrote in 1825 that France had no steady commercial policy like England, irrespective of changes of ministry, and that she did not, like England, co-ordinate her production with her markets. Finally, said Beauvais, France drives away foreign traders by high shipping dues, while England admits them free.[23] It would have been well for France if both the government and his fellow manufacturers had listened to Beauvais.

Audiganne, who wrote often and well about French transportation, industry, and labor, said in 1849 that the French export trade

---

[21] Bachelier, op. cit., 276.
[22] France, Enquête relative à diverses prohibitions, v. 3, p. 627.
[23] Beauvais, op. cit., 34–46.

lacked organization strikingly. Few leaders had enough capital to
wait for returns, so that they generally used pedlars of doubtful
solvency as middlemen.[24] Gras, the historian of the industries of
Saint-Etienne, corroborates Audiganne quite fully, as in a measure
does Hedde, whose observations as a manufacturer of ribbons were
made between 1828 and 1842.[25] It is clear that the ribbon manufacturers of Saint-Etienne were far too numerous, so that no one had
enough capital to organize either production or sales on a large
scale. Competition with Bâle and Crefeld was keen and the manufacturers of Saint-Etienne were unable to meet it effectively either
at home or abroad, because they were busily fighting each other.
Hence they complained that low duties on silks caused excessive
smuggling from Switzerland, while they themselves were actively
engaged in smuggling ribbons into England. Gras agrees that the
pedlars who took the ribbons of Saint-Etienne were mere carters
who took the goods and disposed of them to wholesalers or commission merchants in large centers such as Paris and Bordeaux, and
these in turn seem to have used export merchants. Many payments
and guarantees and much confusion seem to have resulted from this
system, or lack of system, and this is probably the explanation of an
accusation of fraud made by the government against the manufacturers of Saint-Etienne engaged in sending ribbons to Chile when,
unable to meet Swiss competition there in plain ribbons, they were
trying to educate the South Americans to an appreciation of fancy
ribbons. We have no details regarding the alleged fraud and do not
even know the date, except that it was before 1844, when the manufacturers tried again to sell fancy ribbons in South America and
appear to have succeeded.

We must remember, however, that our information is scanty. It
seems almost certain that goods for export were handled better at
Lyons, where, it is known, there was a small aristocracy of rich
merchants. We know also that at Paris there were able merchants

---

[24] Audiganne, *op. cit.*, 995.
[25] Louis Joseph Gras, *Histoire de la rubannerie et des industries de la
soie à Saint-Etienne et dans la région stéphanoise* (Saint-Etienne: Thomas,
1906), 441–43. For numerous articles by Hedde, see chapter on "The Silk
Industry," Note 1.

of whom we can name two: Bertèche, who represented the famous Bonjean firm of Sedan, and Horace Say. At Paris there were also, we are told, a number of American commission houses which were increasing. It seems safe to assume that there were able and efficient merchants in great textile centers like Reims, Elbeuf, and Roubaix. We know that there were at least ten firms of export merchants in Alsace. One or two firms seem also to have had branches abroad, and it seems safe to assume that some French consuls were interested in trade, although it is hard to conceive of anyone less fitted for such a task than Stendhal, who was consul at Civitavecchia. The various *enquêtes* held by the French government, such as those on prohibitions in 1834 and on the linen industry in 1838, all produced witnesses who were merchants and whose testimony often showed an understanding of economic conditions and a freedom from overwhelming provincialism such as we get in writers like Gras and Hedde of Saint-Etienne. Our rather discouraging picture of French foreign trade could probably be brightened by careful research in municipal archives and the libraries of Chambers of Commerce, such as those of Paris and Mulhouse. Yet the salient lines of the picture would not be changed. Most French manufacturers had no interest in foreign trade, knew little or nothing about foreign markets or the needs and wishes of foreigners, and sold goods for export only when they could not sell them at home. This is not surprising when we remember the size of France and the isolation of her many provincial markets from each other, and even from Paris, during the Restoration—and only a little less under the July Monarchy. We must remember also that France lost Canada and India in the eighteenth century, many of her lesser colonies at the beginning of the nineteenth, and the hegemony of Europe in 1814.

CHAPTER EIGHTEEN

Governmental Influences
on Industrial Growth

THE TARIFF

OUR STUDY of French commerce, both at home and abroad, has
shown clearly that costs of production were too high. It is true that
this unfortunate condition was caused partly by geographical or
geological factors such as the location of the deposits of iron and
coal and the quality of each, by the location of most good ports far
from the principal regions of manufacturing, and by the difficulty
of bringing together the various resources of France and marketing
their products through an adequate system of transportation. Many
of the geological and geographical difficulties helped to retard the
mechanization of French industries, as we have seen in the chapters
devoted to that subject. Iron and coal were both expensive and
difficult to obtain in sufficient quantity. Yet in considering these
various phases of the Industrial Revolution in France we have noted
in each the influence of the government, whether through legislation or administration. It is time now to consider the various aspects
of that influence, which was certain to be important in a country
which had been united to an unusual degree by its monarchy and
which had emerged from the long period of revolution and conquest
with a centralized bureaucracy of extraordinary strength and efficiency.

In no field was the influence of the government more important
than in that of the tariff, which was enacted by the Chambers and

the Crown with the approval of most of the political and economic leaders of the country. A high tariff with enormous prohibitions was not new either in France or in Europe, for it was in complete accordance with the traditions of Mercantilism. We must remember also that even England had such a tariff until she recovered from the effects of the Napoleonic wars, and that she abandoned it only when it seemed profitable to do so. Yet the French tariff, if not really unusual, was peculiarly important because of the efficiency of French administration and of the influence of France on the Continent. France was the leader of the Continent, not only in culture and enlightened legislation but also in industrialization. Far behind England as France was in the Industrial Revolution, she was still far ahead of most of her neighbors, and in the case of the three that could perhaps be called her equals, Belgium, Switzerland, and the Netherlands, France had governed them all for a considerable period, and still possessed resources and skills which her size and proximity made potent. The tragedy in the situation to the economic historian is that France was so deeply impressed by the industrial, commercial, and financial power of England that she could not calmly and prudently estimate and rely upon her own strength and ability.

There are other important reasons why France failed to appreciate her own economic strength when the Bourbons returned in 1814. She had just lost, through defeat in Germany and foreign invasion of her own territory, the political hegemony of Europe. After more than twenty years of civil and foreign war, she had forced upon her a peace that, while generous in most respects, was necessarily, in Gallic eyes, humiliating. Her people also were exhausted and fearful of the future. The Bourbons were old and unpopular and their opponents numerous, even if divided. The brief return to power of Napoleon in 1815 was to many a warning of the constant danger of another revolt, if not of another revolution. Not until France had enjoyed six years of peace and Napoleon had died at St. Helena did this feeling of insecurity diminish sufficiently to permit rapid progress in industrial recovery. Many people in France felt quite sincerely in these years that their only hope of economic

survival in the face of a powerful and hostile England lay in a prohibitive tariff.

The bureaucracy which Louis XVIII inherited from Napoleon
had been trained in the administration of high duties and prohibitions and its influence was powerful. Specific duties were liked by
accountants, and were far easier to collect, and the influence of the
administration was generally exercised in that direction. Since frequent variations of prices were disturbing to bookkeepers, it was
much easier to fix the prices on the books of the government and
stick to them. The effect of these two bureaucratic tendencies towards specific duties and fixed official values was, however, unfortunate. The influence of the bureaucracy was harmful, then as now.
The forces unleashed by the Industrial Revolution were too strong
for French administrators to control. For most commodities prices
fell during the period from 1815 to 1848, and in many cases, as in
those of most textiles, they fell drastically, so that in some cases
specific duties, or ad valorem duties based on fixed official values,
increased as much as tenfold or more in terms of actual prices in
the French or foreign markets.[1]

The government of the Restoration favored a protective tariff
without prohibitions, but it was not free to choose or strong enough
to impose its will. Its own unpopularity and the highly restricted
suffrage made it dependent upon the support of the more important
landowners in France. Among these were, of course, most of the
surviving nobles and many ironmasters, raisers of wheat, sheep, and
cattle, and some of the most important manufacturers of textiles.
All of these wanted high protection and many favored absolute
prohibition. In addition, the great ports, with their refineries of

---

[1] Vincent, comte de Vaublanc, *Du commerce de la France: Examen des
états de M. le directeur des douanes* (Paris, 1824), 39–41, 47–51. M. Saint-
Ferréol, *Exposition du système des douanes en France . . . précédée de
quelques réflexions sur les causes qui ont amené l'enquête commercial actuel,
et suivie d'autres réflexions sur les modifications à apporter au tarif actuel
des douanes* (Marseille, 1835). Jean Mantz, "Rapport fait au nom du
comité du commerce sur la situation de l'industrie cotonnière en France,"
Bulletin de la société industrielle de Mulhouse, v. 19 (1846), 182. Paris,
Exposition universelle de 1851, travaux de la Commission Française, "Industrie des cotons," par Auguste Mimerel, v. 4 (Paris, 1855).

cane sugar and their merchant marine, wanted the complete restoration of the old colonial system, with its monopoly for French merchants trading with the French colonies. There is no evidence that the wine industry favored free trade in 1815, or that it realized the injury which a prohibitive tariff might cause it. Even the growers of silk in France feared the power of their rivals in Piedmont and Milan, while the manufacturers thought with alarm of the growth of silk mills in Switzerland, Rhenish Prussia, and England. At the beginning of the Restoration there was no important industry or group that favored free trade; nor, if there had been, would it have been able to exert much influence, because the overwhelming majority of French industries and the more important landowners were for high protection. Even the Crown and many of the communes were important owners of forests and, as such, inclined to support the ironmasters as profitable customers. Such conflicts as arose between different groups of protectionists, such as the raisers of sheep and the manufacturers of woolens and worsteds, were most easily settled by giving both ample protection and then subsidizing the manufacturers through liberal bounties or drawbacks for export. This same system was used to help the cotton manufacturers meet the duties on cotton reinforced by the navigation dues on foreign ships bringing cotton into French ports. Few seemed able to realize that France did not have enough ships of her own and that such subsidies in themselves would not produce more ships for trade or help train sailors for the navy [2]

This prohibitive tariff, established by a series of royal ordinances confirmed by a much smaller number of statutes, was like a cancer which, nurtured in the tradition of Mercantilism and the practice

---

[2] André Cochut, "La Politique du libre-échange: III, Le Régime économique de la France de 1815 à 1860," *Revue des deux mondes,* v. 36 (Nov. 15, 1861), 317–20, 325–27. Arthur Louis Dunham, *The Anglo-French Treaty of Commerce of 1860 and the Progress of the Industrial Revolution in France* (Ann Arbor, Mich.: University of Michigan Press, 1930), 8. Léon Amé, *Etude des tarifs de douane et des traités de commerce,* 3d ed., v. 1 (Paris, 1876), 82, 86, 228. Ernest Pariset, *Histoire de la fabrique lyonnaise* (Lyon: Rey, 1901), 280–87. A. Beauquis, *Histoire économique de la soie* (Lyons, 1910), 272–74. Jean Dollfus, "De l'industrie cotonnière à l'exposition de 1855, *Journal des débats* (July 24, 1855), 20.

of war, started to grow in 1816 and fed upon itself. It never killed the patient, but remedial measures such as the Ordinances of 1834 and 1836,[3] removing the prohibition of fine cotton yarn and certain kinds of woolen yarn, had a superficial effect and did not arrest its growth. Even the drastic operation of 1860 did not destroy the cancer, but merely arrested its growth for between twenty and thirty years. The ravages of the disease were recognized publicly in the consultations, or *enquêtes,* of 1828 and 1834 and were commented upon by a series of writers. They had been called to the attention of the public formally by the prime minister as early as 1825; and two other ministers, Saint-Cricq under the Restoration and Duchâtel under Louis Philippe, tried with some effect to strengthen the patient. But most French leaders refused to recognize the nature of the disease that impaired the vitality of the national economy. They saw only the ever-growing industry and trade of Britain, which they continued to fear with ever-decreasing justification, not because their growth was not a reality but because French industry and trade grew stronger in spite of the tariff. Other symptoms, such as the prevalence of smuggling, were denounced occasionally, and usually hypocritically, by those who profited from them most. The failure of the foreign trade of France to grow normally, and the increasing severity of industrial competition within the country and of industrial crises, were attributed not to the tariff but to the strength of perfidious Albion. Even the very serious effect of the tariff on the relations of France with the states which subsequently formed the German Empire attracted little attention. It seems to have occurred to no one that France should and could have prevented or delayed greatly the growth of the Zollverein.

Before attempting to make a more definitive judgment of the effect of the prohibitive tariff on the growth of the Industrial Revolution in France, we must consider its direct influence on metallurgy and the textile industries. In 1814, when the Bourbons returned for

---

[3] These ordinances are accurately described by Amé and more conveniently by Auguste Arnauné in his *Le Commerce extérieur et les tarifs de douane* (Paris: Alcan, 1911). The Ordinance of 1834 admitted fine cotton yarn and that of 1836 certain kinds of fine woolen yarn needed especially by the manufacturers of mixed cloths.

the first time, iron in France was smelted and refined with wood alone, and English iron processed with coal had not entered France in any appreciable quantity, partly because of the war, and partly because certain necessary improvements in the process as then used in England had not been completed. The French were concerned, therefore, with possible competition from Sweden and Russia, which also used wood. Both the Chambers and the government were interested in keeping up the price of wood, because many important voters and political leaders owned forests, as did the more important ironmasters. Protection of approximately 50 per cent was considered sufficient, and this was confirmed in the Act of 1816.

But, almost immediately after its enactment, English pigs and bars processed with coal began to pour into France in ever-increasing quantities at prices far below those of Swedish iron. The government moved promptly to protect French metallurgy from this new and far more serious danger. It began raising the duty as early as 1817, and this continued until in the Act of 1822 iron smelted and refined with coal had to pay a duty of 120 per cent. In the Act of 1826 various loopholes were plugged up by raising duties on cast steel, sheets, and wire to approximately 100 per cent. Then it was discovered that French metallurgists could not produce enough pigs to meet the needs of their country and that heavy imports of these continued despite the tariff, some coming directly from England and paying the full duty, and others coming in through Belgium, on whose frontier the duty was much lower. Wrought iron was excluded successfully, because refineries in France were learning to use coal more successfully than were smelters, since they needed less fuel and the changes in their plants were less costly than the erection of blast furnaces of sufficient height.

The tariff undoubtedly delayed the improvement of methods in French metallurgy, but as we have seen in studying that industry, it was not the most important factor in causing that delay. Even the government was contradictory in its policy. As guardian of the iron industry, it sought through its mining inspectors to improve metallurgical processes and, particularly, to encourage the use of coal in both smelting and refining; but as the greatest owner of forests, it tried through its forestry service to discourage the growth of the iron industry because the supply of wood was not sufficient for indefinite expansion of the manufacturing of iron. If only metallurgy would increase slowly and decorously, observing *la juste mesure*, the French forests could be preserved and the price of wood kept up to a level that would provide the government with a very comfortable income. But, like the tariff, this conflict within the administration, significant and interesting as it was, was not the most important obstacle in the path of French metallurgy. Far more influential was the scattering of deposits of both iron and coal in France, and the fact that much of the iron could not then be used because of its high phosphorus content, while much of the coal was not suitable for coke. Equally important was the fact that in few cases were the coal and iron near each other and near the industries that needed them, so that an adequate system of transportation was needed badly. Yet it is doubtful if any system of waterways could have solved this problem fully, while railroads were not sufficiently understood before 1830, at the earliest, and when their construction was possible, it was rendered more difficult by the backwardness of the very iron industry for whose development it was needed most. Here was a dilemma for which the tariff was only partly responsible.[4]

Less excuse can be found for the duties on coal and machinery. The cost of mining coal in France was not, in most cases, much greater than that in the majority of English mines, and the cost of carrying coal from Great Britain to France largely offset the cost of transporting it from French mines to the chief centers of consumption. Also, the need for coal in France was so great that, as we have seen in the chapter on fuel, importations from both England and Belgium, large as they were, did not prevent, or even check, the

---

[4] D. L. Rodet, "De l'industrie manufacturière de la France en 1844," *Revue des deux mondes,* Nouvelle série, v. 7 (1844), 722–25. Cochut, *op. cit.,* 323–24. France, *Enquête sur les fers de 1828,* par une commission sous la présidence du Ministre du Commerce (Paris, 1829), 5–9. Adolphe Blaise, *Exposition de produits de l'industrie nationale en 1839* (Paris, 1839), 82–83. Léon Faucher, "Du monopole des fers," *Journal des économistes,* Série 1, v. 14 (1846), 308–9. Arnauné, *op. cit.,* 155. Amé, *op. cit.,* 145–46.

mining of coal in France. The chief handicaps of the French coal industry, such as the irregularity of the veins and the location of the mines, could not be overcome by checking the importation of coal from abroad. The tariff, then, merely injured French industrial growth by raising the price of the fuel, which it must then obtain in part from abroad, as it has done ever since. Reduction of duties on coal in 1836 was a belated and inadequate recognition of this fact.

In the case of machinery there was more justification for protection, for, with the high price of iron and the costly and inadequate system of transportation within France, it was not possible to produce rapidly a great quantity of machinery and machine tools. On the other hand, the most effective protection of the machine industry was not that provided by the French tariff. This was not because of the singular moderation of the tariff in this case, for it imposed a duty of only 15 per cent in 1816 and raised it only to 25 per cent in 1841, but was due chiefly to the prohibition by England until 1843 of the exportation of much of the machinery the French wanted, and to the cost of sending such machinery as England was willing to export. Similarly, it was the cost of coal in France, or the difficulty of obtaining it at all, rather than the duty of 30 per cent imposed in 1818, that checked the increase in the use of steam engines.

The effect of the prohibitive French tariff on the textile industries varied with each industry. In the case of linen it does not appear to have been very important, although widely discussed as of great significance. It does not appear that it did much harm— probably the best that can be said for any high tariff. In the silk industry the French were so skilled in both the production and manufacture of silk that they really needed no tariff at all. There was great anxiety when France was separated from Piedmont, but both the growers of silk in the south and the manufacturers soon became more confident, and duties on silk and its cloths were quickly reduced to moderate proportions. The silk industry suffered much from the tariff, however, because of the protection given coarser textiles of cotton and wool. Foreign nations excluded or levied high duties upon French silks, as they did upon French wines, as reprisals, and these did much harm because the French needed foreign markets very badly indeed.

The cotton industry appeared to have a better claim to protection than any other except iron, because in 1814 the British industry was between three and four times the size of the French. The British had also mechanized spinning and were making rapid progress with the power loom as well. In no other textile industry was machinery used so much or to such good advantage. The French, as we know, were as far behind England in mechanization as they were in the size of their industry. They had a further disadvantage in importing their cotton, because of their small merchant marine, their smaller and less conveniently situated ports, and their more limited facilities for financing large purchases. It was really necessary to obtain much of their cotton through Liverpool, but if it came to Le Havre in English ships, instead of those of France or of the country in which the cotton was grown, navigation dues of 8 to 10 per cent would be charged in addition to the import duty of 3 to 4 per cent. Importation of cotton cloth was prohibited, as was that of yarn until 1834, when very fine yarn was admitted under a duty. In addition, many chemicals needed for dyes were prohibited, or not listed, which was interpreted as prohibition, and those admitted were heavily taxed. As prices fell the duties, which were actually specific, rose in relation to the value of the goods until, in times of depression, they might really be 40 or even 50 per cent ad valorem. In compensation, cottons that were exported received a bounty, although this was based upon the duty on cotton alone and did not include the duties paid on machinery, cylinders, or dyestuffs.

Much of this protection may have been necessary at the start of the period, but even then it was far from being an unmixed blessing, for it encouraged wholesale smuggling of fine yarn, tulle, and muslin for fees that were often as low as 10 to 16 per cent and rose to 30 per cent only when goods were brought into Paris itself. French manufacturers were able to stop this smuggling in each case by improving their own methods and bringing down their costs. This they were able to do in some cases as early as 1834, and in all before the end of the period 1815–48. This, with the prosperity of the French cotton industry and its healthy growth, showed clearly that long before 1848 raw cotton should have been admitted free and yarn and cloth under moderate duties. Yet nothing was done to decrease protection or remove prohibitions except the admission of very fine yarn in 1834. There never was any excuse for a duty on the importation of raw cotton, which France was no more able to produce than England. The result of this unnecessary protection was that the spinners of France made enormous profits in too many cases, while competition within France for the limited market grew in intensity and produced crises more frequently and of greater intensity than was necessary, and prices of cotton goods for the poor were higher than they need have been.[5]

There was no economic justification for the tariff on the woolen industry such as there was in the case of cotton. The French had long been skilled in the manufacture of woolens, and during the period from 1815 to 1848 they built up, as we have seen, a worsted industry of such size and strength that it needed no protection at all. The duty on wool was much too high at all times and was changed on several occasions, so that raising sheep in France became speculative, while the manufacturing of the fine wool of Saxony at home was stimulated, or else it was exported to England far more than it need have been. The prices of woolens and worsteds were thus made so high in France that it was difficult for the poor to buy them. Because of export bounties, manufacturing fine cloths for sale abroad was encouraged and making cheap cloths for the French people was discouraged. As the law stated expressly that proof of the importation of the wool used for the cloths exported

---

⁵ Dollfus, *op. cit.*, 20. Mantz, *op. cit.*, 182. France, *Enquête relative à diverses prohibitions établies à l'entrée des produits étrangers*, v. 3 (Paris, 1835), 617. Horace Say, *Rapport sur le commerce entre la France et l'Angleterre à l'occasion des documents publiés à Londres par George Villiers et John Bowring* (Paris, 1835), 22–24. Louis René Villermé, Jr., *Les Douanes et la contrebande* (Paris, 1851), 143–45.

was not necessary, it was made clear to everyone that the object of the tariff was to subsidize the landowners and manufacturers,[6] while the cost of woolens was raised so high that their sale abroad was difficult. The duty on wool was resented by other countries, such as some of the states of Germany and Italy, with the result that foreign tariffs on French woolens and silks, as well as wines, were raised.

If we consider economic questions primarily, our conclusion must be that the prohibitions in the French tariff in the earlier nineteenth century were unnecessary and the duties nearly all too high. The tariff injured grievously the foreign trade of France, and at home it discouraged improvements and initiative, although it did not, in most cases, check them seriously. It also helped to raise the price of meat and to prevent the prices of wheat and clothing from falling as low as they would otherwise have done. All this made life harder for the poor.

But we must always bear in mind that the tariff was only one of many factors that influenced the development of French industry and that its importance has been exaggerated frequently because information about it and its effects was comparatively easy to obtain. It has been shown that the development of many industries, such as iron and cotton, was affected more by the location of the ports of France and by the location and the quality of the coal and iron. The tariff was not the only reason why the French made cloths of fine quality and high price. They had always loved such products, and their artistic gifts were probably the chief reason for their interest and success in producing them. Even the high cost of food was only partly due to the tariff, because all French towns taxed food on admission through the *octroi,* which was abolished only in the twentieth century. It is well to remember that the philosophy of *laissez-faire,* which prevailed in England also, put the whole force of articulate public opinion and the government behind the employer. Life would have been hard for the workers and wages low without either the *octroi* or high protection. Yet we must condemn the tariff as one example among many of class legislation, and a

---

[6] Cochut, *op. cit.,* 317–20.

rather important one. As such, it was a factor in producing the labor movement in France and such events as the great strikes of the silk workers of Lyons and the widespread disturbances of 1848. The tariff was probably not the chief cause of French industrial backwardness, but it was certainly one of the causes. It is clear that in almost every case its influence was unfortunate, if not definitely harmful.

GOVERNMENT CONTROL AND LEADERSHIP

Among the many paradoxes in the French system of government is the bureaucracy, which controls so many economic activities with such a mass of red tape that it seems to resemble closely the Circumlocution Office described by Dickens. Many French writers during the Restoration and the July Monarchy complained about it, yet one of the most distinguished of them, Michel Chevalier, said rightly that, although the extreme centralization of the administration had created many enemies, the French could not possibly live without it. We must remember also that although these writers usually attribute the bureaucracy of which they complain to Napoleon, he actually only perfected the system which the old monarchy had left behind it when overwhelmed by the Revolution. His codes of law were, perhaps, his greatest achievement, but they were distilled by a group of able jurists from laws and customs of the Roman Empire. This bureaucracy of the Restoration and the July Monarchy was, then, an integral part of French civilization and was so recognized even by its critics. Such a system is characteristic of most continental countries and continues to flourish in the twentieth century despite wars and revolutions. The French have always loved legalism and formality, while they have also been ardent individualists. *Plus ça change, plus c'est la même chose.*

Among the many principles of Napoleon which the Restoration found enshrined in its administration was that authority proceeds from above, confidence from below. This was made the cornerstone under the Consulate, whose intricate constitution was simplified and made workable by Napoleon through the simple expedient of assuming all the power himself. While no Bourbon was ever able to do this, the French administration was full of councils whose members were often men of distinction and ability, but who could discuss only what the minister or prefect brought before them, and who could decide little or nothing. Most of the members of these councils were appointed by an official like the prefect from a group of notable citizens chosen by himself. In many cases, they were themselves members of the official bureaucracy. This was the case, notably, in the Conseil Supérieur du Commerce et des Colonies, which had great influence in economic matters and conducted the *enquêtes* which provided us with such valuable evidence on French industry and trade in the early years of the July Monarchy. Villèle himself in 1824 described this council as consisting of fifteen to twenty members, all officials of the government. Although the king could appoint five who did not sit ex officio, no merchant or other delegate from a body outside the bureaucracy was named.[7]

The merits and defects of the French bureaucracy can be understood best, perhaps, if we consider the work of the Corps des Ponts et Chaussées as discussed by two men who knew it well in the earlier nineteenth century. This was the body that planned the roads of France, the waterways, and the railroads. It also constructed many of them and laid down the rules in cases in which it did not do the actual work. We are told that these engineers spent more time in writing reports than in actual supervision of work, that as soon as an engineer achieved notable success on one subject he was transferred to another, and that much time was given to thwarting any manifestation in the field of public work of individual or corporate initiative. Where there is so much criticism, one suspects the author of insubordination or disappointed ambition. The engineers

---

[7] Alexandre Léon Joseph, comte de Laborde, *De l'esprit d'association dans tous les intérêts de la communauté*, 2d ed., v. 1 (Paris, 1821), 42–50, 64, 70, 95–97, 118–19, 151–52, 261–63. Jean Baptiste, comte de Villèle, "Rapport sur la création du conseil supérieur du commerce et des colonies," *Annales de l'industrie nationale*, Série 2, v. 13 (Jan. 6, 1825), 102–11. Michel Chevalier, *Lettres sur l'Amérique du Nord*, v. 2 (Paris, 1836), 267–69, 273–74.

of this corps were not trained in business or economics, and made mistakes because of this. They used a vast amount of red tape and suffered from it, as did all members of a bureaucracy. They were apt to be critical or contemptuous of private persons or groups active in the field of public works, and their actions were often arbitrary.

We can judge such defects more leniently in the middle of the twentieth century, when we cannot help wondering how much novelty there really is in a new deal. Also, it is perfectly clear that this corps planned excellent networks in all three forms of transportation and that its members were probably the best-trained engineers in Europe in the earlier nineteenth century, as they had been in the later eighteenth. If we compare their work with the waste and incompetence that characterized the construction of public works in so many cases in both England and the United States, we may well wonder if the work of the Corps des Ponts et Chaussées was not the most efficient. More than one French engineer could be compared to the Stephensons in England, and MacAdam learned much from the French engineer Trésaguet. Finally, we should mention the fact that excellent work was done also by the mining inspectors in France, who were a part of the official bureaucracy. And, in conclusion, we should remember that sniping at bureaucrats has always been and still is a favorite sport in all countries that permit free speech.[8]

There is no doubt, however, that the operation of the official bureaucracy, and the laws favoring landowners, were, together with defective means of transportation and the high price of fuel, the chief obstacles to the progress of the iron industry. In the first place, the mining inspectors, who were well-trained engineers and wrote many excellent reports, collected statistics regarding production and then decided the amount of taxes that the ironmaster should pay. Since many ironmasters could remember how the old monarchy had regarded them chiefly as convenient objects of taxation through the

---

[8] Joseph Louis Cordier, *Mémoires sur les travaux publics* (Paris, 1841–42), v. 1, p. xii; v. 2, p. 30–40. Joseph Devey, *Life of Joseph Locke, Civil Engineer* (London, 1862), 225–27.

taille and the *corvée,* they were inclined to give as little information as possible and to minimize their production and, especially, their profits. Then, the ironmaster must ask for official authorization of every improvement, such as starting a new refining fire, or moving an old one. He must have authority to continue the operation of his existing plant unchanged. Official authorization meant in practice publicity, which was most unwelcome, the posting of official notices, the opinion of the mining engineer and the conservator of forests, an investigation, and finally the report of the engineer and conservator to the government. Only after all these steps had been taken could an ordinance or decree of authorization be issued. Such proceedings meant prolonged delay and provided many opportunities for organizing local opposition to the ironmaster by peasants and others who used the forests, the arable land, or the streams that might be affected by his operations. This system, authorized by the Act of April 21, 1810, was in full force until 1866; but, in practice, an intelligent inspector or prefect might give his authorization promptly, running the risk of being overruled by his superior or of having his ironmaster sued in the courts by some irritated landowner.[9]

The law governing the use of streams was particularly obnoxious to the ironmasters. If the stream was too small to be navigable, or to have wood floated down it, the ironmaster might still have his hydraulic motor destroyed, or the water taken for some canal or

[9] George Richardson Porter, *Progrès de la Grande-Bretagne sous le rapport de la population et de la production,* traduit de l'anglais de M. J. R. Porter, chef de Bureau de Statistique Commerciale à Londres, et . . . les progrès analogues pour la France, par Philippe Chemin-Dupontès; précédé d'une préface par Michel Chevalier (Paris, 1837), preface, xxiv–xxv. Frederic Marshall, *Population and Trade in France* (London, 1862), 156. Achille Guillaume, "Du mode de concession des travaux publics," *Journal de l'industriel et du capitaliste,* v. 3 (March, 1837), 154–60. Eugène Flachat, "De l'industrie du fer en France considérée par rapport aux entraves qu'elle éprouve dans le développement de ses moyens de production," *Journal de l'industriel et du capitaliste,* v. 1 (Jan., 1836), 30–43. Albert Auguste Perdonnet, "Industrie minérale: De la législation des mines en France et de l'intervention du gouvernement dans l'exploitation des mines de Rive-de-Gier," *Journal de l'industriel et du capitaliste,* v. 3 (Feb., 1837), 87–91. Comité des Forges, *La Sidérurgie française, 1864–1914* (Paris, 1920), 121. Georges Hottenger, *L'Ancienne industrie du fer en Lorraine* (Nancy: Société Industrielle de l'Est, 1927), 116–17.

the irrigation of a peasant's field, leaving his mill idle. If the stream was larger, anyone desiring to float wood down it could remove a hydraulic motor as an obstruction. If the ironmaster objected and took the case to court he would probably have the support of his mining inspector, behind whom would be the Corps des Ponts et Chaussées, but he would encounter the opposition of the conservator of forests, behind whom would usually be the Council of State, which had long disliked the corps. Under these conditions the decision of the court was highly uncertain, but likely to be adverse.[10]

Other industries must have suffered from legal complications, inspections, formalities, and taxation. One Alsatian writer complained as late as 1845 of the injustice of taxing through licenses individual weavers who worked at home in a cellar or barn and could not really afford to pay any tax while, as they were also agricultural laborers, they deserved protection as doubly useful citizens.[11] It is clear, of course, that this refers to handweavers, who were suffering from desperately low wages because of the progress of the power loom. But the whole subject of the taxation, inspection, and control of textile mills deserves attention and might provide material of great interest to the economic historian. We know that there was a tax on each spindle. The amount of this tax, the basis of assessment, and the method of collection may all have had an effect on the size of mills, the size of spinning machines, and even on the speed with which they were run.

The government did not, however, limit itself to controlling and regulating industry. Even if its attitude was paternalistic, it tried hard to bring in knowledge of foreign methods and machines and to spread it among French manufacturers. This was a tradition inherited from the inspectors of manufactures in the last years before the Revolution and from one or two enlightened ministers, such as Calonne. Their work was important and valuable, as was shown admirably by the late Charles Ballot. It was Calonne who brought over the Milnes to build cotton-spinning mills in 1785. Few mills were built, for the opposition to the new machines, which were jennies and water frames, and even more to the mills, was wide-

---

[10] See Note 9.
[11] Mantz, *op. cit.*, 178.

spread. A little later it proved just as difficult to get the manufacturers to try the mules brought from England. The government realized fully their importance and the advantage derived from their use by the ancient enemy of France, but it made little headway until it opened a competition with a prize for the importer of a mule. It then put the winning machine in the Conservatoire in Paris, where all manufacturers could see it, and sent them invitations to come and copy it. When no replies were received to these invitations, the government sent machines to various industrial centers, where they were finally copied and used in local mills.

C. A. Costaz, who was a veteran bureaucrat, goes on to tell us how the government, realizing how badly cotton was spun, opened a course in spinning at the Conservatoire and sent its graduates out to all parts of France until, by 1816, spinning was reasonably good. Much as the government did accomplish, it is impossible to accept without criticism this account of Costaz. It is quite clear that the spinning of cotton was not generally good until about 1834 and that the improvement was accomplished not by the government alone, but even more by manufacturers like Schlumberger of Alsace and by the unremitting efforts of the Société d'Encouragement pour l'Industrie Nationale.

The government gave further aid to the cotton industry. During the Revolution it presented, or sold at a low price, to many manufacturers, churches and monasteries for use as mills. It also provided them with labor by supplying groups of children from orphanages and other public institutions, as was being done in England at that same time and for years afterwards. In 1816 it gave more aid by publishing designs of the spinning machines used in the excellent mill at Ourscamp near Compiègne, these machines being of the best type then in use in England. But, in general, the government was inclined to help through instruction. Its foundation of the Conservatoire des Arts et Métiers towards the end of the Revolution was significant. Excellent technical courses were given there by recognized experts and a museum open to the public, displayed models of all important machines, even of old and forgotten ones, such as the various looms of Vaucanson that were so useful to Jacquard. A second Conservatoire was established at Lyons, while professors of design were supplied to smaller centers. There were other efforts along this line, such as the excellent School of Mines at Saint-Etienne, and the School of Agriculture at Grignon. Some of these educational schemes had been devised under the Old Regime, but the Convention and the government of the Consulate and the Empire did very important work. It will be recalled that the metric system was worked out under the Convention, which did much for the educational system of France. A decree in 1810 ordered its general use throughout France in 1811; but the fact that a law in 1837 again ordered its general use in 1840 shows that the first decree had not been, or could not be, enforced, and there is abundant evidence to show that throughout the Restoration and the greater part of the July Monarchy French trade was hindered by the use of antiquated weights and measures which varied in different industries, provinces, and even districts. This demonstrates to us again the widespread opposition to new ideas and methods which the government encountered repeatedly in its efforts to help manufacturers and merchants.[12]

Both Barons Costaz and Dupin place much emphasis on the importance of the Chambers of Commerce instituted by the government in twenty-three of the most important cities of France and the *chambres consultatives* in 115 smaller centers. They certainly performed useful services, but they were so closely connected with the official bureaucracy that their importance depended in each case on the intelligence and open-mindedness of the numerous prefects, subprefects, and mayors concerned. It is well to remember the case cited by Michel Chevalier, who was a critic but not an opponent of centralization, of the subprefect who for thirty years sent the government the same set of figures for the industrial production of his district.

More important were probably the national expositions of in-

---

[12] Charles Schmidt, "Jean-Baptiste Say et le blocus continental," *Revue d'histoire des doctrines économiques et sociales,* v. 4 (1911), 149–53; "Les Débuts de l'industrie cotonnière en France, 1760–1806," *Revue d'histoire* . . . v. 7 (1914), 26–55. Claude Anthelme, baron Costaz, *Mémoire sur les moyens qui ont amené le grand développement que l'industrie française a pris* (Paris, 1816), 27, 33, 35, 70. Claude Gabriel Simon, *Observations receuillies en Angleterre en 1835,* v. 1 (Paris, 1836), 179–80.

dustry started by François de Neufchâteau and Comte Chaptal, who was Napoleon's Minister of the Interior, a highly successful manufacturer of chemicals, and the author of a very useful book on French industry published in 1819. These expositions were held frequently after 1819 and provide historians with a mass of useful information; in fact, the carefully prepared reports of the Expositions of 1849 and 1851 are among the most accurate and the richest sources available to the economic historian. On the other hand, they deserve some criticism. Too many exhibitors valued the medals and publicity, while others stayed away because of the expense, the waste of time, and the danger of revealing secrets to competitors. The judges tended also to reward the makers of luxury and artistic products rather than the inventors or improvers of machinery; in other words, they encouraged French manufacturers to continue in the habits that were already too strong, rather than to develop new ones that might be of greater service to their country. Much the same can be said of the numerous *enquêtes* held between 1828 and 1838. These again are a mine of information to the economic historian, but, as a critic has pointed out, the witnesses testified voluntarily without being put under oath. As a result, their evidence was often inaccurate and sometimes deliberately misleading.[13]

Further help was given by publications such as the *Journal des mines,* begun in 1795 and continued after 1816 as the *Annales des mines;* the *Annales des arts et manufactures,* and the *Journal de chimie.* These often published very useful technical information, as did the *Annales du corps des ponts et chaussées.* Some of the reports of mining inspectors on conditions in various parts of France and abroad are of great value; but, on the whole, more good was probably done by the Société d'Encouragement pour l'Industrie Nationale, which conducted many investigations and competitions, usually on technical subjects, gave valuable advice to the govern-

---

[13] Costaz, *op. cit.,* 27. Charles, baron Dupin, "Discours prononcé aux funérailles de M. le comte Chaptal, 1 août, 1832," *Institut national: Funérailles, etc.,* Vol. K (Paris, 1834), 18–20. Porter, *op. cit.,* preface by Michel Chevalier, p. xxliv. Michel Chevalier, "Les Questions politiques et sociales: D'un socialisme officiel au conseil général de l'agriculture, des manufactures et du commerce," *Revue des deux mondes,* Nouvelle période, v. 6 (June 16, 1850), 1035.

ment, and published continuously after 1801 its very useful *Bulletin*. This was a private organization, but it included among its members distinguished scientists and others prominent in the aristocratic world of the Restoration, and it had a committee which worked directly under the Minister of the Interior, who had jurisdiction over industry.

In conclusion, it would appear that the most valuable service rendered by the government in promoting the growth of industry and trade was given by the mining inspectors and the engineers of the Ponts et Chaussées. The Service des Mines saw the dangers of bureaucracy, and on the whole, its policy was enlightened. During the period from 1815 to 1848 it acted as the guide and interpreter of the collective interests of metallurgy and gave to the iron industry proper organization and methods. We should add, however, that it is doubtful that this mining service could have done much if the ironmasters had not been forced into progress by the continued rise in the price of wood which compelled them to substitute coal. But they did render this service in a period when the iron industry did not yet have the leadership of the Comité des Forges. The engineers of the Ponts et Chaussées not only rendered the important services to French transportation that we have discussed but secured for the government and the nation regular reports on mechanical and industrial progress of such countries as England and the United States, so that an important English witness told Parliament in 1841 that France had better information on what was being done in England than England possessed about France.[14]

The Organization of Companies in France

Having considered the influence of the tariff on industrial growth in France, which has been emphasized too much in the past, and the various ways in which the official bureaucracy attempted to control

---

[14] Great Britain, "First Report From Select Committee Appointed to Inquire Into the Operation of the Existing Laws Affecting the Exportation of Machinery," *Parliamentary Papers, 1841*, v. 7, *Reports From Committees*, v. 4 (London, 1841), 69; testimony of Grenville Withers. Hottenger, *op. cit.*, 121–22.

and guide private enterprise in industry and transportation, we must take up our final topic of the legal forms through which private initiative sought to further industrial growth by developing what the French called "the spirit of association." This has been referred to on numerous occasions, and writers were often confused in their references. Sometimes they ascribed to this "spirit" the power to accomplish miracles, and at other times they regarded it as a highly dangerous importation from their commercially minded and profit-seeking neighbor across the Channel. Obviously no tariff could protect them from it. Companies and banks made the French think shudderingly of their sufferings at the hands of the Scotsman John Law. They forgot the complicity of the Regency in that gigantic swindle and the many sound ideas of Law himself, and they forgot also that England went through a somewhat similar experience in the South Sea Bubble, which left her with a marked distrust of large companies in industry and commerce.

By 1825 England had numerous corporations in public utilities, and the next year she legalized joint-stock banks, as Scotland had done some time before. Many insurance companies were organized as very large partnerships with transferable shares. As long as a company did not seek corporate organization it was scarcely troubled at all by legal formalities. But the law did assume that, unless explicitly authorized by the Crown, or by a private act of Parliament, a company was a small partnership of persons mutually well acquainted and all fully and equally liable. Most industrial and mining companies did, therefore, remain small partnerships. They were deterred by the fear of full personal liability for all and the requirement that, unless specifically authorized, a company could neither sue nor be sued through its officers, but must list correctly the name and address of every partner. There was no fundamental change in the laws governing incorporation until after 1848. Yet, despite unlimited liability, the number of firms with many partners and transferable stock increased. This was shown in the number of companies listed by Sir John Clapham in his *Economic History of Britain* for the years 1824 and 1825, most of which succumbed in the crisis that followed that notoriously speculative boom. The number of corporations and joint-stock companies continued to increase, and it would appear that many companies acted as corporations without legal authorization, despite the risks involved. Slow changes in legislation did not, then, seriously retard industrial growth, nor did legislative and administrative severity and caution suffice to check reckless speculation in either 1825 or 1845.[15]

In France permission to incorporate was even more difficult to obtain than in England. There was no French equivalent of an English private Act of Parliament. Legal procedure was governed by the Decree of January 16, 1808, but this laid down no general rule to guide applicants for the reason that each case was so different from every other that individual judgment was necessary. All applicants must, however, have cash or liquid assets and no outside debts, and any organization already in use must be dissolved. After that there were three investigations made: the first, by a committee of the Council of State; the second, by the full Council of State; and the third by the Minister of the Interior. Upon the completion of each of these independent investigations the committee reported to the council and the council to the minister, who then advised the king to sign an ordinance authorizing incorporation.

Very few corporations were authorized up to the fall of the Restoration, but there do not seem to have been many applications. Under the July Monarchy, however, the number of authorizations increased, especially between 1836 and 1839, which was a speculative period at first in France as in England; but the number of applications increased so much that the great majority had to be rejected. It was even asserted that incorporation became a favor

---

[15] John Collyer, *A Practical Treatise on the Law of Partnership* (London, 1832), 622–55. Ronald Ralph Formoy, *Historical Foundations of Modern Company Law* (London: Sweet & Maxwell, 1923), 31–58. Herbert Austin Shannon, "The Coming of General Limited Liability," *Economic Journal*, Supplement: *Economic History Series*, v. 2 (London, 1930–33), 267–82. Bishop Carleton Hunt, *The Development of the Business Corporation in England, 1800–1867* ("Harvard Economic Studies," v. 52; Cambridge, Mass.: Harvard University Press, 1936), 4–44. George Heberton Evans, Jr., *British Corporation Finance, 1775–1850: A Study in Preferred Shares* ("Johns Hopkins Historical Studies," v. 23; Baltimore: Johns Hopkins Press, 1936), 1–15, 149–54.

granted only to friends of the government. While there may have been such abuses of official power, it is also possible that the writer who made this assertion was an opponent of the July Monarchy, for, when he wrote under the Second Empire, most people welcomed an opportunity to criticize the administration of Louis Philippe. It is obvious that the cumbersome method of three independent investigations of every applicant for incorporation would inevitably break down when the number of applications was large. It is also known that the industrial growth of France quickened markedly after 1832 and that, as trading on the Bourse of Paris increased, the amount of each share of stock diminished, so that the purchase and sale of the stock became much easier. This meant also, of course, that the number of persons to be investigated by the government increased enormously. There was no significant change in legislation at this time, but it is clear that the government and its legal advisers were gravely concerned over the increase of speculative activity and felt sincerely that the regulations governing incorporation should be stiffened rather than relaxed.[16]

It is interesting to observe that in Belgium, whose legislation and industrial development resembled the French rather than the English, the corporation was almost unknown until 1834. Then corporate organization was developed in coal-mining and metallurgy during the boom that ended in 1838. When the Belgian government finally issued general rules governing incorporation in 1841 there was no significant number of applications; business had been too unimportant in Belgium and savings had accumulated too slowly. Most industrial enterprises remained private or even family partnerships. The new coal and iron companies organized after 1834 used negotiable shares, but only to a slight extent. Even the *commandite,* which was known to Belgium as well as to France, was uncommon. This Belgian experience, which is easier to follow because on a

---

[16] Emile Vincens, *Des sociétés par actions: Des banques en France* (Paris, 1837), 35–36, 51–52. Charles Coquelin, "Des sociétés commerciales en France et en Angleterre," *Revue des deux mondes,* Nouvelle série, v. 3 (Aug. 1, 1843), 403–30. Cochut, *op. cit.,* 330–32. Ernest Frignet, *Histoire de l'association commerciale* (Paris, 1868), 415–16, 344.

smaller scale, confirms that of France. It is clear that the strict policy of the government regarding incorporation did little harm, because there was little demand for it. Industry in general was not growing fast enough to require incorporation, and had it been freely granted, the people would have been alarmed, because they had not yet come to understand the value or even the need of it.[17]

The French dealt with the problem of incorporation partly by evasion and partly by using a medieval tradition, that of the *commenda*. The rigidity of French law made evasion inevitable, for it would have been impossible to induce the administration to modify the law fast enough to keep pace with industrial growth. To a great extent this was true in England also, because, while English law was a little less rigid and, in general, the English preferred customary or common law to written law and codes, the pressure from industry was much greater than in France because growth was so much more rapid. But the English, while they solved legally the problem of the transferability of shares, did not solve that of limited liability for many years, whereas the French did solve the latter problem quickly. The French succeeded by using the old *commenda* of the Mediterranean world of which they were a part and with which the Netherlands were closely connected. England was so much less a part of this world in the Middle Ages that the *commenda* never took root there and so did not become a part of English law.

In the modern form of the *commenda,* called in France the *société en commandite,* we find dormant partners who were liable only to the extent of their investment. They shared in the profits of the partnership and they could withdraw at will, but they had no actual voice in the conduct of the company's business. The number of such dormant partners was usually small in practice, although the law imposed no limitation upon their number. The Code of Commerce of 1807 brought one very important modification of this organization by authorizing the division of the capital of a *société*

---

[17] Ben Serge Chlepner, *Le Marché financier belge depuis cent ans* (Brussels: Capenhout, 1930), 5–20.

en commandite into negotiable shares. The government did not like this change, and several leading French jurists also disliked it. They saw that it really changed the *société en commandite* from a partnership, even if it had two classes of partners, into a joint-stock company without governmental approval of its by-laws. Their fears seemed justified by the speculative boom that attracted public attention in 1836, although it had begun earlier.

The government introduced a bill in 1838 to forbid freely negotiable shares, but did not press it, because the opposition was too strong. The law was modified to make the manager of a *société en commandite* irremovable, but this proved impossible to enforce. Just as the free negotiability of shares had begun, not with the issuance of the Code of 1807 but in the period of governmental disorder during the Revolution, so now business practice proved stronger than the law. Businessmen insisted that the manager of a *commandite* was removable if the by-laws of the company so stated, that the company could limit his freedom of action and require rules of administration or guarantees. Thus business practices strengthened the influence of the shareholders in the government of the *commandite* and removed the actual differences between this type of company and the joint-stock company.

After 1840 such companies arose on every hand and created a whole army of stockholders interested in spending. If it had taken some twenty-five years after the end of the long period of warfare to make this possible, we must not attribute the length of time chiefly to the endless legal formalities required of all companies, or to the reluctance of the government to grant incorporation. Important as these restraining influences were, the public distrust of banks and of all large companies was more important still. The *société en commandite* was exceedingly useful, because it was much easier to obtain legal authorization for it than for incorporation. Also, it did not arouse the same distrust, despite frequent abuses, because it looked so much more like a simple partnership. When we look back on the period from 1815 to 1848 after the lapse of a century, it does not appear, as it did to contemporaries, that company organization was delayed or hindered seriously either by the government or by public opinion. It seems to have grown more liberal almost as rapidly as the growth of industry and trade required. Greater speed of change would have been just as harmful as greater restraint by the government.[18]

It is difficult to trace the growth of company organization in practice, because contemporaries both expected the government to take the lead in this, as in other matters affecting industrial and commercial growth, and desired the government to exert a restraining influence from their fear of speculation. Not only were these contradictory views widely held, but there was a natural tendency to exaggerate the importance of the progress that was made by magnifying the achievements of its promoters. There was also a general looseness of definition. Thus, plants described as great mills were often in reality small workshops, and a *société anonyme* might be a corporation or simply a joint-stock company. We cannot, therefore, attach much importance to the number of these *sociétés anonymes* until we have more accurate information about their actual powers and the way in which they were used. This situation of confusion and exaggeration is not, however, peculiarly French, but is quite marked in England also in the period from 1815 to 1848.

As in England, so in France we find that companies in transportation and insurance and savings banks were the first to assume corporate organization. In the earlier part of the Restoration it was commonly used by companies building bridges and canals, then by those promoting steamboats, and, finally, by all important railroads. There was some overlapping, for the first railroad in the Loire coal basin dates from 1823. Before the end of the Restoration we find several important iron mines or works and some coal-mining companies obtaining corporate organization. This was secured by the

---

[18] Collyer, *op. cit.*, 622–55. Vincens, *op. cit.*, 16. Coquelin, *op. cit.*, 403–30. Cochut, *op. cit.*, 330–32. Formoy, *op. cit.*, 31–58. Frignet, *op. cit.*, 358–59. Louis Wolowski, *Des sociétés par actions* (Paris, 1838), 6–12, 21, 29, 84. *Journal of the Royal Statistical Society*, v. 1 (1839), 84.

companies of Alais, Audincourt, Decazeville or Aveyron, Imphy, and one or two others, but not by either Fourchambault or Anzin. In 1839 we hear of eleven incorporated railroads; but the five new banks, or *caisses*, organized in Paris after the Revolution of 1830 were *sociétés en commandite*, as were new provincial banks not connected with the Bank of France or wholly approved by it. In comparison with the number of corporations or quasi-corporations, which was clearly small, we have the statement of the Statistical Society in 1839 that between 1822 and 1838 some 1,106 *sociétés en commandite* were registered with the Tribunal of Commerce of Paris, of which 95 were in manufacturing, 60 in metallurgy and coal, 93 in road transportation, 52 in navigation, and 289 miscellaneous.[19]

In the cotton industry the exact form taken by company organization seems to have been of minor importance. In printing there were joint-stock companies and *sociétés en commandite* even in the late eighteenth century, but in Alsace, which did the best printing and weaving, the most common form of company seems to have remained the simple partnership. There were some limited partnerships, or *sociétés en commandite*, probably because this type of organization made it easier to get funds from Switzerland, whose chief financial center of Bâle was near Mulhouse; but, in general, the simple partnership prevailed until towards the end of the nineteenth century. A small number of families from the old bourgeoisie that had controlled the gilds of Mulhouse provided most of the leaders of the cotton industry in Alsace, and they maintained their control throughout the period 1815–48, and even after incorporation became common many years later. These men reinvested their profits in their mills rather than in land, developed large mills where they were needed, built up the chemical and machine-making industries,

[19] Frignet, *op. cit.*, 358–60. Jean Baptiste Vergeot, *Le Crédit comme stimulant et régulateur de l'industrie* (Paris: June, 1918), 65–66. Louis Joseph Gras, *Histoire économique générale des mines de la Loire*, v. 1 (Saint-Etienne: Théolier, 1922), 298–99. Emile Bères, *Manuel de l'actionnaire; ou, Résumé des précautions à prendre pour placer utilement son argent dans les sociétés par actions* (Paris, 1839), 139–345.

and promoted industrial integration where it seemed desirable, or specialization, if that met their needs better. But they did all this as individuals, or as members of small family groups, most of which were closely connected by marriage.

We have not enough information about company organization in other parts of France in the cotton industry to say how important it was, but it would appear that simple partnerships remained the prevalent form and that control by a few families was common, even if not nearly as extreme as at Mulhouse. In the region dominated by Rouen and Le Havre alone is there reason to believe that the industry was not controlled by a few important families, but there is not yet available sufficient evidence to prove this conclusively.[20]

In metallurgy and coal the situation was quite different. There were more cases of incorporation and of *commandites*. Thus the famous mining engineer de Gallois, chief founder of the first French railroad in 1823, organized a company which mined coal and iron in 1818 and obtained governmental authorization in 1820. This firm later took the name of Compagnie des Mines de Fer de Saint-Etienne, although we know it owned at least one important coal mine. How much smelting and refining it did is not clear. We know only that as a business concern it was badly run, perhaps because de Gallois was only a technical expert. The firm failed in 1833, probably as a result of the long depression that had begun in 1827, two years after the death of de Gallois, who seems to have left no capable successor. A rival firm which was much more successful, and was probably a true corporation, was the Compagnie des Fonderies et Forges de la Loire et de l'Isère, authorized in 1822 and engaging in smelting and refining iron on a considerable scale as well as in mining both coal and iron. Its chief leaders were two owners of coal mines, Blumenstein and Roux, and the metallurgist

---

[20] Henri Sée, "Remarques sur l'évolution du capitalisme et les origines de la grande industrie," *Revue de synthèse historique,* v. 37 (1924), 60–61. Henri Laufenburger, "L'Industrie cotonnière du Haut-Rhin," *Revue politique et parlementaire,* v. 125 (1925), 390–402. Achille Penot (ed.), *Statistique générale du département du Haut-Rhin* (Mulhouse, 1831), 367.

Frèrejean, who appears to have been an unusually able businessman. This corporation was still active and prosperous in 1839.[21]

Information about other great metallurgical firms is singularly meager and unsatisfactory. We know that the great Creusot iron works and coal mines were bought by Manby and Wilson and incorporated some time afterwards in 1828. The failure of this firm in 1833 was probably due partly to its combination with the ironworks of Charenton, and to its production of more refined iron and machinery than the French market of that day could absorb, and partly to the high price of iron, which limited its use greatly. Its failure came at the end of the depression of 1827. There is no evidence of reckless speculation in this case. It may well be, however, that the original incorporation of 1828 was not supported by sufficient capital. After Le Creusot was bought by the Schneiders in 1836 the situation was very different. Not only did the new management show consummate ability, but it also secured solid financial support, chiefly from the banker Seillère, who had valuable connections in both Lyons and Paris.[22]

Other examples of company organization that should be considered are the ironworks at Marquise and Denain and the coal-mining companies of Anzin, Aniche, and the Loire. At Marquise, in the Boulonnais, there were useful deposits of iron ore with coal not far away. The first company there was organized by the Pinart brothers as the Société des Minières et Fonderies de Fer de Vimille et de Marquise in 1838 and closed in 1842. In 1843 it was reopened as Barclay, Newman, and Sherwood, and two years later this firm also opened a rolling mill to make rails for the Nord railroad, for which

---

[21] Gras, *loc. cit.; Histoire économique de la métallurgie de la Loire* (Saint-Etienne: Thomas, 1908), 32–47. Comité des Forges, *op. cit.*, 195, 197, 273–76. Jean Jacques, baron Baude, *De l'enquête sur les fers* (Paris, 1829), 89. Louis Reybaud, "Rapport sur la condition . . . des ouvriers [en] fer," *Mémoires de l'académie des sciences morales et politiques*, v. 13 (Paris, 1872), 543–46. Napoléon Vadot, *Le Creusot* (Le Creusot, 1875), 7–10. Henri Chazelle, *Le Creusot* (Dôle: Imprimerie Presse Jurassienne, 1936), 83–84. *Le Pas-de-Calais au XIXe siècle*, v. 3 (Arras, 1900), 425–27. Emile Vuillemin, *Le Bassin houiller du Pas-de-Calais*, v. 2 (Paris, 1880), 348.

[22] See Note 21.

Sherwood was one of the contractors. We cannot be sure whether either company was a corporation, a joint-stock company, a *commandite*, or even a simple partnership; but since the word *anonyme* is not used in the title it seems probable that both the English and the French firms were partnerships of some sort. The title of the French firm does show that strip mining was practiced at Marquise, and the dates show that it was opened just before the depression in France became widespread and serious, and that it failed as recovery got under way, raising the presumption that it failed because of the depression.

In the meantime, another firm was started in another part of the Marquise basin, although its name is not given. This second firm, together with the rolling mill of Guines owned by the Sherwood company, was taken over by a new firm organized by James Morison, a former ironmaster of London, in 1847, as the Compagnie des Laminoirs et Forges de Guines et des Hauts Fourneaux de Marquise, but this last company failed in 1850 and control of all these plants passed through the Gouin company, a firm of Parisian bankers, to the Pinart brothers, who had organized the first of all the companies in 1838. This history tells us little about the form of company organization, but it indicates that Sherwood, the contractor, did not have adequate financial support. This may have been the case with Morison also, yet the failure of Morison was almost certainly due to the crisis of 1847–48 in France, which affected the French railroads very seriously and caused much English capital to be withdrawn from them. Gouin was the banker who became the head of the Caisse Laffitte on the death of its principal founder, the well-known banker Jacques Laffitte. His firm failed in 1848 on the outbreak of the Revolution, but may have been reorganized under his control.[23]

At Denain we have a clear case of the combination of coal-mining and metallurgy. It began in 1835 with the firm of Serret, Lelièvre et Compagnie, almost certainly a partnership, which started a puddling forge at Denain, one of the newer and richer coal-

---

[23] Comité des Forges, *op. cit.*, 195, 197. *Le Pas de Calais au XIXe siècle*, v. 3, pp. 425–27.

mining concessions controlled by the Anzin company, the most
important in France. Two years later this firm opened a blast furnace using as fuel the coal of Denain which made excellent coke.
In 1849 this firm of Serret and Lelièvre was combined with the
Forges d'Anzin, created in 1836 by the Talabots, famous ironmasters
and brothers of the well-known engineer and railroad promoter
Paulin Talabot. The new merger was called the Société des Hauts
Fourneaux et Forges de Denain et Anzin. It seems probable that
this firm was either a joint-stock company or a corporation.[24]

In coal-mining we know that the Anzin company was almost
certainly a *société en commandite*. Its smaller and rather unhappy
neighbor, Aniche, which, as was shown in the chapter on fuel and
power, went through several reorganizations, tried to incorporate
in 1830, but was quite properly refused the necessary authorization
by the government. Another case of governmental hostility was provided by the Compagnie des Mines de la Loire, a gigantic merger or
trust formed gradually between 1838 and 1845. Its request for
authorization to incorporate in 1846 was refused in 1847 on grounds
that a combination of so many coal-mining concessions was dangerous, that its by-laws did not offer sufficient guarantees, that its
partners were not thoroughly responsible, had their controlling
office far from the mines, and had paid far too much for the mines
they had bought. As a result of this refusal, the Compagnie des
Mines de la Loire remained a *société en commandite*. There is no
reason to doubt the soundness of the reasons for the government's
refusal; yet it must be remembered that the previous situation in the
Loire of many small competing mines had been both economically
and financially disastrous.[25]

In conclusion, it can be stated that we have not yet sufficient
information on company organization in France to determine the
effects of legislative and administrative influences. It seems probable
that they retarded progress of incorporation and of organization of
joint-stock companies and thereby helped to force a great increase
in the number of *commandites*. There can be no doubt, however,

---

[24] Comité des Forges, *loc. cit.* Le Pas de Calais, *loc. cit.*
[25] Vuillemin, *op. cit.*, v. 2, 348. Gras, *Histoire . . . des mines*, 298–99.

that there was good reason for the government's great caution in authorizing any form of corporate or quasi-corporate organization. It seems clear also, however, that the hindrance to the development of these organizations by governmental influence was greatly exaggerated by contemporary writers. Economic forces played a much more important part. French industrial growth under the Restoration was not sufficiently rapid to require a large number of corporate organizations. The growth of the *commandite,* by which French manufacturers gradually secured both limited liability and freely negotiable shares, was able to meet most of their real needs. Under the July Monarchy the tempo of industrial growth was stepped up, but as it increased, the difference between the *commandite* and the joint-stock company diminished notably. It has been shown that this was due to business practice rather than to the modification of existing legislation. The government probably helped chiefly through restraining unsound and speculative companies. France seems to have dealt with the problem of company organization quite as well as England, and probably a little better; but she did so chiefly because she possessed the *société en commandite.*

CHAPTER NINETEEN

Conclusion

THE SLOWNESS OF PROGRESS of the Industrial Revolution in France between 1815 and 1848 is well known, but there is still doubt as to what some of the causes of that slowness were. Now that we have escaped from the tariff as our chief source of information on French industrial development, we can fill in many details in the picture. We have tried in this book to study the growth of the Industrial Revolution in France in the light of the country's geography, which was emphasized in the first chapter. It has been studied also in the light of the most striking characteristics of her people, which were partly the result of the country's climate and resources, partly of the racial mixture that made up the nation, and partly of the prolonged effort of the monarchy to create a united nation.

We have seen, first, that France had a much larger area than England and a larger proportion of arable land to the total area. This meant that she could feed a much larger population from her own resources than could the British. It meant also that the people would be less inclined to emigrate; the whole of French history bears this out. France did not really settle Canada, Louisiana, India, or her insular possessions far from home in the period from the middle of the seventeenth to the middle of the eighteenth century, during which she was the strongest and richest of the great states of Europe. The emigration of her Huguenots was the result of religious persecution and, while a grievous loss to French industry and trade, was not due to causes that were fundamentally economic.

Closely related to the love of the French people for the land and their refusal to leave it in great numbers, because there was no need of their doing so, was the fact which we emphasized in the first chapter on France in 1815, that France was more continental than maritime. As we have seen, she was sufficiently maritime always to be interested in expansion overseas, yet not sufficiently to build up as durable a colonial empire as England's. Her interest in the continent of Europe was always stronger, yet not strong enough for her to abandon wholly her maritime interests. In her youth she learned much about industry and trade from the city states of Italy and the provinces of the Netherlands, and she was always more interested in the Mediterranean world than in the American or the Oriental.

When we consider, then, the causes of the Industrial Revolution, we find in France a considerable development of industry, probably greater than that of England up to the middle of the eighteenth century, and a very respectable development of trade; but the industrial development, great as it was, was not made at the expense of agriculture, or because of the inability of the soil to nourish its people. Likewise, the commercial development was never so striking as to constitute what many economic historians, when looking at the growth of trade in England and Holland, have called the Commercial Revolution.

One of the most striking characteristics of the French people as expressed in their art and in their textile industries is their love of beauty. We see this same quality in the Cretans, the Greeks, and the Etruscans, and, in more recent times, in the Florentines, who lived in Tuscany and whose relations with the French were often close. Beauty is sought and expressed among the French in both form and color where both can be present, as in cloth, or in the Gothic cathedrals, or even in the older Romanesque churches, many of whose frescoes have been uncovered after being buried for centuries under coats of modern whitewash. We cannot explain the success of the French in the finest textiles, no matter what fiber they used, simply through a theory like Mercantilism, just as we cannot explain the greatness of Colbert simply through his eagerness to enrich France. Colbert, in his encouragement of the manufacture of fine woolens, was moved by something more than the increase of his country's wealth, dear as that was to his bourgeois heart. To the economic historian Colbert stands for maritime France and a great colonial empire in opposition to the policy of continental expansion favored by Louis XIV and the majority of the nation's leading citizens.

On the other hand we must see, as the French usually have not, the price paid for the gratification of this love of beauty. The conspicuous success of the French in producing the finest textiles and the purest iron meant constant changes in design and form. It made France the arbiter of fashion and taste, but it checked her freedom of action. She could bring herself only with difficulty and reluctance to produce on a large scale goods of ordinary quality and low price. Thus she despised the English for their vulgarity and was puzzled by their astounding success, which she attributed to perfidy. The products of which France was most proud could be sold only to the rich, whether in France or abroad. It was always difficult to find enough customers, while the incessant changes of design and fashion produced crises at home and put France at the mercy of crises and depressions abroad. In the earlier nineteenth century these crises were clearly visible, and they cannot be attributed simply to intense foreign competition in plain silks or similar products. We must remember also that crises meant unemployment, suffering for the poor, and in the final analysis violence, like the strikes of Lyons and the triumphant Revolution of 1848 with all the destruction and tragedy that it produced.

French production was not wholly unbalanced, of course. Normandy produced great quantities of *rouenneries* and cheap prints. Even Lyons used about three quarters of its looms for plain silks, and we hear emphatically, even if only occasionally, of the ever-increasing production of cheap woolens. But one feels that French writers recorded these facts rarely because they were not proud of them. There was something vulgar in their eyes, almost indecent, in the sudden rise of a city like Roubaix largely by imitating in cheaper forms the products of France's greatest designers of fine textiles. Roubaix even had the impertinence to imitate cheaply the

English when they produced goods of fine quality and real beauty. There was probably a far greater production of cloths of poor and medium quality than we know, because too much information has had to be drawn from the reports of expositions, which always featured the products of which the public would be most proud. Clothing for the peasants or the lower middle class, who constituted the great majority of the French people, was not considered interesting by the judges of exhibits and the writers, who were generally socially or professionally prominent. Nevertheless, it is clear that the foreign trade of France suffered because too many of the few exports were high-priced goods of fine quality. They gave France a fine reputation in Europe, the United States, and some of the states of Latin America, but they did not bring a large volume of sales. This gave England a great advantage, for she was well equipped for mass production at a low price. There were many reasons why France was not well equipped, and some were sound ones, but they have been dwelt upon and so are familiar. It is well known that France could not export coal, that her ports were few and inadequate, and that she had little machinery and steam power and few facilities for credit. The situation was better in 1848 than in 1815, but the improvement had not been decisive; in fact, the problem of exports in great volume has continued to be a difficult one for France.

Another cause of the slow development of the Industrial Revolution in France was the marked individualism of the average manufacturer. Small and scattered supplies, costly fuel, inadequate power, and scarce and dear capital are not enough to explain the small size of the vast majority of French firms. Even in Alsace, where capital soon became plentiful, most of the textile firms were small partnerships, usually of relatives, although the mills were sometimes large. In Roubaix, which, like Mulhouse, grew rapidly and showed amazing audacity, nearly all the successful firms were small partnerships, and the great majority of the mills were small also. Most Frenchmen, as we have seen, did not wish to co-operate. In our study of the silk industry we saw how bitter was the struggle between the many small manufacturers in both Lyons and Saint-Etienne and how this tended to hurt business and produce crises even more than the excessive production of fine and costly silks and ribbons.

There was improvement between 1815 and 1848. The size of firms tended to increase, and their capitalization tended to increase even more. But where this happened, we feel that it was forced rather than voluntary. This was notably the case in the coal mines. Amalgamation and ample capitalization came only after years of bitter and ruinous strife and after the supplies of coal obtainable by strip mining had become exhausted, so that shafts had to be sunk and the money found to sink them. This distrust of others by the French manufacturer was ingrained. There is much to be said for it, as we realize now in the twentieth century, when we are trying to help small business to survive. But it is well to remember this determined individualism of the French manufacturer, for it was certainly a restraining influence on large-scale production as well as on the growth of incorporation. The excessive caution of the French government in authorizing incorporation and the rigidity of the laws on the subject expressed well the feeling of most Frenchmen engaged in business. Fortunately, there was considerable progress in this field in spite of the strength of individualism, but the progress was due to a few able leaders willing to take risks and bringing behind them a very distrustful majority and a reluctant government.

Akin to the determined individualism of the manufacturers, and probably more closely so than the manufacturer wished to remember, was the equally determined individualism of the peasant, with his passionate devotion to the land. Frenchmen still feel this devotion, although most of them now are industrial and professional workers and live in towns. It is derived largely from the rich and varied beauty of the country, which can never be forgotten by anyone who has known France from childhood or who has seen her people pass through a long period of intense suffering. This passion for the land is derived also from centuries of struggle to retain possession of it as well as to make it fruitful, for the climate and soil of France have made her supremely desirable to foreign invaders since the beginning of recorded history. It was such peasants who made up the bulk of the industrial workers in the France of the earlier nineteenth century and whose blood was to be found also in many of their employers. Their true devotion was seldom given wholly to their new occupation, and they often sought to spend their summers and even their week ends on the farms, with which they maintained a connection. This peasantry was difficult to turn into a proletariat, although this was achieved in many cases, as Sismondi noted early in the nineteenth century. The difficulty of achieving it had important results. The industrial laborer would work at home and avoid the mill if he could and, if in the mill, would accept low wages because he received food and often some income from the land to which he could often return if factory or urban life became unendurable. There were always movements into industry in times of prosperity and back to the land in times of depression. This meant that the employer could nearly always find an adequate supply of cheap labor and could replace any workman who resented the treatment he received. It meant that in most cases, even if the laws had not rigidly forbidden nearly all forms of organization, an effective labor movement would have been impossible. One effect of this situation is seen in revolts like the strikes at Lyons in 1831 and 1834 and in the coal mines of Rive de Gier in 1844 and 1846, or, still more, in the Revolution of 1848, which proved for the first time that labor in France had become a force that could be ignored no longer. Another effect was to give the domestic system in France a strength that made it almost irresistible. This was probably the most potent of all the causes that made the Industrial Revolution so slow.

All great peoples, like the French, are full of contradictions. We have emphasized repeatedly the determined individualism both of the French peasant, who became an industrial laborer and fought long against working in a factory, and of the employer, who forced him slowly, but inexorably, into his mill. We find also in this gifted nation a gigantic bureaucracy which grew ever stronger and more rigid despite the downfall of the governments which it appeared to serve; and we find in the French people a singular willingness, despite incessant criticism, to submit to its power. This bureaucracy was built up slowly by the old monarchy in its long struggle against feudalism and the tendency to independence of the landed aristocracy, and through the equally long struggle to defend France against foreign invasion. It was accepted by the people because it gave them a security that the aristocracy was never able to give, and because through it the middle class could secure a power which it resented when exercised by the nobles of the court or the provinces, but which it loved dearly to possess and exercise itself. By the early nineteenth century even the lower bourgeoisie and some of the workers could find places in this bureaucracy. Even the humblest *fonctionnaire* was transformed by the possession of a fraction of power with a mass of red tape at his disposal and, if possible, a uniform.

This bureaucracy affected the economic life of every citizen through the administration of the laws, the customs service, the control and regulation of public works and mines, the supervision of industry and labor, and through the *octroi*. In so far as it irritated people through interminable formalities and delays, through the assessment of taxes, and through feuds between the different parts of its great hierarchy or even between the individuals in each part, it served to slow down the progress of the Industrial Revolution. This was beneficial when it checked abuse of economic power or reckless speculation, of which the French are quite as fond as other peoples, despite their prevalent thrift and caution. It was harmful when it discouraged individual initiative of a legitimate sort, or when it imposed legal or technical rules that operated against the best economic interests of a region or an industry. Its evil effects are well known even to foreigners by their own personal experiences and by the constant criticism of the French themselves. They need not, therefore, be dwelt upon here.

The benefits conferred by the bureaucracy, which to the economic historian is difficult to distinguish from the government, were many. We have emphasized in an earlier chapter the high quality of service given by the Corps des Ponts et Chaussées and the Service des Mines, who did more than has ever been acknowledged to make possible the development of the Industrial Revolution in France. The former designed the network of roads, waterways, and railroads; without this fine system of transportation which the corps planned and did much to construct, there would have been no great industrial progress. Our period ends before the full effects of this system could be felt, but the work done before 1848 was excellent and significant. We find an equal degree of enlightenment in the mining engineers of the government, who guided both the coal and iron industries, helped them to learn and apply the discoveries made in England, and themselves made valuable studies and investigations. Like the system of transportation, the development of coal and iron and their fusion were vital to the development of French industry. It was in the period from 1815 to 1848 that both industries were developed and their mutual dependence firmly established. These benefits alone far more than counteracted the harmful effects of French bureaucracy.

Other efforts to educate the manufacturers were made by the government through technical schools of various kinds, the Conservatoire des Arts et Métiers being probably the most notable; through the numerous expositions held in Paris, usually every five years, through exhibits of machinery, and other efforts to make technical knowledge and information available as widely as possible. In this important work, in which both the Restoration and the July Monarchy were keenly interested, important co-operation was given by the Société d'Encouragement pour l'Industrie Nationale, whose membership included many scientists and other scholars of distinction as well as some men who combined scientific knowledge with experience in both business and administration, like Comte Chaptal. Similar services were performed by the *sociétés industrielles* at Mulhouse, Saint-Etienne, and Reims and by other bodies of less importance like the Société d'Emulation of Rouen. The Academy of the Moral and Political Sciences was useful in bringing together many of the country's intellectual leaders and in promoting and financing important investigations, like that of Villermé into the conditions of French labor in the textile industries. Of all these societies the most useful was undoubtedly the Société Industrielle de Mulhouse, founded in 1826, for it brought together a group of manufacturers of extraordinary ability and remarkable breadth of interests. Many of them were wealthy entrepreneurs of great power, most of them were related to each other, and all were interested in making profits; yet it would be hard to find anywhere a more public-spirited group or one more active in seeking to relieve the desperate poverty produced in their region by the Industrial Revolution. This group co-operated readily with the government, but the Société Industrielle was a private organization and did its work through private initiative. It was interested in industrial improvements of all kinds, whether mechanical, commercial, or chemical, and its bulletin, issued continuously since its foundation, is one of the greatest and best sources of information available to the economic historian.

The French government rendered important services in the field of finance. One of the first acts of the Restoration was to insist that all debts must be paid, even those which the exiled Napoleon had incurred as emperor of the French. Through this act, which involved sacrifices for the French people, the foundations were laid for a sound system of public credit without which the great development of industry and of public works would hardly have been possible. The *rentes* were developed into a means of collecting capital from all parts of the nation and were thus made a means by which public works could be financed without alarming the public or endangering the government by a heavy increase in taxation. The Receivers-General of Taxes were also organized into a kind of semi-official syndicate under the Restoration which certainly helped to finance public utilities and probably some industrial enterprises, although we still know little about its actual operations. Other reforms of importance in the financial field under the Restoration were the completion of the *cadastre,* whereby the value of real estate could be estimated accurately for purposes of taxation, the thorough collection of taxes, and the introduction of an excellent system of accounting. The country was poor in 1815 and needed time to recover from the long period of disorder and war through which it had passed. This forced the government of the Restoration to practice the most rigid economy and to forego many economic improvements, but its wise planning and reforms laid the foundation for the much greater progress effected under the July Monarchy.

But the French were not entirely dependent upon the leadership of their government, as was shown by bodies like the Société Industrielle de Mulhouse. They had developed through their own scientists, who, like their engineers, were among the best in Europe, their chemical industry to a point reached by few of their rivals. They learned early to make soda and sulphuric acid on a large scale, and they showed ingenuity; for when monopolistic tendencies in southern Italy, which remind us of papal infallibility in alum in the Renaissance, raised unduly the price of imported sulphur, they substituted iron pyrites. The notable development of chemistry in France at the end of the eighteenth century bore fruit in two important contributions to the Industrial Revolution. When the Continental Blockade cut off the supply of cane sugar French scientists, supported by Napoleon and his government, utilized the work of the Germans on the sugar beet. On the emperor's downfall the new industry nearly collapsed, but a few devoted chemists kept the faith and it revived, sometimes with the help of the Bourbon government, and sometimes in spite of its bitter hostility inspired by the seaports and colonial planters. Among its leading supporters were one of the Delessert brothers, famous in banking, Mathieu de Dombâsle, and Comte Chaptal. The new industry had learned from its chemists how to make animal black, and it had applied successfully the power of steam. Before 1848 it emerged triumphant in the full power of youthful maturity. The other great contribution of French chemists to the Industrial Revolution was the development of vegetable dyes, a natural one, in the light of the keen appreciation the French have always shown of color. Paris, Lyons, Rouen, Mulhouse, and Roubaix, as well as Montpellier in the south, became great centers for the manufacture of dyestuffs and the dying of cloth, and the English were glad to learn the secrets of the dyers of silks in

Lyons when industrial depression, probably aided by pecuniary inducements and frustrated ambition at home, caused one or two of them to cross the Channel.

The French, with all their provincial conservatism and reluctance to co-operate in industrial ventures, produced numerous entrepreneurs who were original and creative. Ternaux was, perhaps, the most successful, until he was ruined by the depression that began in 1827 and helped to bring on the Revolution of 1830, with its further disturbance of business. He was no mere financial wizard, but an able manufacturer and merchant and a real leader of men who rendered great services to the woolen industry of France. Another entrepreneur of importance was Chaptal himself, who was a chemical manufacturer and interested in breeding sheep, raising flax, and producing sugar beets, although he will probably continue to be known best for his work as Napoleon's Minister of the Interior and for his book *De l'industrie française,* one of our few valuable sources for the early nineteenth century. Finally, we should mention in this class Nicolas Schlumberger, probably the ablest spinner France produced in the period from 1815 to 1848, who was the first to show on a large scale that fine yarn could be spun well and profitably. He also kept up with the progress of the best machinists in both France and England, encouraged many of them, and improved many of their machines until they were used successfully in manufacturing. He deserves recognition as one of the heroes of the Industrial Revolution in France.

Among machinists Collyer and Dixon may have been English and Decoster Belgian, although their professional careers were passed almost entirely in France, but the Risler brothers who worked with Dixon in Alsace were French, as were Mercier of Normandy, Hallette of Arras, and André Koechlin and Jérémie Meyer of Alsace, Cavé, Calla *père et fils,* and Pihet of Paris, to mention only a few of the most notable. In metallurgy we have in the earlier part of the period 1815–48 the Boignes brothers and Frèrejean of Lyons and La Voulte and later the Schneider brothers of Le Creusot, who built upon foundations well laid by Manby and Wilson. Many of these men were pioneers who struggled bravely against great odds and won, only, in several cases, to be ruined by depressions which they could not prevent. This was the fate of Ternaux, as we have seen, of the Risler brothers and Dixon and their successors André Koechlin and Jérémie Meyer, all men of outstanding ability. Other great entrepreneurs, again to mention only a few of the most notable, were the designers of mixed cloths such as Paturle-Lupin, Jourdan, Depouilly, and Camille Beauvais; of these perhaps the most versatile and distinguished was Beauvais. These men all had mills, but also had hundreds of domestic workers in the provinces of northern France. Beauvais was also one of the leaders in the movement to import and naturalize in France English breeds of sheep with long and shiny wool. Finally, he was a distinguished scientist carrying on for years careful experiments in breeding silk-worms in his laboratory at Sénart, which rendered great services to the silk industry of France and might have saved it from the disastrous epidemic that came under the Second Empire if the growers of the south had been able or willing to follow him.

France produced not only numerous mechanics and entrepreneurs, some of whom were also inventors, but also several men famous for their notable inventions who were not particularly successful in business. General Poncelet and Fourneyron both invented wheels that increased enormously the utilization of the potential power from the streams of France. De Girard is commonly known as the inventor of a machine for spinning flax under the Empire. His first machine, which won the prize offered by the French government, was far from a complete success, and he was a distinct failure as an entrepreneur. Yet he went on for many years improving the preparation and spinning of flax and contributed more in this field than any other individual. This was recognized, a little grudgingly, by the English, and even more slowly and reluctantly by the French. The greatest inventor of them all was probably Jacquard, who produced his first loom in 1801, improved it a few years later, after studying the looms of the great Vaucanson, and then made still further improvements under the influence, and probably with the financial support, of Depouilly and the practical skill of the mechanic Breton. Finally, we should mention Josué Heilmann of Alsace, who, in 1836, built a power loom that wove silk successfully, although it was used only for certain kinds of plush, probably more because it was not yet feasible to rebuild the mills of Lyons, most of which were small, and the workshops of Saint-Etienne, than because the power loom was defective. In 1845 he invented a comber for cotton which attracted little attention at first; but after his death in 1848 it was found to be ideally suited to treating the short and curly wool of France. Proof of this was provided by the distinguished spinner Nicolas Schlumberger, who took over Heilmann's patent from the Koechlin family, into which he had married. Heilmann was thus post-humously the author of a real revolution in the worsted industry of France.

France in 1848 had developed far beyond the France of 1815, although few of the changes were sudden or dramatic. But research has shown that most of the great changes in England did not come suddenly; it took many years to make Watt's steam engine a commercial success, and the same can be said for the use of coal in smelting and refining iron, for Cort's puddling process, and for the power loom invented by Cartwright. In the period we have studied, France increased her production of coal about sevenfold and her importations tenfold, while her production of pig and wrought iron was increased about fivefold. French textile machinery was first changed from wood to iron, as had been done earlier in England, and then was produced in sufficient quantities, together with the machine tools needed, to be able to meet British competition when England repealed her prohibition of the export of textile machinery in 1843. This was no mean achievement. In other forms of applied metallurgy the French learned, when the need arose after 1842, to make a large part of both the rails and the locomotives they needed for their railroads. They were far more successful than has yet been generally recognized. The spinning of cotton was completely mechanized before 1848, while the victory of machinery in the other textile industries was clearly foreshadowed. The power loom was being used on a large scale in manufacturing cotton and had been introduced into the other textile industries. In transportation, the network of main highways had been greatly extended and that of local roads well begun under the wise provisions of the Law of 1836. The network of waterways had been substantially completed, although much work was yet to be done on the rivers and the canals were not uniform in depth or width or in the dimensions of their locks; nor was there uniformity in the tolls levied upon the traffic that used them. They were valuable to industry chiefly in the north, where they formed a system connecting Belgium with the Oise and the Seine. The network of railroads had been ably planned, but very few lines had been completed and those only in the last five years before 1848. But it can be said that the cost of transportation had been reduced materially and the facilities increased so much that industrial development had been stimulated very greatly indeed.

The period from 1815 to 1848 marks in France the infancy and the beginning of the adolescence of the Industrial Revolution, but not its maturity, which was not attained until after 1860. In 1848 France was still largely agricultural. Mills were more numerous and larger and were coming to play a decisive part in most of the processes of the textile industries. Where this was not quite the case, as in the spinning of flax or the pulling or reeling of silk, it was clear that their part would be decisive in the future. France had learned from England how to use coal and iron together; she had borrowed back some of her own ideas on roads and waterways that had born fruit across the Channel, and she had imitated England in tramroads and, later, in true railroads, while adding herself the important contribution of the tubular boiler, which Stephenson gladly accepted from his friend Séguin. She had gone far towards mechanizing her textile industries. But France in the Industrial Revolution, as in other things, retained her individuality and remained shrewdly realistic. She continued to use much wood because she had it, and she continued to use water power in preference to steam because she had it in abundance and could use it at far lower cost, and she devised water wheels and turbines for its most effective utilization.

France remained chiefly agricultural because the bounty of

nature had made this possible, and even desirable, but she did not return to the past by founding agricultural colonies for un-employed industrial workers, as Villeneuve-Bargemont asked in 1834; nor did she revive the gilds to get relief from the social evils of mechanization, as Sismondi had advised somewhat earlier. She had her visionary idealists, it is true, who were apt to be Utopian socialists with, perhaps, a touch of communism, or anarchism, as in Babeuf, Fourier, or Proudhon; but the most influential of them was Henri de Saint-Simon, whose own life was a complete failure, yet who inspired to high achievement engineers like Michel Cheval-ier and Paulin Talabot, metallurgists like the two other Talabot brothers, merchants like Arlès-Dufour, bankers like the d'Eichthals, and promoters like the Pèreires and Prosper Enfantin. In general, however, the French remained practical. They adopted and im-proved such machinery as they could use with profit; they accepted very gradually an increase in the factory system without ever giving up the domestic system, which met their needs rather well. The sower still went forth to sow his seed, and there were still laborers in the vineyards. The Industrial Revolution might grow, but in France it had to observe *la juste mesure,* and the leading nation of the Continent in the earlier nineteenth century, as before, saw in form, texture, and color the vision of beauty.

Appendixes,
Bibliography and
Index

The Supply of Rails, Locomotives, and Labor for French Railroads

IN CONNECTION WITH THE RAILROAD BOOM in France and the ensuing crisis of 1846–47, the question was raised whether the country could manufacture the rails and locomotives needed and supply the required labor. Some observers believed that France could not possibly meet the needs in these respects, predicted that a serious rise in the prices of materials would result, and that the consequent addition to the cost of building and equipping the railroads would produce a crisis. One highly intelligent writer of great ability, who was, however, close to the Roth-schilds in their financing of French railroads, Léon Faucher, in 1846 asserted that this rise in prices and wages had occurred already and was a very serious matter indeed.[1] It was pointed out that the government ought to help the railroads by admitting rails free, or at a reduced duty, and that the duty on locomotives might also be reduced. French iron-masters quite naturally objected vehemently and succeeded in preventing important concessions; but, while we may condemn them for maintaining a monopoly and reaping large profits at the expense of the country, we must in fairness admit that British interests were promoting French rail-roads not only for profitable investment of capital but also in the hope of providing markets for British rails, locomotives, and coal, which were being produced in rapidly increasing quantities across the Channel. It is a pity that the July Monarchy lacked the courage and strength to lower the tariff enough to compel rapid improvement of French metallurgical methods and to encourage the expansion of the iron industry in France through moderate competition; yet it would be wrong to assume that because the government of Louis Philippe was neither strong nor brave,

---

[1] Léon Faucher, "Les Chemins de fer et le crédit public," *Journal des économistes,* v. 14 (1846), 10–16.

the French iron industry simply sat still and reaped huge profits and thus helped seriously to bring on a formidable crisis.

Price figures for rails are confusing, because they varied greatly according to the distance from the foundry to the railroad where they were to be used. It is clear, however, that prices fell fairly steadily from 1837 to 1844, and then rose again because of the rapidly increasing demand, as they had in England a year or two earlier; but there is no evidence showing that this rise of prices was sufficient to put the French railroads in a critical condition in 1846 or 1847.[2] What evidence we have shows that the French iron industry did expand its facilities for manufacturing rails greatly. Thus, in 1843 there were only six important foundries making rails: those of Alais, Anzin, Aveyron, Creusot, Hayange, and Terrenoire.[3] In that year the Paris-Rouen and Paris–Orléans lines were opened, and it was said that, although they had signed contracts with French firms for 15,000 tons of rails in 1840, when the time came for laying the rails late in 1842 or the beginning of 1843 (both lines were opened in May, 1843) the contracting French companies failed to make their deliveries and the two railroad companies had to send rush orders to England and pay the full French duty on their rails. But they obtained them in time and at a price not very different from that prevalent in France.[4] The truth appears to be that between 1,000 and 3,000 tons of rails only were imported from England by these two companies;[5] that would indicate that in that year French ironmasters were nearly able to meet the demands of the railroads.

Four years later we find several new foundries making rails in France. Two were established in the central part of the country close to the small coal basin of Commentry, and four crossed the frontier from Belgium after the failure of negotiations for a customs union between France and Belgium in 1842 and established themselves on or close to the great coal field of the Nord. We should remember in this connection, however, that the Belgian iron and coal industries had expanded with great rapidity in the period of prosperity ending in 1837 and that they did not resume their expansion in 1841 or 1842, as did the same industries in France. We have reason to believe, also, that older French foundries greatly

---

² *Ibid.*

³ Napoléon, comte Daru, *Des chemins de fer et de l'application de la loi du 11 juin, 1842* (Paris, 1843), 336. Louis Reybaud, "De l'industrie métallurgique en France considérée dans ses rapports avec la construction des chemins de fer," *Journal des économistes,* v. 5 (July, 1843), 393. France, *Rapport du jury central sur les produits de l'industrie française à l'exposition de 1844,* rédigé par Jules Burat, v. 1 (Paris, 1845), 25.

⁴ Faucher, *loc. cit.*

⁵ *Journal des chemins de fer* (July 1, 1843).

increased their production of rails; in fact, it has been said that they doubled their facilities. It is interesting to note that the Est railroad in 1846 signed two contracts with the Hayange establishment of Lorraine, run for many years by the de Wendels—the first in February for 32,000 tons of rails at 350 francs per ton, to be delivered January 1, 1847, and the second for 26,000 tons to be delivered beginning in 1848. All these rails were intended for the eastern part of the line from Epernay to Strasbourg. For the western part from Paris to Epernay they were offered rails by several concerns at prices ranging from 380 to 400 francs, which they evidently considered excessive, and they also felt doubtful of prompt delivery. On the other hand, a contract signed with the Marquis de Boissy for the delivery of rails at 300 francs per ton[6] had to be canceled because it became clear that his lordship could not meet the terms of the agreement. The rails were finally contracted for with the Talabot brothers of Denain, whose establishment used coal from some of the pits of the Anzin Coal Company and who were themselves the brothers and collaborators of Paulin Talabot, the chief promoter of three important railroads in southern France. The two contracts signed with the Talabots provided for the delivery of 37,000 tons of rails between 1847 and 1850, most of them for 345 francs per ton; but the Est railroad company advanced to the Talabots a credit of 2,000,000 francs with interest at 5 per cent.[7]

It seems possible to conclude, therefore, that the French ironmasters did greatly increase their production of rails, and that to do this they enlarged their plants somewhat but had difficulty in obtaining the necessary capital, and that several new concerns entered the field in response to the increasing needs of the railroads. It seems probable, however, that when railroad construction was at its peak in 1846 and the first part of 1847 the foundries, even with enlarged facilities, were unable to meet promptly all the demands of the railroads. With regard to prices, it seems probable that they rose somewhat during the last part of the construction boom, but that the increase was not excessive in most cases. We cannot say, then, that the increasing cost of rails injured the railroads seriously, but we may still wonder if the profits of the ironmasters did not remain excessive, thanks to the high tariff, and it seems certain that railroad construction was delayed a little by inability to get all the rails needed promptly.

The difficulties encountered by French railroads in obtaining locomotives and other rolling stock appear to have been no more serious than

---

[6] Louis Maurice Jouffroy, *Une étape de la construction des grandes lignes de chemin de fer en France: La Ligne de Paris à la frontière d'Allemagne (1825–1852)*, v. 3 (Paris: *Dorbon-Ainé*, 1932), 58–60.

[7] *Ibid.*

those met with in securing rails. Figures of production of locomotives given by some French writers conflict and, for that reason, do not seem safe to use. It is known that under the Restoration France had few good machine shops and that the few that existed were handicapped by shortage of both capital and machine tools; but it is equally clear that under the July Monarchy the situation improved greatly. In or soon after 1834 there were three firms in Alsace able to make locomotives well, the Hallette firm at Arras and the Creusot works, which came under the control of the Schneiders in 1836. All these appear to have built good locomotives, although there can be no doubt that they were expensive. Some were new types, but most were copies of the best English locomotives made by George Stephenson's firm at Newcastle, or by Sharpe and Roberts at Manchester. Another type of locomotive was manufactured by Allicard and Buddicom at Rouen after 1841 and was used to run all the trains on the railroad from Paris to Rouen and later to Le Havre. This firm was really English, brought over by the English engineer Locke and the English contractor Brassey, but their locomotive resembled the American type rather than English or French models. Some of the earlier French railroads were supplied with locomotives from French shops, among them the lines from Saint-Etienne to Lyons, Strasbourg to Bâle, Paris to Saint-Germain, and the two lines from Paris to Versailles. The railroad from Alais to Beaucaire, on the other hand, imported its locomotives from both Stephenson and Sharpe and Roberts, but obtained its cars from French shops in Paris and Lyons, probably those of the Messageries Royales and the Messageries Générales, which we know were used in other cases. It seems probable that in earlier years more than half the locomotives used in France were imported from England. The French duty of 30 per cent on steam engines was lowered in 1837 to 15 per cent, and some writers, including the staff of the usually well-informed *Journal des chemins de fer,* whose editor was an Englishman, have asserted that this almost paralyzed the production of French shops, which recovered only when the ad valorem duty of 15 per cent was replaced by a specific duty of 650 francs per ton in the Ordinance of September 3, 1844.[8] On the other hand, none of the conflicting figures given for the number of locomotives in France indicate any serious increase of importations, and it is well to remember that there was a serious business depression in France from 1837 to 1843, that few French railroads were authorized or built between 1837 and 1842, and that during that period the policy of the French government regarding railroads was very uncertain. It is inconceivable that these economic and political forces did not greatly influence the production of locomotives in France.

There seems to have been a marked revival in the production of locomotives in 1844, whether due to the ordinance of that year or the

---

[8] *Journal des chemins de fer* (April 13, 1844).

boom in railroad construction. The *Journal des chemins de fer* tells us that French shops then supplied the Nord railroad with 58 locomotives,[9] that afterwards they accepted orders for 80 more, and that by 1847 they could easily produce 100 locomotives a year. We know also that in 1846–47 the Est railroad company signed contracts for more than 85 locomotives with two machine shops in Paris, one in Alsace, and one at Angoulême, and that in 1854 Audiganne estimated the French production of locomotives at 500 a year.[10] It seems probable, therefore, that before the outbreak of the Revolution of 1848 France was able to manufacture more than half the locomotives she needed and to import the rest at a cost that was neither prohibitive nor great enough to affect seriously the financial position of French railroad companies. She was probably unable in the later years of the railroad boom to get the locomotives as quickly as might be desired.

With regard to wages we have no figures available except the statement of Léon Faucher in 1846 that the wages of French graders on the railroads had increased from 1.50 francs a day to 3. He states also that good French graders came almost exclusively from Auvergne and Normandy and could not be obtained in sufficient numbers. This may well have been the case, and it would be natural for wages to double and the supply to become inadequate in the face of the rapid increase of railroad construction in France. We know from the accounts of both Joseph Locke, engineer of the Paris–Rouen and Rouen–Le-Havre railroads, and Thomas Brassey, contractor for the same lines, that large numbers of English and Irish navvies were imported to do the heavy work and were paid far more than French laborers, because they had greater strength and expected a higher standard of living. But a later writer tells us that the branch line from Rouen to Dieppe begun in 1847 was built almost entirely by French labor.[11] It seems clear that French laborers learned to work harder and that contractors gave them better tools, so that their higher wages were earned and involved no serious increase in the cost of building the railroads. Another factor that must be considered is the adoption of the steam shovel of the American Captain Cochrane on the Nord railroad in 1843,[12] followed by its extensive use on the lines from Orléans to Tours and Rouen to Le Havre and

---

[9] *Ibid.* (November 29, 1845).

[10] Armand Audiganne, *Les Populations ouvrières et les industries de la France dans le mouvement social du XIXe siècle*, v. 2 (Paris, 1854), 174.

[11] Charles Kenneth Hobson, *The Export of Capital* (London: Constable, 1914), 119–20; quotes from Thomas Brassey's *Work and Wages* (New York, 1872), 79.

[12] *Journal des chemins de fer* (Sept. 30, Nov. 4, Dec. 2, 1843). Leland Hamilton Jenks, *The Migration of British Capital to 1875*, 2d ed. (New York: Knopf, 1938), 143.

probably on others where the fact has not been recorded. This greatly increased the speed of construction and must have decreased the cost considerably. Other aspects of the labor problem on the French railroads cannot be discussed, from lack of information. It would be interesting to know the origin of the supply of labor used on other railroads such as the Est, or the great line from Paris through Lyons to the Mediterranean, and it would be interesting also to know the names and nationalities of the contractors. We cannot assume that because Mackenzie and Brassey together or separately built parts or all of some French railroads, and because Sherwood built part of the Nord line, that all the contractors were British; nor can we accept without reserve the derogatory opinions of English engineers regarding French engineers, mechanics, and machinery.

The Role of Baron James de Rothschild in Financing French Railroads

THE PROBLEM OF FINANCING and promoting railroads must be reconsidered from the point of view of the sources of capital drawn upon and the groups which controlled them. The most prominent figure is obviously Baron James de Rothschild, who had close connections with the French government, with many of the most important French bankers, whether Jews or Protestants from Switzerland, with his English relatives and other English financial interests, and probably also with German financiers. Perhaps the first case of his intervention in the financing of a French railroad was in that of the line from the coal mines of Grande Combe to Alais, Nîmes, and Beaucaire. Proposed as early as 1825 and promoted four years later by Marshal Soult and the Talabot brothers, it took seven years more to overcome local opposition and bureaucratic red tape. Then, in 1836, the railroad company was organized as a *société en commandite*. The first issue of stock failed, and a reorganization of the company also proved ineffectual. The situation was critical. If the railroad was not completed shortly the charter would be forfeited. Then Rothschild intervened suddenly by buying 6,000,000 francs of the railroad company's stock, and the government lent the company 6,000,000 francs at 4 per cent.[1] This assistance brought salvation and the line was fully opened in 1840.

In the case of the Nord railroad, which we have considered in the chapter on railroads, he sought to control the enterprise as early as 1843 and succeeded in 1845. The delay in his success was not due wholly to the hesitations of the French government. The London and South-Eastern Railway, with its terminal at Dover, was anxious to establish control over

---

[1] Gabriel Roselli, *Les Origines d'une ligne de chemin de fer: La Grand'Combe–Beaucaire, 1830–1852* (Nîmes: Université de Montpellier, 1931), 71; covers all aspects of the construction of this line quite fully.

444   APPENDIX B

the Nord railroad and have the French terminal on the Channel at
Calais. Professor Jenks, in his interesting and scholarly book on the
Migration of British Capital, upon which all economic historians of this
period must draw freely, tells us that this English company, acting on
the report of Robert Stephenson, son of the inventor of the locomotive,
and supported by James de Rothschild and the English banking firm of
Glyn, Halifax, and Mills, actually obtained a concession for the Nord
from the French Minister of Public Works, but was obliged to withdraw
because of pressure in the Chambers from supporters of the port of
Boulogne.[2] There was almost certainly opposition from other quarters as
well, for in the next year the branch line from Amiens to Boulogne was
conceded to Laffitte, Blount and Company.[3] They had here the active
support of the municipalities of both Boulogne and Amiens and of the
London and Folkestone Railway, a partnership with the London and
South-Western Railway, with which they had built the Paris–Rouen
railroad and undertaken its continuation to Le Havre, a close personal
connection with Jacques Laffitte, uncle of Charles, and his bank, headed
a year later by the able financier Gouin, and valuable connections with
the French government and possibly with the Crown, for the Duke of
Orléans had been generally regarded as a silent partner in Laffitte, Blount
and Company. It is difficult to believe that Laffitte and Blount would
not have worked actively to oppose Rothschild and the London and
South-Eastern Railway in 1843 and that their pressure would not have
had some effect on the Chambers. We should note also that in 1844 the
Jacques Laffitte Company, on behalf of a consortium of foreign bankers,
proposed to the French government the construction of the whole network
of French railroads planned under the Law of 1842, offering a capital of
500,000,000 francs subsequently raised to 750,000,000 francs.[4] Since
nothing more was heard of this offer, it must have been rejected by the
French government, and it seems reasonable to assume that it must have
been objectionable to James de Rothschild.

Eventually the concession of the Nord railroad was secured by
James de Rothschild, and he directed it much as if it had been his own
enterprise and offered shares in it to his friends as personal favors.
Nevertheless, he was only the head of a merger of which other powerful
financial interests were members, such as the Hottinguer bank, closely
connected with the Labouchères and Barings, Laffitte and Blount, the
d'Eichthals, and Mallet Frères. This coalition was so powerful that it

[2] Leland Hamilton Jenks, *The Migration of British Capital to 1875,* 2d
ed. (New York: Knopf, 1938), 143.
[3] Maurice Wallon, *Les Saint-Simoniens et les chemins de fer* (Paris:
Pedone, 1900), 116.
[4] *Journal des chemins de fer* (March 30, 1844).

secured not only the main line of the Nord but also a parallel line from Creil to Saint-Quentin, first as a separate company in December, 1845, and two years later as an integral part of the Nord company itself.

In other cases Rothschild was less domineering, but hardly less influential. He must have been keenly interested from the beginning in the plans for the railroad from Paris to Strasbourg, often called the Est, yet he did not take a leading part until the final negotiations for merger in the autumn of 1845. We know little regarding the details of these negotiations, but there seems little doubt that Rothschild waited deliberately until he felt that the moment for decisive action had come. He allowed rival interests to take the lead in organizing different companies for the Est, or in pulling wires behind the scenes. The first important company, organized by Comte Molé, soon disintegrated through political strife, but Ganneron, head of an important bank, and Hainguerlot, manager of numerous important canals and supported by de Wendel, the powerful ironmaster of Lorraine, built up strong companies and each obtained 50,000 shares in the merger, while Rothschild was content with 25,000 shares. Nevertheless, it appears to have been Rothschild who fought the banking firm of Gentil and Fol, the financiers supporting the Strasbourg–Bâle railroad and its friends, who evidently sought complete control of the Est railroad. He allowed them to have 50,000 shares in the merger, but he made them merge. When the merger, formed from eleven different companies, had been completed, the deposit required by the government was made on November 24, 1845, by the Rothschilds.[5]

The part played by Rothschild in the organization of the Paris–Lyons railroad company was similar, but more obvious to the public. Although he did not take the lead, he did guarantee the subscriptions for 20,000,000 francs obtained by the English capitalist David Salomons of London, and he joined the Union Company, the strongest unit before the merger.[6] He displayed jealousy of Charles Laffitte, who had more shares in the Union Company and forced a modification in the organization of the company to give him equal influence. Whether he fought directly the interest of the Paris–Orléans railroad in this company or not is not clear, but he was in close relations with Prosper Enfantin and Arlès-Dufour of Lyons, who were outspoken opponents of François Bartholony, head of the Orléans Company, and his friends and colleagues from Geneva. He was close also to Paulin Talabot, an important figure in all three of the companies concerned in building the different parts of the great line from

[5] Louis Maurice Jouffroy, *Une étape de la construction des grandes lignes de chemin de fer en France: La Ligne de Paris à la frontière d'Allemagne (1825–1852)*, v. 3 (Paris: Dorbon-Aîné, 1932), 23–26.

[6] Henry René d'Allemagne, *Prosper Enfantin et les grandes entreprises du XIX⁰ siècle* (Paris: Girard, 1935), 54–75.

Paris through Lyons to the Mediterranean. He had helped Talabot first
in financing the railroad from Alais to Beaucaire, and he supported him
as his banker in organizing a company for the section from Lyons to
Avignon so powerful that it dominated all the others and controlled the
inevitable merger. Yet, in the case of the Marseilles-Avignon Company,
also dominated by Talabot, who had obtained a direct concession in
1843, the part played by Rothschild seems almost hostile. The Marseilles
Company had estimated the cost of construction at about 58,000,000
francs, but found subsequently that at least 70,000,000 francs would be
required. Rothschild appears to have refused the necessary loan after a
considerable delay. The Marseilles-Avignon line then borrowed 5,000,000
francs from the Lyons-Avignon Company and 15,000,000 francs from a
syndicate formed by Gouin and Company, the successor of the second
bank of Jacques Laffitte, the Delahante banking firm of Lyons, and the
Boutoux firm, also of Lyons. All of these firms failed in the crisis of
1847–48; then only did Rothschild come to the support of the Marseilles
Company.[7]

In southwestern France Rothschild played a less prominent part. He
organized a company to compete for the Orléans–Bordeaux concession,
only to be defeated by the Anglo-French company of Laurent, Luzarches,
and Mackenzie. It may be that he did not think the line would be very
profitable, and he must have felt that the concession for twenty-eight
years was dangerously brief, yet within a year he had accepted the
position of banker for his successful rival. In the case of the railroad from
Bordeaux to Cette, Rothschild helped to organize a strong company and
entered the merger, only to have the merger company fail the next year
because of the crisis.

Next to Baron James de Rothschild the strongest financial group promoting French railroads was probably an English one, frequently co-
operating with the Rothschilds yet apparently not controlled by the
English Rothschilds, and often acting independently of Baron James or
in competition with him. This group was represented by the bankers
Denison, Heywood, and Kennard in London, by J. Barned and Company
in Manchester, and by Edward Blount, partner of Charles Laffitte in
Paris. Individual members of the group were Robert W. Kennard,
director of the English North-Eastern Railway and vice-president of the
Eastern Counties Railway, whose firm were the bankers of the Tours-
Nantes railroad company and took 8,000 shares of stock in the Nord
railroad; Thomas Weguelin, director of the Bank of England, member of
an important firm of merchant bankers in the Baltic trade, owner of

[7] *Ibid.*, 67–75.

5,125 shares of stock in the Nord railroad, and director of the Nord and Est companies; and William Gladstone, member of the same firm of merchant bankers in the Baltic trade and director of the Orléans–Bordeaux railroad.[8]

Another group closely allied with the first is found in the English promoters of the Paris–Rouen and Rouen–Havre railroads and consisting in part of the officials of the London and South-Western Railway. Here we find John Moss, a banker in Liverpool and leader in the London-Birmingham railway, a director of the Paris–Rouen–Havre line and of the Nord; Sir John Easthope, Bt., M.P., part owner of the London *Chronicle* and director of the Est and Orléans–Bordeaux railroads; William Chaplin, director of the Paris–Rouen–Havre line and of the Nord, and former owner of the largest coaching business in England; and John Masterman, Jr., member of a London bank, director of the Nord, strong supporter of the Paris–Rouen–Havre line, and organizer of companies for the Nord, Centre, and Paris–Lyons railroads. Finally, we should mention William Mackenzie, the great contractor, rival or partner of Thomas Brassey, chief contractor of the Rouen and Havre railroads and member of both these English groups. He was the chief figure in the Orléans–Bordeaux and Tours–Nantes companies, a powerful member of the merger that won the Bordeaux–Cette concession with the help of David Salomons of London, who found some 13,000 English subscribers, one of the big stockholders of the Est, and a bidder for the concessions of the Paris–Lyons and Lyons–Avignon lines. In addition to all these men, we must note the English Rothschilds, and the Barings, who took 8,000 shares of the Nord railroad and had close connections with the Hottinguers, one of the most important banking firms in Paris and important in many of the French railroads.

When we search for French promoters and financiers of French railroads, it is difficult to go beyond well-known bankers, such as Laffitte and Blount, the Hottinguers, d'Eichthals, Thurneyssen, and Mallet Frères. Next to them in importance we should probably place the Caisse Générale du Commerce et de l'Industrie, organized by Jacques Laffitte in 1837, and taken over by Gouin on Laffitte's death in 1844; the Comptoir Général du Commerce, or Caisse Ganneron, as it was usually called, organized in 1843 with a capital of 7,500,000 francs; and the Caisse Centrale du Commerce et des Chemins de Fer organized in 1846 by Baudon and Michel de Saint-Albin, former Receivers-General of Taxes, and Lehobe, former president of the Court of Commerce. These three banks were useful, especially that of Gouin, but all failed in the crisis of

---

[8] Jenks, *op. cit.*, 144, 378, 379.

1847 or the Revolution of 1848.[9] Of individual promoters we have several names, but little information. We should emphasize the part played by Prosper Enfantin, the former head of the Saint-Simonians and working in part through his former disciples, although he was also in close touch with Baron James de Rothschild and became an astute speculator. He was very active in the organization of both the Paris–Lyons and Lyons–Avignon companies and their mergers, in which one of his closest associates was Arlès-Dufour, the wealthy but socialistic silk merchant of Lyons.

The lists of shareholders published by the *Journal des chemins de fer* give us little information of value, because many companies were organized for nearly all of the French railroads; and since they nearly all were absorbed in the inevitable mergers and were clearly speculative groups, it is difficult to draw from the names of their members economic information of value. The system of public bids insisted upon by the French government, which was supposedly a guarantee of impartiality in the awarding of concessions, proved in practice an encouragement to speculators and gave a decisive advantage to the important bankers, who needed no such assistance from the government. In the complicated and confusing negotiations for mergers, which were usually secret, few individuals or groups stand out, but one or two are prominent and deserve mention. Several companies contained one or more active or retired ironmasters, such as the de Wendels, the Dietrichs, or the brothers of Paulin Talabot; but others of even greater importance, such as the Schneiders, are not mentioned in connection with the railroads. We find also several companies of carters formed to bid for railroads, and occasionally a company of postmasters, but they all disappeared in the mergers, and we are forced to conclude that their financial resources were inadequate. Two other classes of men did survive, however: the Receivers-General of Taxes and the officials of the Messageries Royales and the Messageries Générales; we find them not only in nearly every railroad company, but also in nearly every merger and on many of the boards of directors. It is quite clear that both these groups possessed or controlled large supplies of capital and were sufficiently conservative to inspire confidence. Some of the Receivers-General even organized banks, as we have seen in the case of Delahante of Lyons, and the founders of the Caisse Centrale du Commerce et des Chemins de Fer.

---

[9] André Liesse, *Evolution of Credit and Banks in France, From the Founding of the Bank of France to the Present Time* (Washington, D.C.: Government Printing Office, 1909), 74–75. *Journal des chemins de fer* (March 28, 1846), p. 252. David Morier Evans, *The Commercial Crisis of 1847–1848* (London, 1848), 118.

BIBLIOGRAPHY

THIS STUDY OF THE INDUSTRIAL REVOLUTION in France is based, wherever possible, on the evidence of those who participated in this development and recorded what they saw. It is not feasible to discuss here all of the pertinent books and pamphlets, but the most important may be mentioned. These sources include (1) volumes dealing with the expositions of the products of industry, whether national or international, and particularly with those of 1849, 1851, and 1900, and (2) the *enquêtes* conducted by the French Ministry of Commerce, chiefly between 1828 and 1838, of which the most significant are those of 1834 on prohibitions and of 1838 on linen. Much information is also to be found in contemporary periodicals, particularly the *Revue des deux mondes,* the *Journal des économistes,* the *Bulletins* of the Société d'Encouragement pour l'Industrie Nationale and of the Sociétés Industrielles of Mulhouse and Saint-Etienne, the *Annales des mines* and the *Annales des ponts et chaussées.* Of priceless value, though little known, is the *Journal de l'industriel et du capitaliste,* published between 1836 and 1840 only; its editors were men of unusual ability and integrity and its articles are usually far more reliable than government publications of the period. The *Mémoires* of the Academy of Sciences and of the Academy of Moral and Political Sciences also contain numerous informative essays (they are to be found in several American libraries). In general, books and articles cited are those used in the writing of the present work, but this bibliography is critical also. It omits most books that were not useful to me, but it makes note of some that would generally be thought helpful in such a study but have not been found so.

In this field much information is to be obtained only in scraps, and from sources that are brief and obscure or that deal nominally with another subject. Thus a book about taxation may contain valuable information on roads, or one on banking may shed light on crop failures. Many titles do not indicate the actual contents of the book or article. In addition, most French catalogues do not index by subject and author, nor do they cross-index. This makes research in French economic history exceedingly difficult. The present bibliography contains a good number of items which, for these or similar reasons, have been largely or wholly neglected by scholars. One of the most important of these is the complete set of volumes on the Exposition of 1851, to be found in the library of the University of Michigan. For a fuller listing and criticism of the most important sources related to the many different areas of French economic history in the earlier nineteenth century, see my bibliographical article, "The Economic History of France, 1815–1870," in the *Journal of Modern History,* 21 (1949), 121–39.

For the further assistance of scholars I have indicated in this bibliography one American library which is known to contain the book or article cited. If a book or pamphlet is not known by me to be in an American library, no location is given. Since, in the United States, I have worked chiefly at the University of Michigan and at Harvard University, these libraries appear most frequently; next most common are the Library of Congress and the John Crerar Library in Chicago. The most valuable of the sources used have been marked with an asterisk.

Académie Royale des Sciences. *Mémoires.* Paris, 1729.   Mich.

Académie Royale des Sciences Morales et Politiques. *Mémoires.* Série 2. Paris, 1837–84.   Mich.

Aftalion, Albert. *L'Oeuvre économique de Simonde de Sismondi.* Paris, 1899. 2 vols.

Alazard, Jean. "Les Causes de l'insurrection lyonnaise de 1831," *Revue historique,* 111 (1912), 48–82.   Mich.

Alcan, Michel. *Fabrication des étoffes: Traité du travail de la laine cardée.* Paris, 1867. 2 vols.

Allemagne, Henri René d'. *Prosper Enfantin et les grandes entreprises du XIXe siècle.* Paris: Librairie Girard, 1935.   Mich. (Transp.)

Alméras, Henri d'. *Au bon vieux temps des diligences.* Paris: Michel, 1931.   LC

Amé, Léon. *Etude économique sur les tarifs de douanes.* 2d ed. Paris, 1860.   Mich.

—— *Etude sur les tarifs de douanes et sur les traités de commerce.* 3d ed. Paris, 1876. 2 vols.   Mich.

"Application du barrage mobile de M. Poirée à la navigation de la Seine," *Journal de l'industriel et du capitaliste,* 9 (1840), 19–25.

Armengaud, Jacques Eugène. *Publication industrielle des machines, outils et appareils les plus perfectionnés et les plus récents employés dans les différentes branches de l'industrie française et étrangère.* Paris, 1841–89. 32 vols.   Harv.

Arnauné, Auguste. *Le Commerce extérieur et les tarifs de douane.* Paris: Alcan, 1911.   Mich.

Ashley, Percy. *Modern Tariff History: Germany–United States–France.* 2d ed. London: Murray, 1920.   Mich.

Audiffret, Charles Louis Gaston, marquis d'. *Système financier de la France*. 3d ed. Paris, 1866. 4th ed. Paris, 1876. 6 vols. Harv.

Audiganne, Armand. *L'Industrie contemporaine, ses caractères et ses progrès chez les différents peuples du monde*. Paris, 1856.

—— "L'Industrie française depuis la révolution de févricr," *Revue des deux mondes*, Nouvelle période, 2 (1849), 979–1006. Mich.

—— *Les Chemins de fer aujourd'hui et dans cent ans chez tous les peuples*. Paris, 1858–62. 2 vols. Mich. (Transp.)

—— *Les Populations ouvrières et les industries de la France dans le mouvement social du XIXe siècle*. Paris, 1854. 2 vols. Mich.

Avenel, Georges, vicomte d'. *L'Evolution des moyens de transport*. Paris: Flammarion, 1919. LC

Babbage, Charles. *On the Economy of Machinery and Manufactures*. London, 1832; 2d ed., 1835.

Bachelier, Louis. *Histoire du commerce de Bordeaux*. Bordeaux, 1862. LC

Ballot, Charles. "L'Introduction de la fonte au coke en France et la fondation du Creusot," *Revue d'histoire des doctrines économiques et sociales*, 5 (1912), 29–62. Harv.

—— L'Introduction du machinisme dans l'industrie française. Paris: Rieder, 1923. Mich.

—— "Les Prêts aux manufacturiers," *Revue des études napoléoniennes*, 3 (1912), 42–77. Harv.

*—— "Philippe de Girard et l'invention de la filature mécanique du lin," *Revue d'histoire des doctrines économiques et sociales*, 7 (1914–19), 135–95. Harv.

Ballyet, Antoine Augustin Dominique, baron. *Considérations et recherches sur les voies publiques de France*. Paris, 1827. Mich. (Transp.)
(The University of Michigan copy of this work is bound with the author's translation of the second edition of Richard Lovell Edgeworth's *Essai sur la construction des routes et des voitures*.)

Barrey, Philippe. *Le Havre maritime: La Batellerie et les transports par terre du XVIe au XIXe siècle*, in Vol. 6 of Hayem (ed.), *Mémoires et documents*, pp. 67–126. Paris: Hachette, 1921. Mich.

Baud, Paul. "Les Origines de la grande industrie chimique en France," *Revue historique*, 174 (1934), 1–18. Mich.

*Baude, Jean Jacques, baron. *De l'enquête sur les fers et des conditions du bon marché permanent des fers en France*. Paris, 1829. Harv.

—— "Sur les canaux de la Loire, de Nivernais et du Duc de Berry, concédés à la Compagnie financière des Quatres Canaux," *Société Industrielle de Saint-Etienne, Bulletin*, 3 (1825), 58–78. Mich.

Bazaine, Pierre Dominique. "Considérations générales sur les routes," Société Industrielle de Mulhouse, *Bulletin,* 7 (1834), 320–27. Mich.

Beaulieu, Charles. *Histoire du commerce, de l'industrie et des fabriques de Lyon depuis leur origine jusqu'à nos jours.* Lyon, 1838. Harv.

Beaumont, Gaston du Bosq de. *Industrie cotonnière en Normandie.* Paris, 1901.

Beauquis, A. *Histoire économique de la soie.* Lyons, 1910. Harv.

*Beauvais, Camille. *Essai sur quelques branches de l'industrie française.* Paris, 1825.

Becquey, François Louis. "Rapport au roi sur la navigation intérieure," *Annales de l'industrie nationale,* Série 2, 1 (1820), 138–52, 193–209. Harv.

Benoiston de Châteauneuf, Louis François, et Louis René Villermé. "Rapport d'un voyage fait dans les cinq départements de la Bretagne pendant les années 1840 et 1841," Académie Royale des Sciences Morales et Politiques, *Mémoires,* 4 (1844), 635–794. Mich.

Benoît, Pierre. "Les Tissages de l'Arrondissement de Saint-Dié de la fin du XVIIIe au milieu du XIXe siècle," *Annales de l'Est,* Série 4, 3 (1936), 229–37. Mich.

Bères, Emile. "Mémoire sur les causes du malaise industriel et commercial de la France, et moyens d'y rémedier," Sociéte Industrielle de Mulhouse, *Bulletin,* 6 (1833), 1–177. Mich.

—— *Manuel de l'actionnaire; ou, Résumé des précautions à prendre pour placer utilement son argent dans les sociétés par actions.* Paris, 1839. Univ. Penn.

Berthault-Ducreux, Claude Jean Baptiste Alexandre. *Comparaison des routes, des voies maritimes et fluviales des canaux et des chemins de fer.* Paris, 1839. Univ. Ill.

—— "Constructions et dimensions des diverses parties d'une route en empierrement; largeur de chaussée proportionelle à la fatigue de chaque route," *Annales des ponts et chaussées,* 2 (1831), 259–86. Mich.

—— *Note sur le roulage et les routes d'Angleterre et de France.* Paris, 1843. Chic.

Bertin et Cie. *Mémoire à s. ex. le ministre de l'intérieur sur la navigation de la Seine, du Havre à Paris.* Le Havre, 1829. Mich. (Guizot)

Beyle, Marie Henri (Stendhal). *Mémoires d'un touriste.* Paris, 1837. 2 vols.

Bigot de Morogues, Pierre Marie Sébastien, baron. *De la misère des ouvriers et de la marche à suivre pour y remèdier.* Paris, 1832. Crerar

—— *Du paupérisme, de la mendicité, et des moyens d'en prévenir les funestes effets.* Paris, 1834.

—— *Recherches des causes de la richesse et de la misère des peuples civilisés.* Paris, 1834. (Only 100 copies lithographed.) Harv. (Kress)

Blaise, Adolphe. "Etat de la question des chemins de fer: Exécution de la loi du 11 juin 1842," *Journal des économistes*, 5 (1843), 401–13.
Mich.

—— *Exposition des produits de l'industrie nationale en 1839.* Paris, 1839.

*—— *Exposition des produits de l'industrie nationale en 1844.* Paris, 1844.

—— "Les Chemins de fer en 1845," *Annuaire de l'économie politique*, 3 (1846), 264–79.
Mich.

—— "Les Chemins de fer et le crédit," *Journal des économistes*, 18 (1847), 44–53.
Mich.

Blanchard, Marcel. "Une émeute ouvrière dans l'Isère en 1819," *Revue de l'histoire de Lyon*, 13 (1914), 271–91.
Mich.

Blanchard, Raoul. *La Flandre, étude géographique de la plaine flammande en France, Belgique et Hollande.* Paris: Société Dunkerquoise, 1906.

*Blanqui, Jérôme Adolphe. *Cours d'économie industrielle* (Conservatoire des Arts et Métiers). Paris, 1837–39. 3 vols.
Harv. (Kress)

—— "Des classes ouvrières en France, pendant l'année 1848," Paris, 1849. 1 vol. in 2 parts. Also in *Petits traités publiés par de l'académie royale des sciences morales et politiques.* Paris, 1849.
LC

*—— *Histoire de l'économie politique en Europe, depuis les anciens jusqu'à nos jours,* suivie d'une bibliographie raisonnée des principaux ouvrages d'économie politique. 4th éd. Paris, 1860. 2 vols.
Mich.

Boer, M.-G. de. "Guillaume Ier et les débuts de l'industrie métallurgique en Belgique," *Revue belge de philologie et d'histoire*, 3 (1924), 527–52.
Mich.

Boiteau, Paul. *Fortune publique et finances de la France.* Paris, 1866. 2 vols.
Harv.

Boizard, Emile. *Histoire de la législation des sucres, 1664–1891.* Paris, 1891.
Harv.

Borgnis, Giuseppe Antonio. *Traité complet de méanique appliqué aux arts des machines qui servent à confectionner les étoffes.* Paris, 1818–20. 8 vols.
Mich.

Bourdon, Henri. "Rapport sur l'état de l'industrie séricicole dans le midi de la France," *Société Royale et Centrale d'Agriculture, Mémoires,* 72 (1836), 298–319, 333–36.
U.S. Dept. Agric. (Wash., D.C.)

Bourgin, Georges. "La Crise ouvrière à Paris dans la seconde moitié de 1830," *Revue historique*, 198 (1947), 203–14.
Mich.

"Législation et organisation administrative du travail sous la Restauration," *Revue politique et parlementaire*, 66 (1910), 116–52.
Mich.

Bourgin, Georges and Hubert. *Les Patrons, les ouvriers et l'état: Le Régime de l'industrie en France de 1814 à 1830.* Paris: Picard, 1912–41. 2 vols.

Bourgin, Hubert. *Fourier.* Paris: Société Nouvelle de Librairie et d'Edition, 1905.
Mich.

Bourgin, H. "L'Histoire économique de la France de 1800 à 1830," *Revue d'histoire moderne et contemporaine,* 6 (1904–5), 22–37. Mich.

Bourgin, Hubert and Georges. *L'Industrie sidérurgique en France au début de la Révolution.* Paris: Imprimerie Nationale, 1920. Harv.

*Boussinesq, Georges. *Reims à la fin de la monarchie de juillet et pendant la période révolutionnaire de 1848.* Angers: Société Française d'Imprimerie et de Publicité, 1923. Harv.

Boussinesq, Georges, and Gustave Laurent. *Histoire de Reims depuis les origines jusqu'à nos jours.* Paris: Matol-Brainé, 1933. 3 vols. Harv.
(This work is not so useful for the economic historian as the shorter and earlier work by Boussinesq alone, which has an excellent introduction on the economic causes of the Revolution of 1848.)

Brassey, Thomas. *Work and Wages Practically Illustrated.* New York, 1872. Mich.

*Brayer de Beauregard, Jean Baptiste. *Statistique de l'Aisne.* Saint-Quentin, 1826. 2 vols. LC

Bresson, F. "Rapport de la commission des prix en 1844," Société Libre d'Emulation de Rouen, *Bulletin,* 1844, 94–107. Mich.

*—— "Rapport sur la fabrication des bretelles à Rouen," Société Libre d'Emulation de Rouen, *Bulletin,* 1843, 143–56. Mich.

Bresson, Jacques. *De fonds public français et étrangers et des opérations de la Bourse de Paris.* 8th ed. Paris, 1843. LC

—— *Histoire financière de la France depuis l'origine de la monarchie jusqu'à l'année 1828.* 1st ed. Paris, 1829. 2 vols. Mich.

Briavoinne, Natalis. *De l'industrie en Belgique.* Brussels, 1839. 2 vols. Mich.

—— *Sur les inventions et perfectionnements de l'industrie depuis la fin du XVIIIe siècle jusqu'à nos jours.* In Vol. 13 of *Mémoires couronnés par l'académie royale de Belgique.* Brussels, 1838. LC

*Briez, P. *Notice sur la serrurerie de Picardie.* Abbeville, 1857.

Brisson, Barnabé. *Essai sur le système général de navigation intérieure de la France.* Paris, 1829. Mich.

Bulletin industriel. Publié par la Société d'Agriculture, Sciences, Arts et Commerce de l'Arrondissement de Saint-Etienne. Saint-Etienne, 1823–. Mich.
(Several interruptions in publication and changes of title.)

Burat, Amédée. "Des bateaux à vapeur en France," *Journal de l'industriel et du capitaliste,* 1 (1836), 143–60.

—— "De la fabrication du sucre indigène," *Journal de l'industriel et du capitaliste,* 1 (1836), 319–23.

—— *De la houille: Traité théorique et pratique des combustibles minéraux.* Paris, 1851. U. S. Geol. Surv. (Wash., D.C.)

—— *Géologie appliquée; ou, Traité de la recherche et de l'exploitation des minéraux utiles.* Paris, 1843. Mich.

—— *Le Commerce des houilles en France.* Paris, 1852.

—— *Le Matériel des houillères en France et en Belgique.* Paris, 1860–61. 2 vols.

—— *Rapport sur les houillères de Blanzy.* Paris, 1851.

—— *Situation de l'industrie houillère en 1855.* Paris: Comité Central des Houillères Françaises, 1857–72. 16 vols.

Burat, Jules, "Des voitures publiques," *Journal de l'industriel et du capitaliste,* 6 (1839), 260–69.

—— "Etat actuel de la question du roulage," *Journal de l'industriel et du capitaliste,* 1 (1836), 169–203.

*Burct, Eugène. *De la misère des classes laborieuses en Angleterre et en France.* Paris, 1841. 2 vols. Mich.

Burnley, James. *History of Wool and Woolcombing.* London, 1889. Mich.

Cahen, Léon. L'Enrichissement de la France sous la Restauration," *Revue d'histoire moderne,* Nouvelle séric, 5 (1930), 178–207. Mich.

Calonne d'Avesnes, Albéric, baron de. *Histoire de la ville d'Amiens au XIXe siècle.* Amiens: Piteux frères, 1906. 3 vols. Harv.

Capefigue, Jean Baptiste. *Histoire des grandes opérations financières.* Paris, 1855–60. 4 vols. Harv.

Cavaillès, Henri. *La Route française, son histoire, sa fonction: Etude de géographie humaine.* Paris: Colin, 1946. Mich.

*Chaix, Napoléon (ed.). *Annuaire officiel des chemins de fer.* Paris, 1847–48. Harv.

*Chaptal de Chanteloupe, Jean Antoine Claude, comte. *De l'industrie française.* Paris, 1819. 2 vols. Mich.

Charléty, Sébastien Camille Gustave. *Histoire du Saint-Simonisme (1825–1864).* Paris, 1896. Mich.

Chazelle, Henri. *Le Creusot: Histoire générale.* Dôle: Imprimerie Presse Jurassienne, 1936. LC

Chemin-Dupontès, Paul. *Les Petites Antilles.* Paris: Guilmoto, 1909.

Chérot, Auguste. *Etudes sur la culture, l'industrie et le commerce du lin et du chanvre en France.* Paris, 1844–45. 2 vols.

Chevalier, Jean. *François-Ignace de Wendel.* Metz: Even, 1939.

—— *Le Creusot, berceau de la grande industrie française.* Paris: Dunod, 1935.

Chevalier, Michel. *Cours d'économie politique fait au Collège de France.* 1st ed. Paris, 1842–50. 3 vols. Mich.

—— *Des intérêts matériels en France.* 1st ed. Paris, 1838. Mich.

—— "Les Questions politiques et sociales: D'un socialisme officiel au conseil général de l'agriculture, des manufactures et du commerce," *Revue des deux mondes,* Nouvelle période, 6 (1850), 1033–54.
Mich.

—— *Lettres sur l'Amérique du Nord.* Paris, 1836. 2 vols. Mich.

Chevalier, Michel. "Navigation du territoire," *Journal de l'industriel et du capitaliste,* 3 (1837), 45–54.

*Chevallier, Emile Valentin. *Les Salaires au XIXe siècle.* Paris, 1887.
Mich.

Chlepner, Ben Serge. *La Banque en Belgique: Etude historique et économique.* Brussels: Lamertin, 1926.

—— *Le Marché financier belge depuis cent ans.* Brussels: Capenhout, 1930.
Harv.

—— "Les Débuts du crédit industriel moderne," *Revue de l'institut de Sociologie,* 9 (1929), 293–316.

Chocqueel, Winoc. *Essai sur l'histoire et la situation actuelle de l'industrie des tapisseries et tapis.* Paris, 1863. LC

Clamageran, Jean Jules. *Etudes politiques, économiques et financières.* Paris: Alcan, 1904. Crerar

Clapham, Sir John Harold. *The Economic Development of France and Germany, 1815–1914.* Cambridge, Eng.: Cambridge University Press, 1921. Mich.

*—— *An Economic History of Modern Britain.* Cambridge, Eng.: Cambridge University Press, 1926–38. 3 vols. Mich.

Clarendon, George Villiers, Lord. *First Report on the Commercial Relations Between France and Great Britain.* London, 1834. LC

Claubry, Gaultier de. "Rapport sur les établissemen[t]s de la Compagnie des fonderies et forges de la Loire et de l'Isère," Société d'Encouragement pour l'Industrie Nationale, *Bulletin,* 26 (1827), 163–66.
Mich.

Clément, Ambroise. "De la concentration des entreprises industrielles et spécialement de la réunion des concessions houillères du bassin de la Loire," *Journal des économistes,* 13 (1846), 337–55. Mich.

—— "Nouvelles observations sur le monopole des houilles de la Loire," *Journal des économistes,* 16 (1847), 15–34. Mich.

Cobbett, James Paul. *A Ride of Eight Hundred Miles in France.* London, 1824. Mich.

Cochut, André. "La Politique du libre-échange: III, Le Régime économique de la France de 1815 à 1860," *Revue des deux mondes,* Deuxième période, 36 (1861), 311–46. Mich.

Collignon, Charles Etienne. *Du concours des canaux et des chemins de fer et de l'achèvement du canal de la Marne au Rhin.* Paris, 1845.
Mich. (Transp.)

Collyer, John. *A Practical Treatise on the Law of Partnership,* with an Appendix of Forms. London, 1832. LC

Colmont, Achille de. *Histoire des expositions des produits de l'industrie française.* Paris, 1855.

Comité Central des Houillères de France. *L'Industrie houillère en France de 1811 à 1902* (Circulaire 2640). Paris, 1904. LC

*Comité des Forges. *La Sidérurgie française, 1864–1914.* Paris, 1920. (Privately printed.) Harv.

*Compagnie des Messageries Royales. *Observations de l'administration des Messageries royales sur le discours prononcé le 5 janvier 1841, à la tribune de la Chambre des Pairs, par M. le baron Charles Dupin, à l'occasion de deux petitions d'entrepreneurs de messagerie.* Paris, 1841. Mich. (Guizot)

Comte, François Charles Louis. *Des garanties offertes aux capitaux et aux autres genres de propriétés, par les procédés des chambres législatives, dans les entreprises industrielles et particulièrement dans la formation des canaux, et de l'influence que peut avoir un canal du Havre à Paris sur la prosperité des villes commerciales de la France.* Paris, 1826.

Conseil Général des Manufactures. *Traité belge, Session de janvier, 1846.* Paris, 1846.

Contamine, Henry. *Metz et la Moselle de 1814 à 1870.* Nancy: Société d'Impressions Typographiques, 1932. 2 vols. LC

Coq, Paul. *La Bourse de Paris: Le Marché libre et le marché restreint.* Paris, 1859. LC

—— *Le Sol et la haute-banque; ou, Les Intérêts de la classe moyenne.* Paris, 1850. Chic.

Coquelin, Charles. "Des sociétés commerciales en France et en Angleterre," *Revue des deux mondes,* Nouvelle série, 3 (1843), 397–437. Mich.

*—— "De l'industrie linière en France et en Angleterre," *Revue des deux mondes,* Série 4, 19 (1839), 61–96, 194–234. Harv.

—— "Du commerce extérieur de la France en 1846," *Revue des deux mondes,* Nouvelle série, 13 (1846), 1068–89. Mich.

—— "Les Crises commerciales et la liberté des banques," *Revue des deux mondes,* Nouvelle série, 24 (1848), 445–70. Mich.

—— *Nouveau traité complet de la filature mécanique du lin et du chanvre.* Paris, 1846. LC

Cordier, Joseph Louis Etienne. *Considérations sur les chemins de fer.* Paris, 1830. Mich.

—— *De la navigation intérieure du département du Nord et particulièrement du canal de la Sensée.* Paris, 1820.

—— "Extrait d'une notice sur l'importation et l'éducation des moutons à longue laine," Société d'Amélioration des Laines, *Bulletin,* No. 4 (1827), 41–61. Mich.

—— *Mémoires sur les travaux publics.* Paris, 1841–42. 2 vols. Mich. (Transp.)

*Cordier, Joseph Louis Etienne. *Ponts et Chaussées: Essais sur la construction des routes, des ponts suspendus, des barrages etc., extraits de divers ouvrages anglais.* Lille, 1823. 2 vols. LC
   (The *Discours préliminaire* in Vol. 1 is a brilliant analysis of the whole French transportation system and its effects on the national economy.)

Corti, Egon Caesar, comte. *The Reign of the House of Rothschild, 1830–1871.* New York: Cosmopolitan, 1928. Mich.

—— *The Rise of the House of Rothschild.* New York: Cosmopolitan, 1928. Mich.

Costaz, Claude Anthelme, baron. *Mémoire sur les moyens qui ont amené le grand développement que l'industrie française a pris depuis vingt ans.* Paris, 1816.

Coste, Jacques. *Considérations sur la commandite par crédit, de l'escompte considéré sous son véritable point de vue économique.* Paris, 1841.

Courcelle-Seneuil, Jean Gustave. *Le Crédit et la banque.* Paris, 1840. Princeton

Courtois, Alphonse Charles. *Histoire des banques en France.* 2d ed. Paris, 1881. Mich.

—— "Histoire des institutions de crédit en France depuis 1790: La Banque de France, 1836–1848," *Journal des économistes,* Série 3, 34 (1874), 57–74, 207–34. Mich.

—— "Notices historiques et statistiques sur le canaux entrepris en vertu des lois de 1821 et 1822," *Journal des économistes,* 29 (1851), 213–41. Mich.

—— *Opérations de Bourse.* 3d ed. Paris, 1859. Crerar

—— *Tableaux des cours des principales valeurs négociées et côtées aux bourses des effects publics de Paris, Lyon et Marseille du 17 janvier 1797 à nos jours.* 2d ed. Paris, 1873. Harv.

Creuzé de Lesser, Hippolyte. *Statistique du département de l'Hérault.* Montpellier, 1824. Univ. of Calif.

Crozet, René. "Contribution à l'histoire de la voie ferrée de Paris à Toulouse, et du réseau ferré entre Loire moyenne et Cher," *Revue d'histoire moderne,* 14 (1939), 241–60. Mich.

Daguerre, Pierre. *La Politique de la route.* Bordeaux: Bière, 1926. Harv.

Daru, Napoléon, comte. *Des chemins de fer et de l'application de la loi du 11 juin, 1842.* Paris, 1843. LC

Debon, Paul. *Essai historique sur Louviers.* Rouen, 1836.

—— "De l'amélioration des rivières en France," *Journal de l'industriel et du capitaliste,* 3 (1837), 627–96.

*Demangeon, Albert. *La Plaine picarde.* Paris: Colin, 1905. Mich.
   (Fine bibliography.)

Demoulin, Robert. *Guillaume Ier et la transformation économique des provinces belges, 1815–1830.* Liège: Faculté de Philosophie et Lettres, 1938. Mich.
(Excellent bibliography.)
—— "De notre législation des douanes sur les machines à vapeur," *Journal de l'industriel et du capitaliste,* 9 (1840), 168–83.
Derive, Benoit Louis. *Précis historique et statistique des canaux et rivières navigables de la Belgique et d'une partie de la France.* Brussels, 1835.
Derode, Victor. *Quelques documents pour servir à l'histoire de l'industrie à Lille.* Lille, 1868.
—— "Des lois sur les chemins de fer votées pendant la dernière session," *Journal de l'industriel et du capitaliste,* 8 (1840), 329–65.
Devey, Joseph. *The Life of Joseph Locke, Civil Engineer.* London, 1862.
Crerar
Dewey, Davis Rich. *Financial History of the United States.* 9th ed. New York: Longmans, 1924. Mich.
Dollfus, Emile. "Exposition des produits de l'industrie alsacienne de 1841: Rapport général," Société Industrielle de Mulhouse, *Bulletin,* 15 (1841), 141–266. Mich.
—— "Notes pour servir à l'histoire de l'industrie cotonnière dans les départements de l'est," Société Industrielle de Mulhouse, *Bulletin,* 27 (1856–57), 435–61. Mich.
Dollfus, Jean. "De l'industrie cotonnière à l'exposition de 1855," *Journal des débats,* Paris, July 24, Aug. 13, 1855.
Doublat, Muel. "De la fabrication de la fonte en Champagne," *Journal de l'industriel et du capitaliste,* 2 (1836), 29–35.
Driessche, Jules Emmanuel van den. *Histoire de Tourcoing.* Tourcoing: Georges frères, 1928. 2 vols.
*"Droits sur les cotons en laine," *Mémoire que les manufacturiers de Rouen et du département de la Seine-Inférieure ont l'honneur de présenter à MM. les pairs de France et à MM. les députés des départements (session de 1818).* Rouen [1818].
Droz, Joseph. *Economie politique; ou, Principes de la science des richesses.* Brussels, 1829. Mich.
Dubois, Ernest. *L'Industrie du tissage du lin dans les Flandres,* in Vol. 2 of Royaume de Belgique, Ministère de l'Industrie et du Travail, Office du Travail, *Les Industries à domicile en Belgique.* Brussels: 1900. Harv.
Du Cellier, Florent François. *Histoire des classes laborieuses en France.* Paris, 1860. Mich.
*Duchâtellier, Armand René. *Essai sur les salaires et les prix de consommation de 1202 à 1830.* Paris, 1830.

Duchon, Paul. "Les Mémoires de Jacques Laffitte," *Revue des deux mondes,* Septième période, 8 (1930), 289–92. Mich.

Ducpétiaux, Edouard. *De la condition physique et morale des jeunes ouvriers et des moyens de l'améliorer.* Brussels, 1843. 2 vols. Mich.

*Dufrénoy, Ours Pierre A., et Elie de Beaumont. *Voyage métallurgique en Angleterre.* Paris, 1827. 2 vols. Mich. (Transp.)

Dunham, Arthur Louis. *The Anglo-French Treaty of Commerce of 1860 and the Progress of the Industrial Revolution in France.* Ann Arbor, Mich.: University of Michigan Press, 1930. Mich.

—— "The Economic History of France, 1815–1870," *Journal of Modern History,* 21 (1949), 121–39. Mich.

Dupérier. "De la navigation intérieure," *Journal des économistes,* 7 (1844), 242–65. Mich.

Dupin, Charles, baron. *De l'influence de la classe ouvrière sur les progrès de l'industrie.* Paris, 1835.

—— Forces productives et commerciales de la France. Paris, 1827. 2 vols. Mich.

—— *Progrès de l'industrie française depuis le commencement du XIXe siècle (Discours et leçons sur l'industrie [Technological Pamphlets],* Vol. 7, No. 6). Paris, 1825. LC

Duplessy, Joseph. *Essai statistique sur le département de la Loire.* Montbrison, 1818.

Dupont-Ferrier, Pierre. *Le Marché financier de Paris sous le second empire.* Paris: Alcan, 1925. Harv.

*Dupont-White, Charles Brook. *Essai sur les relations du travail avec le capital.* Paris, 1846. Harv. (Kress)

*Du Puynode, Michel Gustave Partouneau. *De la monnaie, du crédit et de l'impôt.* 2d ed. Paris, 1863. 2 vols. Harv.

(This work is useful for its discussion of the policy of the Bank of France and of mortgages on agricultural lands.)

*Dutens, Joseph Michel. *Histoire de la navigation intérieure de la France, avec une exposition des canaux à entreprendre pour en compléter le système.* Paris, 1829. 2 vols. Mich. (Transp.)

(This work, written in 1820, discusses reasons for the slow development of the French transportation system.)

Duvoir, Léon. *Recherche des tendances interventionnistes chez quelques économistes libéraux français de 1850.* Paris: Rousseau, 1901. Col.

Ellison, Thomas. "History of Cotton Prices and Supply, 1790–1862," *Exchange Magazine* (London), 1 (1862), 306–15; 2 (1863), 45–54.

Estancelin, Louis. *De l'importation en France des fils et tissus de lin et de chanvre d'Angleterre.* Paris, 1842.

*Esterno, Henri Philippe Ferdinand, comte d'. *Des banques départemen-tales en France.* Paris, 1838. Crerar
(The footnotes give valuable information on rates of interest.)
"Etat actuel de l'industrie du fer en France," *Journal de l'industriel et du capitaliste,* 3 (1837), 456–504.
"Etat de la question des chemins de fer," *Journal de l'industriel et du capitaliste,* 7 (1839), 24–51.
Eude, Emile. *Histoire documentaire de la mécanique française: [Frag-ments] d'après le musée central de la mécanique à l'exposition univer-selle de 1900.* Paris: Dunod, 1902. Mich.
Evans, David Morier. *The Commercial Crisis, 1847–1848.* London, 1848. Mich.
Evans, George Heberton Jr. *British Corporation Finance, 1775–1850: A Study of Preferred Shares* ("Johns Hopkins Historical Studies," v. 23). Baltimore: Johns Hopkins Press, 1936. Mich.
Eymard, Paul. *Historique du métier Jacquard.* Lyon, 1863.

Falcot, P. *Traité encyclopédique et méthodique de la fabrication des tissus.* Elbeuf and Mulhouse, 1852. 3 vols.
Falleur, Adrien. *L'Industrie lainière dans la région de Fourmies.* Paris: Université de Paris, 1930.
Faucher, Léon. "Des projets de loi sur les chemins de fer," *Revue des deux mondes,* Nouvelle série, 2 (1843), 357–83. Mich.
—— "Du monopole des fers," *Journal des économistes* [Série 1], 14 (1846), 308–20. Mich.
*—— "Les Chemins de fer et le crédit public," *Journal des économistes,* 14 (1846), 10–16. Mich.
*—— *L'Union du Midi: Association de douanes entre la France, la Bel-gique, la Suisse et l'Espagne, avec une introduction sur l'union com-merciale de la France et de la Belgique.* Paris, 1842. Harv. (Kress)
—— "Mémoire sur le travail des enfants dans la ville de Paris," Académie Royale des Sciences Morales et Politiques, *Séances et travaux,* 6 (1844), 372–79. Mich.
—— "Situation financière de la France," *Revue des deux mondes,* Nouvelle série, 1 (1843), 1017–53.
Faure-Lacroze. "Notice sur les progrès obtenus ou possibles de la fabrique des rubans à Saint-Etienne," Société Industrielle de Saint-Etienne, *Bul-letin,* 17 (1840), 153–61. Mich.
Favre, Adrien. *Les Origines du système métrique.* Paris: Presses Universi-taires, 1931. Mich.
Favre, Jules. *De la coalition des chefs d'atelier de Lyon.* Lyon, 1833. Crerar

Felkin, William. *History of Hosiery and Machine-Wrought Lace Manufactures.* 3d ed. Cambridge, Eng., 1867.   Mich.

Ferguson, S. Jr. *Histoire du tulle et des dentelles mécaniques en Angleterre et en France.* Paris, 1862.   LC

Ferrette, Henry. *Etude historique sur l'intervention financière de l'état dans l'établissement des lignes de chemins de fer.* Paris, 1896.   Col.

Festy, Octave. *Le Mouvement ouvrier au début de la monarchie de juillet, 1830–1834.* Paris: Comely, 1908.   Harv.

—— "Le Mouvement ouvrier à Paris en 1840. *Revue des sciences politiques,* 30 (1913), 67–79, 226–40, 333–61.   Mich.

—— "Sismondi et la condition des ouvriers français de son temps," *Revue d'économie politique,* 32 (1918), 46–72, 118–36.   Mich.

—— "Vicomte Alban de Villeneuve-Bargemont et la condition des ouvriers français aux environs de 1830," *Revue des sciences politiques,* 42 (1919), 78–98, 234–61.   Mich.

Flachat, Eugène. "De l'industrie du fer en France considérée par rapport aux entraves qu'elle éprouve dans le développement de ses moyens de production," *Journal de l'industriel et du capitaliste,* 1 (1836), 31–43.

Flachat, Eugène, et Alexis Barrault. *Traité de la fabrication du fer et de la fonte envisagée sous les rapports chimique, mécanique et commercial.* Paris, 1842.

Flachat, Eugène, and Jules Burat. "Des canaux exécutés par le gouvernement," *Journal de l'industriel et du capitaliste,* 1 (1836), 271–328.

Formoy, Ronald Ralph. *The Historical Foundations of Modern Company Law.* London: Sweet and Maxwell, 1923.   LC

Foville, Alfred de. *La Transformation des moyens de transport et ses conséquences économiques et sociales.* Paris, 1880.   Mich.

France. Bureau de Statistique Générale. *Statistique générale.* Paris, 1835–73. 34 vols.   Mich.

—— Ministère des Travaux Publics. *Les Travaux publics de France,* par MM. Félix Lucas, Victor Fournié et Henri Melchior. Paris, 1883. 11 vols.   LC

—— —— *Rapport au roi sur la situation au 31 mars 1825 des canaux et autres ouvrages entrepris en vertu des lois des 20 juin et 5 août 1821, 17 avril et 14 août 1822.* Paris, 1825.

—— —— *Rapport au roi sur la situation au 31 juillet 1832 des canaux et autres ouvrages entrepris en vertu des lois du 20 juin et 5 août 1821, 17 avril et 14 août 1822, 24 mars et 8 juin 1825, et 29 mai 1827.* Paris, 1832.

—— —— *Rapport au roi sur l'execution pendant l'année 1841 de la loi du 21 mai 1836 relative aux chemins vicinaux.* Paris, 1843.   Harv.

— — — Administration Générale des Ponts et Chaussées et des Mines. *Compte rendu des travaux des ingénieurs des mines.* Paris, 1835–1914. Harv.

— — — — *Résumé des travaux statistiques de l'administration des mines.* Paris, 1834–44. Harv.

— — — — — *Situation des travaux.* Paris, 1836–44. Harv.

— — — — — *Statistique des routes royales de France.* Paris, 1824. Harv.
(This excellent report is the work of François Louis Becquey.)

— — — Direction Générale des Ponts et Chaussées et des Mines. *Annales des mines,* séries 1–4. 1816–51. Harv.

— — — — — *Annales des ponts et chaussées: Mémoires et documents,* séries 1–7. 1831–1900. Mich.

— — — — — *Exposé général des études faites pour le tracé des chemins de fer de Paris en Belgique et en Angleterre,* par Louis Léger Vallée. Paris, 1837. LC

— — — — — *Statistique des ports maritimes de commerce.* Paris, 1839.

— — Ministère du Commerce. *Enquête pour la recherche et la constatation des faits qui doivent servir à résoudre la question de savoir s'il y a lieu de supprimer ou de réduire le droit perçu sur les houilles étrangères, à leur importation en France, tant par mer que par terre, commencée le 13 novembre 1832.* Paris, 1833.

*— — — *Enquête relative à diverses prohibitions établies à l'entrée des produits étrangers.* Paris, 1835. 3 vols. Mich.

— — — *Enquête sur la Banque de France.* Paris, 1866.

— — — *Enquête sur les fers de 1828.* Paris, 1829.

*— — —*Enquête sur les fils de laine longue peignée, tordus, du cordonnet et grillée (décembre, 1836).* Paris, 1836.

— — — *Enquête sur les fils et tissus de lin et de chanvre par le conseil supérieur du commerce en novembre, 1838.* Paris, 1838

— — — *Enquête sur les sucres.* Paris, 1829.

Francœur, Louis Benjamin. "Nouveau système complet de filature du coton, usité en Angleterre et importé en France par la compagnie établie à Ourscamp, près Compiègne," Société d'Encouragement pour l'Industrie Nationale, *Bulletin,* 28 (1829), 563–65. Mich.

François, Jules. *Essai sur l'élaboration du minerai de fer dans le traitement direct: Rapport sur la nécessité d'une forge expérimentale dans l'Ariège.* Paris, 1838.

— — *Extrait d'un rapport à M. le ministre de l'agriculture et du commerce sur la question de l'importation des fers au bois du nord de l'Europe.* Moulins, 1845.

— — *Recherches sur le gisement et le traitement direct des minerais de fer dans les Pyrénées.* Paris, 1843. 2 vols.

Frégier, Honoré Antoine. *Des classes dangereuses de la population dans les grandes villes, et des moyens de les rendres meilleures.* Paris, 1840. 2 vols.   Harv.

Frignet, Ernest. *Histoire de l'association commerciale depuis l'antiquité jusqu'au temps actuel.* Paris, 1868.   Harv.

Gain, André. *La Restauration et les biens des émigrés.* Nancy: Société d'Impressions Typographiques, 1929. 2 vols.   Col.

Gallois, L. de. "Des chemins de fer en Angleterre, notamment à Newcastle dans le Northumberland," *Annales des mines,* [Série 1] 3 (1818), 129–44.   Harv.

Garcenot, A. *Les Bassins houillers du nord-ouest de l'Europe (mines d'Anzin).* Paris, 1884.

Gasperin, Adrien Etienne Pierre, comte de. "Considérations sur les progrès de l'éducation des vers à soie, depuis le commencement du siècle," Académie Royale des Sciences, *Mémoires,* Série 2, 18 (1842), 515–37.   Crerar

—— *Mémoire sur l'éducation des mérinos comparée à celle des autres races des bêtes à cornes.* Paris, 1823.

*Géruzez, Jean Baptiste François. *Description historique et statistique de la ville de Reims.* Reims, 1817. 2 vols.   Mich.

Gille, Bertrand. *Les Origines de la grand industrie métallurgique en France.* Paris: Domat, 1947.   Mich.

Gilroy, Clinton G. *Treatise on the Art of Weaving by Hand and Power.* New York, 1844.   Harv.

Girod de l'Ain, Félix Jean Marie. *Quelques réflexions sur l'importance de l'amélioration des laines en France à l'occasion de l'exposition universelle de 1855.* Paris, 1855.

Gossez, Alphonse Marius. *Le Département du Nord sous la deuxième république, 1848–1852.* Lille: G. Lelev, 1904.   Harv.

Grande encyclopédie: Inventaire raisonné des sciences, des lettres et des arts, par une société de savants et de gens de lettres, sous la direction de MM. Berthelot . . . Hartwig Derenbourg [etc.]. Paris, 1886–1902. 31 vols.   Mich.

Grangez, Ernest. "Des droits de navigation intérieure sur les rivières et les canaux," *Journal de l'industriel et du capitaliste,* 9 (1840), 193–218.

—— *Précis historique et statistique des voies navigables de la France et d'une partie de la Belgique.* Paris, 1855.   NYPL

Gras, Louis Joseph. *Essai sur l'histoire de la quincaillerie et petite métallurgie . . . à Saint-Etienne et dans la région stéphanoise comparée aux régions concurrentes.* Saint-Etienne: Thomas, 1904.

—— *Histoire de la rubanerie et des industries de la soie à Saint-Etienne et dans la région stéphanoise.* Saint-Etienne: Thomas, 1906.   Harv.

—— *Histoire des premiers chemins de fer français . . . et du premier tramway de France.* Saint-Etienne: Théolier, 1924.   Harv.

—— *Histoire économique de la métallurgie de la Loire.* Saint-Etienne: Thomas, 1908.   Mich.

—— *Histoire économique générale des mines de la Loire.* Saint-Etienne: Théolier, 1922. 2 vols.

—— *Les Routes du Forez et du Jarez.* Saint-Etienne: Théolier, 1925.

—— *Le Forez et le Jarez navigables: Histoire de la navigation de la Loire et sur le canal de Givors et des projets de canal de la Loire au Rhône.* Saint-Etienne: Théolier, 1930.   LC

Gras, Marcel. *Du machinisme et de ses conséquences économiques et sociales dans l'industrie moderne.* Paris: Rousseau, 1911.   Harv.

Great Britain. Parliament. House of Commons. "Account Showing the Several Countries to Which Machinery Has Been Exported, With the Official Value, in Each Year, From 1823 to 1827." *Accounts and Papers,* Vol. 18. London, 1827.

—— —— —— "First Report From the Select Committee Appointed to Inquire Into the Operation of the Existing Laws Affecting the Exportation of Machinery." *Parliamentary Papers,* Vol. 7. London, 1841.

—— —— —— "First Report From the Select Committee Appointed to Inquire Into the State of the Law in the United Kingdom, and Its Consequences, Respecting Artisans Leaving the Kingdom and Residing Abroad; Also Into the State of the Law and Its Consequences Respecting the Exportation of Tools and Machinery, 'and Into the State of the Law and Its Effects, so far as Relates to the Combination of Workmen and Others to Raise Wages or to Regulate Their Wages and Hours of Working." *Reports From Committees,* Vol. 2. London, 1824.

Gréau, Nicolas Jean Julien. "Delarothière, inventeur, mécanicien à Troyes," Société Académique d'Agriculture de l'Aube, *Mémoires,* 36 (1867), 83–98.   Mich.

—— *Statistique de la production de l'arrondissement industriel de la ville de Troyes pour l'année 1846.* Troyes, 1848.

Gueneau, Louis. *Lyon et le commerce de la soie.* Lyon: Bascou, 1923.   Harv.

—— "La Première voie ferrée de Bourgogne: Le Chemin de fer d'Epinac à Port d'Ouche," *Annales de Bourgogne,* 3 (1931), 38–65, 224–52.   Mich.

Guépin, Ange. *Histoire de Nantes.* 2d ed. Nantes, 1839.   Mich.

Guéymard, Emile. "Rapport à M. le directeur général des ponts et chaussées et des mines, sur la conduite des fourneaux à l'air chaud," Société d'Encouragement pour l'Industrie Nationale, *Bulletin,* 32 (1833), 386–92.   Mich.

Guillaume, Achille. "Du mode de concession des travaux publics," *Journal de l'industriel et du capitaliste,* 3 (1837), 154–60.

Guilmeth, Alexandre Auguste. *Histoire de la ville d'Elbeuf.* Rouen, 1842.

Guyot, Raymond. *La Première entente cordiale.* Paris: Rieder, 1926.   Mich.

Hachette, Jean Nicolas Pierre. "Mémoire sur les divers modes de numérotage employés dans les filatures et dans les tréfileries," Société d'Encouragement pour l'Industrie Nationale, *Bulletin,* 23 (1824), 349–61.   Mich.

Halévy, Elie. *Sismondi.* Paris: Alcan, 1933.   Col.

Hanotaux, Gabriel (ed.). *Histoire de la nation française.* Paris: Plon, 1920–29. 15 vols.

(Vol. 10 alone is useful for this book.)

Hayem, Julien (ed.). *Mémoires et documents pour servir à l'histoire du commerce et de l'industrie en France.* Paris: Hachette, 1911–29. 12 vols.   Mich.

Hedde, Philippe. "Aperçu sur l'état actuel des fabriques de rubans de Saint-Etienne et de Saint-Chamond en 1828," Société Industrielle de Saint-Etienne, *Bulletin,* 6 (1828), 201–7.   Mich.

—— *Indicateur du commerce, des arts et des manufactures de Saint-Etienne, Saint-Chamond et Rive de Gier, précédé d'un aperçu sur l'industrie de l'arrondissement de Saint-Etienne.* Saint-Etienne, 1831–38. 4 vols.

—— "Notice sur la fabrication des rubans de Saint-Etienne, suivie de la description des métiers mécaniques dits à la barre," Société Industrielle de Saint-Etienne, *Bulletin,* 6 (1828), 123–40.   Mich.

—— *Rubans brodés sur le métier pendant le tissage au moyen des battants brodeurs à aiguilles.* Saint-Etienne, 1842.

Hélot, Jules. *Histoire centenaire du sucre de betterave.* Cambrai: Deligne, 1912.

—— *Le Sucre de betterave en France de 1800 à 1900.* Cambrai: Deligne, 1900.

Helps, Sir Arthur. *Life and Labours of Mr. Brassey, 1805–1870.* Boston, 1874.   Mich.

Henderson, William Otto. *Britain and Industrial Europe, 1750–1870: Studies in British Influence on the Industrial Revolution in Western Europe.* Liverpool: University Press, 1954.   Mich.

Hénon, Henri. *L'Industrie des tulles et des dentelles mécaniques dans le Pas-de-Calais, 1815–1900.* Paris and Calais, 1900.

Héricart-Ferrand, Louis François Etienne, vicomte de Thury. "Rapport au nom du comité des arts mécaniques sur la filature du lin et du chanvre par mécanique, de MM. Schlumberger père et fils et compagnie, à Nogent-lès-Vierges, département de l'Oise," Société d'Encouragement pour l'Industrie Nationale, *Bulletin,* 27 (1828), 33–36.
Mich.

—— "Rapport sur les diverses machines fabriquées par MM. Pihet frères," Société d'Encouragement pour l'Industrie Nationale, *Bulletin,* 28 (1829), 238–39.
Mich.

—— "Rapport sur les nouveaux procédés introduits dans les métiers à fabriquer les étoffes de soie par M. Etienne Maisiat," Société d'Encouragement pour l'Industrie Nationale, *Bulletin,* 27 (1828), 68–73.
Mich.

—— "Rapport sur les procédés, inventions, et perfectionnements introduits par M. Calla père dans la construction des machines," Société d'Encouragement pour l'Industrie Nationale, *Bulletin,* 28 (1829), 235–37.
Mich.

Héron de Villefosse, Antoine Marie. "Recherches statistiques sur les métaux en France," Académie Royale des Sciences, *Mémoires,* 9 (1830), 144–83.
Mich.

—— *Recherches statistiques sur l'état actuel des usines à fer de la France en l'année 1825.* Paris, 1828.

Higby, Chester P., and Caroline B. Willis. "Industry and Labor Under Napoleon," *American Historical Review,* 53 (1948), 465–80. Mich.

Hitier, Joseph. "Sismondi," *Revue d'économie politique,* 13 (1899), 529–82.
Mich.

Hobson, Charles Kenneth. *The Export of Capital.* London: Constable, 1914.
Mich.

Horn, Ignaz Einhorn. *Das Creditwesen in Frankreich.* Leipzig, 1857.
Mich.

Hottenger, Georges. *L'Ancienne industrie du fer en Lorraine.* Nancy: Société Industrielle de l'Est, 1927.

Houdoy, Jules. *La Filature du coton dans le nord de la France.* Paris: Rousseau, 1903.
Harv.

Houtte, J. A. van. *Esquisse d'une histoire économique de la Belgique.* Louvain: Editions Universitaires, 1943.
Mich.

Hunt, Bishop Carleton. *The Development of the Business Corporation in England, 1800–1867* ("Harvard Economic Studies," Vol. 52). Cambridge, Mass.: Harvard University Press, 1936.
Mich.

Hutchinson's Technical and Scientific Encyclopedia, ed. by C. F. Tweney and I. P. Shershov. London: Hutchinson; New York: Macmillan, 1935. 4 vols.   Mich.

Hutt, William Harold. "The Factory System of the Early 19th Century," *Economica,* 6 (1926), 78–93.   Mich.

"Industrie du fer: Des progrès réalisé dans les usines à fer pendant les dernières années," *Journal de l'industriel et du capitaliste,* 5 (1838), 122–24.

Isambert, Gaston. *Les Idées socialistes en France de 1815 à 1848.* Paris: Alcan, 1905.   Mich.

Jackson, William Fritz. *James Jackson et ses fils: Notice sur leur vie et sur les établissements qu'ils ont fondé en France.* Paris, 1893.

Jacquemyns, Guillaume. "Histoire de la crise économique des Flandres (1845–1850)," Académie Royale de Belgique, *Mémoires, lettres, etc.,* 26. Brussels: Lamertin, 1929.   LC

Jannet, Claudio. *Le Capital, la spéculation et la finance au XIXe siècle.* Paris, 1892.   Mich.

Jenkins, Rhys. "A Cornish Engineer: Arthur Woolf, 1766–1837," Newcomen Society, *Transactions,* 13 (1932–33), 55–68. Mich. (Transp.)

Jenks, Leland Hamilton. *The Migration of British Capital to 1875.* New York: Knopf, 1927; 2d ed., 1938.   Mich.

Joinville, Pierre de. *Le Réveil économique de Bordeaux sous la Restauration: L'Armateur Balguerie-Stuttenberg et son oeuvre.* Paris: Champion, 1914.   LC

Jouffroy, Louis Maurice. "Aperçu du développement du réseau férré en Europe de 1830 à 1848," *Annales de géographie,* 40 (1931), 504–18.
                                                                  Mich.

*—— Une étape de la construction des grandes lignes de chemin de fer en France: La Ligne de Paris à la frontière d'Allemagne (1825–1852). Paris: Dorbon-Ainé, 1932. 4 vols. in 1.   LC
       (Excellent bibliography.)

Journal de l'industriel et du capitaliste. Ed. Jules Burat. Paris, 1836–40. 9 vols.
       (Invaluable in study of transportation and metallurgy, with excellent maps. Very rare, now almost unknown.)

Journal des chemins de fer. Paris, 1842–78.   Crerar

Juglar, Clément. Des crises commerciales et de leur retour périodique en France, en Angleterre et aux Etats-Unis. 2d ed. Paris, 1889.
                                                                  Mich.

Julliany, Jules. *Essai sur le commerce de Marseille.* 2d ed. Marseille, 1843. 3 vols.

Kahan-Rabecq, Marie Madeleine. *L'Alsace économique et sociale sous le règne de Louis-Philippe.* Paris: Presses Modernes, 1939. 2 vols. LC

Kaufmann, Eugen. *Das französische Bankwesen.* 2d ed. Tübingen: J. C. B. Mohr, 1923.

Kaufmann, Richard von. *La Politique française en matière de chemins de fer.* Paris: Librairie Polytechnique, 1900.

Kindt, Jules. *De l'industrie du coton, de la laine et de la soie.* Brussels, 1854.
(This study is useful for estimating the influence of changing fashions on business.)

Laborde, Alexandre Léon Joseph, comte de. *De l'esprit d'association dans tous les intérêts de la communauté.* 2d ed. Paris, 1821. 2 vols.
Harv.

*Labrousse, Charles Ernest. "Crise économique et crises politiques en France de 1847 à 1851," *Communication aux journées franco-anglaises d'histoire,* 28 septembre, 1946.

Lacave-Laplagne, Jean Pierre. *Observations sur l'administration des finances pendant le gouvernement de juillet et sur ses résultats.* Paris, 1848.
Crerar

Lafarelle, François Félix de. "Etudes économiques sur l'industrie de la soie dans le midi de la France," *Journal des économistes,* [Série 1] 32 (1852), 17–34, 282–99; Série 2, 1 (1854), 62–85, 191–204. Mich.

—— *Plan d'une réorganisation disciplinaire des classes industrielles en France.* Paris, 1842.
Crerar

Laffitte, Jacques. *Mémoires de Laffitte (1767–1844),* publiés par Paul Duchon. Paris: Firmin-Didot, 1932.

*—— *Réflexions sur la réduction de la rente, et sur l'état du crédit.* 2d ed. Paris, 1824.
Crerar

*Lamé, Gabriel, Emile Clapeyron, et Stéphane et Eugène Flachet: *Vues politiques et pratiques sur les travaux publics de France.* Paris, 1832.

*Lamé-Fleury, Ernest Jules. "Les Arts industriels: De l'impression des tissus," *Revue des deux mondes,* Nouvelle série, 18 (1847), 128–48.
Mich.

La Nourais, Prosper Alexis Gaubert de. *De l'association douanière entre la France et la Belgique.* Paris, 1842. Harv. (Kress)

La Place de Chauvac, Gaston de. *La Crise des finances publiques en 1848.* Toulouse: Marqueste, 1916.

Lardner, Dionysius. *The Steam Engine Familiarly Explained and Illustrated.* 6th ed. London, 1836. Mich.

*Laufenburger, Henri. "L'Industrie cotonnière du Haut-Rhin," *Revue politique et parlementaire,* 125 (1925), 387–415. Mich. (This essay is the best available on the industrial revolution in France.)

Laufenburger, Henri, and Pierre Pflimlin. *Cours d'économie alsacienne.* Paris: Sirey, 1932. 2 vols.

Laurent de Villedeuil, P. Charles. *Bibliographie des chemins de fer* (Préface; Index chronologique). Paris: Librairie Générale, 1906. Mich. (Transp.)

Lavisse, Ernest. *Histoire de France depuis les origines jusqu'à la Révolution.* Hachette, 1903–11. 9 vols., each in 2 parts.

Leblanc, V. *Nouveau système complet de filature de coton, usité en Angleterre et importé en France par la compagnie établie à Ourscamp, près Compiègne.* Paris, 1828.

Leducq, Jean. *Du développement de la production du fer dans le nord-ouest de la France.* Boulogne, 1834.

*Lefranc, Georges. "The French Railroads, 1823–1842," *Journal of Economic and Business History,* 2 (1930), 299–331. Mich.

*Legoyt, Alfred. *Le Livre des chemins de fer, construits, en construction et projetés; ou, Statistique générale de ces voies de communication en France et à l'étranger.* Paris, 1845. Harv.

Lelong, Pierre Siméon. "Aperçus historiques et statistiques sur l'industrie cotonnière dans le département de la Seine-Inférieure," Société Libre d'Emulation de Rouen, *Bulletin* (1834), 218–42. Mich.

Léon, Alphonse F. M. "Considérations sur les différents modes de construction et d'entretien des routes," *Annales des ponts et chaussées,* [Série 1] 11 (1836), 129–79. Mich.

Léon, Paul. *Fleuves, canaux et chemins de fer.* Paris: Colin, 1903. Harv.

Le Play, Piérre Guillaume Frédéric. "Mémoire sur la fabrication de l'acier en Yorkshire et comparaison des principaux groupes d'aciéries européennes," *Annales des mines,* Série 4, 3 (1843), 583–714. Mich.

—— "Mémoire sur la fabrication et le commerce des fers à acier dans le nord de l'Europe, et sur les questions soulevées depuis un siècle et demi par l'emploi de ces fers dans les aciéries françaises," *Annales des mines,* Série 4, 9 (1846), 113–306. Mich.

Lerat, Georges. *Etude sur les origines, le développement et l'avenir des raffineries nantaises.* Paris: Rousseau, 1911. Harv.

Leroy, Maxime. *La Vie véritable du comte Henri de Saint-Simon (1760–1825).* Paris: B. Grasset, 1925. Mich.

Lesguilliez, Alexandre. *Notice historique, topographique et statistique sur la ville de Darnetal*. Rouen, 1835.
(Useful on both the woolen and cotton industries.)

Leuilliot, Paul. "La Renaissance des établissements Japy Frères après 1815," *Franche-Comté, Monts Jura et Haute Alsace: Revue régionale*, 5 (1930), 131–33.

—— "Une Monographie d'établissement industriel alsacien en 1826," *Revue d'histoire moderne*, 5 (1930), 56–61.   Mich.

Leuridan, Théodore. *Histoire de Roubaix*. Roubaix, 1859–64. 5 vols.
                                                                        Harv.

Levainville, Jacques René. *Le Morvan: Etude de géographie humaine*. Paris: Colin, 1909.   Mich.

—— *Rouen: Etude d'une agglomération urbaine*. Paris: Colin, 1913.
                                                                        Mich.

Levasseur, Emile. *Histoire des classes ouvrières en France depuis 1789 jusqu'à nos jours*. Paris, 1867. 2 vols.   Mich.

—— *Histoire du commerce de la France*. Paris: Rousseau, 1911–12. 2 vols.
                                                                        Mich.

*Lévy, Robert. *Histoire économique de l'industrie cotonnière en Alsace*. Paris: Alcan, 1912.   Mich.

Lexis, Wilhelm Hector. *Die französischen Ausfuhrprämien im Zusammenhange mit der Tarifgeschichte und Handelsentwicklung Frankreichs seit der Restauration*. Bonn, 1870.   Harv.

Liesse, André. *Evolution of Credit and Banks in France, From the Founding of the Bank of France to the Present Time*. Washington, D.C.: U.S. Govt. Printing Office, 1909.   Harv.

—— *Portraits des financiers*. Paris: Alcan, 1908.   Mich.

Louis, Paul. *Histoire de la classe ouvrière en France de la révolution à nos jours*. Paris: Rivière, 1927.   Mich.

—— "L'Ouvrier français de Louis XVIII à Louis Philippe," *Revue politique et parlementaire*, 188 (1946), 138–49.   Mich.

Loutitch, L. J. *Des variations du taux de l'intérêt en France de 1800 à nos jours*. Paris: Alcan, 1930.   Harv.

Lucas, Félix Benjamin. *Etude historique et statistique sur les voies de communication de la France*. Paris, 1873.   Mich. (Transp.)

*McKay, Donald Cope. *The National Workshops: A Study in the French Revolution of 1848*. Cambridge, Mass.: Harvard University Press, 1933.   Mich.
(This work includes an excellent introduction on economic crises and an admirable critical bibliography.)

Mallet, Charles. "Rapport sur les ateliers de construction de machines, fondés à Paris par M. John Collier," Société d'Encouragement pour l'Industrie Nationale, *Bulletin,* 27 (1828), 167–70. Mich.

Mallez, Paul. *La Restauration des finances françaises après 1814.* Paris: Dalloz, 1927. Harv.

Malotet, Arthur. "L'Industrie et le commerce des toiles fines à Valenciennes pendant l'époque contemporaine," *Revue du nord,* 3 (1912), 329–94. Mich.

Malvezin, Théophile. *Histoire du commerce de Bordeaux, depuis les origines jusqu'à nos jours.* Bordeaux, 1892. 4 vols. Harv.

Manès, W. *Etudes des gîtes minéraux, publiées par l'administration des mines sur les houilles de Saône-et-Loire.* Paris, 1844.
U. S. Geol. Surv., Wash., D.C.

—— "Notice sur la navigation à la vapeur de la Saône et du Rhône," *Annales des ponts et chaussées,* Série 2, 5 (1843), 10–46. Mich.

Mantz, Jean. "Rapport fait au nom du comité du commerce sur la situation de l'industrie cotonnière en France," Société Industrielle de Mulhouse, *Bulletin,* 19 (1845–46), 163–84. Mich.

Manuel, Frank E. "The Luddite Movement in France," *Journal of Modern History,* 10 (1938), 180–211. Mich.

Margueron, Gustave F. *Le Droit routier: Etude complète, historique, administrative et juridique du régime de circulation sur les routes françaises.* Paris: Dunod, 1930. Harv.

Marion, Marcel. *Histoire financière de la France depuis 1715.* Paris: Rousseau, 1914–31. 6 vols. Mich.

Marshall, Frederic. *Population and Trade in France in 1861–1862.* London, 1862. Mich.

Martin, Germain. *Histoire économique et financière de la France,* in Vol. 10 of Gabriel Hanotaux (ed.), *Histoire de la nation française.* Paris: Plon, 1927.

—— *Le Tissage du ruban à domicile dans les campagnes du Velay.* Paris: Sirey, 1913. Harv.

Masnata, Albert. *L'Emigration des industries suisses.* Lausanne: G. Vaney-Bernier, 1924.

Mauguin. *Etudes historiques sur l'administration de l'agriculture en France.* Paris, 1876–77. 3 vols. LC

Maury, François. *Le Port de Paris hier et demain.* Paris: Guillaumin, 1904. Crerar

*Mehrens, Bernhard. *Die Entstehung und Entwicklung der grossen französischen Kreditinstitute mit Berücksichtigung ihres Einflusses auf die wirtschaftliche Entwicklung Frankreichs.* Stuttgart and Berlin: Cotta, 1911. Harv.

Mémoire général et recapitulatif des travaux de la sous-commission d'enquête pour l'industrie du coton. Rouen, 1829.

Meredith, Hugh Owen. *Protection in France.* London: P. S. King, 1904. Mich.

Molard, François Emanuel Jr. "Rapport sur les fonderies et établisse-men[t]s de l'industrie de MM. Manby et Wilson à Charenton," Société d'Encouragement pour l'Industrie Nationale, *Bulletin,* 24 (1825), 123–26. Mich.

Monier, Charles. *De l'état actuel de la navigation de la Seine entre Rouen et Paris et des moyens de la perfectionner.* Paris, 1832. LC

Montalivet, Marthe Camille Bachesson, comte de. "Le Roi Louis-Philippe et sa liste civile," *Revue des deux mondes,* Nouvelle période, 8 (1850), 112–45. Mich.

Mony, Adolphe. *Histoire d'une mine: Commentry.* Paris: Hachette, 1911.

Moreau de Jonnès, Alexandre. *Le Commerce au XIXe siècle: Etat actuel de ses transactions dans les principales contrées des deux hémisphères.* Paris, 1825. Mich.

*—— "Introduction à la statistique de l'industrie de la France," *Journal des économistes,* 17 (1847), 244–62. Mich.

—— Statistique de l'industrie de la France. Paris, 1856. Mich.

Mortemart-Boisse, François Jérôme, baron de. "Recherches agricoles faites en Angleterre en 1825," Société d'Amélioration des Laines, *Bulletin,* No. 1 (1825–26), 7–26; No. 2 (1826–27), 1–39, 55–66. Mich.

*Mosse, J. M. "Extrait d'une notice sur les routes royales et départemen-tales du département de la Nièvre," *Annales des ponts et chaussées,* 10 (1835), 62–112. Mich.

*Musset, René. "La Canalisation des rivières en France," *Annales de géographie,* 47 (1938), 500–504. Mich.

Navier, Louis Marie Henri. "Considérations sur les travaux d'entretien des routes en Angleterre: Procédés de M. MacAdam," *Annales des ponts et chaussées,* 2 (1831), 132–56. Mich.
(Written in 1822.)

Nervo, Jean Baptiste Rosario Gonsalve, baron de. *Etudes historiques: Les Finances françaises sous la Restauration, 1814–1830.* Paris, 1865–68. 4 vols. Mich.

*Nicolle, André. *Comment la France a payé après Waterloo.* Paris: Boc-card, 1929. LC
(Good bibliography.)

*Nigohosian, V. A. *La Libération du territoire français après Waterloo, 1815–1818.* Paris: Boccard, 1929. Harv.
(Full bibliography.)

Noël, Octave Eugène. *Histoire du commerce du monde depuis les temps réculés.* 2d ed. Paris: Plon, 1906. 3 vols. Mich.

—— *Histoire du commerce extérieur de la France depuis la révolution.* Paris, 1879. Chic.

"Notice sur les mines de houille de l'arrondissement de Saint-Etienne," *Journal de l'industriel et du capitaliste,* 4 (1838), 176–88.

Paris. Chambre de Commerce. *Catalogue de la bibliothèque.* Paris: Hotel de la Chambre de Commerce, 1913. Mich.

*—— —— *Enquête faite par ordre du parlement d'Angleterre pour connaître et pour constater les progrès de l'industrie française et dans les autres pays du continent du 17 février 1824 au 10 mai 1824,* conclusion de l'enquête traduite par M. L. Raymond Balthasar Maiseau et présentée à la Chambre de Commerce de Paris. Paris, 1825.

Harv. (Kress)

(This work is an accurate translation of the following: Great Britain, Parliament, House of Commons. *Parliamentary Papers,* Vol. 5. London, 1824. It contains valuable information on machines—their exportation from England and their use in France, on the supply of skilled labor obtained by France, and on the number and size of French cotton mills.)

—— —— *Statistique de l'industrie à Paris, résultant de l'enquête par la Chambre de Commerce de Paris pour les années 1847–1848.* Paris, 1851.

Paris. *Expositions des produits de l'industrie.* 1819–1900.

(The reports on many of these expositions, here listed chronologically, are available in the United States, the greatest number being in the Library of Congress. However, I know of no other set of the reports of the French Commission on the Exposition of 1851 than the one at the University of Michigan, and of no set of the Exposition of 1849 in this country.)

—— —— *Rapport du jury central sur les produits de l'industrie française à l'exposition de 1819,* rédigé par Baron Louis Costaz. Paris, 1819. LC

—— —— *Rapport fait au jury central de l'exposition des produits de l'industrie française de l'année 1819 sur les objets relatifs à la metallurgie,* par Antoine Marie Héron de Villefosse. Paris, 1820.

—— —— *Rapport du jury central sur les produits de l'industrie française à l'exposition de 1823,* rédigé par Louis Etienne François Héricart-Ferrand, vicomte de Thury, et Pierre Henri Migneron. Paris, 1824. LC

—— —— *Histoire de l'exposition des produits de l'industrie française en 1827,* par Jérôme Adolphe Blanqui. Paris, 1827. Mich.

———— *Rapport du jury central sur les produits de l'industrie française à l'exposition de 1827,* rédigé par Louis Etienne François Héricart-Ferrand, vicomte de Thury, et Pierre Henri Migneron. Paris, 1828.
LC

———— *Rapport du jury central sur les produits de l'industrie française à l'exposition de 1834,* rédigé par Baron Charles Dupin. Paris, 1836. 3 vols.
LC

(Vol. 1 contains an introductory history of French industry since 1789.)

———— *Rapport du jury central sur les produits de l'industrie française à l'exposition de 1839.* Paris, 1840.
LC

(The reports on cotton spinning, by Nicolas Koechlin, and on wool, by Girod de l'Ain, are especially useful.)

———— *Rapport du jury central sur les produits de l'industrie française à l'exposition de 1844,* rédigé par Jules Burat. Paris, 1845. 2 vols.
LC

*———— *Exposition nationale des produits de l'industrie agricole et manufacturière de 1849: Rapport du jury central.* Paris, 1850. 3 vols.

(This source is especially valuable on Roubaix, and for a report on silk by Arlès-Dufour.)

*———— *Exposition universelle de 1851 à Londres,* travaux de la Commission Française sur l'Industrie des Nations, sous la présidence du Baron Charles Dupin. Paris, 1854–73. 8 vols.
Mich.

(This work is perhaps the most valuable single source on the industrial history of France from 1815 to 1848. Vol. 1 opens with P. Dufrénoy's survey of mining operations in a separate volume published in 1873 and marked "Incomplete." There are then 8 parts, of which No. 4 was not published. Vol. 3 includes General Jean-Victor Poncelet's history of machinery, the best of its kind. Vols. 4 and 5 contain excellent reports on the French textile industries by F. Aubry, F. Bernoville, M. Gaussen, C. Legentil, and A. Mimerel. It should be noted that Vol. 2 was never published; Vol. 3 appeared in two parts.)

———— *Exposition universelle internationale de 1889 à Paris: Rapports du jury international.* Paris, 1891. 10 vols.

———— *Exposition universelle internationale de 1900 à Paris: Le Bilan d'un siècle (1801–1900),* par Alfred Picard. Paris: Imprimerie nationale, 1906. 6 vols.
Harv.

———— *Rapport de la commission libre nommée par les manufacturiers et négociants de Paris sur l'enquête relative à l'état actuel de l'industrie du coton en France.* Paris, 1829.

———— *Statistique de la France: Industrie.* Paris, 1847. 4 vols.
LC

*Pariset, Ernest. *Histoire de la fabrique lyonnaise depuis le XVIe siècle.* Lyon: Rey, 1901.
Harv.

Pariset, Ernest. *Les Industries de la soie.* Lyon, 1890.   Harv.
Partington, Charles Frederick. *A Popular and Descriptive Account of the
    Steam Engine.* 3d ed. London, 1836.   Harv.
*Partnership "en Commandite," or Partnership With Limited Liabilities
    (According to the Convenient Practice of the Continent of Europe
    and the United States of America), for the Employment of Capital,
    the Circulation of Wages, and the Revival of Our Home and Colonial
    Trade.* London, 1848.
Pas de Calais au XIXe siècle, Le. Arras, 1900. 4 vols.
Passy, Frédéric. *Les Machines et leur influence sur le développement de
    l'humanité.* Paris, 1866.   Crerar
Penot, Achille. "Notes pour servir à l'histoire de l'industrie cotonnière
    dans le département du Haut-Rhin," Société Industrielle de Mulhouse,
    Bulletin, 44 (1874), 145–60.   Mich.
*——, ed. *Statistique générale du département du Haut-Rhin.* Mulhouse,
    1831.
Perdonnet, Albert Auguste. "Industrie minérale: De la législation des
    mines en France et de l'intervention du gouvernement dans l'exploita-
    tion des mines de Rive-de-Gier," *Journal de l'industriel et du capita-
    liste,* 3 (1837), 87–91.
—— *Voyage métallurgique en Angleterre.* Paris, 1837. 2 vols.   Harv.
Péreire, Emile et Isaac. *Du systeme des banques,* in Conseil Supérieur du
    Commerce, *Enquête sur la Banque de France.* Paris, 1866.   LC
Perrault de Jotemps, Alexandre Gaspard, comte; Fabry, Jr., et Félix
    Jean Marie Girod de l'Ain. *Nouveau traité sur la laine et les moutons.*
    Paris, 1824.
Perrin, Maxime. *Saint-Etienne et sa région économique.* Tours: Arnaud,
    1937.   Mich.
Peyret-Lallier, Alphonse. *Statistique industrielle du département de la
    Loire.* Saint-Etienne, 1835.
Picard, Alfred. *Les Chemins de fer.* Paris: Dunod et Pinat, 1918.   Harv.
*Picard, Charles. *Saint-Quentin: De son commerce et de ses industries.*
    Saint-Quentin, 1865–67. 2 vols.   Mich.
Pigeire, Jean. *La Vie et l'oeuvre de Chaptal, 1756–1832.* Paris: Donat-
    Montchrestien, 1932.   NYPL
Pillet-Will, Michel Frédéric, comte. *De la dépense et du produit des
    canaux et des chemins de fer.* Paris, 1837. 2 vols.   Mich. (Transp.)
Polonceau, Antoine Rémi. *Observations sur les routes, suivies de proposi-
    tions sur leur amélioration et sur leur entretien.* Paris, 1829.
                                                               Mich. (Guizot)
Ponteil, Félix. "L'Alsacien Jean-Georges Humann: Le Brasseur d'affairs,
    l'homme politique (1780–1842)," *Revue d'histoire moderne,* 12 (1937),
    227–45.   Mich.

*Porter, George Richardson. *Progrès de la Grande-Bretagne sous le rapport de la population et de la production,* traduit de l'anglais de M. J. R. Porter, chef de Bureau de Statistique Commerciale à Londres, et accompagné de notes et tableaux présentant les progrès analogues pour la France par Philippe Chemin-Dupontès; précédé d'une preface par Michel Chevalier. Paris, 1837. Harv. (Kress)

—— "A Statistical View of the Recent Progress and Present Amount of Mining Industry in France," Royal Statistical Society, *Journal,* 7 (1844), 281–91. Mich.

Poujade, Marcel. *Etude sur les variations du taux de l'escompte en France et leur conséquences aux XIXe et XXe siècles.* Paris: Editions de la Vie Universitaire, 1923. LC

Poulain, César. *Tableau synoptique de l'industrie lainière, 1789–1878.* Harv.

Proudhon, Pierre Joseph. *Manuel du spéculateur à la Bourse.* 5th ed. Paris, 1857. Mich.

*Quentin-Bauchart, Pierre. *La Crise sociale de 1848: Les Origines de la révolution de février.* Paris: Hachette, 1920. LC

Rambaud, Joseph. *Histoire des doctrines économiques.* 3d ed. Paris: Larose, 1909. Mich.

Ramon, Gabriel. *Histoire de la Banque de France, d'après les sources originales.* Paris: Grasset, 1929. Mich.

"Rapport du jury départemental du Haut-Rhin pour l'exposition des produits de l'industrie nationale de 1839," Société Industrielle de Mulhouse, *Bulletin,* 12 (1839), 555–93. Mich.

"Rapport du jury départemental du Haut-Rhin pour l'exposition des produits de l'industrie nationale de 1844," Société Industrielle de Mulhouse, *Bulletin,* 17 (1844), 166–226. Mich.

(Both these reports are useful on the crisis of 1837–42, and on the introduction of the power loom.)

Ravinet, Antoine Louis Théodore. *Dictionnaire hydrographique de la France.* Paris, 1824. 2 vols. LC

*Rebotier, Maurice. *Les Participations bancaires à l'industrie.* Paris: Sirey, 1935. LC

(This work includes the names of firms in the *haute-banque* and shows the importance of this group in furnishing capital to industry.)

Reboul, Henri. *L'Industrie nîmoise du tissage au XIXe siècle.* Montpellier: Firmin et Montane, 1914.

Reconnaissances de la Seine de Rouen à Saint-Denis en 1829 et 1830, et travaux proposés pour rendre cette partie de la Seine facilement navigable. Paris, 1830. Mich. (Guizot)

*Redlich, Fritz. "Jacques Laffitte and the Beginnings of Investment Banking in France." *Business Historical Society, Bulletin,* 22 (1948), 137–61.   Mich.

Reeves, John. *The Rothschilds, the Financial Rulers of Nations.* London and Chicago, 1887.   LC

Renouard, Alfred J. *Etudes sur le travail des lins.* 4th ed. Paris, 1879. 6 vols.   Univ. Ill.

Revue de l'histoire de Lyon. Lyon, 1902–14, 1921–24.
  (A continuation of the *Revue du lyonnais,* 1825–, whose title is sometimes used.)

Rey, Jean. *Etudes pour servir à l'histoire des châles.* Paris, 1823.

Reybaud, Marie Roch Louis. "De l'industrie métallurgique en France considérée dans ses rapports avec la construction des chemins de fer," *Journal des économistes,* 5 (1843), 390–400.   Mich.

—— *Etudes sur le régime des manufactures: Condition des ouvriers en soie.* Paris, 1859.   Mich.

—— *Le Coton: Son régime, ses problèmes—son influence en Europe.* Paris, 1863.   Mich.

—— "Rapport sur la condition morale, intellectuelle et matérielle des ouvriers qui vivent de l'industrie de la laine," Académie Royale des Sciences Morales et Politiques, *Mémoires,* 12 (1865), 453–808. Mich.
  (Published in book form in 1867.)

—— "Rapport sur la condition morale, intellectuelle et matérielle des ouvriers qui vivent de l'industrie du fer," Académie Royale des Sciences Morales et Politiques, *Mémoires,* 13 (1872), 511–852. Mich.

Reynier, Elie. *La Soie en Vivarais.* Largentière, 1921.

Ricommard, J. *Le Bonneterie à Troyes et dans le département de l'Aube.* Paris: Hachette, 1934.

*Rigaud, Hector. "Mémoire sur la situation des forges de France et de Belgique," *Annales des mines,* Série 4, 8 (1845), 371–496.   Mich.

Rigaudias, Hilde (Weiss). *Les Enquêtes ouvrières en France entre 1830 et 1848.* Paris: Alcan, 1936.   LC
  (Good bibliography.)

Rist, Charles. "La Durée du travail dans l'industrie française de 1820 à 1870," *Revue d'économie politique,* 11 (1897), 371–93.   Mich.

Rivoire, Hector. *Statistique du département du Gard.* Nîmes, 1842. 2 vols.   Chic.

Rodet, D. L. "De l'industrie manufacturière en France," *Revue des deux mondes,* Série 3, 3 (1834), 714–50.   Harv.

—— "De l'industrie manufacturière de la France en 1844," *Revue des deux mondes,* Nouvelle série, 7 (1844), 714–50.   Mich.

Rondot, Natalis. *Etude pratique des tissus de laine convenable pour la Chine, le Japon, le Cochin Chine et l'archipel indien.* Paris, 1847.

—— *Rapport au ministre de l'agriculture et du commerce sur l'industrie lainière de la Belgique en 1847.* Paris, 1849.

Roselli, Gabriel. *Les Origines d'une ligne de chemins de fer: La Grand'Combe-Beaucaire, 1830–1852.* Nîmes: Université de Montpellier, 1931.

Rousiers, Paul de. *Les Grands ports de France: Leur rôle économique.* Paris: Colin, 1909.

Roussel-Defontaine, Charles. *Histoire de Tourcoing.* Lille, 1855.

Sacy, Antoine Isaac, baron Silvestre de. *Notice biographique sur M. le baron Guillaume Louis Ternaux lue à la séance publique de la société d'agriculture le 6 avril 1834.* Paris, 1834.

Saint-Ferréol. *Exposition du système des douanes en France depuis 1791 jusqu'à 1834, précédée de quelques réflexions sur les causes qui ont amené l'enquête commercial actuel, et suivie d'autres réflexions sur les modifications à apporter au tarif actuel des douanes.* Marseille, 1835.

[Sartoris, Urbain.] *Note sur les canaux adjugés en 1822.* Paris, 1832.
Mich. [Guizot]

Say, Horace Emile. "La Crise financière et la Banque de France," *Journal des économistes,* 16 (1847), 193–207. Mich.

—— *Rapport sur le commerce entre la France et l'Angleterre à l'occasion des documents publiés à Londres par George Villiers et John Bowring.* Paris, 1835. Col.

Schmidt, Charles. "Jean-Baptiste Say et le blocus continental," *Revue d'histoire des doctrines économiques et sociales,* 4 (1911), 148–54.
Harv.

—— "Les Débuts de l'industrie cotonnière en France, 1760–1806," *Revue d'histoire des doctrines économiques et sociales,* 7 (1914), 26–55.
Harv.

—— "Une Enquête sur la draperie à Sedan en 1803," *Revue d'histoire des doctrines économiques et sociales,* 5 (1912), 93–109. Harv.

Schwilgué, Jean Baptiste. "Mémoire sur les routes et sur le roulage," *Annales des ponts et chaussées,* [Série 1] 4 (1832), 189–249. Mich.

Sée, Henri Eugène. *Esquisse d'une histoire économique et sociale de la France depuis les origines jusqu'à la guerre mondiale.* Paris: Alcan, 1929. Mich.

—— *Französische Wirtschaftsgeschichte.* Jena: Brodnitz, 1930–36. 2 vols.
Mich.

—— *Histoire économique de la France.* Paris: Colin, 48–51. 2 vols. LC

—— "L'Economie rurale de l'Anjou dans la première moitié du XIXe siècle," *Revue d'histoire économique et sociale,* 15 (1927), 104–22.
Harv.

Sée, H. E. *L'Industrie texile et le commerce du Bas-Maine pendant le premier empire et la Restauration d'après les papiers des Guyard-Moricière (1800–1815)*, in Vol. 12 of Hayem (ed.), *Mémoires et documents pour servir à l'histoire du commerce et de l'industrie en France*, pp. 291–307. Paris: Hachette, 1929. Mich.

—— "Les Progrès de l'agriculture en France de 1815 à 1848," *Revue d'histoire économique et sociale*, 9 (1921), 67–91. Harv.

—— "Quelques aperçus sur la condition de la classe ouvrière et sur le mouvement ouvrier en France de 1815 à 1848," *Revue d'histoire économique*, 12 (1924), 493–521. Harv.

—— "Remarques sur l'évolution du capitalisme et les origines de le grande industrie," *Revue de synthèse historique*, 37 (1924), 47–67. Mich.

*—— *La Vie économique de la France sous la monarchie censitaire (1815–1848)*. Paris: Alcan, 1927.

*Ségalat, Antoine. *L'Impôt des prestations: Son origine, sa législation, sa réforme*. Toulouse: Imprimerie Cooperative Toulousaine, 1906. LC

Séguier, Jules. "Rapport sur les perfectionnements apportés au métier à tisser de Jacquart par MM. Dhomme et Romagny Jr.," Société d'Encouragement pour l'Industrie Nationale, *Bulletin*, 36 (1837), 201–10. Mich.

Séguin, Jules. *Chemins de fer: De leur exécution par l'industrie particulière*. Paris, 1838. Mich.

*Shannon, Herbert Austin. "The Coming of General Limited Liability," *Economic History* (supplement to *Economic Journal*), 2 (1930–33), 267–91. Mich.

Simiand, François. "Essai sur le prix du charbon en France au XIXe siècle," *Année sociologique*, 5 (1900–1901), 1–81. Mich.

—— *Le Salaire des ouvriers des mines de charbon en France: Contribution à la théorie économique du salaire*. 2d ed. Paris: E. Cornély, 1907. Mich.

*—— *Le Salaire, l'évolution sociale et la monnaie*. Paris: Alcan, 1932. 3 vols. Mich.
  (Excellent bibliography.)

Simon, Claude Gabriel. *Observations receuillies en Angleterre en 1835*. Paris, 1836. 2 vols. Harv.

*Simonde de Sismondi, Jean Charles Léonard. *Du sort des ouvriers dans les manufactures*. Paris, 1834. Harv.

*—— *Nouveaux principes d'économie politique; ou, De la richesse dans ses rapports avec la population*. Paris, 1819. 2 vols. 2d ed. Paris, 1827. 2 vols. Mich.

Sion, Jules. *Les Paysans de la Normandie orientale*. Paris: Colin, 1909. Mich.

Société d'Amélioration des Laines. *Bulletin.* Paris, 1825–30. 2 vols. Mich.
(Publication appears to have ceased in 1827 after issue of four numbers. Rare source on importation of English sheep.)
Société d'Encouragement pour l'Industrie Nationale. *Bulletin.* Paris, 1801–.
(One of the best bibliographical sources. Technological.)
Société Industrielle de Mulhouse. *Bulletin.* Mulhouse, 1826–. Mich.
—— *Histoire documentaire de l'industrie de Mulhouse et de ses environs au XIXe siècle.* Mulhouse: Bader, 1902. 2 vols. Harv.
Stainier, Emile. *Histoire commerciale de la métallurgie dans le district de Charleroi de 1829 à 1867.* 2d ed. Charleroi, 1873. Harv.
Surleau, Georges. *Les Réformes financières de M. de Villèle.* Paris, 1901. Harv.

Tarbé de Saint-Hardouin, François Pierre. *Notices biographiques sur les ingénieurs des ponts et chaussées.* Paris, 1884. LC
*Tarlé, Eugène. "La Grande coalition des mineurs de Rive-de-Gier en 1844," *Revue historique,* 177 (1936), 249–78. Mich.
Teisserenc de Bort, Pierre Edmond. *Etudes sur les voies de communication perfectionnées et sur les lois économiques de la production du transport.* Paris, 1847. 2 vols. Mich. (Transp.)
—— "La Crise des chemins de fer," *Journal des économistes,* 28 (1851), 225–43, 337–57. Mich.
*—— *Les Travaux publics en Belgique et les chemins de fer en France.* Paris, 1839. Mich. (Guizot)
Teissier du Cros, Charles. *La Production de la soie dans les Cévennes.* Paris, 1903.
*Thouvenin, Dr. "De l'influence que l'industrie exerce sur la santé des populations dans les grand centres manufacturiers," *Annales d'hygiène publique et de médecine légale,* [Série 1] 36 (1846), 16–46, 277–96; 37 (1847), 83–111. Mich.
Toussenel, Alphonse. *Les Juifs, rois de l'époque: Histoire de la féodalité financière.* Paris, 1847. 2 vols. Crerar
Tribout, Henri. *Un grand savant, le général Jean-Victor Poncelet, 1788–1867.* Paris: Saffroy, 1936.
Truchon, Paul. "La Vie ouvrière à Lyon sous la Restauration (1814–1830)," *Revue d'histoire de Lyon,* 11 (1912), 195–222. Mich.
—— "Les Transports et voies de communication au service du commerce lyonnais sous la Restauration (1814–1830)," *Revue d'histoire de Lyon,* 10 (1911), 362–73. Mich.
Tuan, Mao-Lan. *Simonde de Sismondi as an Economist.* New York: Columbia University Press, 1927. Mich.
Turgan, Julien François. *Les Grandes usines.* Paris, 1866–88. 18 vols.

Ure, Andrew. *The Cotton Manufacture of Great Britain Systematically Investigated.* 1st ed. London, 1836. 2 vols. Mich.
—— *The Philosophy of Manufactures.* London, 1835. LC

Vadot, Napoléon. *Le Creusot, son histoire, son industrie.* Le Creusot, 1875.
Varlez, Louis. *Les Salaires dans l'industrie gantoise.* Brussels: Royaume de Belgique, Ministère de l'Industrie et du Travail, 1901–4. 2 vols. Harv.
Vaublanc, Vincent Marie Viénot, comte de. *Du commerce de la France: Examen des états de M. le directeur général des douanes.* Paris, 1824. Mich.
Vergeot, Jean Baptiste. *Le Crédit comme stimulant et régulateur de l'industrie: La Conception saint-simonienne, ses réalisations.* Paris: Jouve, 1918. Harv.
   (Good bibliography.)
Vidal, François. *De la répartition des richesses; ou, De la justice distributive en économie sociale.* Paris, 1846. Harv.
Villard, Amédée. *Histoire du prolétariat ancien et moderne.* Paris, 1882. Crerar
Villèle, Jean Baptiste Séraphin Joseph, comte de. "Rapport sur la création du conseil supérieur du commerce et des colonies," *Annales de l'industrie nationale,* Série 2, 13 (1825), 102–11. Harv.
Villeneuve-Bargemont, Alban, vicomte de. *Economie politique chrétienne; ou, Recherches sur la nature et les causes du pauperisme.* Paris, 1834. 3 vols. Mich.
Villermé, Louis René. *Discours sur la durée trop longue du travail des enfants dans beaucoup de manufactures.* Paris, 1837.
—— "Notes sur quelques monopoles usurpés par les ouvriers de certaines industries, suivies de quelques considérations sur la situation actuelle des ouvriers dans les bassins houillers de la Loire et du centre," *Journal des économistes,* [Série 1] 17 (1847), 157–68. Mich.
*—— *Tableau de l'état physique et moral des ouvriers employés dans les manufactures de coton, de laine et de soie.* Paris, 1840. 2 vols. Mich.
*Villermé, Louis René Jr. *Les Douanes et la contrebande.* Paris, 1851. LC
Vincens, Emile. *Des sociétés par actions: Des banques en France.* Paris, 1837. Chic.
Vuillemin, Emile. *Le Bassin houiller du Pas-de-Calais.* Paris, 1880. 2 vols. Chic.
—— *Les Mines de houille d'Aniche: Progrès réalisés dans les houillères du nord de France pendant un siècle.* Paris, 1878. Col.

*Wallon, Maurice. *Les Saint-Simoniens et les chemins de fer.* Paris: A. Pedone, 1908. Harv.

Warden, Alexander Johnston. *The Linen Trade, Ancient and Modern.* 2d ed. London, 1867. Mich.

*Weill, Georges Jacques. *L'Ecole saint-simonienne.* Paris, 1896. Mich.

—— *Un Précurseur du socialisme, Saint-Simon et son oeuvre.* Paris, 1894. Mich.

Wolowski, Louis François Michel Raymond. *Des sociétés par actions.* Paris, 1838. Mich.

Wyatt, Matthew D. *A Report on the Eleventh French Exposition of the Products of Industry.* London, 1849.

Wages, 193–98; in Lyons silk mills, 208, 209–10, 317; of railroad workers, 441–42
Wales, coal from, 334
Walincourt, textile mills at, 341
Water frame (throstle), 258, 297, 403
Water power, 8, 9, 10–12, 85, 117–18, 243; use of, in cotton industry, 112, 265; government influence on use of, 89–90, 402–3; use of, in iron industry, 129, 146–47; use of, for lace looms, 315; prevalence of, 118
Waterways, 19, 28–48, 100, 433; Becquey's plan for, 30–31, 35; English, 10, 35, 42–43; traffic on, 42. *See also* Canals; Rivers; Transportation, inland
Water wheels, 112–13, 114, 125, 147, 433
Watt and Boulton low-pressure engine, 41, 114, 120, 184, 432
Webber, Charles, invents silk power loom, 316, 317
Wedgwood Co., 43
Weguelin, Thomas, English banker, 446–47
Wendel, François de, and Wendel family, iron and railroad promoters, 128, 141, 142, 439, 445, 448
Wesserling, cotton-printing at, 265
West Indies, English influence in, 338; as market, 374; slavery in, 373; sugar-cane production in, 238; trade with, 372
Wheat, crop failure, 82 ff.; from Levant, 379; price of, 363, 365, 366, 398
Whitney, Eli, invents cotton gin, 164
Wilson, Daniel. *See* Manby & Wilson Co.
Wines, 391; made at Bordeaux, 215, 369, 372; transported by canal, 32, 46
Wollaston, sheep importer, 154

Women workers, 191–92; as embroiderers, 186; as weavers, 181. *See also* Silk industry, spinning of raw silk *and* raising worms
Wood and forests, 30, 85–91, 393–94; cost of, 86–89, 91, 94–95; in England, 85; government control of, 146; government-owned, 86–87, 391, 393–94; use of, in iron industry, 125–26, 130–31, 132, 138, 146, 148–49, 243; production and supply of, 9, 10, 85–86, 88, 91–93, 93–94, 243
Wool and woolen industry, mechanical carding of, 277–78; mechanical combing of, 275–77; use of combed yarn in, 276–77, 278–82; competition in, 349; vs. cotton, 288, 329, 330, 332; demand for, 287–88, 330; imported raw, 150; mechanization of, 275–82; price of cloths of, 283–84, 362; price of raw, 150, 155–56, 284; production and supply of raw, 157–58, 275, 283; quality of cloths of, 283; mechanical spinning of, 277–82; use of steam in, 113, 116–17; weaving of, 282–83, 285. *See also* Belgium, woolen industry of; Sheep; Worsted cloth *and under various regional and city names*
Woolf medium-pressure engine, 114–15
Worsted cloth, 152, 158, 275, 279, 280, 281, 284–85, 344
Wyatt, Matthew D., on Exposition of 1849, 357

Yonne River, 30, 38; improvement of, 40. *See also* Burgundy canal
Young, Arthur, 14

Ziegler, Martin, tries flying shuttle, 269
Zuber Co., uses cotton-printing machines, 265
Zurich loom (bar loom), 311–12, 320